The Double Perspective

The Double Perspective

Language, Literacy, and Social Relations

David Bleich

New York   Oxford
Oxford University Press
1988

Oxford University Press

Oxford   New York   Toronto
Delhi   Bombay   Calcutta   Madras   Karachi
Petaling Jaya   Singapore   Hong Kong   Tokyo
Nairobi   Dar es Salaam   Cape Town
Melbourne   Auckland

and associated companies in
Berlin   Ibadan

Published by Oxford University Press, Inc.
200 Madison Avenue, New York, New York 10016

Oxford is a registered trademark of Oxford University Press

Library of Congress Cataloging-in-Publication Data

Bleich, David.
The double perspective: language, literacy, and social relations
/ David Bleich
p.   cm.
Includes index.
ISBN 0-19-505173-4
1. Philology—Study and teaching.   2. Literacy—Study and
teaching.   3. Sociolinguistics.   I. Title.
P53.B63 1988
401'.9—dc19   88-11987

9 8 7 6 5 4 3 2 1
Printed in the United States of America
on acid-free paper

Contents

Introduction:
Thinking Double

About thirty years ago, when I first read *1984*, I was dazzled by the neologisms of the "future." "Doublethink" was one of my favorites, and I did not give a second thought to my reading of it as the name for the hypocrisy and lying of public officials, as well as for how ordinary people were implicitly forced to think in self-contradictory ways. The term "double standard" plays an analogous role in the common vocabulary, meaning "doublethink" in regard to the different standards of sexual conduct expected of men and women. Similarly, to think or act "duplicitously," or doubly, is to use "doublethink" in ordinary life. In other words, certain conventions of language and habits of usage made it possible for me to understand "doublethink" in a clear and fixed way.

This use of the term "double" is a conventionalized error, however. In each of the foregoing cases, the term does not really refer to a "double" situation, but to an unequal one. Two parties are stipulated: government and people, men and women, I and you, in each of the cases above, respectively. One of the parties—government, men and I—is in a privileged position and is permitted two or more standards of thought and behavior, while the other party—people, women, and you—is permitted only one standard: the party in the privileged position is in control of the party in the unprivileged one. Thus, the thinking or the behavior described is not double but unbalanced and unfair.

However, the fact that unbalanced and unfair social situations are *called* double says something about the culture that uses this term in this way: there is something wrong with double things, except, perhaps, for chewing gum and ice cream. Double things usually imply ambivalence, ambiguity, uncertainty, particularly when the two parts of a pair are said to be equal in other senses, such as boys and girls. Readers may recall William Rehnquist's confirmation hearing, when it was brought up that he pronounced men the "heads" of families because otherwise the family just won't work. In fact, in our culture, married couples are not considered truly double, but only a pair in which one party is "head." "Double" in the previous instances is thought of as a perversion of what should be single.

The title of this book assumes both a literal sense of "double" and an ameliorated sense of it, as when two almost identical images combine with one another to produce a stereoscopic view. Throughout the study, many familiar pairs of terms and things are considered: mind and body, thought and action, objective and subjective, societies and individuals, mothers and fathers, orality and literacy, indication and expression, subject and predicate, names and things. In my discussion of these pairs, I try to offer them as a fully double perspective whose constituents need one another, belong to one another, are sometimes interchangeable, often superposable to produce a variety of conceptual stereoscopies. However, the perspectival pairs are never subjected to the choice of "either/or." Particularly with regard to language, literacy, and social relations, this book is a study of how pairs and multiples of things go together and work together, and thereby introduce a new perspective, a depth, a third dimension of understanding, even when they seem to be opposites.

I came to these thoughts because of my frustrations as a teacher, because of my discomfort reading blue books, making comments and assigning grades to students to whom I relate, finally, person to person. I felt discomfort lecturing to large numbers of students who I did not think needed to listen to me talk for fourteen hours each semester without "equal time" to answer, to talk back. I was bored and impatient in class because I was no longer participating in conversations, and I was teaching young people not to participate either. I became ashamed of holding the floor in classes of all sizes, of being to one to "call on" others who waited patiently to speak with their hands raised. I became embarrassed that the young women in my classes waited to speak while the young men spoke out and got recognized by me immediately. I became convinced that my own classrooms were moments when students were taught to suppress their language, and where the language habits of sexism and racism were actually promoted. I was repeatedly surprised to find that I could not say how students were in a position to enlighten me and teach me.

I am also writing this book because I feel embarrassed by the conditions of my employment. Of my sixty-five former colleagues in the English Department at Indiana University, ten are women and one is black; of the thirty-six senior faculty, three are women. Over the past ten years and with the presumed authority of affirmative action, the gender and ethnic balance has not changed. In addition, the salary gap between senior and junior faculty has widened considerably, as the nefarious practice of "targeting" has fattened the salaries of us senior faculty, particularly those of us who write books, while penalizing those who think teaching is the main activity of our profession. In my department, junior faculty not only can't pay their bills, but they are constantly worried that they won't get tenure and they are sometimes urged to stop teaching altogether to take the time to write the book that will get them tenure. We are less and less a school, more and more a monastery encouraging the isolated efforts of individual men. There is an obsessional fear in my department that "weak" graduate students will "get through," and an increasing number of memos appear in my mailbox urging me to submit discursive written judgments of students to be utterly sure that students who haven't gotten the highest grades are weeded out, rather than taught and nurtured into a dignified spot in our profession.

I am embarrassed because I worked in a community and in a state that is suspicious of what goes on in the university, particularly in subjects like mine where there is no palpable technological outcome, and no championship to show for hard work. Like it or not, the majority of my colleagues, including me, are affected by this general attitude, since we know and feel that few around us will be responsive to whatever we are lucky enough to achieve. The main result of this widespread attitude is the continued withdrawal into and emphasis on individual achievement in our subject, the continued emphasis on teaching and evaluating individual students and performances, the continued effort to treat the collective of the university, department and classroom as a mere collection of monadic units, each going its own way with little or no sense of common purpose.

What is perhaps most alarming to me is that there are so few people in most of my communities who think that anything is wrong with this state of affairs. The ideology of individualism is so automatic, so taken for granted, so much a part of the history of our culture and civilization, so deeply entrenched in religious practices, business practices, sports, entertainment; so many are enamored of "stars" and other rich people; so few complaints are lodged as outrageous salaries and contracts become public, so widespread is the acceptance of the ideal of becoming individually rich that the destructive collective circumstances that this ideal generates appear to most people as necessary peculiarities and not instances of unfairness and injustice.

This book does not of course treat the problem of the unfair distribution of wealth. But I do consider the ideology of individualism that is responsible for the unfair distribution also responsible for the rigidity of our language use habits, the inertia of our pedagogical mores and traditions, and the isolation of large-scale public injustices of gender, race, and class from our teaching of language and literacy. By teaching these subjects under the ideology of individualism, we are lying about what these subjects really are. We are failing to tell the truth about what it means to speak and to write to one another. We are failing to acknowledge that language does not simply appear in each of us, but that its acquisition is bound up with the individual's family, community, and society. The way we now teach language and literacy depends on our thinking that language is an isolated skill or competence, and that sustained "direct" instruction of individual students is the only real way to achieve success in bringing out literacy.

In this book I view this pedagogical problem of teaching literacy and the academic problem of understanding language as the "same" problem that requires the double perspectives of the classroom and the academy (chapter 1). But it also requires a host of other double perspectives, particularly ones created by an enlightened gender consciousness (chapters 2 and 5). The ideology of individualism is, among other things, a euphemistic way of referring to sexism: the assumption that the masculine perspective is necessarily the main perspective or the prior one, or the one whose historical momentum must be honored. The figure of the "double perspective" is therefore an attempt to say that whatever value we may place on individual consciousness, this consciousness is double in a variety of nonfigurative ways, starting with the fact that for us men, feminine perspectives are already "in" our own, just as for women, historically, masculine perspectives have been part of their ways of thinking. As I discuss it in this book, doubleness means that each gender's ways of viewing, thinking, and speaking always accompany the other's ways, that we use both at once, that we switch back and forth, that each gender's being so fully bound up in the fate and welfare of the other makes it only common sense for us to acknowledge that our perspective is double in this way; and if we do not accept this plurality in our minds, men will consider it right and just to continue our collective political hegemony as it exists in every known human society.

One of the ways in which our society has permitted this hegemony to continue is in its attitude toward the classroom (chapters 1 and 6). In the earlier grades, where the teachers are still mostly women, the salaries are low and the work is too often viewed as an advanced form of babysitting. In the secondary schools, where the teacher population is mixed and the salaries higher, the work load is so great and the curriculum so coercively regulated it prevents teachers from taking initiative, using their imagination, and spending extra time. And in the university, as is well known, "real" men write books; women and other low achievers teach. If this description of things makes any sense, then it is clear that the undervaluation of teaching is linked to sexism and individualism in our society, and the "double perspective" is, in this case, an attempt to claim the political and social necessity of viewing the classroom as just as salient, vital, and important as the academy.

I am also making a narrower case for the double perspective as a description of how language works all the time; this description of language as a local phenomenon implies and requires the wider political thesis. In chapter 4, I try to show that the subject-predicate structure of sentences is also true of the individual word, and that this linguistic structure grows out of the intersubjective grounding of language acquisition as a dialogue of action and words between parent and child from the beginning (chapter 3). Insofar as subject and predicate, thing and name, may be seen as different forms of topic and comment, this latter form is more obviously social in that a topic is the initiative, the comment the response, and we speakers soon learn to internalize the trope of topic and comment, thereby emerging with the capability of naming things and making sentences. To speak, in a sense, is to be able to divide ourselves in two and present our full doubleness—our simultaneous consciousness of ourselves and our speaking partners—to others.

No one chapter makes the "basic" point of this book. The order in which the chapters are presented does not represent a "line" of argument; with suitable adjustments of my narrative voice, a different order of chapters could be just as appropriate, including, for example, interspersing the classroom materials in chapters 5, 7, 8, 9, and 10 with the more abstract theoretical arguments. In large part, I am using the figure of the double perspective to present doubleness and plurality (not pluralism) in general to criticize individualism, particularly as it has influenced knowledge about language and the teaching of language and literacy.

Chapter 2 deals with philosophical knowledge about language, and, while the reader will very soon discover that I am not the sort who thinks "all views are valid," I do try to stress there that many philosophical disputes can be productively viewed not as opposing views, but as complementary ones often making sense as two parts of a single approach to an issue, providing the adversarial axiom of philosophical discourse is reduced radically. Chapter 3 pays attention to language and literacy as social phenomena and suggests perhaps that the doubleness or complementarity I advocate in chapter 2 is bound up with a similar doubleness in the variety of contexts in which practical literacy appears. The larger movements of the first six chapters concern a whole cluster of double thoughts, double relationships, that are involved in gender, teaching, language, and literacy.

I have yet to broach the subject of literature in this introduction. My degree is in literature, my previous work has been on the response to literature, I have been publicly identified as someone who "professes" literary theory. So, where's the literature? I am happy to say that for all my years in academic life, people have whispered behind my back that I am not "really" interested in literature because my courses have books in them which are not literature, in addition to the ones that are. People have said that I would prefer to do therapy on readers that to teach literature, and that, were I "really" interested in literature as my "main" subject I would, like everyone else, have a normal reading list, with normal literature, and I would give tests and write comments on papers and give grades like everyone else. People have said that I don't "really" belong in an English department, but maybe in psychology or education, or somewhere else, in any event.

I can understand why many would be so suspicious. I have had a minority approach to literature. I am, after all, a member of a minority group, and I have followed some of the intellectual styles and traditions of thought that, historically, Jews lucky enough to live in (presumably) free societies have followed. Often, these have been traditions of opposition, as exemplified, perhaps, by the thinking of Freud and Marx, which continues to cause controversy. In any event, when I was presented with Shakespeare and Milton, I read and understood them, but they weren't mine: they belonged to the English, and while I can easily appreciate moving work in my native language, it was also important for me to remember that my native language is not necessarily the language of my historical ancestors. In 1971, I published an essay in *College English* which reflected on how I came to start on a profession of "English." There I noted that it was my reading of Arthur Miller's play "Death of Salesman," which my father urged on me, which led to my vocational decision to be a critic or a student of literature. At the time I first read the play, I did not realize that Miller was a New York Jew like myself, but somehow his language, his issues, his approach to family and vocation spoke to me in ways obviously deeper than how Shakespeare spoke to me. As a college student I could not quite understand why I was immediately moved by I. L. Peretz and just knew how to interpret his work, but had to rely on mastering the formulas and abstractions given to me by Protestant New Critics to interpret T. S. Eliot, whose plays were the subject of my Bachelor's thesis, but which never really moved me at all.

In my earlier work, therefore, I decided that criticism was (or ought to be) "subjective," because I thought that critics never did acknowledge how they were moved by the literature they wrote about. But I also learned that the way critics treated literature was subjective in a different sense, namely, that they, like me, wrote about things in culturally traditional ways and were following the habits and thought styles of their own people, their own values. For me to write about English and American "WASP" literature meant that I had to overtake that perspective, to find a way, at least temporarily, to make it my own. This, I own, was quite hard to do, and I was at least happy to learn how subjectivity and perspectivism actually worked.

Living in this free society, it was comforting to know that there was room for my perspective and style of thought, that I could learn from the majority perspective, and that I could contribute to it what I had gotten from my own traditions of thought. The question of literature for me is, however, not the literature itself, but, in a sense, the principle of what literature is, its local character and horizons of reference, its embeddedness in a host of other cultural elements and features. From this perspective, the literature of one culture can in no way be understood as canonical or greater or prior in some imaginary hierarchy to the literature of minority cultures and languages. For me to teach literature is to teach and learn how a given work may or may not play a role in a culturally and politically situated living person. And this is the connection of literature to literacy and language that I discuss and reflect on in this book.

Just as, for me, "Death of a Salesman" was not Literature (with a capital L) but a slice of my discourse put into a frame and performed on a stage, I assume that literature will play—or fail to play—a similar role for others. In chapters 4, 5, 6, and 7, I try to show how the response to literature—to the framed and separated slice of ordinary discourse—provides special access not only to otherwise concealed aspects of our language use habits, but to the actual picture of how we are culturally and politically involved. Because literature is conventionally separated (it is not given out at any time as just "a piece of language" but instead as a specific genre), because it is itself an institutionalized second or "other" language category, literary reading spontaneously elicits in us a new "second" perspective on language and human relationships. This "double perspective" effect that reading literature always has carries over into whatever psychosocial issues emerge in response to the literary language.

As you can see, the foregoing discussion of literature required me to to identify myself more exactly, to disclose, finally, in some degree, my personal implication in the claims I am making about language, literacy, and literature. Such disclosure need not come just in literary response, though that is where it usually appears in my work; but, in my view, the *habit* of self-disclosure in both a personal and social sense does need to come into the picture at an early point when we teach this subject. In this book, I treat it in detail in chapter 9, where I describe the interaction between Ms. K, a first-year student, and myself in the progress of the course I am discussing. Such pedagogical self-disclosure is not simply a signature but an attempt to enact regular cross-talk in the classroom by designating a space in which there are no privileged members. By virtue of individuality itself, each person brings into the classroom certain privileges, while the teacher brings the lion's share. While my privileges don't disappear, I do contribute my zones of unprivileged existence, and my psychosocial clothing starts to resemble that of the students.

Admittedly, the discussion in chapter 10 of three people in a group barely scratches the surface of what sort of things group work can accomplish. It is very difficult to get textual materials that really show what the collective experience in a group is like. A teacher can't really enter a student group but can only ascertain that work is being done and how good the atmosphere is. Yet I mean to show in these last chapters how much any kind of intra-student collaboration depends on the teacher's willingness to combine the interests and styles of the classroom with some of those in the academy and, therefore, to really behave like a student by submitting local work for collective scrutiny and analysis. This permits students to take the "academic" perspective and to begin professing about language and literature what they feel sure they discover. In this way, I hope, both the classroom and the academy will combine to assume a more flexible, informal and social institution.

A final note on my discussions of students' work. It might not be easy for readers to become fully involved in the long samples of students' writing that I cite. It does take time to grasp the idiom of each person's work. Nevertheless, it would not be possible to show what I think are essential features of language use and literacy without such extensive samples. Often, for example, the student's real insight is embedded in an excess of important but repetitive talk, as in Ms. K's work in chapter 8. Had I just picked out the "good parts" and discussed them, my discussions would not have given a realistic example of what I am pointing to, and then you would not be able to test my claims on your own. One of the fundamental arguments of this book is that any literacy "sample" must be long and extensive, and that no meaningful judgments of someone's language use can be made on the basis of just one or a few pieces of work, or over a short period of time. Because each of our literacy styles is something that has developed over years, it only makes sense to be patient in letting it emerge in the classroom and patient in "getting into" it when it becomes more fully an object of research.

I believe that what we do in English with language, literacy, and literature relates to a host of other disciplines in the humanities and social sciences, and probably in the natural sciences as well. In preparing this book, I have tried to hear what those in other disciplines are saying, tried to adopt their perspectives and adapt to them. I think that our discipline can no longer continue on the autonomous path it has followed in recent generations, and that the time has come for new subject matters that can grow from our "double"—multiple, actually—perspectives on language. This book invites the discourse of other disciplines to join it, and I expect to continue to include "nonliterature" in my literary and literacy reading lists. I feel I need more friends who speak different languages—student languages, feminine languages, nonprivileged languages—as well as those who think about science, economics, sports, food, dishes, laundry, and diapers.

The Double Perspective

1

The Classroom and the Academy

When I first started work as a university teacher, I assumed those in the classroom and those in the academy were members of the same community. The "book" (i.e., thesis) that I wrote to get my degree was a serious contribution to a continuing public discussion of my topic. I was then supposed to read in the same or related areas, so that the courses I taught would deal with the topics of my scholarly work, and I would grow and learn along with those I was teaching. There was to be, I expected, a regular, meaningful, substantive connection between my academic projects and my teaching.

After thirty-one years of university life, I see that, as a rule, the classroom and the academy are not only separate communities, but separate institutions with different memberships, purposes, and histories. Some of these differences are fairly obvious. In the university, as well as in society, a member of the academy has more privileges than a member of the teaching community. If someone who has written several books is also known as a good teacher, the books are always the first credential given, with the good teaching tacked on as a secondary feature. But if someone is known only as a good teacher, their erudition is rarely mentioned: teaching is not expected to be the primary result of erudition. Except in the most indirect ways, a scholar's published work is not an occasion for inquiry, discussion, or debate in his or her classroom. Subjects for courses and seminars are defined according to standards other than what teachers are doing as scholars and critics. Because, often, scholars only begrudgingly function as teachers—it is what they have to do to remain on the payroll—they have an interest in maintaining a curriculum that reinforces the separation of the classroom and the academy.

The institution of the classroom occupies a secondary position because it is taken to be a place where the uninitiated (who could be younger or older people) come to receive enlightenment. From elementary school on, students are viewed as needing induction into some aspect of the "real world." The regular, daily gathering of students is not believed to have an intrinsic value, but, rather, a preparatory purpose. To go to school is to "prepare for life," an education being something you *get* (many people think you actually buy

3

it) in order to do something else, something more real and more important.
It is as if the many years a young person spends in the classroom are not
a part of life equal in interest and consequence to those experiences that
come later on. In this way, the classroom, rather than serving its constituents
directly, is actually serving other institutions. Throughout the earlier grades,
the spontaneous but complex social processes of the classroom are peripheral
to the task of passing on "useful skills and information," as if there were no
connection between the styles of social interaction in the classroom and the
way knowledge and language subsequently function in our society.

As a child moves through the educational system—that is, as the child gets
older and more socially capable—the integration of social and intellectual
activity becomes less and less possible in the classroom. By the time students
enter the university, they understand that the actual authority of the classroom
is held by members of the academy. They see that the social process of
intellectual life that really counts is the coping with academic authority.
Students then either appropriate this authority as a contribution to their
"careers," or let it serve as a model for what they are to become out of the
classroom. In other words, in the university, one learns to *either appropriate
academic authority or adapt to it in a completely private and individual
way.* As a matter of both teaching conventions and the deeper ideology
of our society, academic authority is not often diffused, shared, changed,
or considered as a determinant of whatever knowledge is pursued in the
classroom. The university classroom is just not considered to be the site of
social activity.

Grading,[1] which begins in elementary school, continuously encourages the
conception of the classroom as a collection of individuals as opposed to a
cooperative group. Grading means, in part, that each individual competes
with the others for the teacher's favorable judgment. It also promotes the
attitude that the sharing or negotiation of knowledge among students must
finally be subordinated to the student's performance as an individual. If, as
all students know, the outcome or end of classroom activity is to achieve
a high grade, they also know that whatever social activity spontaneously
arises in the class as a result of the common interest in the subject matter
should be understood as something peripheral to the "moment of truth"
when the examinations are distributed and a purely individual performance
is demanded. Because of this process, "cheating," or the ability to create a
fraudulent individual performance is possible. If the cooperation that took
place before the examination, or independently of the grading situation,

---

1. In chapter 6, there is further discussion of grading, along with some thoughts on what
changes in classroom functioning would allow grading to be abandoned.

appears during the test, it is "cheating." In this way, students learn to "steal" knowledge; but more subtly and more importantly, they are taught that the achievement of knowledge is a purely individual matter, something best done entirely on one's own. This understanding on the part of students conceals, sometimes permanently, the truth that knowledge is always inseparably both individual and collective.

Members of the academy, of course, will deny that they wish to teach this conception of knowledge. They will claim, along with the university administration, that there is no other way to "certify" students. Because each person tries to find work as an individual, there must be an individual record to attest to a person's qualifications. This implies, however, that sixteen or more years of academic competition in school are necessary for a person to get a job. Many do claim life in the "real world" is competitive. This, we can admit, is the truth: competition and individualization are promoted in the classroom because they are values held by our society.

In speaking, therefore, of the nonsocial character of the classroom, we are pointing to a widely held value in society at large. Members of the academy, who, in an abstract way, will deny their implication in this value, actually hold it. In part, as Richard Ohmann has discussed at length in *English in America*,[2] it is a value created by the economic system, and the academy adopts it automatically in order to serve this system. In addition, however, it is a value that is held more by men than by women.[3] As we are well aware, the academy is disproportionately populated by men; few academic departments have more than a fifth of their positions filled by women, and many far fewer.[4] Dating back to when universities were founded in monasteries, scholarly work has historically been the exclusive domain of men. Only very recently has this custom been challenged. It would not be an exaggeration to claim, therefore, that the social psychology of the academy is the social psychology of men functioning among themselves.

The history of the classroom is somewhat different. For many years, women were not educated at all until they finally began entering the educational system as teachers of the very young. When I was in elementary school, of my first seven teachers only one was a man. Both sexes have been going to school in this century, but women have been the custodians of the

---

2. Richard Ohmann, *English in America* (New York: Oxford University Press, 1976).

3. In chapters 2, 3, and 5, there is further discussion of this point, since it plays a very large role in this treatise. However, the most general basis for this claim is Naomi Scheman's essay, cited in the next chapter, which persuaded me that individualism is an ideology that men regularly advocate and which favors their (our) privileged position in a sexist society.

4. In case you don't believe this claim, I advise you to pick up, at random, ten catalogues in your library and tabulate the gender distribution yourself.

schoolchildren. The elementary schoolroom, as we remember, functions in a much more social way than the university classroom. Students are in one group all day, and, as a rule, the same teacher teaches different subjects and conducts different activities. Students, as a result, become much more familiar with one another, and classmates are often residents of the same community for many years; the teachers themselves are often part of that community. Yet, as salutary as this circumstance is, school systems are still run by values of the academy, as principals and superintendents are mostly men trained in the university to insure that schools "prepare" the young either for the university or "the real world." Thus, testing and competition are introduced early, the focus of subjects becomes narrower in the higher grades, "specialists" are introduced, and students are indeed "prepared" for the highly individuated styles of higher education and economic life. The social potential of classrooms populated by women and children is gradually replaced by the values of the academy and the economy.

As subjects of study, language and literacy have been seriously damaged by the unbalanced relation of the classroom and the academy. In elementary school, language still retains some of its early infantile character as a dynamic feature of the children's interaction. The curriculum in the early grades is now called Language Arts, implying that language is something that grows, needing to be cultivated, rather than something that is inserted into people's minds. Gradually, through the middle and secondary school years, the subject becomes Language Skills, which is, at the same time and later on in college, further divided into Reading Skills and Writing Skills. As the classroom becomes increasingly desocialized and under the influence of the academy, language becomes a correspondingly less consequential subject; more of an item to serve individualized interests; a career tool rather than a social capability. In fact, because the purely instrumental use of language starts to predominate, social relations are thought of more as contracts between individuals than as communities with continuously varying mutual interests. The reduction of language as a subject is done in the interest of preserving the academy's monastic character, which, in turn, serves larger and sometimes more sinister values.

In this chapter, I am going to discuss three contexts in which I think such values are at work: the formal study of reading in the middle school grades, the teaching of writing to freshmen and other college students, and the attention to language in contemporary literary theory. Each of these contexts plays an important role, on the one hand, in how the classroom and the academy relate to one another, and on the other hand, in how the subject of language and its use is introduced in the different phases of the school-through-university sequence.

Reading Research Quarterly, sponsored by the International Reading Association, is one of the most influential journals of research in reading. Its main readership is made up of teachers of reading teachers, or those in the academy (in schools of education or comparable divisions of the university) who are responsible for formulating and presenting the issues of reading as a developmental event and guiding younger people in cultivating their reading capability. As an academic project, the study of reading is a large enterprise on many levels, reaching from the university into the elementary schools. Within this enterprise, "research" is usually cited as the basis for a wide variety of initiatives taken to enhance the quality of reading instruction at every level. In other words, many who teach reading in the more elementary grades rely on research to provide new facts, new perspectives, new attitudes, and new ideas, which can be applied to the problems in local school systems or particular classrooms.

One of the main items of this research has long been the comprehension of any written text. An apparently reasonable premise of this research interest is the belief that comprehension may be understood to denote the same sort of thing regardless of which texts are read, so long as the texts have been determined, by a series of measures, to be at a certain "reading level." The only significant variant of texts at the same level of difficulty is their length. Thus, comprehension is studied, at any given level, of words, sentences, paragraphs, essays or short stories. The underlying assumption is that the ability to comprehend a text is not related to the reader's roles and well-being as a social figure. Comprehension is generalized and then subdivided into units on a quantitative basis. This has long been the standard procedure in the natural sciences. For example, to study the process of digestion, one variously studies biting, chewing, swallowing, acid secretion in the stomach, assimilation of nutrients in the colon, and the assembling of waste products. A large process is defined and then studied as a series of subprocesses. Similarly, in reading comprehension, each of the subprocesses is measured by a test. So, if P. W. Bridgman's concept of the "operational definition" is used to define what a scientifically studied entity is, we will conclude that comprehension, when studied scientifically in this sector of the academy, is *that which a comprehension test measures*. The objectivity of the test results—that is, their presumed truth—is insured by a suitable degree of "inter-rater-reliability." In any event, comprehension tests are presented as the bottom line in all studies of comprehension. Designs of studies do vary, but regardless of the overall design (choice of population, of text, of research site, and so on), the "scientific" fact of comprehension and the degrees of its achievement appear mainly through the tests.

As a case in point, consider James F. Baumann's article in the Fall 1984 issue of *Reading Research Quarterly* entitled "The Effectiveness of a Direct Instruction Paradigm for Teaching Main Idea Comprehension."[5] Baumann wishes to show that the technique he developed for teaching sixth-graders how to comprehend the main idea in a paragraph is more effective than the technique used in a basal textbook series and the technique of giving assorted vocabulary exercises. Baumann divided his sixty-six students into three groups, then gave each group five different tests to measure, or help measure, their comprehension after all three techniques of instruction were administered. The five tests were: the "main ideas in paragraph" test, the "details that support main ideas" test, the "main ideas in short passages" test, the "main idea outline" test, and the "free recall" test. The conclusion of the study was that students instructed by Baumann's technique had higher scores on all but one of these tests (the "free recall" test) than those in the other two groups. We should note that Baumann devised all of these tests, with the exception of part of the "free recall" test. Here is the list of units that Baumann taught to the group using his technique: "paragraph main idea (explicit and implicit)," "passage main idea" (explicit and implicit, with "subordinate details"), "passage main idea outline" (explicit and implicit). As we can see, the tests correspond exactly to the units of Baumann's instruction. We can reasonably suppose that the tests tested only Baumann's technique and not that of the other two methods. And we can further conclude that the students' comprehension was not tested after all; the high scores by the students in the main experimental group are attributable to the fact that they had just been taught the very items that the tests tested, while the other students were taught different things.

Because the tests were so closely related to the instruction technique being investigated, I should probably change my claim that only the test defined comprehension. In this case, it was the teaching technique, which the test repeated, that defined comprehension. This, of course, is not the conclusion Baumann sought. It is the result of trying to formulate one's purpose in terms that do not suit it—in this instance, the formulaic application of what Baumann takes to be the "scientific method." Yet it is not a trivial conclusion that the teaching technique defines comprehension, and it is perhaps a more consequential one than what the article put forth. It shows that comprehension is defined by cultural values, particularly the value which endorses "direct instruction" as a classroom format. The instructional situation and the testing situation have more or less the same interpersonal format. This format gives

5. James F. Baumann, "The Effectiveness of a Direct Instruction Paradigm for Teaching Main Idea Comprehension," *Reading Research Quarterly*, 20 (Fall 1984), 93–115.

a clearer picture of what Baumann and many other researchers and teachers assume without question, and which they permit to define, consciously or unconsciously, as comprehension.

The interpersonal structure of the testing format is familiar: an authoritative adult enters the room with a stack of tests, and the students do their best to follow instructions. The tests are then scored and the results announced, each student accepting the judgment given by the teacher. But consider how Baumann said the material was taught. There are five steps: introduction, example, direct instruction, teacher-directed application, and independent practice. Here is how Baumann describes what happens in the introduction: "In this step, the students are provided a purpose for the ensuing lesson, and they are told why the acquisition of the skill will help them become better readers." Consider the two passive constructions: the students "are provided a purpose" and "they are told." If we insert the missing subjects, we get, "I tell the students the purpose" and "I tell them why this purpose is good for them." It is not an innocent use of a science-reporting convention to describe an instruction with the passive voice; it is a means of concealing or attempting to conceal, through language, the fact that specific real people have made choices. In this case, Baumann and his team made the choices. The use of the passive voice tries to imply that the only thing that happened during the introduction was that information was transferred. What actually happened was that the students were *warned* that they now must follow instructions. Here is how Baumann describes "direct instruction," the third step:

> Direct instruction, the real heart of the instructional strategy, consists of the teacher telling, showing, demonstrating, modeling, the skill to be learned. In direct instruction, the teacher is leading the lesson; that is, responsibility for skill acquisition rests solely with the teacher. Students should be involved with learning, but the transfer of responsibility to students comes in the following steps.

The "heart of the instructional strategy" is this: the students must do what the teacher does and what the teacher says to do: they must imitate the behavior of the teacher. The meaning of the term "direct instruction" is: the teacher tells the students what to do. In the fourth step, the teacher-directed application, Baumann writes, "the teacher is still present for guidance and feedback, but the students are forced to apply the skill previously taught." In this sentence we see the passive construction "students are forced." While this phrase is not meant in a malicious sense, its translation to an active, "I force the students to do what I taught them" suggests coercion both in the instructional technique and in the many tests students must take. The "scientific" format of the research presentation is coercive in a similar way: it is falsely assumed that because the results were counted and tabulated and statistically balanced, they must be epistemologically authoritative. The actual authority at work is quite another thing. In the fifth step, Baumann claims, "the transition from full teacher responsibility to full student responsibility is complete." The students "are provided" new exercises to do on their own. The only fair way to describe this responsibility is to say that the students are responsible for doing the new exercises in the way the teacher would want them to. The students are responsible to comply; they are not responsible to think through a problem, but to think through *how someone wants them to solve it.* This is the meaning I think students well understand when they hear the instructions.

In another article in the same issue of *Reading Research Quarterly*, the purpose of seeking student compliance is almost explicitly stated. This piece, "Direct Instruction of Summarization Skills" by Victoria Hare and Kathleen Borchardt, deals with the same instructional technique.[6] Here is what they say at the end of their essay, in the "discussion" section:

> We are no longer sure of children's ability to identify main ideas as we were, . . . and we know that younger readers—particularly poorer ones—may possess their own, different notions of importance. . . . We know that particularly with the content area, expository texts, students often do not know enough about the passage context to be able to identify what is important. This lack of background knowledge causes them to play a guessing game when naming top-level ideas.

While this account of the problem seems reasonable enough, consider their proposed solution:

> What can be done to increase students' sensitivity to adult conceptions of importance? Unfortunately, summarization instruction, i.e., teaching of macrorules, did not enhance identification of implicit main ideas. Nevertheless, we suspect that redoubled, more focused efforts to teach the stubborn invention half of the topic sentences rule, i.e., recognizing implicit main ideas, may succeed where instruction failed.

It is probably not a coincidence that Baumann's article, a few pages away in the same issue, describes just such "redoubled, more focused efforts" and the "success" they yielded. More pertinent, however, is Hare and Borchardt's statement of just what the problem of comprehending main ideas is and thus its implied solution. The key phrase is "increase student sensitivity to

6. Victoria Chou Hare and Kathleen M. Borchardt, "Direct Instruction of Summarization Skills," *Reading Research Quarterly*, 20 (Fall 1984), 62–78.

adult conceptions of importance." This pedagogical purpose suggests that what students *already* see as important can't be important except as it agrees with adult conceptions. In the classroom, there is usually only one adult, moreover. I wonder how many adults are willing to say that their sense of the importance of any paragraph or story or essay is representative of "adult conceptions." I have worked with groups of secondary school teachers where we all shared ideas of "importance" in works of literature. Since there were no "adults" in that classroom, we had to conclude that each person's sense of importance contributes something to the collective understanding of the particular text. This situation for middle-school students should not be much different. If the students actually worked with one another, perhaps in small groups, they would learn to understand paragraphs or any other text they are capable of reading. More likely it is the usual authority structure of the classroom which discourages collaboration and encourages compliant "recitation," rather than the failure of any given technique used within that structure that accounts for young students' frustration in learning to read. Articles such as Baumann's, and Hare and Borchardt's seem unaware of the authoritarian premises of ideas like "direct instruction," and, even worse, seem to advocate a kind of "get tough" policy which depends even more on these premises than traditional juvenile didactics.

Let me cite one more instance of the social potential of the classroom being nullified by the conventional use of the academic-scientific research style. In the main text, under "Method," Hare and Borchardt write, "Eighty-four low-income minority high school juniors were randomly assigned. . . . students attended school in a large Midwestern city." In the Baumann article, under "Method," it says, "sixty-six sixth-grade students from an elementary school in a rural midwestern community participated in the study." If we read the fine print of the Hare/Borchardt article (that is, the footnotes), it turns out to mean: "Eighty-four Chicago inner-city poor blacks and Hispanics, with a smattering of whites, and three times as many girls as boys, were paid minimum wage one summer to help us with our work. Some of them did not show up, so we had to reduce our population to 44." In the Baumann article, the actual report should read: "The Principal of Frontier Elementary/Middle school in Brookston, Indiana, let me and my team into his school so I could test out my method with 66 of his students."

In the first case, indigent inner-city students were paid to cooperate with a relatively privileged group whose underlying purpose was to teach them to adapt to a feature of the majority culture. In the second case, collaboration between the researcher and the school principal permitted the normal classroom routine to be interrupted by strangers pursuing their own goals. In both of these cases the need to keep up an academic formalism (both in doing the studies and in presenting them in print) takes priority over what the classroom had already planned: there is something doubtful about paying students (who really do need the money) to participate in a study that makes no other contribution to their own lives; and there is cause to wonder at two men (the principal and the researcher) in powerful positions temporarily agreeing to convert a classroom into a research site which serves only the interests of the researcher. The methods, attitudes, procedures, and content ("direct instruction") of both studies contribute much more to academic than to classroom interests, and work not to enrich the classroom but to keep its (mostly) female and juvenile constituents in their place.

Richard Ohmann's several discussions of Freshman Composition[7] show the relation of the classroom and the academy in a similar light. He argues that both high school and college teachers, through their strong dependence on standardized handbooks, tend to suppress their social awareness because of the conflicts it would bring out:

> English teachers, like their books, do teach students that a speaker or writer runs a constant risk of betraying through his language some shameful inferiority. A recent article shows that both high school and college English teachers proclaim standards of usage they themselves, along with many of the most famous writers of English and American history, often violate. The author, Mary Vaiana Taylor, goes on to suggest that:
>
>> English teachers establish and protect absolute standards for linguistic performance because in so doing they are establishing and protecting their own prestige, and they feel it necessary to establish and protect it because they are themselves linguistically insecure.
>
> Others have shown that these insecurities are greatest among the middle and lower class, and among women—the groups to which most school teachers of English belong. So the anxiety and the sense of linguistic hierarchy they teach to students are deeply involved with class and status, and are felt by English teachers themselves.[8]

Ohmann is arguing that those working primarily in the classroom are silently coerced by an external standard represented by the handbooks and further traceable to the cultural-economic (and ideological) demand for as static a social class structure as possible. The uniformity of writing standards found

---

7. Richard Ohmann, *English in America*; "Use Definite, Specific, Concrete Language," *College English*, 41 (December 1979), 390–97; "Reflections on Class and Language," *College English*, 44 (January 1982), 1–17.

8. Ohmann, *English in America*, pp. 169–70.

in handbooks, he argues, hides the fact that different styles of language use are the means by which students learn of different social class interests. The use of an official standard tends to devalue the already rich strains of language use in less privileged classes and prevents them from contributing their special kinds of "knowledge."[9] Ohmann implies that there is, perhaps, something militaristic about the handbooks' quiet pressure for a fixed standard of English.

Ohmann summarizes this standard in his essay, "Use Definite, Specific, Concrete Language," the title being a composite of an instruction given by almost all composition handbooks. The instruction is a syndrome of substrategies that add up to what Ohmann characterizes as a "preferred style" with an implied set of both language and social values. This style "focuses on a truncated present moment"; it "favors sensory news, from the surfaces of things"; it "obscures the social relations and the relations of people to nature that are embedded in all things"; it "foregrounds the writer's own perceptions," which lead to an excessive involvement in oneself; and it urges the "denial of conflict" by picturing a world in which, for example, "the telephone has the same meaning for all classes of people." In general, Ohmann continues, these handbooks

> push the student writer always toward the language that most nearly reproduces the immediate experience and away from the language that might be used to understand it, transform it, and relate it to everything else. The authors privilege a kind of revising and expanding that leaves the words themselves unexamined and untransformed.

This is a standard not of language use but of "writing skills," particularly the skill of transmitting information. Uses of language that give attitudes, opinions, feelings, generalizations, guesses, and doubts—commonplace, socially interactive behavior—are understood to interfere with the basic need for "clear information." The affirmative purpose of this standard, Ohmann suggests, is to train people to use language (as opposed to cultivating language capability in people) in such a way as to best serve corporate purposes—language which doesn't question or challenge, but tends to narrow its focus to discrete tasks. The more negative purpose of this standard is to suppress the tendency of active language use to encourage the formation of social subgroups and to enlarge the feeling of a collective consciousness. In any

---

9. A related case that has the same social pertinence is the recent vote in California to make English the "official" language. While this move will not, suddenly, render Spanish an impoverished language, it will increase the tension between English and Spanish speaking communities, especially since no extra funds were voted to intensify the teaching of English.

case, students are taught to treat their language as a tool, as if it were not already ineradicably bound up with their individual histories as social beings, as if it can be cut and shaped into an all-purpose conduit of "thought." The alternative to this strategy, Ohmann observes,

> would mean having students develop their writing skills in the process of discovering their political needs, and as an aid in achieving those needs. It would mean encouraging students to form alliances with one another based on real life interest, and letting the skills of writing grow through collective work. And of course some of these alliances would come into conflict, since different students are of different classes, races, and ages. In short, it would mean bringing politics—everyone's politics—into composition, rather than just the politics of the establishment, which are now implicit in the course and made to look like no-politics.[10]

Although Ohmann is emphasizing issues of world- or macro-politics throughout his work, he is careful to stress politics as something inherent in social existence, as something which reaches from the smallest groups to the largest societies. He wants to show that language is taught as if it could be socially disinterested, when in reality it is bound up at every point with social or collective interests.

Ohmann generally refers to such interests as *class* interests. Of course we do not need to revise his sense of class as descriptive of large socioeconomic groups. It might be helpful, however, to remember that the idea of "class" in "class interests" relates to the "class" in "classrooms." Ohmann describes what we could take as an important common element—the idea of class or classroom as a social event:

> I have been using a notion of class that is structural and static. In this way of thinking, a class is defined by its relationship to the means of production and to other classes. The concept is incomplete unless joined to one grounded in the continuous movement of history. In this second view, I do not simply and eternally *belong* to the professional and intellectual portion of the working class. Rather, in all my doing from day to day, I and the people I mingle with and am affected by constantly *create* my class position. As, for instance, I confirm it by writing in this way to this audience, by continuing to work with my mind and my mouth more than with my hands. . . . From this perspective, class is not a permanent fact, but something that continually *happens*.
>
> As soon as we look at it this way, a still different relationship of class and language comes into focus. My way of talking, whether "caused" by my class or not, is one of the important means by which I, in my relations with other people, recreate my class, confirm it, perhaps alter it.[11]

---

10. Ohmann, *English in America*, p. 160.
11. Ohmann, "Reflections on Class and Language," 15.

According to this description, class is a human process, a name for organized sectors of collective interaction; but it is also the basis for phenomenological subjectivity and its result. The individual "way of talking," which is the principal way we relate to others, at once marks this class—identifies it to and for others—and *changes* it. The act of language use, is, in principle in each case, something that changes one's class either relative to other members or other classes.

The principle of "direct instruction" keeps the social structure of the class-room unchanged. It promotes a classroom paradigm that is found in almost every university and is regularly kept in force by the grading system. Stasis is achieved, as Ohmann describes, by *fixing* the class roles of teachers and students, which means, *by not allowing the language use in the classroom to change the class*. In part, this entails a restriction of vocabulary; mainly it involves restrictions in speaking and thinking for *both* parties (teachers and students). For example, turn-taking, the common regulation of group conver-sations, appears in the classroom as the alternation between the teacher speak-ing and a student speaking. In this way, the teacher speaks half the time (usu-ally much more), and each student extremely little—and most don't speak at all. In this situation, as has been well documented by Dale Spender,[12] men feel freer to take over the conversation; if the teacher is a man (in most cases), he becomes even more of a controlling factor. Because the academy is mostly men, the classroom becomes the means for men (and the academy) to perpetuate their political privileges as a social class. The class*room* is being denied as a class that contributes to and changes the academy.

The student's use of language is usually limited to what he or she "hands in," a practice that almost no one questions. "Handing in" means submitting one's language for judgment by the academy. The teacher's binding judgment is given not in his or her commentary, but in the grade. Thus, for the language that really counts in the classroom, *there is no dialogue at all*. Both students' and teachers' language is considered to be a fixed entity; actually the teacher does not finally contribute his or her language—only a letter! On the one hand, the teacher speaks most of the time in class; but on the other hand he (sometimes she) contributes very little "language" that does not bear on what grade the student can get. Students' actual use of language in class "recreates and confirms" a receiving or an adapting class; the teacher's actual use of language recreates and confirms membership in the "grading" class, a membership that students cannot regulate or participate in. For the classroom to be an authentic scene of discussion, negotiation, and exploration, all members must participate as equals. Also, each member's

12. Dale Spender, *Man Made Language* (London: Routledge & Kegan Paul, 1980).

language must be studied and used in an evenhanded way, so that exchanges of language matter in themselves and are not "officially" overruled by a last word (the letter) of one member, and, as the responsibility for teaching is shared, the task of coming to new knowledge is collective.

Sometimes it seems as if, within the academy, the presentation of new thought is collective; sources are cited, acknowledgments are given, apologies and guesses are made, and notes of uncertainty about the future are often struck. In some cases there are two or more authors for important volumes. These are the senses in which scholarship has been traditionally understood to be communally held and generated. They are also the features of more recent scholarship being contributed on behalf of clear political causes. Yet the individualist identity of scholarly and critical work remains its primary identity. Even the recent forward-looking volume, *Changing the Subject*,[13] aiming to enact something like collective authorship, presents essays by five different authors, making the volume unique only in that there is no "editor" who collected the work. The essays themselves show no substantive point where collaboration brings in something individual authorship could not. Humanistic thought is understood to be privately generated, and the conditions of its production are highly individualized. Scholars work *out* of the classroom, in libraries or other private places. When papers are given in public, there is rarely any discussion; performance is the main event. When a series of essays is presented in a learned journal, they rarely have anything to do with one another; most editors don't take the trouble to assemble an issue to address a collective concern.[14] And, virtually no work appears that studies the social or collective basis of language and knowledge, or that enacts this basis in some serious way.

There is no ready explanation for this situation. We are dealing with customs and traditions that date back to classical, biblical, and even prebiblical times, in that literacy has always been, by and large, a privilege of men. Only in this century, when literacy has begun to become universal, have we seen any signs that the academy's constituency will change, and this only under strong pressure from feminist interests.

Of particular concern in the present discussion is that even "advanced" theoretical work in language and literature is often governed by individualist and masculinist ideology. For example, the concept of "reading" in the academy

13. Julian Henriques, Wendy Holloway, Cathy Unwin, Couze Venn, and Valerie Walkerdine, *Changing the Subject: Psychology, Social Regulation, and Subjectivity* (London: Methuen, 1984).

14. A notable exception to this claim is Ralph Cohen's effort, over the past twenty years, to make virtually every issue of *New Literary History* cohere around a single topic and to include contributors from a variety of disciplines as well as from different countries.

has moved away[15] from Louise Rosenblatt's original concept of classroom-based, interactive reading, toward abstract concepts of "the" reader and "the" text and models that would apply to *all* instances of reading. These models presuppose the idea of a single person facing a single text as a reasonable or even natural way of coping with the subjectivity of reading. But as this position is articulated, the "reader" is more of a purely hypothetical being. In very few instances does the critic actually study his or her own readings, much less the readings of others, while the great majority of discussions focus on the texts. Theorists such as Iser, Culler, and Fish have documented their models not by inquiring into the variety of actual readings in some real-life context, but by presenting their own readings as exemplary or even fundamentally objective. The actual human use of texts and language, which would mean bringing in considerations from the history, psychology, and sociology of literacy, for example, is not taken to be part of the subject matter of "reading." Rather, the academy, led, for example, by Culler's recent work on deconstruction, has celebrated more and more the idea of the primary autonomy of language—an idea supporting Janusz Slawinski's fear that the scholar would like "to detach himself from the community of readers to which he belongs, to liberate his method from the cultural and literary constraints of time and place."[16] While many who have adopted this theory in language claim they are drawn more into history and community, the actual result has been the opposite. What has emerged instead is a kind of "academic fraternity with a French accent," intensifying the individualist style of scholarship and criticism.

Let's consider now how several different renditions of this idea of "the primary autonomy of language" have contributed to the traditionally nonsocialized university classroom, preserving the academic psychology of social detachment and, usually, the emphasis on intramasculine interests. The common element in these renditions is the figure of language as a ludic activity, resulting in terms such as "the game of language," the "free play of language," or "the play of difference," as if language were only a constraining force that is beyond human regulation. These terms mark the deep philosophical position that language regularly poses frustrations, mysteries, paradoxes, and problems, and that there is no escape from this situation.

15. Actually, the "academy" never endorsed Rosenblatt's work to begin with when it first appeared. The "moving away" I am referring to occurred more recently—in the late sixties and early seventies—when deconstructionist thought began to seem academically much more attractive than the uncertain, complicated, and ungainly studies of real readers, my own work being a case in point.

16. Cited by Michal Glowinski, "Reading, Interpretation, Reception," *New Literary History*, 11 (Autumn 1979), 78.

In his 1962 essay, "On the Problem of Self-Understanding,"[17] Hans-Georg Gadamer describes first the general idea of the "game" and then that of the "language game."

> . . . for human subjectivity the real experience consists in the fact that something that obeys its own set of laws gains ascendancy in the game. . . . The back and forth movement of the game has a peculiar freedom and buoyancy that determines the consciousness of the player. . . . Whatever is brought into play or comes into play no longer depends on itself but is dominated by the relations that we call the game, . . . the individual . . . conforms to the game or subjects himself to it, that is, he relinquishes the autonomy of his own will. [In the case of two men using a saw], it appears . . . that the primary fact is a kind of agreement between the two, a deliberate attitude of the one as well as the other. But this attitude is still not the game. The game is not so much the subjective attitude of the two men confronting each other as it is the formation of the movement as such, which, as in an unconscious teleology, subordinates the attitudes of the individuals to itself. . . . The individual self, including his activity and his understanding of himself, is taken up in a higher determination that is really the decisive factor.

> The common agreement that takes place in speaking with others is itself a game. Whenever two persons speak with each other they speak the same language. They themselves, however, in no way know that in speaking it they are playing this language further. . . . So we adapt ourselves to each other in a preliminary way until the game of giving and taking—the real dialogue— begins. It cannot be denied that in an actual dialogue of this kind something of the character of accident, favor, and surprise—and in the end of buoyancy, indeed of elevation—that belongs to the nature of the game is present.

Gadamer characterizes the ethical action of the mutual exchange of thought as "the game of giving and taking." The terms "buoyancy" and "elevation" suggest that "real dialogue" rises above the mutual acceptance of rules, the use of a common vocabulary, and the disciplined observance of turn-taking. The game element that is present is the "higher determination that is really the decisive factor." (Later in the essay, Gadamer identifies this "higher determination" with a religious transcendence, suggesting the monastic and/or spiritual element usually found in academic social psychology.) But instead of seeing this new element in social and ethical terms, Gadamer keeps to the "game" figure to such an extent that it begins to influence how we understand the whole passage: the idea of the sport or leisure-time activity overtaking the person, as in "golf plays John." Instead of the implication of social action

17. Hans-Georg Gadamer, *Philosophical Hermeneutics*, trans. and ed. David E. Linge (Berkeley: University of California Press, 1976), pp. 53–54, 56–57.

taking place in the dialogue, there is the implication of social inertia and passivity on the part of the speakers. This suggestion is strengthened when Gadamer traces his concept of language to Heidegger's later thought which "'banished not only the concept of consciousness from its central position, but also the concept of selfhood as such." Furthermore, "the primacy that language and understanding have in Heidegger's thought indicates the priority of the relation over against its relational members—the I who understands and that which is understood." This is a relation not between people, but between knower and the known (the concept underlying "the reader and the text"), something fully bound to an individual mind on the one hand, yet apart from human relationships altogether. The virtual interaction between a reader and a text is claimed to be both a universal feature of reading and a description of a private experience. The responsibility of one reader to another, of groups of readers to previous and subsequent groups, as well as of writers to one another and to readers, do not enter this relation as active terms.

The work of Roland Barthes suggests an enactment of Gadamer's and Heidegger's idea: the joyful surrender to the text or to the act of reading. Barthes, in admitting the "game," celebrates its ludic potential for sheer pleasure.

> Our literature is characterized by the pitiless divorce which the literary institu-
> tion maintains between the producer of the text and its use, between its owner
> and its customer, between its author and its reader. This reader is thereby
> plunged into a kind of idleness—he is intransitive; he is, in short, serious:
> instead of functioning himself, instead of gaining access to the magic of the
> signifier, to the pleasure of writing, he is left with no more than the poor
> freedom either to accept or reject the text: reading is nothing more than a
> referendum.[18]

Although Barthes seems to identify contemporary reading styles as socially detached and isolated (the various "divorces" he cites), his solution seems to be a completely private one—to "'gain access to the magic of the signifier"— rather than a redoubled attention to the relationships that have been severed. In *The Pleasure of the Text*, Barthes suggests a possible approach to reading:

> . . . our very avidity for knowledge impels us to skim or to skip certain passages
> (anticipated as "boring") in order to get more quickly to the warmer parts of the
> anecdote. . . . we boldly skip (no one is watching) descriptions, explanations,
> analysis, conversations; doing so, we resemble a spectator in a nightclub who

18. Roland Barthes, *S/Z*, trans. Richard Miller (New York: Hill and Wang, 1974), p. 4.

climbs onto the stage and speeds up the dancer's striptease, tearing off her clothing, but *in the same order.*[19]

From the writer's point of view, Barthes describes,

I must seek out this reader (must "cruise" him) *without knowing where he is.* A site of bliss is then created. It is not the reader's "person" that is necessary to me, it is this site; the possibility of a dialectics of desire, of an unpredictability of bliss; the bets are not placed, there can still be a game.[20]

On the one hand, one can appreciate Barthes' attempt to foreground the affective engagement of readers and writers in the literary experience. Feelings and passion have always been fundamental in the use and history of literature. On the other hand, his sense of affective experience is so fully centered on the (masculine) individual's fantasy life that even the idea of the erotic seems devoid of its necessary social dimension. Barthes characterizes the reader's action as a licensed aggression, where this reader is faithful to the idea of the dance yet permitted to intrude on its performance in order to gain an erotic pleasure while "no one is watching." In his description of the writer, Barthes celebrates the writer's unconsciousness of the other, the reader, as well as of self. It is the "site" of bliss that counts, the field or board on which the game is played that finally matters. The "dialectics" have no conscious or rational components, no calculations or "bets." The individual readers finally give themselves over to play, foreplay, fantasy, and "magic." In the cause of opposing an inhibiting "seriousness," Barthes also suspends judgments, arguments, and opinions—items which define and express the common sense of interpersonal responsibility that inhabits every use of language and literature.

Wittgenstein's concept of the language-game seems less affective and more pragmatic than Gadamer's and Barthes'. Rather than mystery and pleasure, Wittgenstein emphasizes paradox and frustration as underlying features of our necessary embeddedness in language. These latter features are offered as final, limiting factors that language presents to human initiatives. Here are several of his characteristic formulations:[21]

I shall . . . call the whole, consisting of language and the actions into which it is woven, the "language-game" (section 7)

19. Roland Barthes, *The Pleasure of the Text*, trans. Richard Miller (New York: Hill and Wang, 1975), p. 11.

20. Ibid., p. 4.

21. The following citations are all from Ludwig Wittgenstein, *Philosophical Investigations*, trans. G. E. M. Anscombe (New York: Macmillan, 1953).

. . . The term "language-*game*" is meant to bring into prominence the fact that the speaking of language is part of an activity, or a form of life. (section 23)

We see what we call "sentence" and "language" has not the formal unity that I imagined, but is the family of structures more or less related to one another. (section 108)

Philosophy is a battle against the bewitchment of our intelligence by means of language. (section 109)

The results of philosophy are the uncovering of one or another piece of plain nonsense and of bumps that the understanding has got by running its head up against the limits of language. (section 118)

Philosophy may in no way interfere with the actual use of language; it can in the end only describe it. (section 124)

Wittgenstein describes a situation in which intelligence is "bewitched" by language, but all philosophy does is disclose this situation. Philosophy is itself bound by language games, each of which has no clear boundary but is defined by its connectedness in a "family" of similar games. Furthermore, these games are not purely linguistic but are "forms of life," not unlike children's ritualistic games. While this pragmatistic note has been taken up in several quarters recently in speech act theory and linguistic pragmatics, Wittgenstein himself had a relatively meager idea of just how social a "form of life" is, and he had no language to include its social character in his own thought. In fact, even in the contemporary elaboration of the pragmatic theme, social interaction is conceived as small units of a ritualistic cast, very much as Wittgenstein conceived them.[22] Wittgenstein is ready to let language stand as a paradoxical entity: something which cannot be explained because it is the only means of explanation.

Jacques Derrida's response to this paradox is to plunge into it and make it the hallmark of his discourse. He is thus given to such formulations as, "The verb 'to differ' seems to differ from itself," or "*Differance* is neither a

---

22. A typical example might be John Searle's discussion of "promising." This word definitely bespeaks social interaction, but can one remove "promising" as a "form of life" from the complicated psychosocial context in which it is routinely done? The question not taken up by linguists, as a rule, is just what is a "form of life." In chapter 6, I discuss Shirley Heath's idea of a "literacy event" which does provide a fuller and more recognizable life unit, but still the key elements of the underlying relationships of the speakers are not as prominent as they should be. Some work in sociolinguistics that is beginning to study real sorts of generic conversations — such as teacher-student or doctor-patient — are more promising paths toward finding how language use and forms of life are related.

word nor a *concept.*"[23] Derrida, using sources in Nietzsche, Saussure, and Heidegger, claims that such usages, and the thinking they encourage, mark a new phase, even a new era, in the history of Western metaphysics. The result, however, is that he renders discourse more important than explanation, formulation more important than ideas, and texts more important than contexts of history and intersubjectivity. It is not as if discourse, formulations, and texts are not important; it is that for Derrida, explanation, ideas, and contexts are all principal terms of the "old" metaphysics and therefore obsolete in some fundamental sense. In his preoccupation with the space between terms and with the gap between poles, people's living experience of the balance of terms, and of this balance's "feel" in daily life is utterly ignored, and he seems to endorse thought that is abstract and tied up in purely academic action.

We should not be surprised, therefore, to find that the game metaphor enters his work in significant ways.

> Contrary to the metaphysical, dialectical, and "Hegelian" interpretation of the economic movement of differance, we must admit a game where whoever loses wins and where one wins and loses each time. (p. 151)

The game image articulates a paradox that purposely subverts the meaning of winning and losing, as well as the common sense of change and continuity. Hegel's idea of the movement of history stresses history's path toward rational synthesis. The idea stipulates that at any moment some forces prevail over others. But if Derrida's "game" phrase is admitted to discourse, language would become ineligible to identify social developments. Any attempt to do so cannot "win," and any such act by anyone at any time can always be also read as a loss or defeat. Naming can no longer wield social authority.

A similar effect takes place when Derrida argues that difference is prior to Being (understood here as consciousness and self-consciousness).

> Being has always made "sense," has always been conceived or spoken of as such, only by dissimulating itself in beings; thus, in a particular and very strange way, differance (is) "older" than the ontological difference or the truth of Being. In this age it can be called the play of traces. It is a trace that no longer belongs to the horizon of Being but one whose sense of Being is borne and bound by this play; it is a play of traces or differance that has no sense and is not, a play that does not belong. There is no support to be found and no depth to be had for this bottomless chessboard where being is set in play.

---

23. Jacques Derrida, "Differance," in *Speech and Phenomena*, trans. David B. Allison (Evanston: Northwestern University Press, 1973), pp. 129, 130; hereafter cited in text.

The main predication here is: differance, the bottomless chessboard, is the scene of being. The play of traces is prior to the division of Being into separate individual consciousnesses. The ordinary sense that there are different minds which act in affirmative ways is illusory (Being "'dissimulating itself in beings")—or, at least only characteristic of the previous era of Western metaphysics. Just as Wittgenstein claims that philosophy "cannot give any foundation" (*Philosophical Investigations*, section 124), Derrida claims that any such foundation is a "bottomless chessboard," some comparative space which allows linguistic terms to look positive while hiding their implication in the play of traces. For Derrida, to *say* the game is to play it, to present the performance of textuality, to enter fully into the play of traces (the intermixing of texts, intertextuality) without regard to the experience of consciousness and self-consciousness. For academic deconstructionist critics, reading is similarly anchored in the bottomless chessboard, and attempts to view it as anchored in the nonludic domain of social experience and rational purpose are not considered to be enlightened critical discourse. Intertextuality is the academic "game" that has come to overtake the purposes, intersubjectivity, and historicity of reading communities found in university classrooms.

Several sources within the masculine pale of the academy have presented views which don't join the game. Gerald Graff argues, for example, that as long as the referentiality of language is a part of language, there must always be room for taking the referentiality of literature seriously, that the self-reflexiveness of language cannot be an ultimate category.[24] Ralph Cohen's theory of the historical evolution of literary genres shows that a genre has never been, and can never be, a language category that functions independently of a social purpose and history, and that no text is only a text, but is also a textual kind defined by its social and historical life.[25] Saul Kripke's idea of the "rigid designator" suggests that any instance of naming or identification has a psychological fixity and objective uniqueness that does not admit arbitrary change or fluent substitution.[26] I will take up these arguments later on. Now I would like to consider the game figure in a more psychosocial and, perhaps, political light.

Carol Gilligan's book *In a Different Voice* cites a 1976 study by Janet

24. Gerald Graff, *Literature Against Itself* (Chicago: University of Chicago Press, 1979).

25. Ralph Cohen, "The Attack on Genre" and "The Regeneration of Genre," The Patten Lectures, Indiana University, 24–25 September 1984. I elaborate on Cohen's thought below, toward the end of chapter 4, where I view the idea of text-and-genre as an instance of the double perspective.

26. See, again, chapter 4, which takes up Kripke's arguments in some detail.

Lever which investigated the differences between how boys and girls play games. Here is the citation from Lever:

> During the course of this study, boys were seen quarreling all the time, but not once was a game terminated because of a quarrel and no game was interrupted for more than seven minutes. In the gravest debates, the final word was always to "repeat the play," generally followed by a chorus of "cheater's proof." [27]

In contrast, Gilligan summarizes, "the eruption of disputes among girls tended to end the game. Lever seems to have confirmed Piaget's finding that 'girls . . . have a more "pragmatic" attitude toward rules,' regarding a rule as good as long as the game repaid it." "Girls are more tolerant in their attitudes toward rules, more willing to make exceptions, and more easily reconciled to innovations." (p. 10) The play of girls, Gilligan continues,

> tends to occur in smaller, more intimate groups, often the best-friend dyad, and in private places. This play replicates the social pattern of primary human relationship in that its organization is more cooperative. . . . It fosters the development of empathy and sensitivity necessary to taking the role of "the particular other" and points more toward knowing the other as different from the self. (p. 11)

Gilligan is contesting the idea that men are more ethically advanced because of their tendency to want to continue the game and uphold the rules, while women are less advanced because they treat rules more flexibly: "Rather than elaborating a system of rules for resolving disputes, girls subordinated the continuation of the game to the continuation of relationships." (p. 10) The consequence of this conclusion is not that the socially masculine "ethic of rights" should be replaced by the socially feminine "ethic of responsibility and care" but that each ethic ought to have more or less the same claim on each person's sense of social destiny.

From Gilligan's perspective, the game idea as a psychological orientation is contrasted with the relationship idea, and the contrast more or less matches the general contrast of gender-identities in contemporary society. I think there is something socially and historically masculine in the interest in rules and games, which accounts in part for the strong role of the game idea in (masculine) theorizing about the problems of language. Barthes' work in particular, which is perhaps more emotionally daring than most academics', discloses its implicit affective meaning: the autonomous interplay of reader and text is the "site" of a masculine "game"—the striptease fantasy which follows the order of the dance (that is, keeps the rules of the game), and

---

27. Carol Gilligan, *In a Different Voice* (Cambridge, Mass.: Harvard University Press, 1982), p. 9; hereafter cited in text.

pursues the erotic purpose while "no one is watching." For neither Wittgenstein nor Derrida does an actual human relationship enter into their use of the game-figure, while for Derrida, "play" is something that happens all by itself in language. Gadamer does describe a human relationship (abstract and masculine), but one in which the human relationship is subordinate to the autonomous action of the game. Even Derrida, who, in a deep sense, is looking for ways to name illusory aspirations in the tradition of Western thought, cannot find a language other than the "bottomless chessboard" and a series of new abstractions and figures to urge alertness to a crisis of false idealism. Instead of looking beyond the "game" to issues of need and value in human civilization, he intensifies his immersion in the individual performance of language, and, in a sense, makes a spectacle of his own language, his own individuality, his own academic virtuosity.

The game idea is part of the ethical and psychosocial mentality of the academy: the classroom, with its more flexible rules, ragged edges, unpredictable paths of development, and more gender, race, and class-balanced populations, has a different mentality altogether. Basically, the academy neither wishes to deal with it nor change its own style of functioning. I have tried to outline briefly how even when the academy applies itself to a careful review of the problems of language and literacy, as it has done in recent decades, it cannot seem to find its own right language to execute the social changes required to reduce its frustrations. In the chapters to follow, I will try to say, in my own language, how we can change the way we think about our subject, and through another simultaneous perspective, can change how we are the citizens of our various communities—in the classroom and in the academy.

2

Language, Knowledge, and Intersubjectivity

The opposition between the classroom and the academy could, conceivably, be resolved by encouraging more men to become elementary schoolteachers and more women to be administrators; teaching literacy in a variety of collective situations and relying very little on "direct instruction"; rejecting the academic idiom of excessive abstraction and waiting for the fad of the "language game" to pass. One could reasonably predict that these things could be made to happen. Yet, when John Dewey was exercising his influence on American education, such initiatives were taken—and they still go on in many quarters—but they also went out of style and have not taken root in any permanent way. It is quite remarkable to see how the teaching of writing announces the same complaints and problems today as it did a hundred years ago.

In retrospect, we see that Dewey's work, and its lack of social staying power, amounted only to an attempt at a local solution to the frustrations of the classroom. It was not attached to a popular movement or to a constituency that suffered under the existing social arrangements. Dewey's initiatives were, in the American tradition of education, finally not permitted a political or even psychosocial identity, but had to be content with only a moral identity. Until very recently, American schools and universities did not consider themselves part of the political process: the tradition has been that the states and local governments were responsible for education. No matter how clear it is that there are national patterns, customs, and habits of educational practice, and that these patterns are connected with social and political interests, there is overwhelming resistance to recognizing these connections and a stubborn clinging to the sentimental relationship between the classroom and the academy, in which the academy is the priestly shepherd and the classroom the unenlightened flock.

We have seen that there was at least one social constituency that was being harmed by separatist thinking and that successfully opposed it: the black communities. Because of their political efforts, classrooms and universities across the country are radically changed: different subjects must now be taught, different techniques must be used, different approaches to language-learning have been introduced. The social character of school experience has been transformed by the multiracial classroom. At the same time, the nature of knowledge has changed, as has the meaning of what it is to know anything at all.

Partly alongside the successes of the black movement, and partly because of them, the feminist movement has acquired purposes more far-reaching and more urgent than any it has had in the past. As a political movement it is unlike most others we have known in that it aims to share and diffuse political power rather than to gain and hold it for itself. Toward these ends, accordingly, there is no sign that war will be one of its strategies. In the feminist movement, militancy is the unrelenting exercise of free speech and the continual announcement of the changes that are being sought. On the basis of this regular action, political initiatives are taken, candidates selected, votes organized, money raised, and so on.

Seen in this light, the feminist movement is trying to enact what men have said they wished to enact but have never really succeeded in doing: transforming fights and wars and "militant" action into purely social and verbal forms of conflict resolution. It seems likely, therefore, that from a feminist perspective, matters of language and knowledge are academic "subjects" especially in their status as the only real path toward social peace. Neither violence toward others or self-destructive behaviors are acceptable as the "or else's" should free speech continue to yield only frustration. If men who also will not accept extinction as the "or else" following the failure of free speech join those women, then the common initiatives of this enlarged "feminist" constituency should be welcomed as changes in our basic senses of language and knowledge.

Although feminists do not mention it frequently, the feminist project does address its work to the long-term survival of the human race. In the traditional fixed psychosocial complementarity of men and women, Dorothy Dinnerstein sees a "human malaise," a species-wide psychopathology that has been "chronically uncomfortable and at this point [1976] critically life-threatening."[1] She sees both the psychopathology and the present urgency for change as equally "natural" developments. While the "prevailing male-female arrangements" are "part of nature," "our impulse to change these arrangements is as natural as they are, and more compatible with our survival

---

1. Dorothy Dinnerstein, *The Mermaid and The Minotaur* (New York: Harper & Row, 1976), p. 4; hereafter cited in text.

on earth [italics in original]." These arrangements have continued over so long a historical stretch, she argues, because of a "massive communal self-deception," which, if allowed to continue, will be "suicidal" for the human species. The root of this self-deception is

> a so far taken-for-granted condition of our existence: that the auspices under which human infancy and early childhood are lived out are predominantly female auspices. (p. 8)

Throughout her study, Dinnerstein traces a variety of topical features of the traditional gender arrangements to the universal condition of mother-exclusive or mother-dominant child-rearing. Some of these features are: the "double standard"—monogamy for women, polygamy for men; men working out of the home, women in it; men achieving identity through separation, women through attachment; the masculine politics of power and force, and the feminine support of it and victimization by it. She views the human race as limping along through history, sustaining recursive damage, enslaved to an ethic of gender configurations immediately, but not ultimately, advantageous to men, and now arriving at a political, psychosocial, and ecological pass, through which the human species cannot move unless the limp is overcome by human beings' "special abilities to pool knowledge and to build social structures based on the interpenetration of subjectivities."(p. 8) In each of Dinnerstein's chapters, she shows how a different aspect of psychosocial functioning can move toward an intergender, intersubjective style once it is admitted and understood that mother-exclusive child-rearing is ultimately in no one's best interests.

Dinnerstein's argument is that adult gender identities become exaggerated and distorted—women into "mermaids," men into "minotaurs"—because infants' exclusive attachment to their mothers is unnatural. For both sexes, the early, overwhelming attachment to the mother becomes the dominant, though usually repressed, model for all subsequent relationships—especially sexual relationships. Because the mother is the primary parent to the child for several years, not just the first few months, the early habits of physical intimacy are gradually authorized into social intimacy, thus rendering the mother-child relationship psychologically more vivid and vital to each child than is healthy. The strength of this relationship makes the masculine gender self-definition more urgent or desperate than it need be, and the feminine gender self-definition more subject to a sense of a divided self. In his sexual mentality, a man will overobjectify women, tending to see them as sex "objects," while a woman will experience her normal attachment to both sexes as a conflict of interest: women, as adults, will too easily see themselves as "mothers"—

one who ministers to both sexes—then repress this perception in the cause of getting a man. Because of the repression, a woman's wish to rediscover the mother in the man becomes opposed to the man's extraurgent need to remain "masculine," i.e., not a woman. The usual reaction to this conflict is for the man to separate himself more decisively from the home, often adopting the "double standard," while the woman becomes an ever more assiduous mother, thus preparing the path for the cycle to continue into the next generation. In this way, the family relation continues as an institution but also perpetuates the "psychopathology" of excessive infantile attachment to the mother and intergender opposition in adults. In a sense, motherhood continues in its strong role because, to both men and women, it is the only really "clean" relationship. Dinnerstein's point is that it is not clean, either, but its damaging effects on the child don't appear until adulthood, and the damaging effects on the mother have been ignored.

Nancy Chodorow's account[2] of the weakness of the sex-gender system has the same basic emphasis as Dinnerstein's, but she includes a more detailed account of the actual acquisition of gender-identity in childhood. Of particular pertinence is her description of the comparative states-of-mind or general perspectives of boys and girls. Here is how she characterizes the genders as they grow out of the oedipal period (about 5 or 6):

> Girls emerge from this period with a basis for "empathy" built into their primary definition of self in a way that boys do not. Girls emerge with a stronger basis for experiencing another's needs or feelings as one's own (or thinking that one is so experiencing another's needs and feelings). . . . From very early, then, because they are parented by a person of the same gender . . . girls come to experience themselves as less differentiated than boys, as more continuous with and related to the external object-world and as differently oriented to their inner object-world as well. (p. 167)

The oedipal period is when a child identifies with the parent of the same sex in order to overcome the potential rivalry with that parent for the parent of the opposite sex. For boys to identify with their fathers means that they further differentiate themselves from their mothers. For a boy, to form a self is to continue the infantile process of individuation that normally takes place for all children, entailing *separation* from (in most cases) the mother. For girls, however, to identify with the mother is, as Chodorow puts it, to retain the pre-oedipal attachment to the mother. The girl, in a sense,

2. Nancy Chodorow, *The Reproduction of Mothering* (Berkeley: University of California Press, 1982); pages cited in text.

"mixes" the initial modes of attachment with the basic separation and with the oedipal identification. To identify oneself as a girl means to be *both* attached to and separate from the mother. As a result, Chodorow argues, girls can empathize more easily, put themselves in another's place, more easily consider themselves as continuous with the external world. Chodorow claims that these differences ultimately mark general personality characteristics in adult life:

> Women's mothering, then, produces asymmetries in the relational experiences of girls and boys as they grow up, which account for crucial differences in feminine and masculine personality, and the relational capacities and modes which these entail. . . . Feminine personality comes to be based less on repression of inner objects, and fixed and firm splits in the ego, and more on retention and continuity of external relationships. From the retention of preoedipal attachment to their mother, growing girls come to define and experience themselves as continuous with others; their experience of self contains more flexible or permeable ego boundaries. Boys come to define themselves as more separate and distinct, with a great sense of rigid ego boundaries and differentiation. The basic feminine sense of self is connected to the world, the basic masculine sense of self is separate. (p. 169)

> . . . Masculine personality, then, comes to be defined more in terms of denial of relation and connection (and denial of femininity), whereas feminine personality come to include a fundamental definition of self in relationship. Thus, relational ability and preoccupations have been extended in women's development and curtailed in men's. . . . This points to boys' preparation for participation in nonrelational spheres and to girls' greater potential for participation in relational spheres. (pp. 169–170)

In Dinnerstein's work, the correspondence between her psychological analysis and her political interest is clearer than in Chodorow's. Like Dinnerstein, Chodorow, at the end of her book, advocates shared parenting as a clear need. But it is not obvious that the analysis cited above leads to the principle of shared parenting. This analysis is offered as an account of gender-identity psychology as it is now, the psychology governing the "reproduction of mothering." Chodorow's book is not as clearly a critique of mothering as Dinnerstein's, even though she opposes its exclusive exercise by women. The view of men and women as having, respectively, less and more "permeable ego boundaries" seems to lead more in Carol Gilligan's direction, namely, toward an inherently gender-specific ethical style. It seems Chodorow wants to provide an account of feminine developmental psychology that will obtain alongside the psychoanalytic account of masculine psychology. She seems less willing to see the reproduction of mothering as pathological, and more as an item, which, if understood in its actual complexity and scope, would make shared parenting a possible universal value.

Nevertheless, Dinnerstein's perspective is broader than Chodorow's, and, in that respect, convincing. Dinnerstein connects the psychopathology of the sex-gender system to the predominance of war and tyranny in human history. In following this line of thought she starts with the fact that women have been "immune" "from the risks and exertions of history-making." (p. 213) Both sexes make use of this feminine immunity, and "their mutual motive in fostering it is in my view the morbid core of our sexual arrangement. To uncover it is the main point of this book." (p. 213; italics in original) Dinnerstein claims that men have "legitimate internal misgivings" about how they conduct the political-historical process from behind the "men only" sign, but that when women consent not to participate in this process they are helping both genders conceal from men "the feeling that there is something trivial and empty, ugly and sad, in what he does." (p. 214; italics in original) The need of both men and women to retain the custom of mother-dominant parenting urges women to insulate their roles from the everyday risks of power politics and military life. While on the one hand this strong feminine role helps to preserve life, on the other it provides a continuing justification for the adversarial and militaristic psychology used by men to conduct international relations: the "innocent" depend on them for protection. In addition, Dinnerstein suggests, the value of power, either openly or tacitly understood by most to be the bottom line of history, is given its public validation by the assumption, within the family, that masculine authority finally overrules feminine authority.

By placing the issue of gender arrangements in this broad context, Dinnerstein implies that many other aspects of culture should be reviewed with an eye toward how they may or may not reflect gender-specific social values. For example, the principle of the divisibility of knowledge as institutionalized in academic departments is open to question. Although it may not be a self-evident good to see the relatedness of seemingly unrelated subjects, the fact is that the increasing pressure in academic life for "interdisciplinary" and "multidisciplinary" issues and projects is directly related to the political forces that brought Victorian Studies, American Studies, and now, Black Studies and Women's Studies into major view in most universities. A large part of the resistance to interdisciplinary studies is, obviously, the traditional (masculine?) respect for boundaries, the (masculine?) need to guard one's "turf," and sometimes, the bizarre yet characteristically masculine view that different departments compete with one another and thus that collaboration of the more powerful with the less powerful departments will dilute or otherwise impoverish the rich and powerful departments.[3] In any event, Dinnerstein's argument says that this historical moment calls for a collaborative strategy of relating to one another, a purposeful seeking after sites for the "interpenetration of subjectivities," for the recognition, in a sense, of the doubleness of the single species as well as the separateness of its parts. The "ethic of responsibility and care" given by Gilligan, and which grows from the work of Dinnerstein and Chodorow, is at once an answer to the malaise of a single constituency—women—and the attempt to make all constituencies responsible to one another without denying their boundaries or their right to cultivate their own identities. A more complicated but more useful sense of the relation between human sameness and human difference is being proposed. This project involves seeing knowledge as "interested" as much or more than it is "disinterested."

The feminist critique of knowledge centers on the standard of objectivity. Michael Gross and Mary Beth Averill observe, for example, that

> The sciences—as the paradigm of modern academic disciplines—maintain the self-serving if misleading pretense of "dispassionate objectivity," an attitude which promotes a sense of separation between self and other, observer and observed, scientist and nature.[4]

In biology, they relate concepts such as "scarcity" and "the survival of the fittest" to the ethical perspective implied by "dispassionate objectivity." They therefore question, and perhaps reject, the assumption that underlying the evolution of life is a struggle for scarce resources and a necessity for competition. They suggest that if the ideas of abundance and cooperation played an equal or stronger role in the presuppositions of evolution, there would be both a different kind of knowledge and a different attitude toward getting it to begin with.

Evelyn Fox Keller pursues this general point by observing that "scientific ideology [prescribes]" a very specific relation between "the knower (mind) and the knowable (nature)":

3. I feel certain that my department, which is more privileged in my university in terms of its overall treatment by the central administration, has, over the past twenty years, not sought, and, usually, actively discouraged, collaboration with the language branches in the School of Education. Efforts on my part to start such a collaboration have been met with, for example, a refusal by my department to cross-list courses, or, more usually, remarks by my colleagues about the incompetence of the education faculty.

4. Michael Gross and Mary Beth Averill, "Evolution and Patriarchal Myths of Scarcity and Competition," in *Discovering Reality: Feminist Perspectives on Epistemology, Metaphysics, Methodology, and Philosophy of Science,* ed. Sandra Harding and Merrill B. Hintikka (Boston: D. Reidel, 1983), p. 82.

Not only are mind and nature assigned gender, but in characterizing scientific and objective thought as masculine, the very activity by which the knower can acquire knowledge is also genderized. The relation specified between knower and known is one of distance and separation. It is that between a subject and object radically divided, which is to say no worldly relation. Simply put, nature is objectified. The "chaste and lawful marriage" is consummated through reason rather than feeling, and "observation" rather than "immediate" sensory experience. The modes of intercourse are used so as to insure emotional and physical inviolability. . . . In this process the characterization of both the scientific mind and its modes of access to knowledge is indeed significant. Masculine here connotes, as it so often does, autonomy, separation, distance. It connotes a radical rejection of any commingling of subject and object, which are, it now appears, quite consistently identified as male and female.[5]

In the process of being genderized by predominantly masculine values, the practice of science creates a gender-specific sense of knowledge. To get to know something is to see it as if it were isolated from the already-socialized scientist, to see it as existing independently of its human pertinence ("no worldly relation" between people and what they know). Keller cites studies which show that scientists themselves are men with a reduced repertoire of social capabilities who tend to "avoid interpersonal contact." (p. 201) In taking a social view of science, she sees both scientific work and its practitioners as belonging to a continuous ethic involving a fixed sense of what knowing is and of what social roles scientists play, an ethic which bears out the psychological speculations of Dinnerstein and Chodorow.

Naomi Scheman presents a reflection on psychology analogous to Gross and Averill's on biology. She sees individualism as the governing epistemological presupposition in psychology. This assumption renders people as separate objects but also sees feelings and behaviors as separate entities, as things-in-themselves. In opposing this view, she argues that the objects of study in psychology are so

only with respect to socially embodied norms, and thus any reduction would have to proceed via the whole social system, explaining a particular object as an object-with-respect-to-that-system.[6]

Considered in this way, the system to which feelings are related is a relationship or set of relationships. The feeling is not something in and of itself but an item within an intersubjectivity, a signal of how people are relating to one

5. Evelyn Fox Keller, "Gender and Science," in Harding and Hintikka, *Discovering Reality*, pp. 190–191.

6. Naomi Scheman, "Individualism and the Objects of Psychology," in Harding and Hintikka, *Discovering Reality*, p. 228.

another. In this style of thought, the whole concept of individual psychology is called into question: one's mental life is no longer only one's own.

Scheman's sense of what psychology is moves her toward a different ethical sense of what knowledge is. She traces epistemological individualism back to traditional modes of family life: the individual has become so important because there was only an "individual" (that is, one person who "really counted" as a) parent. In consequence, not only have philosophy and science been practiced mainly by men, but the language of these disciplines is "socially masculine." What most understand to be "objective" thought, she claims, is actually governed by the (masculine) ideal of a "world filled with self-actualizing persons pulling their own strings, capable of guiltlessly saying 'no' to anyone about anything, and freely choosing when to begin and end all their relationships." To include feminine styles equally with masculine styles in our concept of the "ideal" person would make the idea of the individual more flexible and thereby suggest

> . . . that the psychological individualists might be wrong, and [that] we are responsible for the meaning of each other's inner lives, that our emotions, beliefs, motives, and so on are what they are because of how they—and we— are related to the others in our world—not only those we share a language with, but those we more intimately share our lives with.

As things are now, the "underpinning of philosophical psychology, metaphysics, epistemology, ethics, and political theory [are] the essential distinctness of persons and their psychological states, the importance of autonomy, the value of universal principles in morality, and the demand that a social theory be founded on an independent theory of persons, their natures, needs, and desires."

Related to the epistemological ethic of individualism is the "Adversary Paradigm" in philosophy. Janice Moulton argues that under the rule of this paradigm, philosophy

> is seen as an unimpassioned debate between *adversaries* who try to defend their own views against counterexamples and produce counterexamples to opposing views. The reasoning used to discover the claims, and the way the claims relate to other beliefs and systems of ideas are not considered relevant to philosophic reasoning if they are not deductive.[7]

In this description, Moulton contrasts the technique of the dyadic contest or competition through deduction with the technique of relating whole belief

7. Janice Moulton, "A Paradigm of Philosophy: The Adversary Method," in Harding and Hintikka, *Discovering Reality*, p. 153.

systems and reasonings with one another. In inquiring adversarily, each thinker is forced to assume the premises of the other, even if erroneous, and the argument must proceed point by point. A mutual evaluation of premises is not considered part of the process and very likely can yield no "winner" of a dispute. Without this evaluation, Moulton argues, proponents of certain views remain locked into their systems, and understanding is retarded or completely missed because the less deductive, less certain part of mutual evaluation is inadmissible. The purpose of adversarial techniques is extremely narrow: "to convince an opponent" (p. 159). Moulton shows that because many others, in addition to opponents, may need to hear a point of view, other kinds of reasoning may be more suitable. Adversarial behavior lacks this social alertness, being virtually obsessed with merely prevailing in an argument. When philosophical discourse is overtaken by an adversarial attitude, it is in danger of losing its ability to be a social force, since its intention is to win an argument. Basic questions, Moulton goes on, such as "Why is this argument important?" are not considered pertinent to the argument itself: "one can consider not only whether Descartes' proofs of the existence of God are valid, but what good reasons there are for proving the existence of God." (p. 161) It is considered unfair or beyond the "rules of the game"[8] to raise the question of *why* Descartes wanted to offer his proofs to begin with, rather than simply going along with the premise that a proof is necessary. This unspoken rule about accepting one's opponents' premises makes it possible for one thinker, holding more social authority, to dominate a particular inquiry. This is just what happens in the ordinary university classroom: the premises of the academy are not subject to scrutiny. Since the premises of one's arguments are usually rooted in one's social situation, the custom of not bringing up premises tends to keep philosophical discussion separate from possibilities for social action.

Moulton's final point will have repeated bearing on the discussion in this study: "experience may be a necessary element in certain reasoning processes." (p. 162) She writes that most philosophical discussion proceeds "as if experience plays no essential role in the philosophical positions one holds."[9]

8. Yes, I am implying here that the adversary method is a variant of the game-interest of men. Notice how strongly upholding the rules of the game keeps the game more strongly separated from the nongame world around it. The same argument would obtain about the concern for "law and order" in the late sixties and early seventies: obsessive upholding of the "law" keeps those most protected by it separate from everyone else.

9. My reading of this claim is that the vast majority of philosophical discussion simply does not either refer to or bring in actual things experienced by real people. In analytic philosophy, the tendency is to bring in hypothetical instances or made-up verbal propositions. In the holistic Continental philosophy, the tendency is to reflect at length on major generalizations such as "being" without citing features of human experience that they might refer to.

Yet in many cases, if not most or all, one's own social and developmental experience certainly plays a major role in what one claims to be a "position" or a "philosophical point of view." Experience does not, of course, present itself in formal philosophical language, but appears in conversation in much less governable forms. Philosophical reasoning, however, admits *no* form that enables real human experience to be reported. This is so, even if we know, secretly perhaps, that abstract systems become comprehensible *only* when we can identify features of our experience to which they correspond. Yet to move back and forth from experience to argument, to conduct a dialogue or dialectic of reasons and experiences, is not viewed as admissible philosophy. There is, we may add, a tradition of deliberately *excluding* experience, of aiming to "purify" thought of experience and feeling, so that some ideal of pure truth may somehow (miraculously) be isolated from the confusing flux of people's daily experience.

Thomas Kuhn's revisionary view of the history of modern science has taken some important steps in the directions Scheman and Moulton propose. Rather than seeing the origin of new ideas as the isolated individual effort of geniuses, Kuhn stipulated that several workers participate in new forms of thought which grow from incremental changes in how the world is perceived. He suggested that new beliefs about what is true have a great deal to do with changes in historical priorities and with the passing of, and interaction between, generations. One of the sources for Kuhn's ideas, Ludwik Fleck (whose work Kuhn claims, rightly, to my mind, is considerably different from his own) had much earlier proposed a conception of scientific work that anchors it more completely in social experience than Kuhn's book does. In Fleck's 1935 monograph, *Genesis and Development of a Scientific Fact*, he proposed the existence of "thought styles"—which are very similar to Kuhn's "paradigms"—but he additionally proposed that thought styles were always borne by *thought collectives*.

Fleck sees those who are doing work on a scientific problem as being socially connected. When a thought style is shared, the linkage among the sharers is much greater and more important than the linkage Kuhn sees between subscribers to the same paradigm. Here is Fleck's description of a thought collective:

> A thought collective exists wherever two or more people are actually exchanging thought. He is a poor observer who does not notice that a stimulating conversation between two persons soon creates a condition in which each utters a thought he would not have been able to produce either by himself or in different company. A special mood arises, which would not otherwise affect either partner of the conversation but almost always returns whenever these persons meet again. Prolonged duration of this state produces, from common

understanding and mutual misunderstanding, a thought structure that belongs to neither of them alone but nevertheless is not at all without meaning. Who is its carrier and who its originator? It is neither more nor less than the small collective of two persons. If a third person joins in, a new collective arises. The previous mood will be dissolved and with it the special creative force of the former a small collective.[10]

The salient difference between this description of the collective nature of a conversation and Gadamer's (in chapter 1) is that Gadamer's "relation" transcends the two parties. But notice Fleck's usage: the carriers and originators of the thought structure "are neither more nor less than the small collective of two persons." Instead of there being "elevation," there is in Fleck a "mood," that is, something accessible to psychological description and understanding. At no point in Fleck's monograph does the idea of the game enter in to describe collective experience. Rather, it is understood to be something essentially social in all its dimensions, and something that relates to other aspects of social existence—particularly the size and values of a social group. Just as the mood changes when one collective grows, a single person is always a member of several different collectives in addition to that in the workplace—"the political party, a social class, a nation, or even a race," (p. 45) and each has an emotional character as well as a rational purpose: "the concept of absolutely emotionless thinking is meaningless. There is no emotionless state as such nor pure rationality as such." (p. 49)

Fleck cites a series of sociologists and humanists such as Durkheim and Levy-Bruhl to support his conviction about the social origins and character of knowledge. He then observes that all of these humanists "exhibit an excessive respect, bordering on pious reverence, for scientific facts." (p. 47) Subsequently, citing the work of the Vienna Circle epistemologists such as Carnap and Schlick who were trained in the natural sciences, Fleck says that they construe human thinking as "something fixed and absolute" and scientific facts as variable. He then notes that "it is characteristic that both parties [the humanists and the scientists] relegate that which is fixed to the region with which they are unfamiliar." (p. 50) Fleck's own point follows:

> Would it not be possible to manage entirely without something fixed? Both thinking and facts are changeable, if only because changes in thinking manifest themselves in changed facts. Conversely, fundamentally new facts can be discovered only through new thinking.

10. Ludwik Fleck, *Genesis and Development of a Scientific Fact*, ed. and trans. Thaddeus J. Trenn, Robert K. Merton, and Fred Bradley (Chicago: University of Chicago Press, 1979), p. 44; hereafter cited in text.

The fruitfulness of the thought collective theory is revealed especially in the facility with which it enables us to compare primitive, archaic, naive, and psychotic types of thinking and to investigate them uniformly. It can also be applied to the thinking of a whole nation, a class, or any group no matter how it is constituted. I consider the postulate "to maximize experience" the supreme law of scientific thinking. (p. 51)

By experience, I take Fleck to mean something very similar to what Moulton means: those historical, lived-through, reportable happenings which manifest themselves in self-awareness. As both a subjective and an intersubjective event, experience is the connection between the thought collective and the creation of scientific fact. Fleck is also suggesting that *any* facts, scientific or humanistic, become so only by virtue of their embeddedness in a thought collective—a community of real people with common interests. Fleck writes that

> the summarized report about a field of research always contains only a very small part of the worker's relevant experience, and not even the most important. Missing is that which makes the stylized visual perception of form possible. It is as if the words of a song were published without the tune. (p. 96)

Fleck argues that, although Wasserman's account of discovering a "serodiagnosis of syphilis" claims that Wasserman had searched for exactly what he found, what actually happened was that "from false assumptions and irreproducible initial experiments an important discovery has resulted after many errors and detours." (p. 76) Fleck says that all discoveries come about this way and are then presented as rational narratives of individual action, with the actual character of the experiences purposely omitted. He then makes the key point:

> Epistemologically the problem is insoluble from an *individualistic* point of view. If any discovery is to be made accessible to investigation, the *social point of view* must be adopted; that is, the discovery must be regarded as a *social event.* (p. 76)

Both facts and truth appear in a thought collective as constraints on the thought style. They are both—facts and truth—"a stylized solution" (p. 100) to local problems and are always collectively held. Because the original collective experience is omitted from scientific reports, truths and facts always appear absolute and immutable, and, usually, as the result of a deliberate individual effort to "discover" them. Furthermore, Fleck reflects, only the experience of having searched and failed among one's colleagues and students—Fleck explicitly mentions the membership of both in the same collective—makes it possible for any subsequent results to become "reproducible and practical." Therefore, the individual and collective *experience* of work, which is always the determining factor in establishing knowledge, is the factor that is always left out of the formal reports and claims of knowledge.

If we briefly consider Freud's work in the light of Fleck's, it becomes clearer why Dinnerstein and Chodorow were able to find in Freud a configuration of ideas and attitudes that could be productively translated for contemporary feminist psychosocial and political interests. One of the main turning points in the development of psychoanalysis was the deliberate use of conversation between doctor and patient as both a diagnostic and a therapeutic procedure: this was a change in the usual relationship between doctor and patient. Since Freud, the main technique of psychotherapy has been conversation either between two people or among groups of people. In psychoanalysis, as anyone like myself who has gone through it will testify, the moment of insight, in which the patient "knows" for the first time how to identify certain thoughts, behaviors, or dream patterns recurring in his or her personal history, is always a moment of finding the right language, the right name for something that has before been only disturbing or frustrating. The actual origin of this language is of no consequence—it can come either from the therapist or the patient—but its efficacy as being "right" depends on the feeling of its rightness to *both* patient and therapist. In Fleck's sense the therapeutic relationship is a thought collective because the "facts" not only appear through a free-associative path, but they are rendered facts only by the collective decision to identify them as such. When patients feel better, or feel that progress has been made, the parties in the collective share, in language, the sense of congruence between knowledge and experience.

All of the reflections on gender psychology and epistemology I cited earlier should be seen as another step in the development from Freud, Fleck, and Kuhn. In psychology, biology, and chemistry/physics, respectively, the idea of the origin of knowledge in individuals has been gradually replaced by the belief in its origins in groups, in history, and in social purposes. The role of language is fundamental in all. But this sense of "language" is no longer familiar: it is not a code or a self-enclosed system of rules and words, or any other entity that is separable from the social interests and collective experiences that emerge in public as language initiatives. The gradually growing belief in the social character of knowledge is one of the factors that has led to such widespread inquiry into the nature of language in this century, and has led many to see language as the fundamental problem of contemporary philosophy. In spite of this immense effort to reunderstand language, however, there are ever fewer answers and ever more frustrations. The tendency to move toward a "game" concept cannot be seen as the manifestation of any *local* masculine psychology, but more as a kind of masculine retreat from the real frustrations created by the "natural" pursuit of what feminists have called "socially masculine" thinking.

The term "masculine retreat" is appropriate, however, only if the feminist perspective is exaggerated into a dogma. (To use the term "retreat" is already to have militarized a peaceful shift of opinion among men.) Many have understood "language game" thinking as a positive loosening of philosophical attitudes toward language: the concept of the "play of language" (the feeling that language, by itself, actively creates unanticipated possibilities for thought and meaning) seems to make room for the peremptory idea, for the unexpected changes that would take place as literate discourse becomes the idiom of all groups in the human community. Nevertheless, the tone, style, and accent accompanying the belief in the primary autonomy of language has led to an all-too-familiar narrowing of academic attention, excluding in the usual way what Moulton and Fleck have called, "the experiential basis of knowledge."[11]

As an extended example, to show the difference between narrow and broad ways to take advantage of new thinking in language philosophy, consider Derrida's critique of Husserl in the 1967 study, *Speech and Phenomena*— a work whose historical function is just as interesting as its substantive argument. This work should be credited with opening a new set of issues and with producing a different style of inquiry, especially in the study of literature. Far from being a mere game, the practice of deconstructing a text is a careful, intense examination of its language, as well as a provocative reflection on the problems posed by even the contemplation of specific language.[12] At the same time, it has become a formula (mostly in the hands of Derrida's followers), the application of which leads to a predictable conclusion. When a text is deconstructed, its meaning has been "problematized," and every positive feature of the text—its "literal" meaning, its plot, the relationships among characters, for example—is reconceived in terms of inner contradiction and logical paradox. The critical community then becomes involved in controversy over whether anything new and useful has really been offered. While such controversy is in many respects a salutary development, its beneficiaries have been almost exclusively members of the academy.

11. In *Professing Literature* (Chicago: University of Chicago Press, 1987), p. 241, Gerald Graff gives a brief but what seems to me conclusive critique of the ultranarrow criticism that has been produced by those who accept the premise of the primary autonomy of language.

12. This point looks like a qualification of the claims I made in chapter 1, but it is not: it is a continuation of the point that the language game idea is a socially masculine intellectual preference that accents, biases, or localizes the issues being discussed—but this emphasis alone need not nullify any man's total project. In the following discussion, I am trying to separate what I consider the politically and intellectually insular and backward elements in Derrida's work from the useful and progressive elements.

The form of thought itself has no political constituency except the academy from which it sprang. While relationships among academic practitioners can be said to have changed insofar as different kinds of essays are written, so far no changes have been seen outside this community. This sort of academic work makes language and literature even less accessible for the classroom population than it was while the similarly academic New Criticism was defining the literary teaching style. From a social point of view, Derrida's work helped to preserve the institution that has historically perpetuated the attitudes of "Western metaphysics" that his intellectual program opposes.

Seen in the light of the "adversary method," Derrida's critique of Husserl scores a victory. Derrida presents a strong argument that Husserl failed to establish an absolute foundation in subjective consciousness for the pursuit of science and the establishment of knowledge. He shows that Husserl's work uses the same illusory ideas that governed Plato's thought and Western metaphysics since then. He argues that in spite of the change, developments, and struggles that can be seen in Husserl's texts, the "germinal structure of the whole of Husserl's thought" that appeared in his earliest work in 1900 remain the "conceptual premises" of his last works written almost forty years later. These premises are, more or less, that a certain basis for knowledge can be found by purifying subjective consciousness of the distractions of ordinary experience to such an extent that the sense of "presence" or, perhaps, self-awareness, creates the subjective certainty of a mental here-and-now that can not be considered illusory. Husserl calls this sense "transcendental subjectivity," which, in his later works, he tries to use to derive a more general idea, "transcendental intersubjectivity," which is to be an even more authoritative foundation for the process of knowing. Although Derrida *reads* Husserl's full body of thought, he does not approach the problem in terms of the salient "differences within" this body but in terms of its (in Derrida's view) complete dependence on a single conceptual premise found in Husserl's *Logical Investigations* (1900). Derrida argues that if this premise is defeated or shown to be false or invalid, Husserl may then be thought of as the last in the parade of thinkers carrying the flag of Platonic idealism. In following the adversary method, Derrida entertains Husserl's premises, shows that they do not lead to a certain subjectivity, and "wins" the argument—making room for the substitution of his own premises and the program that follows from it. Behind both Husserl's argument and Derrida's is, however, the unspoken premise of adversarial thought: either my argument is right or it's wrong. If right, it will "prevail"; if wrong, it will be recorded as yet another error. What does not enter into Derrida's critique is that there may be reasons for accepting Husserl's program, for using it, reworking it, and, above all, adopting its special language and habits of thought that are pragmatically and experientially based—just as there are similar reasons for using Derrida's program. Finally, although one may agree with Derrida that Husserl's search for certainty was in some sense misguided, it was Husserl, more than Derrida, who brought to our attention the overwhelming potential of intersubjective experience as a new basis for changing not just how people know, but how knowledge and social experience may be continuous within the human community.

Derrida finds the germinal structure of Husserl's thought in the latter's discussion of "the sign" (which could also be described as the linguistic symbol or the name or the word, though in German it is *Zeichen*). This is a significant move because the "sign" plays a strong role in Husserl's thought, but not nearly as strong a role as it does in Derrida's. Language is far more thoroughly Derrida's issue than it is Husserl's, who addresses a variety of philosophical concepts, including time, knowledge, and self-and-other. For Derrida, language is not only a subject to treat, but the key instrument, whose self-conscious handling is found in his every study of the many texts he entertains. Each time Derrida takes up a new text, both its language and his become the subject, very much as it is Joyce's subject in *Finnegans Wake*. But language is not the only thing that matters, or lives, in Husserl's work. Derrida's approach to Husserl sees his illusion as being *about* language and finds that Husserl's premise for his philosophy is only and singularly a premise about language. This move, in traditional scholarly practice, is legitimate under the assumption of the one-on-one custom: one scholar may pick any text in the history of the subject, sever it from its "thought-collective"—the actual human context of its production and reception—and test it for illusions or "errors." In this way, Derrida succeeds in making his point and gains the means to substitute his own issue for Husserl's. However, in a nonadversarial tradition, such success would not be sought. More likely, room will be found, as in part it already is, to see how each perspective, each premise, each issue may become useful to the social experience of today's reading communities.

The point at issue, Derrida argues, is whether the sign, or, more generally, any piece of language, may be understood in the two senses Husserl claims for it: expression (*Ausdruck*) and indication (*Anzeichen*). Or are these two senses, as Husserl also acknowledges, so "interwoven" that they cannot be separated? Husserl's view is that while, in any actual use of language, the two senses cannot be separated, in the "solitary mental life," or in "transcendental subjectivity," only expression exists, because indication— the referring of something to someone, or of someone to something—is not a feature of this private (nonlinguistic and subjective) area of meaning. Derrida's argument is that a private area of meaning can have no relation to language—cannot be thought of as part of the sign—because to use the idea of "sign" is to presuppose its already having been established in its combined form of expression and indication. To imagine a separation between the ordinary indicative meaning and some inner expressive meaning is to stipulate a meaning somehow more fundamental, more "primordial" than the meaning which came about from the recursive *use* of language to begin with. To think of a meaning at all means to acknowledge the primordiality of the sign itself.

Derrida explains how the concept of "presence" makes it possible for Husserl to clear away indicative meanings from expressive ones. Presence may be described as an irrefutable momentary consciousness of sense that is separable from consciousness as tied to language. The mere fact of self-consciousness (or self-presence) intuitively demonstrates its priority to language. In this way, Husserl stipulates the unchangeable palpability of subjectivity, an ineradicable self-possession on which all mental life is founded. Derrida argues that this momentary experience of certainty is illusory because the moment cannot be held, because it is a feature of time, because the "now" is a series of *repetitions* of consciousness, because the "digital" character of self-presence is founded on the digital character of language, and, in particular, of speech. The human voice, Derrida argues, gives at once the illusion of the subjectivity of meaning and the demonstration of its permanent exteriority. When one hears oneself speak, the speaking and the hearing coincide with one another, giving the sense of "absolute proximity" of meaning and subjectivity. There seems to be an incontrovertible bond between the "meaning-intention" and its expression in sound while it is at the same time heard. Because of this bond, the act of speech seems "alive." At the same time, however, the exteriority of the sound and its necessary movement in time forces all other exteriority to appear, creates the occasion for "the world" to appear as a noninterior phenomenon: "the voice *is* consciousness." (p. 80) It is this view that leads Derrida to reject any possibility of a split either between indication and expression, or between these two and some inner silent subjective "sense" that precedes the word. Husserl is seen as Western metaphysics' last effort to preserve the ideality of that subjective sense because of his extraordinary effort to make it the cornerstone of a new edifice of utterly certain knowledge.

The key thrust of Derrida's critique is perhaps less to deny the existence of an authoritative subjective sense than to declare its contingent relation to the materiality ("exteriority") of the word. It is this materiality that he calls *writing*. Any palpable rendition of language is necessarily written. In actual writing, this exteriority is obvious. But to understand speech also as writing is to unify all manifestations of language as having the same sort of palpability, the same inextricability of indication and expression, and the same relation to the "bottomless chessboard" of subjective being. Rather than being in some fixed relation to a series of subjective "senses," language is only the "trace" of sense, and its use the "play of traces."

Before returning to some implications of this concept of language, consider first the extent to which Derrida has actually won a point against Husserl. First, we should acknowledge the cogency of his critique of Husserl's idea of the sign. It is reasonable to doubt (and perhaps to deny) that one can isolate a substrate of sense *from* the sign but still claim the sense is associated with it in some essential way. It is also reasonable to dispute the primordiality of this sense because one is led to it only through language: only if one is already self-conscious-through-language can one, in imagination, arrive at this primordial sense. On these grounds, Derrida is "right" about Husserl's concept of the sign.

At this point, however, questions arise about the usefulness and consequences of being "right." Does it mean, for example, that Husserl really is the last and most elaborate exemplar of Western metaphysics? Is there any indication that the "metaphysics of presence" was, or is, really a guiding principle of thought in the West? What does it mean to say that such an abstract item as metaphysics is either a description or an explanation of two thousand years of history? Is it correct to say that Husserl's stipulation of the primacy of transcendental subjectivity is the same as saying that "the human soul is eternal," both of which, presumably, derive from the "metaphysics of presence"? And are these the same as saying that the "idea" of a chair is its "essence"? Is the search for a foundation for knowledge the same as the search for a proof of God or the belief that God exists eternally? If each of these questions is taken to have emerged from *specific societies*, and if the meaning of each is understood in that community-specific way, would Husserl then seem to be the contemporary spokesman of an alleged two-thousand-year-old tradition? Would Derrida's critique of Husserl then imply a critique of other formulations—even if in the same or a similar language—given in radically different moments of history?

These questions are intended to suggest that the texts of Derrida and Husserl cannot be considered as just texts. At each point, already, Derrida refers to such things as "Husserl's thought" or "Husserl's program." And by thinking in still other ways about Husserl, Derrida sees him as a member of some community, "Western civilization." In his *Grammatology*, Derrida explains that this kind of "obsolete" language must nevertheless be used since there is no other language: to use language at all is to displace its "present" meaning. Yet one wonders if the use of a term like "Husserl's thought" should be understood as some form of "differance." Wouldn't it be easier to say that for any given reading community and reading occasion, some terms are in fact "rigid," even while admitting that this rigidity is *not* intrinsic to the (exterior) language, to the text? Isn't it also true that the actual social dissemination of any text, the actual event of people buying and reading a text, and their gradual familiarization with it, depends on some form of "common knowledge" among these people, some socially constructed rigidity of interest that actually renders the text meaningful, causing us to see that any text is already meaningful, and that the separation of meaning from language is not a useful description of reading? And even though, finally, we can view language productively as a "play of traces," isn't it the case that any one text—any one instance of language–is understood to "want to say" ("mean," in English) in consequence of how it fares among a specific group of real people, in consequence of nameable human actions taken with the text (even if the actions are the production of other texts)?

It is because of Derrida's own argument that one always writes a new text, Derrida's own textual revision of "Western metaphysics," his own interesting reformulations of the "whole projects" of Husserl, Freud, or Rousseau, that one finally doubts that limits to thought are exclusively linguistic, that one finally needs to include the *language of purpose and interest*, and to actually declare purpose and interest as, at one time or another, in one situation or other, belonging to a different kind of human action, a kind, that, with suitable thought and imagination, may be understood to be as separate from language as subjective "sense" is from expression and indication. This is how I think Husserl's transcendental turn to subjectivity and intersubjectivity may be used by us, now, without being concerned that it may involve a contradictory conception of language.

Maurice Natanson reports that Husserl died still "discontented . . . with the problem of intersubjectivity."[13] In reading Derrida's account of Husserl, one gets the impression that Husserl's changes in emphasis and language as he grew older are less important than the alleged "germinal structure of the whole of Husserl's thought."[14] But, instead of continuing to contemplate this germinal structure, suppose we contemplate the meaning of the *change* in Husserl's concern as he continually rethought his phenomenological purpose. Suppose, for example, that Husserl formulated a concept of the sign, and then moved toward a concept of transcendental subjectivity as something that needed to be understood because of the problems raised by his concept of language, and then reflected on an idea of transcendental intersubjectivity

13. Maurice Natanson, *Edmund Husserl: Philosopher of Infinite Tasks* (Evanston: Northwestern University Press, 1973), p. 195.

14. Jacques Derrida, *Speech and Phenomena*, trans. David B. Allison (Evanston: Northwestern University Press, 1973), p. 3.

because of problems raised by the emphasis on the "solitary mental life." Suppose Husserl was living at every moment in a fluctuating "now" (the kind of ungraspable present that Derrida describes) and that each new text is a "trace" of that moment. Suppose, therefore, that Husserl was a historically situated figure (like everyone else) and that each new moment changes the biological, psychosocial, and historical perspective marked or "inscribed" in each text. This suggests that it might be helpful to overcome the temptation to decide on a "germinal structure" and to understand how Husserl's path of change opens up our own.

An important change in Husserl's life was his shift from a prospective career in mathematics to one in philosophy. This meant, in his life, a change of attention from the machinery and formalism of science to the study of its purposes, presuppositions, and functions in human life. If the formulations in his last major work (*The Crisis of European Sciences* [1937]) are any guide, this project remained the same throughout his career as a philosopher:

> The point is not to secure objectivity but to understand it. One must finally achieve the insight that no objective science, no matter how exact, explains or ever can explain anything in a serious sense. To deduce is not to explain. To predict, or to recognize the objective forms of the composition of physical or chemical bodies and to predict accordingly—all this explains nothing but is in need of explanation. The only true way to explain is to make transcendentally understandable.[15]

Husserl's main pursuit was first to challenge the empirical authority of science: the belief that when a logical formalism seems to describe real events in nature it is explaining them. He observed that this belief rests on "portentous prejudices" which "shared in the responsibility for the European sickness." (*Crisis*, p. 272) He therefore sought to "explain" the belief in this sort of explanation. His new form of explanation—that which will make things "transcendentally understandable" is the phenomenological method.

The basis of this method is what Maurice Natanson has called the "egological" point of view. Rather than claiming that one's sense of certainty derives from the manifest palpability of physical things or events, Husserl stipulated that one's *consciousness of* these phenomena is knowledge of which one is much more certain, if not "apodictically" certain": one's awareness of an experience is much more certain than the item "itself" being experienced. This awareness being one remove from "real" experience, to "live" in this awareness is to "reduce" experience to its most certain element; and in its

---

15. Edmund Husserl, *The Crisis of European Sciences* (1937) (Evanston: Northwestern University Press, 1973), p. 189.

certainty, it transcends experience in general. This "transcendental reduction" can be performed by any thinking individual, and, if done, provides a common ground for any knowledge-seeking project, humanistic or scientific. In fact, Husserl argues, it must be done as an answer to the situation in which European thought finds itself in the 1930s. He is proposing a new level of what it is to be an individual, a new approach to develop the capability of the individual mind. Here is Natanson's formulation:

> Radical certitude is Husserl's goal; radical certitude must be phenomenology's method. [italics in Natanson] The person who strives for such certitude must turn to himself as the locus of ultimate rigor, for all of the translations made of history and of the deeds of fellow men in the worlds of spirit and politics must finally be made by the individual for whom reality exists to be comprehended. Past any cheap "subjectivism" and beyond all merely idiosyncratic attitudes, the *egological* [my italics] structure of experience stands as the last criterion for philosophical accountability. (Natanson, p. 11)

In support of this claim, Natanson cites a passage from Husserl's *Cartesian Meditations*:

> Anyone who seriously intends to become a philosopher must "once in his life" withdraw into himself and attempt, within himself, to overthrow and build anew all the sciences that, up to then, he has been accepting. Philosophy— wisdom . . . —is the philosophizer's quite personal affair. It must arise as his wisdom, as his self-acquired knowledge tending toward universality, a knowledge for which he can answer from the beginning, at each step, by virtue of his own absolute insights. (Natanson, p. 11)

Husserl himself had gone through this process at the turn of the century, about thirty years before this passage was written. He had gone through the fundamental questioning of science and come to think that knowledge could be refounded on a universal capability of consciousness to "reduce" itself to only the utterly certain. In spite of Derrida's demonstration that such a place cannot be found in consciousness, Husserl's argument is in part given as an *ethical* one, both because his program is an individual choice and because it is a response to a public "sickness." The talk of "scientific" certainty aside, "radical certitude" is a psychosocial ideal. If this were not the case, Husserl could not propose in seriousness that others like himself could actually go "within" themselves and "build anew all the sciences." Although it would be right to say that Husserl never dropped his egological perspective, and particularly its capacity for radical certainty, it is not quite pertinent to propose that one has to find the locus of such certainty through a formal demonstration. In other words, if, "reduced" consciousness is practiced collectively, the sense of certainty will acquire an altogether new character, and it will be that new character which matters, not the fact that its existence eludes a formal philosophical proof.

It is noteworthy that Derrida is so much more patient with Freud than he is with Husserl. Freud also had no proof of the "unconscious"; rather, it is the principle of eternal suspicion in Freud that Derrida sees as the important contribution to Western thought. Yet how different is Freud's steadfast intention to "replace" the "it" with the "I" from Husserl's continuing belief in a starting point of certainty within a transcendentally reduced consciousness? When it works successfully, psychoanalytic treatment does lead each patient to an "egological" state of vastly increased *affective* certainty. It is a certainty not necessarily about facts, but about the values governing one's life. Like the transcendental reduction, psychoanalytic treatment is a highly individual process, almost completely oriented around "building anew" the history of one's life. But Derrida is fascinated not with the reconstructive process that had always been part of the psychoanalytic program, but with its own starting point: where the human mind appears as a "mystic writing pad" that bears only "traces" of the past. Derrida holds out this conception of the mind as evidence for the final impalpability of consciousness. Again, he is "right." The mind never does lose this character. But Freud the rationalist does just what Husserl does: fix on the continuing "presentness" of consciousness as the instrument of the active path to psychosocial change.

For both Freud and Husserl, it is impossible to speak of "the" self. Instead, they spoke of the "I," the word that always (already) alludes to its utterer and cannot bear the definite article. To speak of an "I" is to speak of a *sense* of self rather than *the* self. To replace the id with the ego, as the authorized translator of Freud does, is not the same as replacing the "it" with the "I," as Freud actually wanted to do. The id and the ego are both objects which live inside strong boundaries "in" one's mind. The it and the I, on the other hand, are both in our own language, our own subjectivity—a fact lost, as Bruno Bettelheim has recently discussed, by the English translations of Freud. Since both the unconscious and the conscious are parts of the subjective person, change is a matter of supplanting the unconscious parts with the conscious parts: the declaration of the new "I" is the accession to self-knowledge, rather than just the acquisition of a new self or an improved ego. In psychoanalysis one never speaks of what one's self "really" is, only of what *value* we place on ourselves, of what *confidence* underlies our use of "I." If we think of a person who places great value on consciousness, a person for whom self-awareness is ever to be pursued, we may well think of the person who has "transcendentally reduced" his consciousness not to its "contents," but to its awareness—that active condition of *dominion* over one's knowledge recognized as certainty. Because this dominion is as much a feeling and a value as it is an ordinary piece of propositional "truth," one cannot be wrong to claim its transiency or its impalpability. But one can find no better use for this inward sense of dominion that is both the starting point for the reconstruction of one's social being, and the starting point for the pursuit of knowledge.

In the next chapter I will discuss the reconstruction of one's social being as it entails ideas of selfhood and language. Consider now, more carefully, just how Husserl presents the task of pursuing knowledge, and just what values he claims for the egological perspective. In a 1935 lecture, "Philosophy and the Crisis of European Humanity," Husserl characterizes "the subject matter of the so-called humanist disciplines":

> Here theoretical interest is directed at human beings exclusively as persons, at their personal life and accomplishments, and correlatively at the products of such accomplishments. Personal life means living communalized as "I" and "we" within a community horizon, and this in communities of various simple or stratified forms such as family, nation, supranational community. The word *life* here does not have a physiological sense; it signifies purposeful life accomplishing spiritual products: in the broadest sense, creating culture in the unity of a historical development.[16]

One of the problems others have found repeatedly in Husserl's work is that, if transcendental subjectivity is "primordial," how do communication and other forms of social relations take place? This point has made it attractive to accede to Derrida's strong criticisms as well as to the program he derives from those criticisms. But in the foregoing passage, which appears in the very early part of his lecture, Husserl observes in a fairly casual style that "personal life means living communalized as 'I' and 'we' within a community horizon." This sentence, and especially the word "means," seems to suggest that Husserl is citing a self-evident truth. However, in the Fifth Meditation, and in parts of the *Crisis* that I will cite shortly, Husserl takes pains to derive a concept of transcendental *inter*subjectivity from the starting point of the transcendental reduction. Husserl wants to show that the intentional constitution of others within "the primordial sphere" is the experience of community that makes "personal life mean living communalized." In other words, he is at pains to deny any paradox that could be associated with the primordiality of subjectivity and the necessary communal existence of personal life.

In section 51 of *Cartesian Meditations*, Husserl stipulates the phenomenon of "pairing" as "occurrence in configuration as a pair and then as a group,

16. Ibid., p. 270.

a plurality [to be] a *universal* phenomenon of the transcendental sphere,"[17] where "pair" and "group" mean pairs and groups of people in which "I" am included. In a "pairing association," within the "transcendental sphere,"

> the characteristic feature is that, in the most primitive case, two data are given intuitionally, and with prominence, in the unity of a consciousness and that, on this basis—essentially, already in the pure passivity (regardless therefore of whether they are noticed or unnoticed)—, as data appearing with mutual distinctness, they *found phenomenologically a unity of similarity* and thus are always constituted precisely as a pair. If there are more than two such data, then a phenomenally unitary group, a plurality, become constituted.... we find, more particularly, a living mutual awakening and an overlaying of each with the objective sense of the other. This overlaying can bring a total or partial coincidence, which in any particular instance has its degree, the limiting case being that of complete "likeness." As the result of this overlaying, there takes place in the paired data a mutual transfer of sense—that is to say: an apperception of each according to the sense of the other, so far as moments of sense actualized in what is experienced do not annul this transfer, with the consciousness of "different." (CM, p. 113)

While it could be claimed that this description applies to something going on inside an individual's transcendental subjectivity, therefore leaving the paradox intact, such phrases as "mutual awakening" and "overlaying of each with the objective sense of the other" and "mutual transfer of sense" suggest some sort of dialectic action. The passage could be reasonably read as a description of how an individual comes to a certain transcendentally subjective *representation* and/or *experience* of social mutuality.[18] In other words, the subjective action which "founds" the "unity of similarity" is necessary to the founding of any social intersubjectivity. Put in more common terms, any "objective" social mutuality requires the participation of one's transcendental subjectivity. In this sense, transcendentally subjective pairing is consistent with Fleck's description of the "thought collective"; Husserl may even be said to add a note of individual responsibility to Fleck's formulation.

Without trying to decide here whether Husserl considered individual transcendental subjectivity to be a comprehensive or absolute priority, it is enough to note his effort to *reconcile* his spontaneous sense of the commu-

17. Edmund Husserl, *Cartesian Meditations*, trans. Dorian Cairns (The Hague: Martinus Nijhoff, 1960), p. 112.

18. This abstract description, this "guess" about how a sense of mutuality may be generated inside an individual's mind, corresponds very well to Helen Keller's description of her realization of self and other with her teacher Anne Sullivan, as I first discussed in chapter 2 of *Subjective Criticism* (Baltimore: Johns Hopkins University Press, 1978), and as I continue to explore in chapter 4.

nality of human life with his equally spontaneous but more elaborate sense of individual subjectivity. After all, it was opposition to his community as a youth that led him to "withdraw into himself" in order to "overthrow" and "rebuild." Later in life, he could correctly say that a new community had grown up, one (presumably) in some position to "rebuild" the "European Sciences" out of their "sickness." The question of community reappears in Husserl's work, therefore, not as a formal necessity or even as a response to individual critics alone, but to the historical development of his own life and society. In the *Crisis*, Husserl presents a further approach to "the paradox of human subjectivity" and a resolution of it in the wider context of the then-contemporary change in the character of science.

Probably his simplest formulation of the paradox appears in the title to Section 53 of the *Crisis*: "Being a subject for the world and at the same time being an object in the world." (p. 178) The more rigorous formulation, however, shows that this is a problem of intersubjectivity more than of subjectivity:

> But precisely here lies the difficulty. Universal intersubjectivity into which all objectivity, everything that exists at all, is resolved, can obviously be nothing other than mankind; and the latter is undeniably a component part of the world. How can a component part of the world, its human subjectivity, constitute the whole world, namely constitute it as its intentional formation, one which has always already become what it is and continues to develop, formed by the universal interconnection of intentionally accomplishing subjectivity, while the latter, the subjects accomplishing in cooperation, are themselves only a partial formation within the total accomplishment?

> The subjective part of the world swallows up, so to speak, the whole world and thus itself too. What an absurdity! (pp. 179–180)

Husserl responds to this paradox in two parts, the first being an acknowledgment of how transcendental subjectivity leads to the absurdity:

> . . . what was lacking was the phenomenon of the change of signification of [the form] "I"—just as I am saying "I" right now—into "other I's," into "all of us," we who are many "I's," and among whom I am but *one* "I." What was lacking, then, was the problem of the constitution of intersubjectivity—this "all of us" from my point of view, indeed "in" me. (p. 182)

Here Husserl says that what was lacking was a collective meaning for the singular pronoun "I." The "I" as an individual should be understood as just the "component part" alluded to in the longer paragraph above, even though in it Husserl suggests that "universal intersubjectivity" is also only a "component part" of the world. In what sense, therefore, is it not absurd for a "component part" to constitute a whole?

Husserl's resolution is that there are *two perspectives*—one "transcendental" and one "concrete":

> Concretely, each "I" is not merely an ego-pole but an "I" with all its accomplishments and accomplished acquisitions, including the world as existing and being-such. But in the epoche and in the pure focus upon the functioning ego-pole, and thence upon the concrete whole of life and of its intentional intermediary and final structure, it follows *eo ipso* that nothing human is to be found, neither soul nor psychic life nor real psychophysical human beings; all this belongs to the "phenomenon," to the world as constituted pole. (p. 183)

There is no paradox as long as one remembers that the epoche is a *deliberate performance*—a decision made by a person and not a pregiven condition. It is therefore a deliberate performance for an individual to "bracket out" and constitute transcendental intersubjectivity. "Bracketing," we recall, is not a denial of the objective world but a purposeful putting it "on hold," a task undertaken (by philosophers or anyone else) to achieve as radical a certainty as possible. The only real paradox Husserl saw late in his career was that his formulations and reflections had not previously taken into account all the "other 'I's." This is what he tried to do in the Fifth Meditation and in the following discussion in Section 54b of the *Crisis*.

Husserl opens this section by observing that although "the epoche creates a unique sort of philosophical solitude," "in this solitude I am not a single individual who has somehow willfully cut himself off from the society of mankind . . . or who is cut off by accident." Rather, this "I" *renders* the concrete world a phenomenon in the face of his ineradicably belonging to it; otherwise, the philosophical solitude would have no meaning. The transcendental "I" (or "ego-pole")

> Starting from itself and in itself, . . . constitutes transcendental intersubjectivity, to which it then adds itself as a merely privileged member, namely as "I" among the transcendental others. This is what philosophical self-exposition in the epoche actually teaches us. It can show how the always singular "I," in the original constituting life proceeding within it, constitutes a first sphere of objects, the "primordial" sphere; how it then, starting from this, in a motivated fashion, performs a constitutive accomplishment through which an intentional modification of itself and its primordiality achieve ontic validity under the title of "alien-perception," perception of others, of another "I" who is for himself an "I" as I am. (p. 185)

This is perhaps a complicated way of saying that for transcendental intersubjectivity to be realized, it needs to be *rendered so* by individuals. Even though I only want to claim that intersubjectivity needs to be *recognized* (because, as I will discuss in Chapter 3, we ought no longer assume the ontic priority of the individual), Husserl's point is that an individual is *responsible* for either recognition or constitution of others "who are for themselves 'I's as I am." Here again we hear the ethical resonance of Husserl's argument.[19] A person constitutes others "in a motivated fashion." That is the need, reason, and obligation to pay deep attention to others "constitutes" them in our own minds. Both the world of objects and of people are constituted in this deliberate way. The object world, Husserl writes a few lines later, joins transcendental intersubjectivity as a "world for all." Each "I" "coconstitutes" the world and is itself constituted as a human being "within intersubjectivity."[20]

As he grew older, Husserl's intensifying concern with intersubjectivity was always rooted in his ongoing search for "radical certainty," or a way to render knowledge universal. This led him to formulate that both the sphere of "objects" and of intersubjectivity are constituted through the same mental initiatives. But this implied a change in what sorts of knowledge are to be more highly valued or more vigorously pursued. He originally pursued mathematics and logic. He gradually saw that knowledge of "physical or chemical bodies" "explains nothing but is in need of explanation." This looks like a statement of his philosophical task, but consider this passage which appears some pages later:

> All of modern philosophy, in the original sense of a universal, ultimately grounding science, is, according to our presentation, at least since Kant and Hume, a single struggle between two ideas of science: the idea of an objectivistic philosophy on the ground of a pre-given world and the idea of a philosophy on the ground of absolute transcendental subjectivity—the latter being something completely new and strange historically, breaking through in Berkeley, Hume, and Kant.
>
> Psychology is constantly involved in this great process of development, involved, as we have seen, in different ways; indeed, psychology is the *truly decisive field*. (For by beginning as objective science and then becoming transcendental, it bridges the gap.) It is this precisely because, though it has a

19. In *Toward Deep Subjectivity* (New York: Harper & Row, 1972), Roger Poole also discusses how Husserl's work is particularly valuable in its ethical and political implications. The fact that more ethical and political readings of Husserl are not available is testimony only to the insularity and parochiality of academic philosophy and other academic subjects. It is considered more or less irrelevant to take abstract ontological thinking like Husserl's as a description of the everyday reality of how people, or nations, get along.

20. Perhaps I should say again that I am not overlooking the fact that Husserl almost certainly did think of the individual as "prior" to the collective human race. But I am also claiming that his whole structure of thought, but for this premise, is a careful and valuable formulation of how individual responsibility is in no way reduced once we accept the simultaneous "double" priority of both subjectivity and intersubjectivity.

different attitude and is under the guidance of a different task, its subject matter is universal subjectivity, which in its actualities and possibilities, is *one*. (pp. 207–208)

Although Husserl once said that he did not wish to be construed as an advocate of depth psychology, here he nevertheless reconceives the discipline of philosophy, itself the second discipline in his academic career. This is the result of Husserl's own "constitutive accomplishment" or "intentional modification of [him]self," as well as an authentic critical contribution to the European community, a plea for the public recognition of a common situation, and a proposal for change that actually requires—not simply advocates—a "decisive" status for both psychology and his own intersubjectivity. What we traditionally read as the formulation of a "philosophical position" is more usefully understood as a many-sided social event, a development from individual history which is embedded in social history.

Recalling Natanson's observation that Husserl died unsatisfied with his idea of intersubjectivity, we ask if this was because of his primary attempt to establish a basis for "certain" knowledge. Husserl could not say that he had achieved his purpose; he was dissatisfied partly with the ideas themselves and partly with their failure to bear fruit on the matter of epistemological certainty. However, in view of the kinds of thought he was pursuing, particularly the troublesome idea of "transcendental intersubjectivity," one cannot seriously entertain Derrida's point that Husserl was the last and most perfect exemplar of a "failed" two-thousand-year-old tradition of the "metaphysics of presence," regardless of how "right" Derrida may be in his formal philosophical refutations. It is no coincidence that Fleck and Freud, Husserl's near contemporaries (as well as others such as G. H. Mead and L. S. Vygotsky, who I will discuss in chapter 3), came up with formulations very similar to those of "transcendental intersubjectivity." Highly alert to how individuals were bound up in the destinies of their families and communities, they, like Husserl, related this growing conviction about social life to their basic attitudes toward knowledge.

Ironically, it is because of Derrida's highly individual focus, the rootedness of his own discourse—his own language use habits and strategies—in the constricting, masculine-accented traditions of academic writing, that he is unable to see Husserl as a figure in a more promising movement among "scientists" toward social alertness and responsibility. Because Derrida concentrates on the texts, on their literal meanings and on their relatedness to other texts, he emerges with a view of Husserl as a collection of texts and not a growing, developing individual with a namable community of cosubjects and cothinkers—"coconstituters."

The questions that Moulton asks, like "Why is this argument important?," are the questions which alert us to the political nature of our own work, to the interests of those who are reading this text, to the constituents of our own communities—the classrooms, often enough—those who are likewise coconstituting intersubjectivity, those who with necessarily subjective and individual interests in mind are nevertheless aiming to "intentionally modify themselves" so that collective life can be experienced within individual subjectivity as well as in its natural public territory. Scheman's critique of individualism is not a rejection of subjectivity, but of a collective ethic in which subjectivity means not being "responsible for the meaning of each other's inner lives." Notice how important *having* an "inner life" remains in Scheman's thinking. Husserl, being a pioneer in the matter of intersubjectivity, still spoke in the idiom of his childhood, just as Freud did, the idiom in which the "primordiality" of the individual was unquestioned. But unlike his socially inert and politically promiscuous student Heidegger, Husserl did not cave in to mysticism, religiosity, or nationalism when he saw the problems in the received idiom. Even though that idiom may not have been adequate, causing major intellectual frustrations, it still mattered, and it does now, because our own communities are shifting their focus toward the very issues which frustrated Husserl.

The work of the feminist movement, particularly its epistemological thinking, puts intersubjectivity in a light which, perhaps now in retrospect, explains many of Husserl's frustrations: his academic community was thoroughly and profoundly masculine. Dozens of social features of this community were so heavily tied to modalities of individualism, strong boundaries, adversarial attitudes, and even to the direct preservation of an exclusively masculine population for academic projects, that there was neither intellectual nor social room for an idea like intersubjectivity. In a sense, there was little room in Husserl's own elaborate edifice for it, much less in the rest of the German-speaking academy, an institution which today actively discourages women from joining it. What can intersubjectivity ever mean if the fundamental relations of the two genders remain in the background of cultural inquiry and under the political rug? Either it means what it always has—a quiet agreement among men—or something that "peripheral" figures like Husserl, Freud, or Fleck can think about, so long as it is not taken "too far."

Until recently, the study of language has borne the usual social and epistemological marks of the masculine academy. As I discussed in chapter 1, one can detect certain symptoms of intellectual and emotional discomfort in both the fascination with mystery and paradox in language and in the nagging sense of resignation to their regular appearance. This discomfort may also indicate that the paradigm is about to change out of the necessity to normalize the balance of genders in the academy. In the last two decades or so, this balance has improved, and not surprisingly the nature of this subject has, perhaps, also begun to change. Accepting the view of modern philosophy that language is far more important in determining knowledge and culture than had ever been supposed, one sees in the contemporary development of the subject at least some means of removing it from the narrow social concerns of the traditional academy and making it the occasion for new social growth. This means, for one thing, reconceiving the idea of literacy.

3

Reconceiving Literacy

One of my reasons for juxtaposing contemporary feminist thought with the "socially masculine" style of thought in Derrida and Husserl was to demonstrate their potential complementarity. In Derrida's work, for example, the idea of the exteriority of language makes it possible (as deconstructionist criticism has suggested) to see the more characteristic feminist principle of *flexibility* in the understanding and explanation of language. Individual words and texts are not "bound" by a fixed meaning (that can be articulated in words other than the original word or text themselves), while different texts and different parts of the same text are understood to affect one another in ever new ways. In Husserl's work, his intensifying effort to conceptualize intersubjectivity is probably one of the distant analogues of the feminist interest in relatedness and mutuality. Even though the feminists' initiatives emerge partly in order to oppose men's desire for business as usual, they nevertheless aim for nonoppositional styles in the study of language and knowledge.

The socially masculine style of thought, however, has two features which tend to perpetuate it and its predominance in the academy, and which therefore reduce access to the problems it treats: the interest and respect for "paradox" and the axiomatic use of hierarchical thinking.[1] Each of these features is usually presented as a fact of reality. Derrida's "bottomless chessboard" is

---

1. Of course, there are many instances where hierarchical thinking can be useful—whenever, for example, we need to decide the extent to which certain things are more important than others. I am only calling attention to the fact that, for many scholars, hierarchical thinking is an unquestioned presupposition. A typical example of this is when there are two equally good explanations for something, but because of the hierarchy axiom, the thinkers feel they need to pick only one. Physicists took a while to reach the consensus that light "is" both a particle and a wave, or that light "can be either" a particle or a wave, instead of continuing to wring their hands over the fact that two different explanations seemed to obtain depending on the circumstances. In literature, we have finally understood that no one reading is really the "best" or the "most accurate," and so on. The hierarchy axiom is responsible for prolonged disputes only because both parties assumes that only one "right" answer exists: and they feel unable to entertain a variety of good answers which suit *different conditions* in which the question is raised.

given as a part of reality which makes the more common parts, like the feelings of consciousness and "being," illusory. The resulting paradox is: since consciousness depends on language and language depends on this abyss, then consciousness must also have no certain foundation. While Husserl is less willing to accept a condition of paradox, he also characterized the problem of subjectivity as a paradox, i.e., "the paradox of human subjectivity."[2] If the paradox had a "resolution," as he claimed it had, why did he need to pose the paradox of human subjectivity in the first place?

The axiom of hierarchical thinking is closely related to the interest in paradox: in Derrida's case, the fact that he sees no foundation for consciousness is itself a paradox: it is presented in the language of self-contradiction, as when he writes that "differance is neither a word nor a concept." In other words, the inherent paradox of language is the fundamental fact, a fact more fundamental than the apodictic certainty of consciousness sought by Husserl. Derrida, in seeing Western metaphysics as "illusory," implies that his own "metaphysics of absence" is a more fundamental truth. Yet, why is it not more reasonable to suppose that the fundamentality of paradox is a historically situated perspective in exactly the same way as Derrida sees Western metaphysics: why is it not *only one* perspective in today's historical situation? What need is there, therefore, for claiming some primordial status for the "bottomless chessboard"?[3]

In Husserl, the hierarchical thinking is much more overt: he starts his project with the announced purpose of finding a new and completely certain basis for knowledge. His paradox is not an actual one, but a logical one: if subjectivity means being totally "within" oneself, why doesn't this mean that one is denying or ignoring "the world." If, however, transcendental subjectivity were not thought of as this "ultimate" basis, this necessary starting point for all knowledge, it could very well exist alongside the "real world." It is the logic of going for the "ultimate" that leads Husserl into the paradox. As I suggested in the last chapter, Husserl unconsciously resolves the paradox not as he claimed, but by casually, almost inadvertently, acknowledging a "concrete reality" that continues to function while one is performing the transcendental reduction.

Any paradox is purely the result of the recursive application of purely logical processes to a beginning thought or "axiom." Take, for example, the "one-sided" piece of paper, the Möbius Strip. There are no one-sided pieces of paper; the Möbius Strip is demonstrated by taking a two-sided

---

2. Husserl, *Crisis*, p. 178.

3. When Fleck says that there is *no need* for certainty in either the sciences or humanities, it expresses a different attitude from Derrida's ironically affirmative claim that *there is* no certainty.

strip, giving it a half twist, and then gluing the two ends together. While one can reasonably *think* of this paper as having only one side, the single side is really only a construction of one's imagination; the demonstration has the same correspondence to the idea that a movie set has to the scene it represents. In various mathematical situations, one can stipulate the "one-sided plane," or "the square-root of minus one," or other similarly "irrational" entities, and work with other mathematical operations to achieve a variety of interesting formulations. But the "irrational" entity does not itself appear "in reality"; only the formulations may be usefully "applied." Similar reasoning obtains for verbal paradoxes such as "This statement is false." By using the language, one can invent any number of self-denying statements, but they never play a role in a social speech situation, in which the "this" always refers to some other statement even though it may, logically, refer to itself. In this connection, recall Derrida's statement, "The verb 'to differ' seems to differ from itself." However, to *use* a self-denying statement (as Derrida sometimes does) is not necessarily a claim for its truth; the full human act of this use—the special formulation, its appearance in a certain kind of text, its eligibility for discussion by certain kinds of people, the actual discussion which takes place in response, and so on—create the dimensions of its linguistic life. There is no "paradox itself" which has any effect on anything else.

Consider Derrida's answer to Husserl. Husserl says: we may establish an ultimate foundation for knowledge in such and such a way. Derrida answers: we may not, because the "ultimate foundation" is finally a paradox; there are no ultimate foundations. Notice that Derrida's refutation presupposes that either he or Husserl is "right." How would Derrida's answer look if one denied that paradoxes exist in the "real world," and there had to be a "right" choice between Husserl and Derrida? Both Derrida's critique and Husserl's original formulations would then each have a certain degree of plausibility. What will determine which aspects of their work are valuable will depend on how the structure of each one's thought can be appropriated in any given situation. There are circumstances, for example, in which both the "primordiality of transcendental subjectivity" would be a sensible way to describe experience, say, in a moment of psychoanalytic insight. But there are other circumstances in which subjectivity is a burden, and the solid exteriority of language is the "foundation" on which to understand a situation, for example, in public statements by public officials. A literary text could be usefully read either way. On the one hand, its meaning is a function of a completely subjective and/or a completely intersubjective "constitution" of it, while, on the other hand, there is no other meaning for the text than that given by its unique set of words: the only way the text "says" is the way it actually says. In the history of criticism, both of these points of view are represented, and both are recited in the many new situations in which literary texts are reread. Even though criticism is a discipline occupied almost exclusively by men, it is also one, for reasons I will discuss shortly, whose history shows at once the interest in paradox and in hierarchical searches for "truth," and the ability to repeatedly draw on readings and ideas from ever more distant historical periods and cultures.

If we think of criticism as the socially organized commentary on a culture's significant texts, we will see it as a contemporary descendant of a long series of social institutions governed by biblical and legal hermeneutics, oral and written. In dealing with sacred or legal texts, hermeneutics always had a concrete purpose: to construe either the Word of God or The Law in such a way as to clarify what social action to take. Of course, other matters about the "meaning" of the texts always came into play, even if there was no immediate need. Nevertheless, the process of interpretation was usually related to some form of action or behavior, even if only in ritual form. Because of the social and pragmatic grounding, it was possible to "read" the law in more than one way, even if one way predominated for long periods of time. Interpretation of the law works more or less the same way today, as when the various ways of understanding "obscenity" are discussed in courts. The specific case under review usually plays some role in urging how the law will be read. In this way precedents are set and "the law" undergoes an incremental change in meaning. In any event, because of this "social" history of hermeneutics, criticism not only continues to tolerate contradiction, but often makes use of it or seeks it out, notwithstanding the fact that direct action often is not taken as a result of how a literary text is read.

Susan Handelman, in her study of the historical origins of contemporary literary theory, contrasts the hermeneutic thought style—which she loosely associates with the traditional Rabbinic thought-collectives—with the Classical Greek thought style of deductive logic. She indicates that "for Aristotle, the Law of Contradiction is 'the firmest of all principles.' "[4] This law—" 'It is impossible for the same thing to belong and not belong to the same thing in the same respects' "—carries with it the primary principle of bivalence— either P or not-P—and the primacy of the syllogism. This set of axioms, she argues,

> is a cornerstone of Western philosophy, but it is also dependent on certain unexamined ontological assumptions. . . . Freud, for example, recognized the *logic* of an unconscious where the Law of Contradiction does not operate.

4. Susan Handelman, *The Slayers of Moses* (Albany, New York: SUNY Press, 1982), p. 13.

Rabbinic thought can also at times suspend the Law of Contradiction. The same is true of poetry, rhetoric, metaphor, and so forth, all of which play with the equivocalness and ambiguity of words, and all of which Aristotle banished from the realm of pure science and logic. Yet, it should be noted, their "play" is no less serious than Aristotle's play with the forms of reasoning and statement. Aristotle, however, did not recognize any play within his system; he took his formulations of general statements as axiomatic rules of inference rather than as theses. For example, in the type of syllogism which is called *conditional*, where the formula is "*If*, every M is L, and every S is M, then every S is L," the *if* becomes more or less forgotten, and statements are considered axioms. In fact, Aristotle does not examine conditional statements within his theory of logic, nor consider the kind of argument based on them as comparable to the syllogism. (Much of Rabbinic thought, in contrast, is oriented around conditional statements, where *if* becomes the key that opens the discourse to an almost endless play of argument based on all manner of seemingly unrelated conjecture. *If*, in literary terms might also be said to correspond to the faculty of the imagination, the *what if* that opens and creates new and alternative visions of what *is*.) Aristotle, following Greek ontology, is more concerned with *what is* than *what if*. For Aristotle, all valid arguments involve syllogistic reasoning. (pp. 13–14).

Although Handelman's concern is to demonstrate the contemporary appearance of Rabbinic thought-styles, let us entertain only her contrast between the logical and the hermeneutic as two different *concerns with language*, two different senses of how rational thought can proceed.

Handelman implies, from her own perspective, that hermeneutic thought is a minority style: the major, most authoritative style is that of deductive logic, of mathematics. The most authoritative kind of knowledge is the discovery of mathematical arrangements in nature. Deductive logic is a "cornerstone" of Western thought in that it is preferred and honored more than hermeneutic thought. The two styles have, therefore, been *hierarchically* juxtaposed, so that both the *superior value of deductive logic* obtains *and* the *presupposition* of hierarchical arrangement. When Evelyn Fox Keller seeks to reduce the separateness of subject and object in science, of knower and known, of people and nature, she implicitly opposes thinking of these pairs as hierarchically arranged.[5] The feminist challenge to science is a statement that the presumably value-free standard of logical thought is, like all other thought, interest bound, with this interest coming, as Handelman suggests, from Classical Greek values and intellectual priorities.[6]

5. See chapter 2, pp. 32–33.

6. In the Harding and Hintikka volume, *Discovering Reality*, there are three feminist essays that challenge Aristotle—by Lynda Lange, Elizabeth Spelman, and Judith Stiehm. Also

The contrasting ways in which the conditional is treated is particularly germane to questions of knowledge. In a conditional syllogism, Handelman says, "the *if* becomes more or less forgotten." This means that the "if" is routinely read as a "when," but then the approach to real cases is characterized by a search for instances where the "when" is stipulated as an "is." The way this syllogism is actually used is to *try* to find cases where the "if" is taken out of the question in order that the fixed and completely predictable deductive process apply. Kuhn's conception of "normal science" follows this pattern. Once a theory is stipulated, its conditional premise is forgotten, so that the "logical" or necessary consequences of the theory may be pursued. In the textbooks, the knowledge is then presented in this self-enclosed way, so that the conditional premise of the knowledge is taken out of the pedagogical process as well as out of the "normal science" process.

One wants to say that the "if" was removed accidentally, but this cannot be the case. In a sense, it was not really removed; it was, rather, read as a way to find objectively predictable instances of natural phenomena. In other words, the way the "if" was used represents a certain syndrome of *human values*, a predilection for behaving in certain ways, an expression of certain desires, and an initiative to organize the public interest in knowledge in certain ways. In Handelman's contrast of this use with the stronger "what if" usage, she is implicitly pointing to a different set of values and a different approach to knowledge, and at the same time, pertinently for us, a different approach to language.

The principle involved here is that it is as important to question the premise of any inferential procedure as it is to find instances of the consequences. In Janice Moulton's critique of the adversarial technique discussed in chapter 2, she advocates approaching the "classic" philosophical questions in just this way. It means not simply searching for an answer or developing a proof, but identifying the issue's motivating context—the matter of why the questions were raised to begin with. The way she puts it, "Why is this argument important?" shows that attention to the premises is necessarily a disclosure of the human interest or stake in the question. She assumes that any important philosophical question must be motivated by some human concern, that there must be some experiential basis for abstract inquiry and that this basis always

pertinent is Sandra Harding's *The Science Question in Feminism* (New York: Basic Books, 1986). Greek thought goes unchallenged in today's intellectual life as a repository of values and intellectual schemata. Usually it is a question of either Aristotle or Plato, but virtually no one conceptualizes the great period of Athens as a masculine-dominated, sexist, slave-holding society whose conceptions of knowledge may actually be serving those degenerate values. The arguments by Handelman and the essays by Lydia Lange, Elizabeth Spelman, and Keller and Grontowski in the Harding and Hintikka volume give some grounds for pursuing this challenge to the unthinking admiration and credit given to Greek thought in intellectual life today.

plays a role in the style and substance of the inquiry itself. This is a point similar to the one Fleck made in his analysis of biological research.[7]

The issue may be seen as the need for at least two attitudes toward knowledge, neither of which is to be considered more primordial or more authoritative. The traditional attitude concentrates on relatively abstract procedures and the search for predictable results. Keller, Handelman, and Fleck (for example) concentrate on teleological questioning—on the purposes, aims, and consequences of seeking knowledge to begin with; and they also seek understanding that does not necessarily predict the subsequent fate of the matters under study.

While philosophy has been addressing the question of language for most of this century, Chomsky sought to break the conceptual deadlock by advocating a series of premises that made its "scientific" study attractive. These premises included the ideas that (1) language was acquired much too rapidly and masterfully by children to suppose that it was acquired through imitation, (2) each newly constructed sentence is achieved by applying transformational rules to a series of fundamental language elements, and (3) language exists in two senses, competence and performance, only one of which can be studied scientifically. The (hypothetical) conclusion from these premises was that the controlling mental machinery for the acquisition of language must be part of the genetic code. In this discussion, the first two premises need not be investigated, while many are already investigating whether the conclusion is true. Our interest is in the third premise—that the phenomenon of "language" can be divided into an abstract capability eligible of scientific inquiry and a concrete manifestation that remains "mysterious" and ineligible of such treatment. Instead of "performance," however, I will call this manifestation first "language use" and then "literacy." These two categories—competence and performance—should be understood as outgrowths of the two attitudes, or approaches, to knowledge I described above. Why, then, might Chomsky have begun with such a distinction?

The early studies of language acquisition and use done by Clara and Wilhelm Stern in 1907 presented a great deal of information about the physical development of language—vocalization and articulation—as well as about the gradual emergence of vocabulary and grammatic speech. The scientific literature mainly *disclosed* typical cases of how language appeared. However, no reliable theoretical understanding came out of such studies. The observational technique concentrated on the individual child since the presupposition was that language acquisition was altogether part of individual ontogenesis. Chomsky made his proposals to a research scene which presupposed the primacy of the individual and which collected a great deal of "empirical" data.

7. See chapter 2, pp. 36–38.

His division of language into a theoretical component, competence, and an empirical component seemed to be a bold move because it freed researchers from having to account for the bewildering variety of materials one gets when one actually records what infants say. It was enough for him to show how complex a task language acquisition is and how rapidly it takes place. Stipulating the existence of competence suggested that the data be organized as the sequential *emergence* of ever-more complex abilities, each of which could, in principle, be described abstractly in terms of the transformational rules being used. Once it became plausible that there was such a successive emergence of (unconscious) rule-use, it became possible to formalize the rules and then suggest that there is a complex logic of rules—a set of rules for making rules—that is conceivably written into the genetic code. In this way, the primary work of the linguist was to conceptualize the rules in the best possible formal way. For many years after Chomsky's first proposals, linguists studied language the way physicists studied nature: assuming an inner, concealed *logical* order, and then reflecting on which order best fits the phenomena. As a result, the paradigm of the primacy of the individual was retained, while an authoritative theoretical technique was applied.

The study of language use does not fit into this procedural combination on the one hand because the data from individuals is so complex, and on the other because language use always takes place when *more than one person is present*. If the presupposition of the study of language was that language is necessarily manifested in a social situation, it would not be as simple to also stipulate that individual competence was the mental essence of language. In other words, the division of competence and performance *depends on* conceiving language as a purely individual matter. If language is thought of as "dialogue," for example, then competence would have to include a category like "ability to interact with another person," while performance would have to include much more than just linguistic data. At the same time, it might not be necessary to persevere with the distinction at all, since it does not seem plausible to look for a genetic coding for "the ability to interact with others." It might be possible, in other words, to conceptualize "language" in a way that can yield explanations but does not demand a formal description. Or, it might be that whatever formal descriptions obtain, it would still be erroneous to consider them an identification of some mental essence of language, as it would be to say that the genetic code for leg musculature explains all forms of locomotion. Two sources cast doubt on Chomsky's distinction. One is the set of problems researchers have encountered in formulating competence in some complete way, and the other is the interesting results obtained by those who view language as being at least as fundamentally tied to social existence as it is to individual biological development. The study of language has seemed more and more to require the epistemological shifts proposed by Scheman, Moulton, and Handelman, and less and less to be susceptible to the treatment which views a purely logical conceptualization as the most authoritative understanding.

In changing our attention from the issue of "language" to those of "language use" and "literacy," we are aiming to think with a new set of values in mind and with a sense of social purpose. The constituency of "language" has been the academy, but the constituency of "language use" and "literacy" is any social group whose interests and makeup can be identified, including the academy but in new ways. These new subjects require a new sense of what research is, something more akin to what Fleck described, a self-conscious sense of working within a shared thought-style and a known community of interest. Such research is still in the investigation of language, but by seeing it as language use and literacy, we are also aiming to include our own language use strategies as part of the object of research. To use the term language in the usual sense is to invite abstraction and to discourage specification of which or whose language is being studied. By claiming that it matters whose language we are studying, we are trying to include the premises of our study as part of the object of investigation. Most studies merely name which "population" is being used. But it is a different matter to understand in some depth the special psychosocial features of *this* population in analyzing their language use. It is still further necessary to recognize the relativity of the subject population's use of language to the presuppositions of our own. These cascading sets of intrasocial involvements are definitely not as "clean" as those studied by transformational linguistics. But they show more clearly what the subject really is. Rather than resigning ourselves to either its paradox or its mystery, we are trying to be more faithful to the normal *experience* of language, to its phenomenological appearance in our minds. In so doing we also aim to be more respectful of the sense that we are never alone when using language, that we are necessarily bound up with others at all linguistic moments, and that there are ethical and political forces which go to the heart of all language use.

Perhaps the term "literacy" alludes to ethical and political matters in a way that "language use" does not. Consider two senses in which this is the case. In literate societies, the illiterate belong to a less privileged class. Being literate is a privilege usually associated with other social and economic advantages, and literacy is a feature of many subsets of privileged communities. The particular style of language use which includes reading and writing is also a style that carries certain values associated with, for example, wealth, technology, and an underlying sense of access, potentially, to the best that society has to offer. In the world at large, where there are still whole societies and large communities which are not literate, in addition to their less privileged status, the question arises how their ethical integrity is to be respected by the more powerful literate world. Studies of these societies (some of which I will discuss shortly) suggest that they carry values which can and should be adopted by literate societies, but which cannot be because the syndrome of "literate" values inhibits it. By becoming an unquestioned standard of language use, the values of literacy have made it seem that acquiring literacy is as necessary as growing into adulthood. At the same time the meaning of literacy has been grossly underestimated. As a rule it is conceived of and presented as a skill something like driving: something more or less easy to learn, necessary for handling the technology of contemporary civilization, but something nevertheless "transparent," not in itself carrying values or urging any social conduct, and only providing the capability to achieve things that have little to do with literacy and language use themselves. Those who cannot or do not become literate are understood to be deficient in some way—sick or lazy or self-indulgent. Because literacy is not regarded as a complex cultural feature, comparable to religion,[8] it is assumed that it can be acquired regardless of the culture a person has been born into, or the approaches to language use a person already has.

Derrida's concept of "writing" (briefly discussed in chapter 2) helps to explain the broader concept of literacy I am exploring. If writing is taken to mean both oral and written language, to mean, in addition, the wide variety of symbolic behaviors that are refined and represented in art forms, then writing is a more general term than "speech," as reading is, by implication, more general than hearing or listening. The important point is that the term "writing" connotes better than "speech" the palpability of symbolic gestures and, hence, the principle that *these gestures matter*. To speak or use language in a certain way means not that there is a meaning "behind" the words, but that the presentation of the words themselves is the nucleus of social behavior. It is not the "intention" motivating the words but what the words are that matters. Contributing one's words to a conversation is an interpersonal act that *counts*. No matter how rapidly one's conversation is forgotten, it still marks a key moment of a social achievement, the establishment of an intersubjectivity, the reidentification of a human relationship. To be "literate"

---

8. There are some religious people who think that anyone can join their religion and give us to believe that all it takes is an act of faith. We see these people (as well as their corruptions) on television. It is not a coincidence that they are also the ones now advocating censorship in the schools. Those who think literacy and religion are isolated commitments are also those who refuse to recognize their own politics.

means to be a social being. One is committed to "read" the inner life of others, and to "write" one's own life on the blank space of one's pregiven relatedness to others. In these terms, any literate act is a development of one's implication in the lives of others, and the cultivation of literacy always entails psychosocial, ethical, and political practice. These considerations cast doubt on the usefulness of the distinction between competence and performance. If every appearance of language is a choice made by an inherently social being, if the gradual appearance of language in the mind of the infant is inextricably bound up with the infant's relationships, it cannot be that performance is "triggered" into being. The acts of knowing and saying must be so tied to one another that to think of them as separate is actually to suppose that there is another phenomenon than what is actually developing. It cannot be that the capacity to choose the words is separate from the capacity to acquire them "properly." Even to say that language is "acquired" would be wrong. Rather, language is the natural machinery of human socialization and the means of intrasocial regulation. *To cultivate literacy is to refine and enhance our mutual implication in one another's lives and to discover and exercise our mutual responsibilities.*

Let me review work from several sources to further clarify this point. In his discussion of the "higher psychological functions," L. S. Vygotsky presents an analytical description of how an infant's grasping behaviors turn into pointing. Subsequently, he gives a similar argument for the conversion of sensorimotor intelligence (in the child) into linguistic intelligence:

> We call the internal reconstruction of an external operation *internalization*. A good example of this process may be found in the development of pointing. Initially this gesture is nothing more than an unsuccessful attempt to grasp something, a movement aimed at a certain object which designates forth-coming activity. . . . When the mother comes to the child's aid and real-izes his movement indicates something, the situation changes fundamentally. Pointing becomes a gesture for others. The child's unsuccessful attempt engenders a reaction not from the object he seeks but *from another person*. Consequently, the primary meaning of that unsuccessful grasping is estab-lished by others. . . . At this juncture there occurs a change in that move-ment's function: from an object-oriented movement it becomes a movement aimed at another person, a means of establishing relations. *The grasping move-ment changes to the act of pointing*. . . . It becomes a true gesture only after it objectively manifests all the functions of pointing for others and is under-stood by others as such a gesture. Its meaning and functions are created at first by an objective situation and then by people who surround the child.[9]

9. L. S. Vygotsky, *Mind in Society*, ed. Michael Cole, Vera John-Steiner, Sylvia Scribner, and Ellen Souberman (Cambridge, Mass.: Harvard University Press, 1978), p. 56.

The keynote of Vygotsky's work on the development of language and thought is the principle that social action on motor behavior creates *internal* intelligence. This case is paradigmatic: the interpersonal response to physical movement converts it into *gestures*, which, normally, are understood to be deliberately initiated by people. This implies that intelligence has no meaning as an independent faculty, but only as an internal part of the capacity for social adaptation. We should add an additional factor to this picture, one not often mentioned by students of cognitive development: the process of internalization must also be, as Maureen Shields (more of whose work will be cited shortly) put it, "soaked in affectivity." In the case of the gesture, the grasping function has first met with *frustration* which is seen by the caregiver (usually the parent) and then taken up by her or his (i.e., the caregiver's) response. In the individual child, the frustration creates an intensified alertness to oneself. Social response then recognizes this affective condition and helps convert it, at the same time, to self-awareness and gesture. The social response is affectively restorative and pedagogical. When the gestures become ordinary, the original affective load drops out and only the "learned" item seems visible. Notice how gestures are easily construed as pieces of "writing." In one sense the gesture is "neutral" or completely objective: the history of its acquisition is not detectable. However, the gesture becomes "meaningful" to the child and others in part because it is already meaningful in the child's community. At the same time the child did not acquire the gesture "by rote"—by sheer imitation; rather, the child had to exercise its own desires and senses, had to interact step by step, to "win" the "knowledge" of making gestures. The child became "gesturally literate" by simultaneously growing, knowing, and interacting.

One of Vygotsky's most seminal essays discusses "the relations between speech and tool use," and introduces his conception of language. He argues that an adult human's tool use is different from an ape's or infant's tool use primarily because language is bound up with it. Although speech functions and other (nonspeech) motor developments can be seen as separate from one another, they are actually growing toward one another in a reciprocal relationship: "The history of the process of the *internalization of social speech* is also the history of the socialization of the children's practical intellect." [10] Vygotsky also implies something Piaget described: when "practical activity" (sensorimotor intelligence in Piaget) and speech converge, language has been acquired. The child sees, in one act or one mental stroke, the congruence of speech and behavior, of names and things. To internalize speech is both to make language into a specifically human tool, and to make tool use into a specifically social behavior. Language acquisition is both the internalization

10. Vygotsky, "Tool and Symbol in Child Development," in *Mind in Society*, p. 27.

of social speech and the socialization of individual, practical "sensorimotor" intelligence. This dialectic must also "run" in an affective vein (though Vygotsky, again, does not make this point). Tool use and language use are regulated by feelings of confidence, mastery, achievement, ambition, love, generosity, and so on. Such feelings mobilize memory and action and in this way prompt and inhibit the use of language. The feelings themselves are "about" the intrapersonal tasks, and they mark these tasks with social value. They could be thought of as a biological "ink" that holds the knowledge in memory by contributing its social pertinence. This simultaneously practical and mental capability is tool-using literacy.

A concept absent from Vygotsky's work but which bears on his approach to language is "the self." The work of G. H. Mead, which stresses practical experience less, presents a social perspective similar to Vygotsky's; it does not discuss experimental data but includes extended reflection on the self as needing explanation if the priority of social processes is assumed:

> . . . if you regard the social process of experience as prior to the existence of mind and explain the origins of minds in terms of the interaction among individuals within that process, the . . . origin of minds [and] the interaction among minds cease to seem mysterious or miraculous. [11]

Mead outlines how the individual mind has always been considered the primary datum in Western thought, and that in this century it has come to be understood as "biological both in its nature and its origin." (p. 224) If this is so, he argues, the act of explanation is solipsistic. The mind explains both itself and other minds. The idea of sharing knowledge, or of an explanation being accepted by another, must be understood as either a mystery or the result of a power struggle in which one mind prevails. Recall, in this connection, how Chomsky viewed language performance as a "mystery": performance must be an instance of "the interaction among minds," while the ultimate parameters of Chomsky's concept of language come from the assumption of the "biological nature and origin" of mind and language. In assuming the priority of the individual mind, the common phenomenon of mutual or intersubjective knowledge would have to be understood either as having been declared so by one authoritative person, or as being an inexplicable duplication without any account of how such a duplication could take place. On the other hand, according to Mead, if you assume that intersubjectivity is the prior item, it is easy to see how an individual mind is *derived* from it, how a single person can define and feel that singleness as the result of individuation. Mead then makes a similar argument regarding the self:

11. G. H. Mead, *Mind, Self, and Society*, ed. Charles W. Morris (Chicago: University of Chicago Press, 1962), p. 50; hereafter cited in text.

... self-consciousness involves the individual's becoming an object to himself by taking the attitude of other individuals toward himself within an organized setting of social relationships and unless the individual had thus become an object to himself he would not be self-conscious or have a self at all. Apart from his social interactions with other individuals, he would not relate the private or "subjective" contents of experience to himself. (pp. 225–226)

For experience to acquire meaning, for it to be known as private experience to begin with, an individual must have first performed self-objectification, and to have done this is to have internalized "the attitudes of others" toward oneself. Self-objectification is the key to understanding subjective experience as intersubjectively grounded. Here, Mead is dealing with issues quite similar to those with which Husserl laboriously struggled. The difference between them, aside from their tone and levels of intensity, is that Husserl did not relent in his belief in the primordiality of individual subjectivity. Mead, however, unhesitatingly declares the priority of social relationships. Yet, it is still not a question of one or the other being "right." What is important is that both sought ways to view the individual subject (mind and/or self) in terms of others, and to articulate the mutual implication of selves and communities. Once this mutuality is understood, a statement like "I am in pain" may be said to have a "primordially subjective" meaning, but it may also be seen as inseparable from the meaning "I need help from you."[12] *Literacy is being able to read or write or say such sentences while being alert to the simultaneity of their subjective and intersubjective meanings.* This is the sense in which all people, in some degree, are already literate, and in which, at the same time, social relatedness can be continuously used to cultivate literacy.

Only recently has the study of infantile development and language acquisition begun to make use of these early reflections on intersubjectivity (i.e., Husserl, Vygotsky, Mead). While Chomsky's work has created a new and intense interest in infantile development, the efforts resulting from this interest have pointed up the need for a more comprehensive social perspective. Margaret Donaldson, for example, finds Piaget's and Chomsky's work to distort the process of childhood mental development. She rejects the transformational perspective for the same reason both she and Chomsky reject the associationist program—its reduction of the individual to mechanistic behaviors:

Chomsky's LAD is a formal data processor, in its way just as automatic and mechanical as processes of an associationist kind. In go the linguistic data, out

---

12. The matter of how a declaration of pain is to be understood will be discussed in another context in chapter 4, where Saul Kripke's use of this example is the topic.

comes a grammar. The living child does not seem to enter into the business very actively (not to say fully) in either case.[13]

But it is not the individual child alone that Donaldson seeks to reintroduce; rather it is this child in the "situation involving direct and immediate human interaction." (p. 31) In her view,

> The primary thing is now held to be the grasp of meaning—the ability to "make sense" of things, and above all to make sense of what people do, which of course includes what people say. On this view, it is the child's ability to interpret situations which makes it possible to him . . . to arrive at a knowledge of language. (pp. 32–33)

Donaldson cites several instances which show how the unfamiliar laboratory environment and experimental procedures contribute to the Piagetian view of how children's intelligence is *limited*. She observed that children's answers to Piaget's questions were cued by the schedule of questions, when the schedule was changed so that the questions implied much less that the children's answers were wrong, their answers were "right" much more often. When the situation of inquiry was less intimidating, either because fewer questions were asked or experimental materials that were already familiar to the children were used, their "performance" was much better, and they seemed to know more at an earlier age than Piaget's measure suggested. Donaldson is concerned to show that cognitive activity, and particularly language, is fundamentally tied to a "matrix of personal relations." (p. 90)

Perhaps more than other researchers, Colwyn Trevarthen and Penelope Hubley have taken the concept of intersubjectivity seriously as a research project. They claim that it is "innate," because they see no other way to account for the many spontaneous infantile behaviors that guide and orient infants in response to and in relations with other people:

> . . . the infant is both a subject and a person. Even if the infant lacks a differentiated image of "self" and even if the communications of infants lack all referential content, the manner of expression of a two-month-old in face-to-face play with the mother has human or personal characteristics. It regulates an interpersonal field of action between them. This claim is at variance with the fundamental postulates of traditional psychoanalysis and with Piaget's conception of the sensorimotor period.[14]

13. Margaret Donaldson, *Children's Minds* (New York: Norton, 1978), p. 34; hereafter cited in text.

14. Colwyn Trevarthen and Penelope Hubley, "Secondary Intersubjectivity: Confidence, Confiding, and Acts of Meaning in the First Year," in *Action, Gesture and Symbol: The Emergence of Language*, ed. Andrew Lock (New York: Academic Press, 1978), p. 325; hereafter cited in text.

While it is probably not necessary to believe the claim to be at "variance with the fundamental postulates" of other concepts of child development, Trevarthen and Hubley's work emphasizes a different kind of infantile developmental schedule. In the first year, they suggest, there are two noticeable phases of intersubjectivity, punctuated, in between, by a period of consolidation. "Primary intersubjectivity" is observable at about two months (smiling begins at about six weeks), and "secondary intersubjectivity" begins at about nine months:

> Given what 2-month-olds can do in mutual awareness with their mothers, it seems simplest to conclude that at 9 months there is attainment of functional control, of intrinsic origin, for the use of innate and practised communicative abilities so they can be related to physical objects that have been brought inside the field of shared experience and shared knowledge. All of the above examples [they list about fifteen interactive behaviors] fit the hypothesis . . . that development of the infant mind brings together newly elaborated intentions to things and the giving of messages to people. We see no evidence that this achievement is the result of practice of specified rituals (rules of conduct) learned with a consistent companion. We think the acquisition of specific practices gives necessary definition to a process which is caused by change in the structures of intelligence at a deep level; one which is basically the same for all infants [and which are] inherent and self-regulating. (p. 223)

In presenting an innateness hypothesis for intersubjectivity, Trevarthen and Hubley are proposing that the "structures of intelligence" are "at a deeper level" structures of intersubjectivity. What most researchers study as purely cognitive development is here understood to be intersubjective development, and it is taken further than Piaget's findings and in a different direction from Chomsky's. In Chomsky's case, the formal description of the "steady state" adult language is supposed to provide the formulae for genetic findings. In the present case, repeatedly observed *qualitative behavior styles* which, they claim, "regulate the individual enjoyment of action and experience from the start of psychological existence" (p. 338), are taken as evidence for the intersubjective character of this existence. Trevarthen admits to being far from finding any physiological correlative for intersubjectivity, but he and Hubley do show, in a way related to Mead's, that to *think* of mental development in terms of intersubjectivity promises a more comprehensive understanding of how mind, language, society, and culture evolve together from the beginning. *Literacy begins with psychosocial development.*

Attention to intersubjectivity brings out two elements not usually found in purely cognitive approaches to language: affect and dialogue. Maureen Shields emphasizes these items in her work on infantile development. Like Trevarthen and Hubley, she aims to change and enlarge the concept of cognition:

The impact of the personal and social world on the child is almost always described in terms of affective rather than cognitive consequences. Yet [it has been shown] that attachment, the most powerful manifestation of affect, must be closely tied up with perception and the development of stable representations of identity for the caretaker and other familiar family figures. Such representations are of course soaked with emotional meaning, and this makes them more significant and powerful, but in what way does this make them less cognitive than the representations of physical objects? Furthermore [it has been pointed out that] the child acquiring language develops a whole repertory of verbal labels and speech acts concerned with the activity and feelings of persons. There are words about thinking, wanting, liking, being friends. There are claims for possession, assignments of roles, words for sharing play proposals, threats, protests, appeals to social rules. In so far as children can use this repertory, it appears reasonable that the terms of it refer to internal representations of behaviour as much as words like *mug* and *chair* refer to representations of experienced objects.[15]

In the same way, as Shields discusses, that there is no separating the cognitive from the affective in children's mental development, there is no way to separate the individual's capability for and use of language from the continuing situation of dialogue—the necessity to speak with someone else. Shields observes that "the young baby appears to be genetically programmed to give preferential attention to the human voice and the human face, and to respond with pleasure to human exchanges."[16] She therefore proposes that "dialogue is the basic form of thought" and that language should be understood as "the internalization of the voices of others. . . . the subject-to-subject relationship will promote and develop our ability to act as our own subjects when we consciously examine our ideas and think things out." (pp. 30–31) Shields maintains that the affective character of interpersonal relations makes them the orienting point in the growth of mental life. In addition, the innateness of intersubjectivity makes possible *both* the dialectic of object cognition and the dialogue that governs object cognition. Intersubjectivity is the framework for the intermingling of the cognitive and the affective, and it makes it possible to conceptualize language as dialogic or interactional.

In pursuing this more comprehensive idea of literacy as a series of culturally encouraged language-use strategies beginning in infancy, it is important to challenge the habitual notion that literacy and orality are fundamentally different from one another. Consider what Lévi-Strauss observes in his short essay, "A Writing Lesson." Ordinarily, "one might suppose that [writing's]

15. Maureen Shields, "The Child as Psychologists: Construing the Social World," in Lock, ed., *Action, Gesture and Symbol*, pp. 530–31.

16. Maureen Shields, "Dialectics, Dialogues, and the Social Transmission of Knowledge," unpublished essay, 1984, p. 30; hereafter cited in text.

emergence could not fail to bring about profound changes in the conditions of human existence."[17] He continues, however, that "the only phenomenon with which writing has always been concomitant is the creation of cities and empires, that is, the integration of large numbers of individuals into a political system, and their grading into castes or classes." In general, writing "seems to have favored the exploitation of human beings rather than their enlightenment," and in contemporary civilization, "the fight against illiteracy is . . . connected with an increase in governmental authority over citizens. Everyone must be able to read so that the government can say: ignorance of the law is no excuse." We should not, of course, construe these remarks to mean that literacy is not also a means of political emancipation, as Paulo Freire has discussed (and as I will consider further in Chapter 6). The point is that writing—in its usual sense—like every other tool or device that has emerged in civilization, is immediately a function of the prevailing social styles and interests, and it becomes one of a wide array of customary opportunities and capabilities. If, for example, in a society, the written word is thought to have magical power, it is because that society considers other things also to have this power. As Lévi-Strauss narrates in his essay, when an outsider brings writing into a nonliterate group, it is assimilated to the existing practices of social interchange. Similarly, even though the transistor seemed like a "revolutionary" device, Western values which urge the production of new consumer goods are exactly the same after the transistor as before it.

A more recent, elaborate, and consequential view of the continuity of communal values as they affect the growth of literacy and its ties to orality is Shirley Heath's ten-year-long study of three small communities in the Carolinas. Her work is especially valuable because she became a contributing member of the communities she studied, a methodological departure from the traditional "scientific" detachment that gave her a much more intimate access to the communities. The kind of understanding that she achieved could only have come from being both a trusted and contributing figure of the communities. For the study of literacy, it is essential that the researcher be involved or integrated. That is, the researcher herself had to become "literate" in those communities.

Here, then, are three general propositions she derived from her inquiry:

First, patterns of language use in any community are in accord with and mutually reinforce other cultural patterns, such as space and time orderings, problem-solving techniques, group loyalties, and preferred patterns of recreation. In

17. Claude Lévi-Strauss, "A Writing Lesson," in *Tristes Tropiques*, trans. John Weightman and Doreen Weightman (1955; New York: Atheneum, 1973), p. 298.

each of these communities, space and time usage and the role of the individual in the community condition the interactional rules for the occasions of language use.

Second, factors involved in preparing children for school oriented, mainstream success are deeper than differences in formal structure of language, amount of parent-child interaction, and the like. The language socialization process in all its complexity is more powerful than such single-factor explanations in accounting for academic success.

Third, the patterns of interactions between oral and written uses of language are varied and complex, and the traditional oral-literature dichotomy does not capture the ways other cultural patterns in each community affect the uses of oral and written languages.[18]

Each of these formulations urges us to abandon the idea of literacy as a trainable skill and to establish the principle that attention to literacy in any of its aspects entails attention to the community, the culture, and the process of language socialization. Heath observes, for example, that "Roadville [the White community] parents bring up their children in the drama of life by carefully scripting and rehearsing them for the parts they must play." (p. 346) This means that a great many instructions are given to show how to behave in church, say, or at the dinner table. As the child enters school these "scripts" become a model and a preparation for the formal writing done in school. (In discussing the work of Deborah Tannen, shortly, I will elaborate on this point.) It is an ethical and cultural matter to "train" children in certain kinds of behavior and to do it in just this scripted way (in the White community). These ways greatly resemble the social rules in school, as well as the technical rules of reading and writing. The underlying mental, social, and affective structures of school literacy are, in other words, already part of the children's culture throughout the first five or six years of growth. About the Black community, Heath says: "In the drama of Trackton life . . . children will experience numerous shifts of scene and cast, and players will take on different roles on different occasions. . . . As they become conversationalists, they draw from their viewing of others' performances on the plaza, they imitate motions, facial expressions, and extraneous sounds to set the background for their discourse." (pp. 346–47) This situation, of course, is not scripted in advance by the parents; children, in a sense, socialize themselves—not in any less complex way—but in a way which is definitely not the way of the American school. The family life and socialization style of the black families, even through and perhaps because of generations of slavery, have spontaneously retained their ancestral forms,

18. Shirley Brice Heath, *Ways with Words* (New York: Cambridge University Press, 1983), p. 344.

without, that is, some purposeful attempt to retain what is "theirs" in the face of white domination. This spontaneous dramatic style is no less firm as a cultural style than the "scripting" style, but its natural inclination to grow is abruptly halted. The black child's entrance into school is a radical cultural disjunction. The original style remains (in the child's mind) in a secondary, and perhaps subversive role, while the new habits are laboriously learned from scratch. One can see, in this light, that one cannot "teach" literacy as if it can be acquired on top of any community and family background a child happens to have. Put in the more abstract terms I used in chapter 2, the materiality or exteriority of language—that is, the cultural modes of literacy—are stable in a particular culture, while different cultures have different *kinds* of materiality, both oral and written. Heath sees the need to weaken the oral-literate dichotomy because language use, whether oral or written, is always attached to deeper, underlying socialization patterns in the community or society. Any attempt to "teach" literacy is unlikely to succeed unless, somehow, the existing patterns of literacy—in the more general sense I am advocating—are recognized and actively engaged.

Heath, in a 1984 essay,[19] demonstrates in some detail what it takes to teach "white" literacy to a young woman whose existing modes of literacy and social relations already had a significant momentum of their own. The woman, T, is sixteen years old and has two infant sons, De, about seventeen months, and a newborn she had during the study. Because of her complex family life, including embarrassment about being a black pregnant girl in school, T was not able to go to school on a regular basis, though she did start out in a ninth-grade "basic" English class. In this class, Heath had a working professional relationship with the teacher, B, and also corresponded with the class herself. B had set up a letter-writing program in which the ninth-graders wrote to eleventh-graders in order both to exchange thoughts and write. When T had to leave school, Heath encouraged her to continue corresponding with the eleventh grader, L, as well as with her teacher, B, *and* with her, Heath. Because Heath had already introduced into that ninth-grade class the idea of taking "field notes"—which meant that the students could do the same kind of *work* that Heath does—Heath successfully urged T to take field notes on the language development of her older son, De. This became the topic of the correspondence between T and B and between T and Heath. The two teachers (B and Heath) helped T to provide a (white) literacy environment for her son by teaching her to read to him and to make the use

    19. Shirley Brice Heath with Charlene Thomas, "The Achievement of Preschool Literacy for Mother and Child," in *Awakening to Literacy*, ed. Hillel Goelman, Antoinette Oberg, and Frank Smith (Exeter, New Hampshire: Heinemann, 1984), pp. 51–72.

of books habitual. In these ways, T developed habits of writing and teaching her son which she believed would make it easier for him to subsequently assimilate himself into the school system.

What, then, are the salient elements of this arrangement? Two, I think, should be noted: First, T retained and did not distort her usual family relationships in order to go to school. She is able to continue, more or less, the literacy style that marked her own upbringing and the childrearing circumstances of her own sons. At the same time, the public world and its own literacy style is represented in her life in a special way—through individual attention from three figures: L, the student, B, the teacher, and Heath. She has three partners who encourage her to be a teacher, a "fieldworker" and a student. Such encouragement is not gratuitous because T is herself a concerned mother; it is, in fact, her motherhood that is the main instrument of her accession to the majority literacy style. Moreover, all the relationships are reciprocal: the written correspondence goes back and forth, and it is as if a new community is established not just to serve T, but to serve its other members as well. As a pedagogical arrangement, this is an ingenious and remarkable achievement. If continued, it would no doubt have a major effect on T and her children, as it already has had a strong effect on B and Heath.

However, the effectiveness of this arrangement points up just how complicated it is to transfer the literacy mores of the majority into the life-structures of the unprivileged minority. What is achieved in this situation cannot be achieved routinely in school. In addition, a simple assimilation of the minority cannot really take place: a culture cannot voluntarily abandon its history and customs of socialization. What Heath's arrangement shows is that literacy styles are *mutually* assimilable.[20] Her own conceptualization of the literacy style of Trackton—the "dramatic" style—implies that when members of this community, and others like it, becomes part of the *same* community in the schools, there must be the means for a reciprocal overtaking of one another's style of language use. If there is no value attributed to the minority culture, it is not likely that this culture will accept contributions from the majority. And just as T herself became a teacher and a fieldworker, the minority members must also assume pedagogical authority so that the complex cascading of roles that took place in Heath's arrangement can become part of the school's social vocabulary.

As willing as the white majority may be to "integrate" the schools, the majority concept of literacy is itself an obstacle to the mutual assimilation

20. In the conclusion of this book, "Literacy and Citizenship," I discuss other problems raised by Heath's pioneering initiatives and how they might be reduced.

of language styles. Western literacy has carried with it, for many centuries, certain features of elitism and exclusivity. Walter Ong's study *Orality and Literacy*[21] is useful in alerting us to some of the history of oral and written forms in the West, but he seems eager to retain a strong dichotomy between orality and literacy and to make a case for the superiority of literacy.

Ong tries to show that "writing restructures consciousness":

> By separating the knower from the known, writing makes possible increasingly articulate introspectivity, opening the psyche as never before not only to the external objective world quite distinct from itself but also to the interior self against whom the objective world is set. Writing makes possible the great introspective religious traditions such as Buddhism, Judaism, Christianity, and Islam. All of these have sacred texts. (p. 105)

Ong claims that because in writing the audience is not immediately present, the possibility for introspection is enhanced; the resulting growth of introspection into a cultural habit is one of the bases of the "great" religions. But Ong states further that writing made it possible to use "Learned Latin," a language which, he claims,

> effects even greater objectivity by establishing knowledge in a medium insulated from the emotion-charged depths of one's mother-tongue, thus reducing interference from the human lifeworld and making possible the exquisitely abstract world of medieval scholasticism and of the new mathematical modern science which followed on the scholastic experience. Without Learned Latin, it appears that modern science would have got under way with greater difficulty if it had got under way at all. (p. 114)

In addition to being "insulated from the emotion-charged depths of the mother-tongue," Learned Latin is "devoid of baby talk, insulated from the earliest life of childhood where language has its deepest psychic roots." (p. 113) Finally, Learned Latin was "written and spoken only by males," based in academia "which was totally male" and learned "outside the home in a tribal setting which was in effect a male puberty rite setting, complete with physical punishment and other kinds of deliberately imposed hardships." (p. 113)

What, then, are the features of "consciousness as restructured by writing"? Objectivity, religion, and science—in their *decisively masculine form*, with puberty rites and punishments. Ong actually provides evidence for Naomi Scheman's claim, cited in chapter 2, that the language of science is "socially masculine." He pays homage to detachment, strongly emphasizes the value of insularity for thought, and seems to fear the consequences of proceeding

---

21. Walter Ong, *Orality and Literacy* (New York: Penguin, 1982); hereafter cited in text.

with cultural work in the mother-tongue with its roots in baby-talk. In large part, the case for separating literacy from orality, and for seeing literacy as superior, is a case for prolonging purely masculine cultural forms, exclusively masculine groups, and for ignoring, and perhaps even opposing the complex forms of intersubjectivity that Husserl, Fleck, Mead, Chodorow, Keller, Trevarthen, and Shields have claimed are the defining features and values of human life. If Ong's claims are taken seriously, one would wish to advocate learning dead languages to be used by purely masculine groups. The social circumstances of studying Learned Latin are not unlike those faced by the Trackton children as they enter the American school. An original, family-based literacy style and its affiliated values and social forms are to be rendered secondary to a new "scripted" language which is to be mastered *because* it does not retain the emotional and social history of the mother-tongue. One wonders where this idea of literacy is still advocated. Ong must advocate a separate and better literacy because he is himself a member of an exclusively masculine group having known social, political, and intellectual interests in the structure of society. His argument might seem less dangerous if he announced these interests and included them in his discussion. Scheman's and Heath's views are no less political, but they are explicitly so, and they aim to enhance the interests of groups that are less exclusive, less privileged, less masculine, and less white. Like Lévi-Strauss, Heath sees for traditional literacy no special power. In her essay on T, she writes:

> In spite of all the claims about the consequences of literacy, recent research has shown that the changes which have come with literacy across societies and historical periods have been neither consistent nor predictable. We cannot yet make generalizations about literacy as a causal factor, nor indeed as a necessary accompaniment of specific features of a society. The prior conditions and co-occurring contexts of literacy in each society determine its forms, values, and functions.[22]

In discussing Alexander Luria's study of illiterates in the Soviet Union, Ong discerns that the language use of the purely oral person seems incommensurable with that of the literate questioner. What Ong does not entertain is that the difference is *ethical*, a difference that Heath's perspective makes it possible and valuable to see. The standards, rules, and purposes of oral, context-bound behavior also represent values with long histories, which, if sympathetically identified, are eligible for life in literate societies. And, in fact, as Deborah Tannen's work (which I will treat shortly) suggests, these values often function among us, though unidentified as such.

---

22. Heath, "Achievement of Preschool Literacy," p. 68.

Here is a short sequence from Luria's *Cognitive Development: Its Cultural and Social Foundations*,[23] which Ong discussed in *Orality and Literacy*. The respondent is a 22-year-old illiterate peasant:

Q: Try to explain to me what a tree is.

A: Why should I? Everyone knows what a tree is, they don't need me telling them.

Q: Still, try and explain it.

A: There are trees here everywhere; you won't find a place that doesn't have trees, so what's the point of my explaining?

Q: But some people have never seen trees, so you might have to explain.

A: Okay. You say there are no trees where these people come from. So I'll tell them how we plant beetroots by using seeds, how the roots goes into the earth and the leaves come out on top. That's the way we plant a tree, the roots go down. . . .

Q: How would you define a tree in two words?

A: In two words? Apple tree, elm, poplar.

About the first question, Ong observes that this intelligent respondent reacts to the question by "trying to assess the total puzzling context (the oral mind totalizes)." (Ong, p. 56) Why the peasant's answer is particularly oral, I can't tell. (On most occasions that I had to take intelligence tests, my thought about the test questions were: no one generally wants to know the answer to these questions; it has an ulterior political purpose where my dignity is on the line. My response "totalized" the context, and I was the epitome of the literate student.)

As I read the sequence, the peasant is less unable to play the game than *unwilling*. The researcher's interrogative behavior is intrusive, personally and culturally. The respondent's view is that the explanation of what a tree is may be necessary if he were really in a place where there were no trees and someone really needed to know. When this hypothetical purpose is finally explained to the respondent, the description of tree *planting* is perhaps a

23. Alexander Luria, *Cognitive Development: Its Cultural and Social Foundations*, trans. Martin Lopez-Morillas and Lynn Solatoroff, ed. Michael Cole (Cambridge, Mass.: Harvard University Press, 1976), pp. 86–87. It is hard to judge what Luria's views of his materials are. What he says seems to be doctrinaire Marxism and seems to assume the superiority of the literate mind. Also, with few exceptions, Marxism is generally not responsive to the feminist epistemological claims, though there are feminists, such as Zillah Eisenstein, who see their interests bound up with Marxian values — not an unreasonable view. However, when nonfeminist men present Marxist views they do not seem terribly alert to their own implication in historical sexism. Often, in fact, as Gerda Lerner's book *The Creation of Patriarchy* (New York: Oxford, 1986) shows, they are eager to use "Marxian" views, such as the belief that private property preceded sexism historically, to "win" a point against the feminist view of history, which sees patriarchy as the earlier ideology.

more than reasonable response, because the peasant includes information not only about what a tree *is* but what *his relation* to it is: planting. However, the questioner is looking for an abstract essentialist *definition* of a tree, some kind of description, often found in Latin in science books, in genus and species terms, i.e., a plant of such and such variety and structure. It does not seem to be a consideration for Ong and for the researcher that such a definition may actually be useless to someone who works with trees and needs other kinds of knowledge. Meanwhile the passage shows something about the respondent's own sense of what language is, namely, something that ought to bear some *correspondence to the social relation of the speakers*. The respondent is resisting the questioner's initiative because, to him, such questions seem illegitimate. When the respondent asks, three times, "what's the point?" the questioner does not answer truthfully (the truth being, "the point is to demonstrate that you can't give an abstract essentialist definition of a tree.") The first two of the researcher's questions are in the imperative voice, while the answers are in the interrogative. On these grounds alone the inquiry is suspicious. But once we know that the researcher is coming to the peasant "from above," and surmise and the peasant sees this, it is easy to conclude that the problem with the inquiry lies in the embeddedness of language in social relations, the assumption of this principle by the peasant, and the attempt to use language in its less social "literate" form by the researcher.

Recalling Margaret Donaldson's critique of Piaget's experimental handling on his subjects, Luria's treatment of the illiterate subject may be susceptible to the same criticism. Neither Piaget nor Luria come to their subjects with the purpose of *contributing* to their lives and situations. In their roles as observers, and perhaps as manipulative observers, they superimpose an intimidating authority situation on the social scene of the people being studied. Working in the standard idiom of objectivity, that is, isolating one parameter while ignoring any others, the meaning and role of the research scene is overlooked—really, understood to be inert—by the researchers, and the knowledge claimed is given out as pertaining only to the subjects under study, rather than to the subjects-in-the-interpersonal-research-situation. In contrast, Heath announced herself to be a part of her research situation. She came to join other communities, learn about them, and, as a teacher, contribute to them in lasting ways. This involvement of the researcher, this deobjectification of her perspective is, in one sense, to adopt "oral" values. But, in Heath's case, it is also to adopt the values of the communities under scrutiny, recognizing the integrity of that community and marking her implication in its life. In a sense, Heath has helped *render* the difference between the oral and literature less important, though she has also shown the fundamental but heretofore concealed ground they share.

Deborah Tannen has approached the relatedness of the oral and the literate in a somewhat different way, though, significantly, she too studies situations in which she is herself actively involved. In her 1983 essay, "Oral and Literate Strategies in Spoken and Written Discourse," she concludes with the following speculation: "Oral strategies may underlie successful discourse production and comprehension in the written as well as the oral mode."[24] The essay examines oral discourse, such as in elementary schools and in adult conversations, and written discourse, such as literature and expository writing, defines some basic characteristics of each, and then shows that and how each mode uses features of the other. Her speculations, however, seem to unsettle this balance, implying that the two modes of discourse are not symmetrical with one another. In our culture, while the two are usually required for one another, there is a certain sense in which the written requires the oral but the oral does not require the written.

In her long study of "two and a half hours of naturally occurring conversation at Thanksgiving dinner among six participants [one of them was Tannen] of various ethnic and geographic backgrounds,"[25] Tannen observed a language use trope she calls "overlapped or simultaneous speech" among three of the participants. Her reflection on this feature bears on her sense of the relation between oral and literate discourse styles:

> The preference for overlapping talk in some settings has been reported among numerous ethnic groups—Armenian-American, Black-American, West Indian, Cape Verdian-American, to name just a few. This preference sacrifices the clear relay of information for the show of conversational involvement, and in that sense, it is typically interactive or oral as opposed to literate in style. The effect of overlapping or "chiming in" with speakers who share this style is to grease the conversational wheels. But when speakers use this device with others who do not expect or understand its use, the effect is quite the opposite. The other speaker, feeling interrupted, stops talking. A paradoxical aspect of this style clash is that the interruption is actually created by the one who stops talking when she or he was expected to continue. Yet this reaction is natural for anyone who assumes that in conversation only one person speaks at a time. Such a strategy is literate in style in the sense that it puts emphasis on content, on uttering a complete message, on a kind of elaborated code. (CS, p. 86)

The basic difference between the oral and literate styles is that the former is context-dependent and the latter content-dependent, or "lexicalized." What gives expository writing its independent cast is the extra vocabulary and

---

24. Deborah Tannen, "Oral and Literate Strategies in Spoken and Written Discourse," in *Literacy for Life: The Demand for Reading and Writing*, ed. Richard W. Bailey and Robin Melanie Fosheim (New York: MLA, 1983), p. 92.

25. Deborah Tannen, *Conversational Style* (Norwood, New Jersey: Ablex, 1984), p. 85.

extra explanation that comes, so to speak, with the "main thought." It looks as if it did not matter who the author and who the reader is. The oral style, on the other hand, requires the participation of the other speakers in any one speaker's contribution. The "extra language" of expository or literate discourse comes, in oral situations, from other participants. So that, preliminarily, one can stipulate a certain equivalence between oral and literate styles.

But only preliminarily. What Tannen is describing are different styles of social conduct, which she observes in her study of discourse, but which appear in other forms of social behavior in each group. This discourse is itself not the full issue but only a part of general attitudes toward interpersonal comportment. Thus, if "chiming in" is important, if interruption is expected, if "cheerleading" (i.e. the response of a black congregation to a sermon) is appreciated, all of these add up to a certain mode of relatedness among people, where the speech is in a literal sense a speech *act*, or a palpable element in a relationship. This is a demonstration of the "exteriority" or "materiality" of language. Of course, the meanings of the words count and are necessary, but meaning is not just in words but in the modes of exchange, in the choice of when to present the words, in the pre-established systems of mutual uptake, and in the way all speakers sense that the exchange of language is an exchange of responsibility, commitment, caring, and involvement.

In the literate style, even though Basil Bernstein calls it an "elaborated code," the discourse depends much more narrowly on the meaning of the words. To interrupt, when this style obtains, is to injure the presentation of "meaning." The language itself takes on a much fuller referential sense: what the discourse refers to—something beyond the speaking situation—is understood to be the point of the contribution. More words, perhaps involving holding the floor longer by oneself, enhance the contribution. Notice also, however, how much more prominent the individual speaker becomes, how much more set off he or she is from the group in this style of conversation. We are reminded of the Greek rhetorical style admired by Ong, which, not coincidentally, found its way, through the universal use of the word "rhetoric" to describe writing textbooks, into the contemporary approach to teaching writing in all colleges and universities. We are furthermore led to Ong's other values—abstraction, objectivity, and the desire for insularity when attending to how to say things. The literate style tends to mute the social presence of any group and implicitly depends on an elitist social organization, recalling the time when literacy and privilege were intimately associated.

The literate style is weighted in favor of an individual-priority sense (i.e., an individualist style) of society, even as we move, historically, into contemporary times. Ong's point about how introspection is enhanced by writing is related to the idea that *thought*, or meaning, is "more basic" than words (consider the familiar freshman complaint, "I know what I want to say but I just can't find the right words"), which in turn relates to the idea that an inviolably private human soul lies "deeper" than the observable social and bodily presence of the individual. In the religious view of things, individual souls are "saved" because of their private acts of contrition, their completely private pact with God, a pact to which other people can have no access or knowledge. The gradual separation of literacy from orality in the West developed from these values of the priority of the individual. But, in the light of Derrida's and Handelman's considerations, it was in no sense a necessary development. In fact, to take the word seriously as a human, social speech act shows the strong kinship of literacy and orality; what is required for that kinship to emerge is the adoption of values which do not give priority to either the individual or community. Each simultaneously constitutes the other. This mutuality is reflected in the "overlapping" conversational style, in context-dependent talk, and a series of other verbal-interaction strategies that are not permitted to disturb the decorum of formal adult life in the West. As I discussed in chapter 1, a child's spontaneous oral style is slowly "refined" away while he or she is growing up. In successive school years, classrooms become more and more quiet, as the teacher becomes an increasingly priv-ileged figure and the students become more and more "literate." The fact that the "oral" habits continue in a secondary and sometimes subversive role impoverishes the teaching of literacy and inhibits our efforts to understand it.

One of the arguments Tannen uses for her concluding speculative point about the key oral elements in written discourse is her claim that "imaginative literature has more in common with spontaneous conversation than with the typical written genre, expository prose."(p. 89) While I will take up this point in further detail at the end of the next chapter, we should ask why this claim should come as a surprise. In the memory of almost all people living today, I would answer, "literature" is something that first appeared in schoolbooks as something "taught." (Bedtime stories are rarely understood by children as "literature.") Even though there are increasing similarities between British and American styles of education, in Britain, literature is much more part of everyday life: more often than here, schoolchildren have some other acquaintance with the indigenous national literature than through school, and the literature itself has more of an independent life outside of school, in the media, for example. But if our familiarity with literature comes mainly from the stiff, "literate" presentational forms of the school, Tannen's claim that "literary language builds on and perfects features of mundane conversation" (p. 90) will seem surprising. It is because there is so little practice, in the schools, of "interpersonal involvement" that Tannen must conclude, after careful study, that "literary language, like ordinary conversation, is dependent for its effect on interpersonal involvement." (p. 90) But where else could literary language have come from? It is only because the spontaneous social connections between literacy and literature are systematically severed, only because written texts become "sacred," because interpreters become privileged clerics, that the "oral" character of literature is lost, and the means of distinguishing between literature and expository prose are obscure.

The concept of literacy is changing. At the same time, circumstances urge that we interested parties help change it. Many, like Husserl, have thought that in the interrelated areas of language, knowledge, and intersubjectivity, "psychology is the truly decisive field." Here, too, there is doubt about how to understand, in the same framework, individual and social psychologies, how to create "more permeable boundaries" between two disciplines, two genders, two "incommensurate" perspectives. Our task is to show that these are not paradoxes or other mysterious burdens of life, but are practical matters of language use that will need to be renamed and renewed in used language.

4

The Double Perspective:
New and Used Language

One of the least challenged aspects of transformational linguistics is its premise that infants and small children utter new sentences so prolifically that their sentences could not be the result of imitation or conditioning. Because, as we grow, we continue to utter new sentences in our daily speech, the "novelty" premise has a deep plausibility, an intuitive ring of truth so strong that we often consider it a fact. Yet, if we go through the many samples of infants' speech, or even if we scrutinize our own sentences, it will not be easy to say just what about them is "new." The two-word "sentences" put together by infants are made up of words we know they have previously used, and, while the combination is often "new," we probably would not want to say that the combination itself is what makes the sentence seem new; after all, some of the combinations don't seem to make sense and therefore would not qualify as new sentences. By the same reasoning, if we examine any of the sentences in this paragraph, it will, in one sense, be easy to say it is new, even though piece by piece, word by word, phrase by phrase, structure by structure, we can also say with assurance that I, and thousands of others, have made very similar sentences before, so similar, in fact, that the variations may even be called trivial. We might then want to say that, yes, the sentence resembles other sentences, but that somehow a new "meaning" comes out of the new sentence that makes it seem new. We should recall, however, that Chomsky did not claim that children create new meanings, but that they created new sentences. If, from another standpoint, we wish to identify sentences with their meanings and say they are one and the same, that would not accord with the idea of the transformational program, which considers meanings more a part of the performance of language and not an essential part of the speaker's grammatical competence. Chomsky's reluctance to say that new meanings are really generated by the grammar is justified, since the prospect of devising a "grammar" of meaning with a finite set of rules does seem like a fool's errand. The problem I pose, therefore, is how to accept the convincing intuition that all of our sentences are new while understanding that, really, none is.

This is not a phenomenological riddle but a practical matter, especially since we feel no constraint to understand the problem as a logical paradox. We are dealing with *two different perspectives* on the sentence and considering the consequences of each. *Our aim is to understand how all sentences are, at one and the same time "new" and "already" used, and that the reasons for this simultaneity are traceable to the social circumstances of language use, or, in the other term I have been using, the institutions of literacy.* The paradoxical cast of this problem disappears once the presuppositions of a hierarchical order of things and a search for essences are dismissed. In place of these thought-strategies, we use a principle of the simultaneity of multiple perspectives, which I am calling, for simplicity, the double perspective—an idea I have used in a less general sense as "cognitive stereoscopy,"[1] with both of the foregoing concepts being closely related to and consistent with the idea of innate intersubjectivity explored in the previous chapter. My emphasis on these various forms of "doubleness" aims to make the idea of language compatible with both individual and social presuppositions. To say that both perspectives obtain at once makes it possible to use either without assigning it an absolute priority.

I first used the idea of "cognitive stereoscopy" in my analysis of how Helen Keller came into language in her relationship with Anne Sullivan. The term refers to a mental schema that governs the ability to name things, the ability to make sentences, the ability to distinguish oneself from others and from everything else, and the characteristic human (species-specific) self-awareness. A key feature of stereoscopic vision is usually referred to as "depth perception," a term whose practical meaning is "the ability to experience one's own distance or spatial relation to physical objects outside one's body." Similarly, "cognitive stereoscopy" refers to an intersubjective "depth-perception," while it practically means the ability to know one's "distance" from other entities and people—the sense of the otherness of others and the objectivity of oneself. Whereas visual depth perception is achieved by the integration of two superposed images, cognitive depth perception is the result of integrating the simultaneous sense of the separateness of others (people and things) and the objectivity of oneself. As Vygotsky, Trevarthen, and Shields implied, child development can be described as "double" or dialogic in many different areas. The process of individuation, of acquiring the sense of the singleness of one's self—in the middle of the second year—

---

1. I first used this term in *Subjective Criticism* (Baltimore: Johns Hopkins University Press, 1978), p. 40, in my discussion of how I thought language was motivated into existence.

has actually been going on since birth, always through *inter*action with the important caregivers. Early sensory skill, like the ability to fix the visual focus and to locate the source of sounds, to coordinate sight and sound and then to integrate the two "data" into a single "perception," all take place in a condition of mutual dependency and attachedness, a condition which renders each new skill as "making sense" yet which permits the use and knowledge of that skill to function and grow *outside* its original context of appearance.

To say that all people think stereoscopically is not only to describe an individual capacity, but to call attention to the implication of all individual thought, sooner or later, in interpersonal contexts. The relationships which enable individuation to occur—most of the time, those with one's parents or other family—remain well into adult life. We do not merely have an adult "responsibility" *to* those people—that is, to see to their welfare as they once saw to ours—we are, rather, permanently implicated in their lives, and any new relationships we develop are seriously affected by our historical implication in our foundational relationships. As Shields described, individuation is affective and dialogic as well as cognitive and monologic: it is all of these things at once. For this reason, we cannot separate items such as "cognition" or "language" and study them as if they had the unity of an organ, because, as with biological organs, close scrutiny reveals the meaninglessness of their (cognition's and language's) being and function without reference to the rest of the socially situated person. Cognitive stereoscopy is meant to describe the full range of experiences subject to conscious mental regulation, as well as many experiences that appear in our lives without such regulation. It is meant to help remove the paradoxical status held by such problems as that of "other minds" or of "the one and the many," so that these problems may be seen in a less abstract, more urgent, and yet more manageable context.

In trying to present the general idea of the double perspective and its special usefulness in the study of language, I will first review several elements of my earlier discussion of Helen Keller's acquisition of language, connect this discussion with issues raised by Derrida and by Saul Kripke about words and names, and then consider how these narrower aspects of language relate to how we might wish to think about discourse, dialogue, society, and literature. I hope to suggest that *from the smallest to the largest scales of language experience, any language/literate act depends on double or multiple perspectives held by members of the speaking community, and that to analyze any language/literate act, the stipulation of double or multiple perspectives will be part of the explanatory procedure.*

Helen Keller understood how to use language about a month after Anne Sullivan arrived at her home. They had established an intimate relationship of constant togetherness, with Anne "speaking" to the child (through hand spelling) in the regular and casual way any parent speaks to a child. From published accounts, the moment of language acquisition was when Helen "recognized" the "name" for the "thing" *water*. In part, it only took a short time for Helen to catch on because of a not-too-frequently mentioned fact: Helen had already learned the "word" for water before she became ill at nineteen months of age and lost her sight and hearing. In her account, Helen speaks of the "misty consciousness of a returning thought," and it seems fairly certain that the new knowledge of the word for water—as well as the new knowledge that all things had "words" for them—had been already "there" at the time of her illness. Only the loss of the physical means for developing that knowledge held her in the prelinguistic state until Anne Sullivan's success enabled the resumption of growth. The long delay between the establishment of the prelinguistic perspective and the emergence of the linguistic perspective permits us to see that two perspectives are actually involved. In the normal child the development is fluent and, as child-language researchers have repeatedly indicated, it is not easy to decide on the existence of fixed acquisitional stages. We should think of what happened to Helen as the mutual assimilation of a past perspective on language experience with a present one.

Piaget's term, "internal reciprocal assimilation," can help—though not completely—clarify this process.[2] In a footnote, he gave an instance from adult life to illustrate his point. While driving his car, he had occasion to use a handkerchief. When he was finished using it he needed to put it in a secure place and so he stuffed it in a crevice inside the car. Later it began to rain, and he needed something to keep his windshield only slightly open (his car had a windshield which swung open from the bottom). His insight came when he remembered having stuffed the handkerchief in the crevice and "realized" that he could remove the handkerchief and stuff it into the crevice between the top of the windshield and the frame of the car. The schema of "stuffing the handkerchief" was assimilated to the schema of "holding the windshield open." The one schema was associated with the past need and the other with the present need. The two schemata were assimilated to one another to form a new schema. In this way, the "new" knowledge of how to keep the windshield slightly open can be described as the internal reciprocal assimilation of the two schemata, or, in the terms I am using, the mutual superposition of two perspectives: the solution to the problem was a moment of cognitive stereoscopy.

One could conceivably understand Piaget's car success as "applying" pre-

2. Jean Piaget, *The Origins of Intelligence in Children* (1952) (New York: Norton, 1963), p. 345.

vious knowledge to a new situation, and Piaget invokes this idea often enough. However, I am emphasizing our conceptualization of the moment of knowledge. In that moment, two situations appear in our minds and the *combination* creates the sense of illumination. One can't claim that the earlier schema is "more basic" since several earlier schemata *could* have been used in the present situation. Furthermore, the task of keeping the window slightly open did not necessarily imply "stuffing" something into the crevice: a solid item might have been used to prop it open. It is just that, through mental process which cannot be further specified, the window problem was perceived as a "stuffing" situation which then lent itself to the assimilation of the earlier stuffing behavior. It could well be that the earlier stuffing of the handkerchief urged Piaget to see the later situation as one which needed a "stuffing." For this reason, the *reciprocity* of the assimilation is the important point.

The case must be similar for Helen Keller's relearning of the previously known "name." One can't claim that either the present experience was assimilated to the memory of the past alone, or that the past memory was assimilated to the experience of the present. Rather, the moment of insight should be understood as the mutual assimilation of memory and experience. The memory is in fact "present" in the experiencing mind, and success is a matter of associating the memory with the experience. It would be just as true to say that the new way of naming—the touch-words—was assimilated to the "old" idea of a name as it would to say that the "old" idea was "brought into" the new system of naming. The best way to describe what happened, I think, is to say that the assimilation went in both directions at once; the two ideas dissolved into one another so that the present moment was rendered stereoscopic and Helen experienced that moment of insight: the touch-words are the "same" as the names she had learned about five years previously.

Paying attention to the moment of insight and to the formulaic character of the mutual assimilation of schemata is part of the familiar ontogenetic perspective found in most studies of cognitive development. Helen Keller's case, however, suggests the limitations of this perspective alone. The question is, really, why *at that moment* did the insight come? An individualist answer will be: only then did Helen have the vocabulary of touch-words that gave her the "tools" to come to the insight on her own. This is a plausible answer and will stay "true," in at least some degree, regardless of other explanations I will adduce. It is also true, though, that no one "spoke" to Helen until Anne Sullivan arrived. The many accounts of her prelinguistic childhood show Helen to have been "spoiled"—permitted to do almost anything she wished including disruptive behavior such as taking food from anyone's plate during dinner, or eating with her hands. Helen had in her sign-vocabulary a number of gestures which helped her navigate through the various people—primarily her mother—in her household. She functioned in about the same style that she left off before she became ill, a style similar to the way chimpanzees now function when brought into a human situation: with distinct signs of intelligence that will not grow any further. The level of social dexterity and the level of intelligence were more or less the same. What Anne Sullivan's arrival accomplished—from my point of view—was to demonstrate the mutual inextricability of intelligence, language, and social awareness.

The relationship that Anne first created with Helen was immediately political: Anne demanded a discipline from Helen that no one had previously demanded, and which Anne physically enforced. Her early "teachings" of the sign language took place in a context where Helen was forced to accede Anne's superior strength and authority. Anne's strategy was to create a "priority" relationship: one in which both behavior and speaking were oriented around the one person, and where previous habits of behavior, oriented around the indulgent family, would be deauthorized. Anne made her relationship with Helen the completely supervening fact of Helen's life. This also meant—as I will elaborate in chapter 6—that this relationship was the main item in Anne's life as well. This intense mutual focusing served (at least) two purposes: disrupting Helen's social, affective, and political lethargy of the previous five years, and creating a situation in which the full range of human behaviors is expected. It was not just the sign language that Anne brought; it was that language in the context of an authentic human relationship, one that, regardless of how understanding her family was, could not have been achieved by that family because it had not the *cultural values* that would naturally permit doing what Anne Sullivan did. Helen saw Anne as an intrusive, tough, demanding person—even a revolutionary one—who finally required a new self which had within it the *sense* of that self, the self-awareness previously absent.

The achievement of the new self was reflected in the drama of the old and new dolls: the old doll being the one Helen had before Anne arrived, the new doll having been brought by Anne.[3] In a tantrum just before her insight, Helen broke the new doll; but after her insight, she realized what she had done and wanted to put the new doll together. Previously I had understood the two dolls to be the two different "selves," but now want to add that the "new" doll was the "doll of relationship," the socially implicated self that is "identified" with Anne who brought it, while the old doll was the isolated

---

3. A detailed discussion of how the dolls worked into Helen's achievement of the sense of self is in my *Subjective Criticism*, pp. 60–62.

individual with no responsibilities to those around her. Anne said that she wanted to teach Helen "obedience and love," but this meant responsibility in the sense of, literally, *answerability*: the obligation to answer, to take one's own speaking turn, to participate, and to reciprocate. To have a self is to be, at once, a separate self and an implicated self. Anne took Helen through the stages of dependency, separation, and reattachment (as any mother does spontaneously). The last, reattachment, coincided with the consciousness of self and the illumination that "everything had a name."

To know that things have names is the recognition of the double character of one's self—the experiencing self and the self that knows it is experiencing. It is the naming capability that makes them seem separate. On the one hand, you experience the "good taste of pizza," while on the other hand you know that you are experiencing the good taste of pizza. The act of naming "the good taste of pizza" is the act of knowing that you are experiencing it. Without the naming you only experience it, and as an infant does, or perhaps a dog or a cat, you only gesture or move toward the experience again, reflexively. With the capability to name, all experience acquires this double character, a character that in fact cannot be split apart any longer into its elements. This is the upshot of Derrida's critique of Husserl presented in chapter 2. For a human being, there is no experience outside of its being named. But the relationship of Anne and Helen also shows that there is no doubleness of self, no distinctly human self without its simultaneous implication in others. To name oneself—to "know" one's doubleness, is at the same time to know oneself as *distinct from and as implicated in* other people. The doubleness of naming is itself double. Just as one cannot separate the experiencing from the knowing (after naming has been achieved), one cannot separate the knowing of oneself from the knowing of others.

The relationship of Helen and Anne points up still another feature of language acquisition that I mentioned in connection with Shields's view of innate intersubjectivity: affect is mobilized and regulated only in connection with others. From birth on, a "dialogue" of crying and frustration and attention and relief is established between mother and infant. For the infant, to be fed is also to be held and looked at. As the child becomes older, the increasing length of separations and aloneness remain punctuated and regulated by occasions of reunion and togetherness. This dialogue in Helen's life never left the peremptory or demand stage. Because of her illness she was *considered* functionally an infant, and so it was all right to respond to her on a demand basis and not all right to enforce demands made on her. In this way, she wasn't required to develop the usual capacities for affective self-regulation, to rationalize and cope with delay, and most of all, to understand why restrictions and demands could be made on her. The more dramatic moments of Anne's and Helen's prelinguistic relationship were those in which Helen's feelings were not permitted free license to translate themselves into action, when frustrations were not allowed translation into tantrums, and when affection was something that could be expressed in various ways to various people, not something experienced principally as a closeness to mother. Anne's normal and usual idea of love led her to try to *discipline* Helen, both to receive affection from her, Anne (as well as from her mother), and to motivate her to give affection to others.[4] The relationship was so tight and so demanding that Helen's feelings became focused on *another* person who, initially, was both an enemy and a friend, an alien and an intimate. Once Helen felt pain from her separation from Anne, she began to seek ways to relieve it herself. At first this was through obedience, since obedience made peace and relieved the pain without thought: it was compliance. However, it very soon became possible to relieve the pain actively, through initiative: and language was the instrument of this initiative which took the priority away from the need to comply. Language—touch-words—was what Anne brought Helen, a new mother-tongue that, as with any infant, became the normal and usual mode of sharing, of controlling feelings and expressing them, and of preparing for action and understanding it. *Without that relationship with its political and psychological demands, its increased level of pain and difficulty, there can have been no affective machinery, no motivation, no interest or purpose in Helen's mobilizing the rest of her mind to "get" the "mystery of language."*

In view of these considerations, one cannot rest with the idea that Anne brought a viable sign-system. *All* of what Anne brought should be understood as language: namely, the means of speaking as invested in the principles of mutual responsibility, interpersonal attachment, and public discipline. You might want to say that if Helen's mother had had the signing system mastered, she may have accomplished what Anne had. This may be true, but consider this circumstance: Helen's mother saw her child as a profoundly afflicted being, not as a normal child with a bad handicap or even a handicap that could be surmounted. Her wishes for Helen were that she be taught something, that she be taken off the path she was then on to see what else can be done. It was probably inconceivable to her to think of Helen as a normal child, and even

---

4. The strong role I am claiming here for affect is consistent with Naomi Scheman's idea of feeling in one person being a marker of mutual implication; that is, the feeling has no purely individual reference—another person is always associated with each of our feelings. In my *Readings and Feelings* (Urbana: National Council of Teachers of English, 1975) I discuss in some detail how a reader cannot present an intelligible affective response to literature without also exemplifying the affect in terms of a real relationship in that person's life. For example, a reader has to distinguish sibling jealousy from marital jealousy and cannot report only "jealousy" without it remaining too vague for others to understand.

less likely that she should think of *treating* Helen normally. For reasons I will return to later (chapter 6), Anne Sullivan had already learned the necessity of treating handicapped children normally from her own childhood experiences and she understood how to do this. It was this ordinary sense of human relationships toward the handicapped that Anne "brought" to her relationship with Helen, and it was the one item that made the so-called miracle possible.

It has long been understood that the prolonged periods of human infantile dependency plays a strong role in making adults what they are. In view of the claims made by Trevarthen and Shields about intersubjectivity, and of my own claims about Helen Keller and Anne Sullivan's relationship, human infantile dependency should be understood as something *mutual*. Mothers, caregivers, and families become dependent on infants even though these adults would not be physically endangered if the infants were not there. We should not be reluctant to understand mothers' attachments to their infants as dependency of a deep psychosocial kind, probably related to the biological factors of child-carrying, child-bearing, and nursing. Mothers (and families) and infants are dependent on one another according to their age or place in the life cycle. Thus, while infants and parents are mutually dependent on one another in equally strong ways, the differences in *kinds* of dependency should not be permitted to conceal the basic fact of its mutuality.

As we have seen in Helen Keller's case, the internalization of the mutual dependency led to the sense of self and the cognitive ability to use "names." I would like to show now how affective dependency is bound up with the "cognitive" achievement of syntactical language, and how both naming and sentence-making require the affective process of separation, individuation, and psychosocial "return" in order to assume their characteristic form in normal language use. The familiar structures of language usage are founded on and continuously bound up with such a variety of psychosocial interdependencies that one is hard put to claim the existence of an independent capability for language which develops autonomously. *Even the smallest feature of language use, such as naming, determines and is determined by social relations in the same ways that sentences, paragraphs, and novels are so constituted.*

We are accustomed to thinking that there is a "relation" between a name and a thing, usually understood as "semantic." The two categories, names and things, are routinely separated, as when Helen Keller reported that she "learned" that "everything had a name." In this perspective, a name can "mean" a thing, but a thing does not "mean" a name. It looks as if there were no mutuality of meaning, that the "direction" of meaning, so to speak, is only from names to things. When this view is generalized to language, language then appears to be a "medium," or a conduit, through which meanings are transferred from one person to another. However, Helen Keller's achievement may be seen in another light. In her mind, there were two categories: the touch-words (that were spelled into her hands) and the *experiences*—so that she was dealing not with one category in her mind and one outside it, but with two categories both inside her mind. To have "gotten" language is to have unified the two categories into a single one, so that it could be said that names and things are one, and that the knowledge articulated with names is "stereoscopic." By claiming this achievement is implicated in the relationship of Helen and Anne, I am also suggesting that this relationship motivated, or provided the affective energy to make it happen. The process of separating from Anne, and the need to "return," is the affective-social "force" that makes the names and things "return" to one another. The schema of returning to another person is assimilated to the schema of "returning" the word to the thing, while the latter schema is being simultaneously assimilated to the former: the affective and cognitive processes are mutually assimilated to one another in the naming act, and this is experienced as the special authority or force that naming has. The unification of word and thing is so strong—permanent, in fact—because of the necessary permanence of the mutual dependency of persons. *Social affiliation and our affective sense of it is a kind of "glue" that at first creates the identity of words and things and then maintains it as the "words" enlarge into sentences, texts, and the varieties of human discourse.*

There are key cases in which names are not permanently tied to things but where the change of a name must take place, and where this change is part of and instrumental in a simultaneous social change. These cases help to confirm the foregoing claims about naming and social dependency relations. Thomas Kuhn discusses the case the swinging stone becoming the pendulum, as well as related cases of naming (such as phlogiston and the "naming" of light as either a particle or a wave).[5] It looks as if the "same thing" switched from the name "swinging stone" to "pendulum." With "pendulum," a different mode of mathematical description was used and it was thus a different phenomenon from the one described by "swinging stone." The point Kuhn makes is that a pendulum is really some*thing* other than a swinging stone. Similarly, space "named" by Riemannian geometry is some*thing* other than space named by Euclidian geometry. In all of these scientific cases of name-changing, Kuhn shows how a new perspective (i.e., a paradigm) comes to be accepted, and he describes the path to the name change as a gradual social change, which, at some unidentifiable moment, leads into, or produces, the name change that in turn consolidates the slow process of social change, which, in the

---

5. Thomas Kuhn, *The Structure of Scientific Revolutions* (Chicago: University of Chicago Press, 1962), p. 168. See, in particular, chapter 10, "Revolutions as Changes of World View," pp. 111–35.

cases he presents, culminates in a fundamentally new attitude toward "the world." By the same reasoning, Helen Keller's "acquisition" of language was the culmination of a gradual social process that changed in character once language entered the picture: the process of interpersonal separation and reaffiliation is now governed by language and may also be called "literacy" in the wider sense I discussed in chapter 3. When important names change, it is as much the reconstitution of a community as when the parent-child relationship is reconstituted with the child's acquisition of language.

Each name gets its lasting power in a person's mind because of the affective "mark" left by the reciprocal assimilation of the name's two "parts." Each time Helen Keller asked for and got the new name for something, the power and importance of that name came out of the history of tension between the "experience" category and the "touch-word" category associated with her relationship to Anne, and also, therefore, associated with the experience itself. To then ask for and get the new name from Anne was to utilize that tension between having an experience and not being able to give it back, so to speak, to "reinsert it" into the relationship. Naming permits one to "grasp" an experience, in the sense of being able to hold on to it for the purpose of, at some indefinite time afterward, "reinvesting" it into either the conversation or the relationship, or into some other conversation or relationship. The naming ability comes out of the socializing process, and then goes back into it and changes it, thus regulating social development. Because of the affective character of name-acquisition, an affective potential in naming is always there, and any name reinvested into a conversation can have a special affective weight at any time, though most names (words) have only a small weight in any given discourse.

When naming is conceived as an internalized "doubleness" or stereoscopic event, the idea of what is "semantic" changes: meaning now moves in both (opposite) directions at once. It is reasonable to think that an experience means a word as much as a word means an experience. Because the doubleness is made single by a motivated psychological integration of word and thing, this doubleness, in its reciprocal character, is separable and reversible. In this light, to change a name is not just to take a new name and "apply" it to the "same" experience, it is to make a new subjective combination of an experience and a word. It would be as correct to say that the "swinging stone" experience "means" "pendulum" as—normally—to say the reverse. In conversation, when one searches for a way to express a certain sentiment, one often, mentally, tries out certain combinations until one finds the verbal configuration that "means" the sentiment. Because of the cultural habit, however, we refer to such events only as "finding to right words for what I want to say," thinking that we are looking for words to label the experience, rather than that the experience, as-desired-to-present, is authorizing and giving meaning to the words. Actually, a matching process is taking place, in which experiences and words, conceptualizations (including images of perhaps a nonverbal nature) and sentences are tried until some "right" combination suggests itself. Usually, many of these attempts are public as well as private, and the success of the process finally *requires* multiple confirmations of "rightness" from a variety of individuals and communities. Also, as Kuhn describes, a new name is created when two or more previously unconnected people or groups come up with similar names which are then unified into a single name through negotiations and further thought. The process of getting a new name is just as much the process of deciding on what new experiences people are having and "fitting" these experiences to a word that had already been familiar for a long time. To see naming as the outcome of a series of "matching" events which take place subjectively and intersubjectively is to reconceive it as a *syntactic* phenomenon, a two-directional dialectic that can be analyzed and understood in the same way that sentences are—as a single entity in which two main interchangeable "parts" can be identified, each of which is dependent on the other.

The syntactic structure of sentences allows us to understand them as names in the sense I just described. Sentences have two parts, the subject and predicate, each dependent on one another, but not arranged symmetrically in the sentence: each part has a different role, but when the sentence is considered as a whole, its two parts are implicated in one another. Its two parts produce the sentence's "stereoscopy," or, in the familiar terms of elementary school grammar, the sentence expresses a "complete thought." Complex sentences, paragraphs, and even larger units of discourse are a "nesting" of a series of smaller sentence-names in such a way that these larger units may also be understood—and customarily are—as "complete thoughts" in the same limited sense as above.

Consider two relatively well-known "complete thoughts" from the poetry of Shakespeare and Keats, respectively: "To be or not to be, that is the question" and "Beauty is truth, truth beauty—that is all/Ye know on earth, and all ye need to know." The first part of both of these thoughts is divided from the second by a "that is . . . " clause. The first part of each also has two components: in the Shakespeare they are variants of the verb "to be," while in the Keats they are two sentences with the subject and predicate reversals of one another. Each second component of each first part opposes—either through denial or reversal—the first component. Each second part beginning "That is" functions as a predicate thought for each first part, so that each whole thought can be readily seen as a topic and a comment, the comment being introduced by the phrase "that is." In "Hamlet," the comment is a simple sentence with a simple predicate, while in "Ode on a Grecian Urn," the comment is a simple sentence with a compound predicate—one bearing two different clauses.

"To be or not to be" is itself a sentence in the sense I have been discussing. In spite of the fact that an "or" separates the two opposing components of this phrase, each component is predicated on the other. In the phrase itself, the way it was originally presented renders "to be" the "subject" and "not to be" the "predicate" because the language condition of English is such that the subject comes first. Although the "or" has a specific meaning in regard to Hamlet's feeling the need to choose to live or die, the simple presentation of the proposition and its denial in the same phrase (or "sentence") makes it possible to enrich the dramatic situation by "reading into" it an "and." Custom and language use suggest that "Not to be or to be" is less preferred, but these same customs permit the "and" reading, in that we see it as meaning "life or death" and "life and death." This latter phrase is rarely formulated as "death or life" or "death and life," but the *preference* for the "life and death" sequence is the ground on which the reversal of the phrase makes sense, i.e., we interpret the passage as: "Hamlet is contemplating suicide," not "Hamlet is contemplating living on." The "not to be" is actually understood as the "subject" of the sentence, and not the predicate; but the possibility of suicide is predicated on the fact that Hamlet is alive. The "stereoscopic" package of "To be or not to be," in other words, is the mutual implication on the one part of the phrase and its denial; and the various paths of interpretation may stress *either* part with equal success just because the subject and predicate are interchangeable.

Unlike Shakespeare's phrase, Keats's phrase literally reverses the subject and predicate in succeeding sentences. "Beauty is truth" comes first presumably because the "beauty" of the urn is the "subject" of the poem. "Truth" is then the "predicate" for the "subject" "Beauty." The first element reads "beauty is predicated on truth," so that it appears that truth *names* beauty (i.e., gives its meaning). However, this thought is immediately *predicated* on its reverse, "truth [is] beauty," so that the doubleness implicit in the previous act of predication is exposed[6]—a language tactic not unfamiliar in ordinary usage,[7] but then again not all that common. By announcing the

---

6. Not only are the two single terms, beauty and truth, announced as being predicated on one another, but also both *propositions* must be mutually predicated in spite of the fact that the sequence begins with the "beauty is truth" form.

7. For example, "more expensive clothes are better" and "better clothes are more expensive"; or, "wealth brings power" and "power brings wealth." Freud wrote of the "antithetical" sense of "primal" words, commenting on how certain words have come to have opposite meanings at once. The reversibility of ordinary sentences suggests how such words may be developing

reversibility of subject and predicate in this way—the announcement being itself a generic language act of a specific character—the poem calls attention not only to the doubleness of its interests, truth/beauty, but, like many other highly crafted poems, to language's radical flexibility that is based on the mutual dependency of subjects and predicates underlying all acts of naming. The reversibility of naming discloses its syntactic character and reveals the customary semantic sense of it as much less general or comprehensive than the syntactic sense.

"To be or not to be" registers in our minds sooner or later as a *single* thought, the "subject" that is then "predicated on" "That is the question." Here again, the latter sentence "names" the former: "to be or not to be" is *identified* as "the question" as opposed to something else, say "the issue" or "the lie." To see the necessity of the specific word "question" one need only entertain the idea, "What is the question?" as the subject of the whole sequence I am discussing. If "the question" is the subject, the predicate is "to be or not to be," which *identifies* the question, a meaning readily available from the actual lines in the text. That is, if we conceive the whole phrase, "To be or not to be, that is the question" as a "complete thought," it is clear that the completeness of the thought, or the *subjective sense* of its completeness, derives from our sense of the reversible—syntactic—dependence of its two parts, bearing in mind, of course, that when the reversal takes place, the reversed form has a new meaning owing to the lack of symmetry of subject and predicate. Perhaps the thought makes sense in the first place because of the "togetherness" of its two parts, a togetherness or doubleness only provisionally separated by the linear presentational form in the text. The same situation obtains between the first phase of the Keats thought and "That is all/ Ye know on earth, and all ye need to know." This sentence identifies the beauty/truth pair while the beauty/truth pair identifies this sentence (which, in its compound character, is also understandable as a mutual dependency[8]). That is, the sense of the complete thought requires us to identify "That is all . . . " as "Beauty is truth, truth beauty" and requires us to identify the latter as "That is all . . . " The two discrete directions of identification (or naming) are simultaneously present in our minds and yet separable and separated.

---

at every moment. Hart Crane's mother wrote to him once that "love is a sickness." But a key feature of Crane's behavior was that sickness was love; he was loved when he was sick. In his life, sickness and love were predicated on one another. However, many people not carrying Crane's emotional burdens become "lovesick," a term which presents the mutual predication of sickness and love in a relatively ordinary and unspectacular way, and as the unified name for a common feeling.

8. By which I mean, "all ye need to know" and "all ye know" are, in that phrase, predicated on one another; in reading the phrase in the poem, "all ye need to know" appears to modify "all ye know."

These two instances seem "made" for this point about reversibility. However, the same permutations could be made for any sentences, and as particular sentences and paragraphs in literature or in other discourse become important and/or frequently read and commented upon, their reversibility becomes ever more apparent. The key issue is that it is inherent in naming and sentence-making (which I am proposing ought to be understood as the "same" thing) to be reversible, with this reversibility marking their stereoscopic function as knowledge. One of the achievements of Fleck and Kuhn is that they show the reversibility of naming and proposition-making in the process of scientific knowing. Additionally, Fleck shows the necessary social basis for this reversibility, the conversational or dialectic context from which scientific "sentences" (propositions, facts) grow. Because scientific facts are nodal points in collective knowledge, and because the verbal formulation of such facts is in one sense arbitrary and in another sense necessary,[9] both "ends" (the swinging stone being one "end" and the pendulum the other) of the stereoscopic knowledge are themselves variable, while the predicated combination (i.e., "the swinging stone is a pendulum") comes to feel fixed and permanent, intuitively unified and, therefore, certain. Because of the stereoscopic character of its formulation, a scientific fact feels as certain and authoritative as Helen Keller's "name" for water. The difference between those sentence-propositions presented as science and those presented as poetry lies wholly in the condition of "the desire for certainty" being historically associated with the social institutions of science, and the "expressive flexibility of language and experience" being historically associated with the social institutions of "literature."[10]

Some literary theorists have tried to say that "language itself" is different in scientific and literary discourse, that there are two (or more) "kinds" of language whose "features" could be distinguished if only the taxonomical effort were rigorous enough. Because the social functions of language are completely bound up with any instance of language use, the meaning of a text (oral or written) cannot be separated from its language. There are no "pure" linguistic entities. *Words and sentences, as syntactic stereoscopic construc-*

---

9. This is similar to Ralph Cohen's point (discussed later in the chapter) that generic naming is both necessary and loose.

10. As a result, "old" interpretations of what a work of literature means, like "old" poetry, accumulate and coexist alongside newer readings and newer poems. While some readings and poems may go out of style, none actually becomes obsolete. In contrast, "old" scientific knowledge always becomes obsolete: scientific knowledge first formulated long ago is never considered to belong, somehow, to a bygone historical period if it is still in effect today, while many old theories are considered erroneous if a new theory about "the same" phenomena is accepted. Science and poetry are similar operations on language but motivated and regulated by different social purposes.

tions, cannot be said to have meanings but are themselves meanings that are identical with the elementary social acts of uttering (writing) within the intersubjective situation: to choose words and sentences for "use" is to choose moves between people, to make adjustments in mutual juxtapositionings to foster the growth of relationships.

To see words and sentences as identical with their meanings is also to see all language experience as unified: while it could be said that verbal sounds are "enriched" by their meaningfulness, it is not possible to separate the enrichment from the sound or writing. When a sound is taken as language, it is experienced as a unified extradimensional sound (i.e., significant) and not a series of related elements. In Ernst Cassirer's reflections on the common origin of language and myth,[11] he describes what he considers a more primitive language experience that corresponds well to my foregoing description of regular language experience:

> When Kant defined "reality" as any content of empirical intuition which follows general laws and thus takes its place in the "context of experience," he gave an exhaustive definition of the concept of reality in the canons of discursive thought. But mythic ideation and primitive verbal conception recognize no such "context of experience." Their function, as we have seen, is rather a process of almost violent separation and individuation. Only when the intense individuation has been consummated, when the immediate intuition has been focused and, one might say, reduced to a single point, does the mythic or linguistic form emerge, and the word or momentary god is created. . . . At this point, the word which denotes that thought content is not a mere conventional symbol, but is merged with its object in an indissoluble unity. The conscious experience is not merely wedded to the word, but is consumed by it. Whatever has been fixed by a name, henceforth is not only real, but is Reality. The potential between "symbol" and "meaning" is resolved; in place of a more or less adequate "expression," we find a relation of identity, of complete congruence between "image" and "object," between the name and the thing.[12]

Since Cassirer, the ideas of "primitive" languages and cultures have been discredited. It seems reasonable, therefore, that insofar as there is an intuitive identity between word and thing, it would be discoverable in our own use of language. Cassirer pointedly describes important primordial names as coming from moments of "violent separation and individuation," a phrase which also accurately describes Helen Keller's acquisition of language. To say that "the word" or the capacity to name is a "momentary god" is to indicate the

---

11. Cassirer ultimately presents discursive language as the developed outcome of mythic language, a thesis which I will, shortly, argue against.

12. Ernst Cassirer, *Language and Myth* (New York: Dover, 1946, 1953), pp. 57–58.

transcendental quality of feeling able to name, to speak, to get along with others for the first time in this characteristically human and social way. *It is, in fact, a decisive social reunification of person and person that language use effects.* To name things and persons, compared to not being able to do so, seems transcendent, godly. Helen Keller finally learned just who Anne Sullivan was: "Teacher." This particular generic word, which would be used by almost no one else in intimate relations, obviously had a special quality for both women because of the climactic situation of its emergence. One sees its arbitrariness because we would not use such a name; but one also sees its special transcendent unity *relative to that relationship*, where it seems to make sense to say, more than in most naming situations that are more familiar to us, that the name and the person had become one and the same in both women's minds. According to Cassirer's account, the moment in which the name "Teacher" enters their mutual vocabulary is when the "momentary god" is created: the "other" is revealed to both. The "real" Helen emerges for Anne, and the "real" teacher emerges for Helen, and the name does seem like a god. Cassirer then argues that the conventionalization of the name (in civilization, and, in this case, Helen's and Anne's subsequent relationship) is the important move to discursive thought, and the primitive or mythic "origin" loses its pertinence. The mythic unity of word and thing is, to Cassirer, preliminary to the emergence of the "spiritual power" of language:

> It was a long evolutionary course which the human mind had to traverse, to pass from the belief in a physico-magical power comprised in the Word to a realization of its spiritual power. Indeed, it is the Word, it is language, that really reveals to man that world which is closer to him than any world of natural objects and touches his weal and woe more directly than physical nature. For it is language that makes his existence in a *community* possible; . . . [But] the Word has to be conceived in the mythic mode, as a substantive being and power, before it can be comprehended as an ideal instrument, an organon of the mind, and as a fundamental function in the construction and development of spiritual reality.[13]

From this passage it seems as if "spiritual power" refers to the capability for abstract discursive thought, as in philosophy, and that the term might be synonymous (as *geistig* is in German) with "mental" or "intellectual" power. Yet "spiritual" also refers to the religious and mythic feelings that Cassirer is associating with the "primitive" power of naming. By retaining the term "spiritual," he wants to retain the tie between the "civilized" and the "primitive."

One wonders, however, if it is really necessary to think of mythic nam-

13. Ibid., pp. 61–62.

ing as original in phylogenetic sense.[14] If language "makes existence in a community possible," then communities and language must have developed at once, and the histories of language development and community development must be interwoven at every point.[15] The apparently magical quality of naming and language is a metaphor for the social character of language, while the mythic, religious, or superstitious function that names often have appear so only when the myths, beliefs, and superstitions are not our own. What Cassirer refers to as the unrecognized mythic creativity of language may be better understood as the misperception (the suppression, actually) of its social reach and the politically motivated substitution of religious mystery for social responsibility by the ruling or dominant elements in societies in order to keep power. If anything is told by the modern history of language philosophy (in which Cassirer is a major figure), it is the *inability* of this discipline to replace its stubborn religious habits of thought with an interest in acting on our knowledge of the social character of language use.

In the course of his argument for the mythic origin of language, Cassirer implies a substantive connection between the idea of the identity of the name and the thing, and the idea of language as enabling human communal existence. Earlier, in my discussion of Derrida's idea of writing, I implied a connection between the exteriority, or materiality, of language and its social character, even though Derrida conspicuously omits any discussion of language as a social phenomenon. I would like now to pursue these two implications.

The idea of an identity between name and thing has been discussed recently by Saul Kripke, though not exactly in Cassirer's terms. Nevertheless, Kripke's arguments lend support to the kind of phenomena Cassirer discusses and help bring Cassirer's idea closer to the issue of language use in general. In his first book, *Naming and Necessity*, Kripke begins his discussion of names by exploring only the use of proper names. His argument is that a

14. The instance I discussed in note 7 above also questions this necessity. Crane's mother's formulation, "love is a sickness" appears in what Cassirer might call the mythic dimension— the primary teaching of a mother to an abnormally dependent son. The term "lovesick," which undoubtedly existed in Mrs. Crane's vocabulary at the same time, enabled, in part, her formulation; yet her formulation, in part, enables the conventionalization of a term like "lovesick." At any point in history, language communities have both "mythic" and "spiritual" forms of the "same" predications.

15. Clifford Geertz, in claiming that "human thinking is primarily an overt act conducted in terms of objective materials and only secondarily a private matter," that is, in presenting another argument for the materiality of language, also claims that this argument rests on "the fact that the large human brain and human culture emerged synchronically, not serially." [*Interpretation of Cultures* (New York: Basic Books, 1973), p. 83] Geertz, like others I cited in chapters 2 and 3, sees the concept of the materiality of language (the "overtness of thinking") as implying an end to the ideality of private, individual thought.

name necessarily fixes a reference. There is something unique about a name such that no description of the person, no list of that person's "properties," no language substitute whatsoever, counts as "another name for the same thing." Put in its radical philosophical form, the proper name fixes the reference "in all possible worlds." Any proper name is in this way a "rigid designator." Here is Kripke's formulation:

> In these lectures, I will argue, intuitively, that proper names are rigid designators, for although the man (Nixon) might not have been the President, it is not the case that he might not have been Nixon (though he might not have been *called* 'Nixon'). Those who have argued that to make sense of the notion of rigid designator, we must antecedently make sense of 'criteria of transworld identity' have precisely reversed the cart and horse; it is *because* we can refer (rigidly) to Nixon, and stipulate that we are speaking of what might have happened to him (under certain circumstances), that 'transworld identifications' are unproblematic in such cases.[16]

It looks as if the intuitively fixed reference of the proper name precedes the identification of attributes or features of the person in question, that rigid designation is *a priori*. But this is not the argument. Kripke in his next paragraph makes the distinction between *a prioricity* and necessity, and rigid designation is a form of necessity rather than of *a prioricity*. Kripke isolates the necessary character of fixed reference naming by refuting the value of stipulating a "transworld identity" of any person—or imagining, that is, whether and if and how a person would be the "same" person in other "possible worlds." His point is that no amount of imagining can come up with a case where some definite description would *necessarily* refer to the same person designated by (for example) "Nixon." The only reference that necessarily points to Nixon is "Nixon." The nub of Kripke's argument is that there is *no substitute* for the name of a person fixing the reference. There may be other ways of referring to the "same thing" in certain contexts, but each way of referring must nevertheless be unique in its own way.

For the present argument, the idea of necessity requires a more extended inquiry. Kripke relies mainly on the *intuitive* nature of this necessity and defends his approach in this way:

> Of course, some philosophers think that something's having intuitive content is very inconclusive evidence in favor of it. I think it is very heavy evidence in favor of anything, myself. I really don't know, in a way, what more conclusive evidence one can have about anything, ultimately speaking.[17]

16. Saul Kripke, *Naming and Necessity* (Cambridge: Harvard University Press, 1972), p. 49.

17. Ibid., p. 42.

Kripke's strategy is to show that intuition is the only reliable thing left once the formal arguments against rigid designation have been rejected. However, before inquiring further into both necessity and intuition, it will be helpful to mention the few other cases in which Kripke implies that rigid designation obtains.

The names for natural kinds, Kripke suggests, may also be rigid designators:

> According to the view I advocate, then, terms for natural kinds are much closer to proper names than is ordinarily supposed. The old term 'common name' is thus quite appropriate for predicates marking out species or natural kinds, such as 'cow' or 'tiger.' My considerations apply also, however, to certain mass terms for natural kinds, such as 'gold,' 'water,' and the like. [18]

Or, again:

> . . . my argument implicitly concludes that certain general terms, those for natural kinds, have a greater kinship with proper names than is generally realized. This conclusion holds for certain various species names, whether they are count nouns, such as 'cat,' 'tiger, 'chunk of gold,' or mass terms for natural phenomena, such as 'heat,' 'light,' 'sound,' 'lightening,' and, presumably, suitably elaborated, to corresponding adjectives—'hot,' 'loud,' 'red,' . . . [19]

> . . . the present view asserts, in the case of species terms as in that of proper names, that one should bear in mind the contrast between the *a priori* but perhaps contingent properties carried with a term, given by the way its reference was fixed, and the analytic (and hence necessary) properties a term may carry, given by its meaning. For species, as for proper names, the way the reference of a term is fixed should not be regarded as a synonym for the term. [20]

In extending the range of rigid designation to natural kinds, collective nouns, and adjectives, Kripke restresses that whether the reference was fixed by either contingent or essential properties of the item is immaterial. The fixity of the reference emerges as a feature of naming that, Kripke implies, is unrelated to the elements of the item being named. Furthermore, in adding common collective nouns (notice he refers to "common nouns" as "common names," suggesting that the whole idea of a noun is implicated in his reflection on "naming") to proper names as instances of rigid designation, he makes the case for rigid designation more daring because more comprehensive: proper names seem obviously to "belong" to a person—such-and-such is *his* or *her*

18. Ibid., p. 127.
19. Ibid., p. 134.
20. Ibid., p. 135.

name; the possessive is always used to describe the relation of the name to the person. Whereas in cases like "gold," "tiger," and "heat," we don't feel as easily that the word belongs to the thing, especially not distinctly to any class of things; the words seems more of a label than a name. Kripke goes through considerable trouble, however, to show that the use of the word "gold" does not even necessarily imply "atomic number 79" because most who use the word do not need to know this essential property in order to use the word correctly. The phenomenon of rigid designation occurs not because of an objective relation between a word and a thing, but because that reference has been fixed by thought. The items Kripke adds to proper names are "common" also in the sense of their being familiar or ordinary, so that an analogy is implied (though not explicitly mentioned by Kripke) between an individual's ownership of his or her own name and the common (in both senses) ownership by tigers and heat of their "names." Of course, it is only human collective ownership of these references that really exists, just as an individual's name is collectively recognized as such.[21]

In his study of Wittgenstein, Kripke brings up two other instances of naming, though not quite with the same announced purposes as in his first book. Here is one important point he makes about Wittgenstein: his "main problem is that it appears that he has shown all language, all concept formation, to be impossible, indeed unintelligible."[22] Wittgenstein, Kripke argues, has introduced a most radical sort of skepticism which makes language appear, more than inefficacious, unsusceptible of understanding. He views Wittgenstein, in other words, as having posed the problem that the idea of rigid designation solves.

Without calling the word "plus" a name, Kripke follows Wittgenstein's radical skepticism to a point where we allow that any new use of "plus" has not been already determined by previous instances of addition. To a skeptic, one can never know that "68 + 57" will once again turn out to be 125, because there is a reasonable doubt about the new use of the "word" "plus". Kripke accepts Wittgenstein's rejection of his own "truth conditions" theory of a word's meaning, but finds in Wittgenstein's own later formulations some ground for overcoming his skepticism:

21. One may wish to question the word "ownership" in this connection, since its implication that names are "properties" of some sort would be just what I am *not* suggesting. Perhaps the meaning of "own" in the phrase "my own mother" better suggests the sense of "ownership" I am using here.

22. Saul Kripke, *Wittgenstein on Rules and Private Language* (Cambridge: Harvard University Press, 1982), p. 62.

Wittgenstein asks that we discard any *a priori* conceptions and *look* (Don't think, look!") at the circumstances under which numerical assertions are actually uttered, and at what roles such assertions play in our lives. [23]

As we know, when Wittgenstein looked, he found the "language games" which help to enlighten thought about language. In consequence, Kripke is then able to speak of "numerical assertions" rather than "mathematical truth." Contrary to the familiar sense of addition as an act "containing" some unshakable truth, it is instead viewed as a "numerical assertion" — always *by someone*, we should add — where the "word," or "name", "plus" plays a crucial role. It then seems that numerical assertions are language acts which in a fundamental sense belong in the same basket with proper names and common nouns.

Kripke's means of coming to such a point, however, are different from those he used in *Naming and Necessity*. By engaging Wittgenstein's reflections on rules and private language, he adds many salient particulars to the idea of the "common name," a category, I think, that could in principle cover any use of language. The main thoughts that Kripke takes from Wittgenstein are that the language-game concept means that all rules are public or communal; that private language is more or less meaningless (though statements could be made about it in certain circumstances); and that words like "plus" acquire their fixed reference by public rules, are regulated by such rules, and their use and reference cannot be accounted for by considering the thought processes of an isolated individual:

> . . . if one person is considered in isolation, the notion of a rule as guiding a person who adopts it can have *no* substantive content. There are, we have seen, no truth conditions or facts in virtue of which it can be the case that he accords with his past intentions or not. As long as we regard him as following a rule 'privately,' so that we pay attention to his justifications alone, all we can say is that he is licensed to follow the rule as it strikes him. This is why Wittgenstein says, "To think one is obeying a rule is not to obey a rule. Hence it is not possible to obey a rule 'privately'; otherwise thinking one was obeying a rule would be the same thing as obeying it." [24]

Kripke's new move in his later book is to consider an individual as "interacting with a wide community." [25] From the communal perspective, three items emerge (in Kripke's reading of Wittgenstein) that "solve" the so-called

23. Ibid., p. 75.

24. Ibid., p. 89 [Wittgenstein, *Philosophical Investigations*, trans. G. E. M. Anscombe (New York: Macmillan, 1953), p. 202].

25. Ibid.

skeptical paradox of not being able to adduce "truth conditions" for words like "plus": agreement, checkability, and public criteria. First, it is already accepted by members of a community that they all agree on how to use "plus." Second, because they agree, each member can check on every other member's usage and in this way regulate or keep the usage stable. Third, there are agreed-upon criteria for checking on others' usages: that is, it is also already understood how to go about deciding if a given usage is acceptable.

In making this argument, Kripke may be either equating the "intuitive" sense of a fixed reference with the social fixing of reference, or he may be replacing the intuitive idea with the social idea. From the present perspective, we will want to say that the intuitive is bound up with the social and the social with the intuitive, and that we should understand the fixity of reference in the use of language in this *double* way. In any event, Kripke's discussion of Wittgenstein winds up by strongly emphasizing the material in Wittgenstein's work that could be read to reject private language and private rule-following:

> . . . following section 243, a 'private language' is usually defined as a language that is logically impossible for anyone else to understand. The private language argument is taken to argue against the possibility of a private language in this sense. This conception is not in error, but it seems to me that the emphasis is somewhat misplaced. What is really denied is what might be called the 'private model' of rule following, that the notion of a person following a given rule is to be analyzed simply in terms of facts about the rule follower and the rule follower alone, without reference to his membership in a wider community. (In the same way, what Hume denies is the private model of causation: that whether one event causes another is a matter of the relation between these two events alone, without reference to their subsumption under larger event types.) The impossibility of a private language in the sense just defined does indeed follow from the incorrectness of the private model for language and rules, since the rule following in a 'private language' could only be analyzed by a private model, but the incorrectness of the private model is more basic, since it applies to all rules. I take this to be the point of section 202.
>
> The falsity of the private model need not mean that a *physically isolated* individual cannot be said to follow rules; rather than an individual, *considered in isolation* (whether or not he is physically isolated), cannot be said to do so. . . . Our community can assert of any individual that he follows a rule if he passes the tests for rule following applied to any member of the community. [26]

This passage is noteworthy, first, because Kripke acknowledges but then goes beyond the "logical" argument against private language, even though that argument is "not in error." What seems important to him is the im-

26. Ibid., pp. 109–110.

plied connection in Wittgenstein's work between a rule and a community. Furthermore, it is not the rule itself that matters most, but the *rule follower* and the necessity of understanding such a being only in reference to his or her membership in a "wider community." Pointedly, if parenthetically, he draws an analogy with Hume's argument about the causation of individual events, saying that several events—and implying that several observers—are needed to fix a case of causation. He then goes on to put "language and rules" together as items that are not comprehensible from an individual standpoint. Whether or not an individual is physically alone has no bearing on this issue, because "our community" can "consider" that person a member, even if only hypothetically. As a general matter, Kripke is concerned with *when one can assert something* rather than with if any single assertion has some intrinsic weight. Although Kripke does not draw this conclusion explicitly, it seems clear from his argument that the communal conditions of assertability create the intuition of fixed reference in this particularly difficult case of "plus" or, in general, mathematical assertions.

Consider, finally, Kripke's treatment of a word that seems to denote something completely private, "pain." Like the other instances he uses, "pain" is a member of a large class of words, in this case, "sensation" words, with which individuals seem to be reporting their subjective states. Here is his commentary on Wittgenstein, which appears in the "postscript" discussion of "other minds":

> In section 244, Wittgenstein introduces his well-known account of how, in the case of sensations, "the connection between the name and the thing [is] set up"—"Words are connected with the primitive, the natural expressions of the sensation and learned in their place. A child has hurt himself and he cries: and the adults talk to him and teach him exclamations and, later, sentences. They teach the child new pain-behavior. . . . the verbal expression of pain replaces crying and does not describe it." Thus Wittgenstein thinks that avowals of pain are new, more sophisticated pain behavior that adults teach the child as a substitute for the primitive, non-verbal expression of pain. It is a new way that the child *evinces* his pain. At the same time, as was emphasized in the main text, adults reckon the teaching of the child to have been successful precisely when his natural behavioral manifestations (and, perhaps other cues) would lead them to judge of him that he is in pain. This tendency is, according to Wittgenstein's view, essential to the idea that the concept of pain is to be ascribed to the child at all. Thus we need no longer worry that each of us attributes pain in two unrelated senses, one applying to 'myself,' the other a behavioristic ersatz 'I' apply to 'others.' On the contrary, the first-person avowals would not make sense without the third-person use.[27]

27. Ibid., p. 134.

In the "main text" discussion Kripke alludes to here, he makes the point that when a child uses "pain" it means the same thing as when we—who taught the child—use it, thereby showing how easily we identify "sameness" or fixity of reference. In this passage the point is much stronger—that first person avowals of pain would not make sense to begin with without the already coexisting third-person usages. Kripke seems to want to presuppose a spontaneous identification of persons with one another as an argument for rigid designation. He cites Wittgenstein's aim to explain how "the connection between the name and the thing" is established. If, as we may reasonably assume, Kripke already thinks that connection is "rigid," he is commenting on how the rigidity in the mind of one person cannot exist without a comparable rigidity in the mind of the other. When the child learns to substitute a word for a cry, it is not any word, but the right word—that is, the word that the parents have already substituted for the cry and which has been, so to speak, passed along—rather than taught in the simple sense, as in a natural growth process. Kripke goes beyond Wittgenstein's argument by saying that it matters that that particular word is used for us to know the child is in pain—behavioral manifestations not being enough for us to know it after a while. Kripke asks: "why have such a locution as 'He is in pain'? Why don't we always rest content with specific descriptions of behavior?"[28]

His general answer to this question elaborates the point made in the passage just cited, namely that first, third, and implicitly, second persons are all, perhaps necessarily, related to one another:

> I, who have myself experienced pain and can imagine it, can imaginatively put *myself* in place of the sufferer; and my ability to do this gives my attitude a quality that it would lack if I had merely learned a set of rules as to when to attribute pain to others and how to help them. Indeed, my ability to do this enters into my ability to identify some of the expressions of psychological states—it helps me to identify these simply as expressions of suffering, not through an independent physicalistic description of them. What plays the appropriate role in the formation of my attitude is not a 'belief' that he 'feels the same as I,' but an imaginative ability to 'put myself in his situation.'[29]

Kripke then even finds a sentence in Wittgenstein to support this claim. In *Philosophical Remarks*, Kripke cites, " 'When I am sorry for someone else because he's in pain, I do of course imagine the pain, but I imagine that *I* have it.' "[30] In these passages, Kripke is implying a fundamental, underlying relatedness of persons, a spontaneous putting of oneself in the other's position

28. Ibid., p. 136.
29. Ibid., p. 140.
30. Ibid.

that accounts for our usage of the "same" sensation-word for the same thing. Is this spontaneous identification with the other person something other than a community?—that is, when one puts oneself in community with another person, one understands his or her language. At the same time, when one understands another's language, even about subjective sensations, one must *already be* in community with that person. This is a matter of both language-in-general and, more pointedly, about particular words.

Behind the idea of rigid designation for individual words—that is, the phenomenon of a word seeming to keep its reference fixed, and of language being instantly identified as *our* language—is the psychosocial relatedness of persons, the spontaneous interpersonal attachment, which is also implied in the ideas of innate intersubjectivity and intrasocial thought collectives. Kripke's argument helps reduce any need to look for a priority—either individual or social—in the task of conceptualizing language. His description implies neither priority and shows, rather, the mutual interimplication of individual mental acts and interpersonal circumstances of life.

Let me now return to the ideas of necessity and intuition as they work in the arguments for rigid designation in Kripke's four cases—proper names, common species names, mathematical functions, and sensation words. If one accepts all the arguments as given, it will be difficult to find any other instance of language use that could not be described as rigid designation. Once any reference is fixed, that name has a *necessary* referent. As Michael Spikes has argued against Kripke's point, even "the inventor of bifocals" is a rigid designator because this person, whatever his name, was the only such person.[31] The fixity of the reference is the basis for the *intelligibility of the term* and not for whether it applies in such and such a case. Kripke on several occasions suggests that the necessity of rigid designation is an intuitive perception. In particular, the intuition is that one cannot substitute another word for any particular word as used on this given occasion. As above, we need to *say* "pain," and not describe its symptoms.

One practical result of accepting the intuitive necessity of rigid designation is that *every word always counts*. In each instance of language use, we will find that if other words are used, a slightly different "language game" is being played, a slightly different "form of life" is being evoked. When we go beyond Wittgenstein's relatively reduced usage and think in terms of "community" and "intersubjectivity," as Kripke, in part, does, we see that each word counts so much because it is an element in the zone of relatedness between each of us and the persons to whom we are speaking. Just as the

31. Michael Spikes, doctoral dissertation, Department of Comparative Literature, Indiana University, 1986.

words themselves "count," each speaker "counts on" each word and *depends on* the other's usage by virtue of each one's pregiven dependency on others. One cannot get out of counting on others' usages. The fixity of reference marks our sense of identity with other people. Our relatedness to and dependence on others is necessary by virtue of these two seemingly different perspectives: the sameness of verbal reference, and the sense that we are all the same—the latter being, as Shields and Trevarthen have argued, something perhaps innate. It is certainly perceptible in the earliest interactions between infants and parents. Language and interpersonal identification coalesce at any early age—in the second year—to produce the intuitive sense of necessity in the "common" meaning of words. Any misunderstanding or dispute about words is inseparable from disputes about relatedness. If the intuition of verbal fixity were not already there, or if the sense of relatedness were not already there, then there would be no cause for dispute. *The subjective identification of word and thing is bound up with the subjective identification of person and person.*

In Kripke's work, the attitude that every word counts bespeaks a strong sense of both individual (intuitional) consciousness and of intersubjective involvement. In contrast, Derrida's concept of "writing"—of the exteriority or materiality of language and symbolic forms—shows *neither* of these senses. Yet Derrida's attitude is just as emphatically behind the idea that every word counts as Kripke's. From Derrida's perspective, the word counts because it is at every moment fading into its opposite, its assertion simultaneously implies its denial. In the "I am in pain" example, its meaning gains force from the obvious implication of something like "not-pain"; "Nixon" is distinguished by implicit juxtaposition with everyone who is not Nixon; "gold" with all instances of "not-gold"; "tigers" with "not-tigers." These are not idle claims, since pain versus "health" or "pleasure" can have two (or more) different accounts; the same is true for gold versus silver or fool's gold; Nixon versus Humphrey or Eisenhower; tigers versus lions or versus antelopes, and so on. Because of the infinite potential of which "versus" we may have in mind or imply in our speech, or know other speakers to have in mind, the argument that the word's actual reference always "depends" gains force, even as it is clear that the word itself is treated as palpable, as exterior to individual subjective consciousness, and "counts" to the fullest possible degree. From Derrida's standpoint, much more of the spontaneous richness, subtlety, and complexity of language is engaged by seeing the continuously self-erasing potential of the word. In an important sense both Kripke and Derrida are hemmed in by a long tradition of narrow philosophical discourse; the small gestures toward community in Kripke and the feverish struggle with paradox and "absence" in Derrida are certain signs of the inadequacy of this tradition.

The idea of the double (and/or multiple) perspective, in its revision of the exclusively individualistic attitude, and in its disciplined program of "looking at" how groups actually work, is my response to the philosophical frustrations that surround both Kripke's and Derrida's reflections on language.

I have repeatedly implied that the double perspective applies beyond the small units of language (names, words, and sentences). This chapter has tried to show that basic mental functions result from the unification of two perspectives, and that both the ability to "name" (or to identify something with a word) and the ability to make a sentence are results of this combining activity. In this way I have tried to account for both the satisfying affective experience of language use and its necessary appearance in groups of two or more people, two fundamental features of language that are not treated by the transformational theory of language. I have also tried to suggest that because of cognitive stereoscopy and the double (individual and social) orientation toward language, a name (or a sentence) may be reasonably understood to fix a referent (or to use an already fixed reference) or to challenge or subvert its referentiality, perhaps fixing and challenging at once.

At this point, it will be useful to consider what the role, status, and functions of literature are in order to enlarge our perspective on language by seeing how language, literacy, and literature work together. Earlier in this chapter, I used two literary sentences to claim that the double perspective implies a "syntactic" conception of language rather than a "semantic" one. This was meant to show that while the subject and predicate of any sentence are not symmetrical, they are, in principle, reversible. While the fact that they appear in a certain order means that a certain reference has been fixed— it is that order and not some other order that "counts" at that point—it is also true that the potential reversibility of subject and predicate is also "part" of that sentence, as in the simple pairs of formulations I cited in note 7. The style of literary interpretation that grew out of Derrida's view of language looks for and finds reversals, inversions, permutations, and so on, within whole individual literary works and by studying "intertextual" relationships among several works. On the other hand, many critics, such as Gerald Graff for example, are concerned to respect, as a matter of fundamental critical strategy, the order already fixed in the text as necessarily binding in some way on those of us who consider the text important.[32] For the last two decades or so, literary theorists have been arguing this case back and forth. At least part of the reason the argument can go on for so long is that conservative academic

---

32. While Graff does not treat the topic of "order" directly, his point, in *Literature Against Itself*, that any argument for the variability of meaning depends on at least a provisional stability of meaning, implies the binding character of the language-as-first-given by any text.

interests are usually enhanced by such debates, while the participants feel no need to arrive at some practical result or program. This lack of concrete social purpose diminishes the value of the debates by keeping them "academic" (in the pejorative metaphorical sense as well as the literal). [33]

Historically, literature (including its more general reference to any sort of text) has been an enterprise which temporarily fixes a culture's uses of language. Even in nonliterate societies, a literary event (a performance, for example) is a pause in everyday life marked by a gathering of people with the common purpose of experiencing the event. As is often the case today, when the same play is presented in various versions, or when oral literature is given different presentations, any one of them is nevertheless a moment of collective "holding" the text in a single unique form. The subject matter of such performances is usually widely known, and while in part the new performance's purpose is to resay what is already known, its purpose is also to give the repetition a new accent, so that the whole event appears in some sense as "new language." With written literature, even though the text remains more or less the same over long periods, each new reading, or set of readings that develops historically, is equivalent to a new performance of oral literature. In this way, there is always an inevitable sameness to each new literary event and there is always an inevitable uniqueness; the literary event, oral or written, is always social and always entails some sort of "language fixing," as each reader remembers the reading experience by fixing it. By understanding literary events (literature) in this social and collective sense, its relation to language and writing seems to be more visible.

Toward the end of chapter 3, I cited Deborah Tannen's observation that literature has more in common with conversation than does expository prose. In conversation, Tannen showed, a variety of liberties are taken—abrupt changes of subject, for example—and then a return to the original subject. She cites dialogues, metaphors, jokes, and so on, and she makes it clear that as formal as literature can become, it always uses essential and familiar features of ordinary conversational language to win attention. In all literature, a variety of different voices is heard—and deliberately recreated, for that matter—whereas in expository discourse, such as this text, only one voice is really heard; voices that are cited only appear briefly and in the service

---

33. The term "at stake" is usually jargon in deconstructionist criticism. It is used repeatedly in arguments that aim to disclose opposing terms of dualistically used pairs of words and/or ideas, as in the generic usage, "what is at stake in the confrontation of a and b is . . . " I have yet to find in such criticism, and perhaps in the whole debate between poststructuralists and "referentialists," a clear statement of what is "at stake" in the actuality of our academic lives should we take one or the other view in this debate.

of the "author's" voice. Tannen also points out that literature is context-dependent rather than content-dependent, and that the context includes not only the one developed by the text, but the society into which the text is introduced, i.e., communities, classrooms, clubs, or congregations that decide which book is worth discussing. Furthermore, in today's literate societies, literature is actually introduced into children's lives as something "oral"; even though stories are read to children, the children really only hear the story, requiring the teller to be present. Always, for young children, the literary experience involves two or more people. Literary events begin to "count" for children in the same way that conversations count as moments of interpersonal attachment in which the details of the language interaction — the specific words, tones, and emphases and their role in the total experience — stick in their minds and accumulate toward their social identities. As I suggested in chapter 1, academic values begin to break down the child's sense of language as social and gradually isolate literature by pursuing the retrograde religious habit of understanding written texts as "holy" and oral texts as trivial and juvenile.

In this and previous chapters, I have tried to gather certain sources together in an approach to language, literacy, and literature that is more faithful to how they are experienced subjectively and intersubjectively. Ralph Cohen's recent work on the concept of literary genre belongs in this group. As Cohen develops it, the idea of genre bears certain resemblances to Kripke's sense of what a name is. But more than Kripke, Derrida, and the majority of Marx-accented critics, Cohen seeks to articulate the idea of genre as something bound up in historical and social processes. He is at pains to separate genre theory from the more purely taxonomical efforts such as Northop Frye's and from the conventional idea of genre as a fixed guide for "placing" literature.

In his critique of Derrida, Cohen observes that it is of no help to think of literature or writing as just that: "One does not write 'writing,' " he observed, "one writes novels or plays or poems or letters, and the like."[34] Any specific form of writing is connected with other writings in the same or similar forms, and which use still other forms as "subgenres" in a variety of ways. These forms, in turn, are determined by social purposes and historical circumstances while they are in the process of helping to change these purposes and circumstances. In other words, a genre is an identifiable kind or species of language, the understanding of which must proceed in social and historical terms. It could be called a Wittgensteinian "form of life" or "language game," but it also must be called a manifestation of historical development and social purpose. As we recall, Kripke took some trouble to argue that species

---

34. Informal conversation, 24 September, 1984.

names such as "tiger" fix a reference in ways similar to how proper names do. His argument suggested that the names of things have a kind of strength or inertia, rooted in both mental and communal life, that had heretofore gone unrecognized. Cohen's argument is not that writing must take one main form, but that it always appears in at least one form and is always made up of several subforms which, like the principal form, must be understood as being in the midst of social and historical change. Of significance for my argument is the idea that larger linguistic units are formally, though temporarily, fixed and identifiable, and that they matter *for the same reasons* that names (proper or common or generic) matter and cannot be replaced by other names and definitions. Even though, for example, someone may wish to call *Finnegans Wake* something other than a novel, say, a "dream tract," and even though it may be called a "dream tract" in the year 2088, it is now treated as a novel and not as something else. This treatment, in turn, implies something about this society in this historical moment, and because of those implications, the genre may be said to be fixed. If someone wishes to start a movement to "place" the work with other dream literature, say *Piers Plowman*, the starting point would nevertheless be that Joyce's work is now a novel; reasons would then be given why that is not the case, others would join in, and, gradually, the "name" would change.

Cohen's first central argument, then, is that literature always appears at once as both a text and a kind of text; it is "double" in this fundamental way, which is comparable to Cassirer's and Kripke's ideas that literature is always a thing (the physical, inert texts) with a name (the kind of things as defined by various people and communities—authors, critics, classes of people, for example). This doubleness of text and kind of text is always unified so that name and thing, and subject and predicate, are unified. Cohen then pursues a second main point: that genres themselves are always mixed or "combinatory." At each point in literary history, he shows, any one genre has been made up of a variety of others. Since this is so, what then defines a genre is its "manner of combination."[35] Thus, to identify any one genre, one finds its locally given general category *and* its particular historically developed, socially governed manner of combining other genres from other phases of history and other cultures. Genres identifiable in these ways are the television spot, the miniseries, women's journals, slave narratives, as well as the more traditional ones. Each of these has a principal but local form

---

35. Ralph Cohen, "The Autobiography of a Critical Problem," lecture presented at annual meeting of the Midwest Modern Language Association, Bloomington, Indiana, 4 November, 1984, p. 6.

whose social and historical purposes are then fulfilled by the inclusion of a variety of other forms combined in a (usually) new way according to the situation. Here is one of Cohen's formulations:

> Naming a text a "novel" or a "non-fictional novel," a "mini-series," or a "soap" identifies it and pins down what is unpinnable; in Derrida's terms, genre-naming fixes what is necessarily unfixable, encloses in boundaries that which crosses boundaries. Nevertheless if we think of people instead of maps, we know that border crossings are common practice in some countries (like our own) and that the reasons for such crossings are social and economic. Every time such a crossing occurs, it places the person in a dual relation—with his own and with a foreign country. . . . The point is that if texts cross borders or boundaries, they must have borders or boundaries to cross; they need group or class names to identify them. If all we have are textual crossings, we can make no distinctions between novels, non-fiction novels, and autobiographies that are also fictions and non-fictions. Genre naming or grouping is inevitably both necessary and loose; critics may change the boundaries and the name. But they then continue with other strategies that, nevertheless, involve renaming and remapping. [36]

Neither the general name for the genre nor the specific manner of combination can stand alone: genre naming "is inevitably both necessary and loose." [37] To put it another way, the two naming procedures (identifying both the genre and its manner of combination) take place at once, each contribution to the other.

Finally, neither one nor both of these efforts of identification can be understood as abstract taxonomical activities, since the use of both sets of names requires their being related to history or social purpose—relative to the works under study and to the critical community doing the naming. Cohen gives two instances of this step. First he cites "those tragedies in England that were initiated by George Lillo with *The London Merchant* which Lillo called 'tragedies of private life.'" Cohen continues:

> . . . in Germany in the 18th century up to the present these were and are still called "bourgeois" tragedies; later in England they were called "domestic

36. Ibid., p. 11. I would like to call attention to an indirect point being made here by Cohen: if texts are to be treated more like people than like maps, the question of generic naming is much less of a problem and certainly not the paradox Derrida described—the unnamability of things. The variability of people's official nationality poses some problems in identifying them, but this in no way reduces the need, even the necessity, to continue to identify people in a stable way. Derrida tends not to entertain the social character of this necessity and concentrates instead on the logical problems raised by the intuition of the fixed name.

37. This is the discussion alluded to in note 9.

tragedies" and in our time they have been called "dramas of sensibility" and
sentimental tragedies." In each of these classifications or genres, the tests
referred to and the features discussed were somewhat different though there
was much overlapping.

Cohen then gives a sketch of how the explanation of such renamings might
proceed:

> Lillo and John Hughes called such plays "tragedies of private life" because
> they wished to see them as an extension of Aristotle's notion of tragedy. Their
> contribution was to extend the characters and themes of tragedy from affairs of
> state carried on by the holders of power to the sad and criminal lives of members
> of the lower classes. A major genre was used to embrace and enhance a class
> that had an inferior status. We can note the strategies involved: an undermining
> of classical tragedy by claiming merely to extend it, the demotion of tragedy as
> a genre dealing only with aristocratic protagonists, the elevation of commoners
> as capable of tragic emotions. The same plays were called "bourgeois tragedies"
> in Germany to stress the innovative role of this class and the need for it to
> possess a genre that characterized it. In our time when the bourgeois were not
> an innovative class, the classification of many of these plays as "dramas of
> sensibility" resulted from a desire to attack Enlightenment departures from a
> classical norm that led, in the views of these critics, to the collapse of 20th
> century values. It was, of course, an attack on the bourgeoisie. This generic
> classification of "sensibility" sought to classify a literary tendency assumed to
> be socially and literarily dangerous, and it thus made possible the attack upon
> this group of texts in comparison to others that upheld appropriate values.[38]

This account of the historical changes marked by the reception of these
plays also explains the meaning of the generic names for the plays. The
taxonomy of the names themselves is almost meaningless. But once the social
movements associated with the plays are disclosed—movements that were
familiar parts of the then-contemporary social experience—the stereoscopy
of the generic names becomes apparent. The fixing of a generic name is the
marker of a social event, just as is the fixing of a proper name or the use of
common names on more ordinary occasions. Thus, Cohen observes,

> The purpose of naming a type of writing "feminist literary criticism" or "slave
> narratives" or "legal briefs" is to establish an identity that is socially and
> literarily related to other identities, to make a political assertion that is for one
> group and against another, to announce that a literary act cannot be dissevered
> from social action, to reject the belief that anonymity stimulates fairness.[39]

38. Cohen, "Autobiography," pp. 12–13.
39. Ibid., p. 13.

In Cassirer's account, the name and the thing were conjoined by moments of mythic or religious or "spiritual" insight; in Kripke's account they were conjoined by an intuition of necessity. Cohen's reflections adduce social and historical purpose as the elements which render literary generic names, in our own terms, stereoscopic. But more than this is being proposed by Cohen and by the arguments of this chapter. The development of literature through its multifarious forms itself *names* social circumstances. As critics proceed with "merely" identifying literary types, they are bringing to the fore the variety of "names" that the society, through its different forms of "writing," is using to identify its actions and to regulate its social developments.

By bringing up unusual categories—such as legal briefs and soaps—in his instances of literary genres, Cohen is himself declaring new boundaries for the study of "literature." In a sense he is actually accepting the wide scope implied by Derrida's comprehensive term "writing," but he is also insisting on the necessity of the name and on the discoverability of the circumstances in which names are fixed, regardless of how temporary this fixity may be. This broadening of the subject, this renaming of it with special consciousness of its names is, as his own perspective suggests, a social act, which changes the idea of literature to such an extent that it begins to entail a series of other subjects whose own texts then become the natural topic in "English" departments. At the same time, the subject remains "kinds of writing," which also names the topics of language use and literacy we have been discussing.

Cohen has outlined a program which, in the present view, has made multiple use of the double perspective and stereoscopic thinking that I have described. As I implied early in this chapter, once the principle of the double perspective takes root in infancy with the more or less simultaneous onset of naming, syntactical speaking, and self-awareness, it becomes a principle of how one knows through language. The use of several perspectives is the recursive syntheses of one or some of the "old" schemata with the "new" situation. Very much as Piaget described the mutual assimilation of schemata in his windshield example, Cohen's description of how a ballad is transformed into a play may also be understood as such a mutual, syntactic combination of forms to produce a "new" form—the "tragedy of private life"—that answers a social question of that society at that time. Even in Cohen's brief outline of the political forces that may be at work as a genre is renamed, such forces are analogous to the frustration Piaget felt that motivated him to make the new synthesis. Political forces are collective motives mobilized affectively in ways similar to how individuals' feelings and thoughts are mobilized to identify things in new ways. But even in individuals, the schemata available for personal use, so to speak, are likewise generated from collective sources—from one or more others who at some point validated or otherwise helped provide a name for what is then reintegrated privately. Thus, whenever knowledge is to be presented as a literacy act or literacy event, one will always be able to identify at least two perspectives coalesced to give a unique, apparently "new" sense of how things are.

In this sense, all language is "new" and "used" at once. Its novelty comes from the fact that it always answers to a new social situation, a new historical moment, a new set of circumstances. But also, as Derrida argues, not only is the language "used" as soon as it appears, it was, of course, already used before the present use—it could not have been used now if it had not already been used, that is, was not already a part of the social history of the speaker. In a bizarre way, the transformational approach seems to honor novelty while viewing the circumstance of performance as a mystery; and it seems to be able to view rules and regularities of usage only as the product of a genetic plan. For us, however, language is naming in the various ways discussed above, but it is particularly the manifestation of the double perspectives of individual minds and the unified perspectives of several.

5

Gender Interests in Language and Literature

In one of his inquiries into the question of genre, Ralph Cohen presents the following observation:

> Genre has its source in the Latin "genus" which refers to "kind" or "sort" or "species" or "class." Its root terms are "genere," "gignere,"—to beget, generate and (in the passive) to be born. In this latter sense it refers both to a class and an individual. And it is, of course, derived from the same root terms as "gender." It is not necessary for me to point out that one of the creation stories of gender involves the formation of the female from the male; the creation of one genre from another. The ancientness of genre procedures lies here in one of the creation myths (however prejudiced) of man and woman. [1]

In pointing to the fact that genders are genres and that, if we discount their prejudice, early writers and readers of Genesis could be said to have conceived of either gender as coming out of another (as opposed to woman "coming from" man), Cohen is indirectly calling attention to the "double perspective" available to all people, which is marked by the two genders that are both separate and necessarily implicated in one another. But by suggesting that the biblical account of the origin of genders is prejudiced, Cohen also exposes the masculine accent of the Genesis myth.

For example, why is woman depicted as coming out of man, when both genders actually were born from women? Or, why were not human beings depicted as having emerged from two ur-genres (ur-genders), as they do in real life? Why did there have to be an originating "point": why did God have to be one figure with one gender? I don't know that these questions really do pose any mysteries. The Genesis story *reverses* the fact of birth so that the masculine gender, both in God and in Adam, is the originating gender. Thus God, "He," created men first, then, like a mother tending after our needs, saw that "it is not good for the man to be alone" and created a

1. Ralph Cohen, "The Attack on Genre," Patten lecture, Indiana University.

121

"helper, as if opposite him" (my Hebrew translation), or as the Hebrew word "neged" might also be translated, a "helper, as if *against* him." The term "eyzer" (helper), in addition to referring to the person who appeared second on the scene, clearly admits the social priority of the man whose presumed "primary" role requires "help." In view of the considerations presented by Dinnerstein, Chodorow, and Gilligan, discussed in chapters 1 and 2, it seems quite unlikely that women composed this story, and that, rather, men, writing and thinking under the usual socially masculine conditions, made it up and perpetuated it in their own interests. Would women in a gender-equal society have sought an originating point, a sense of hierarchy, and, finally, an adversarial or oppositional relation between men and women? Cohen's idea is that genres come out of *one another*, that there is no absolute priority of genres or kinds, and that they are intertwined with one another. It is a view of genre and species-naming that we ought to project backward, so to speak, in order to conceive of the two kinds of human beings, as, yes, two kinds, but also two perspectives, both of which inform each other, thus forming a unified human perspective capable of discerning the ethical and social distances among all people and the relationships that these distances mark.

In this chapter I want to show that the perspectives of the two genders together form a double perspective, and that, while the specific features of each perspective (each "genre") may change with history, whatever form each takes in any period should be understood as the result of a combination of biological, psychological, social, and cultural factors. I can only discuss this double perspective as it appears today, in our own historical epoch. Each generic part contains the sense of the otherness of the other perspective, and both need one another to function at all.

As I have developed it so far, the idea of a generic (double or single) perspective has a very long reach; however, our main interest now is in how these perspectives emerge in literary response and then, by implication, in language use. My discussion will not yield any incontrovertible conclusions, but it will present what I consider convincing styles of literary response and language use by each gender, styles consistent with the accounts of child development and gender socialization given by Chodorow and Gilligan. I will also consider the possibility of these styles being biologically linked, yet not biologically necessary, traits that often exist as part of a discernible gender identity, yet that are not necessarily tied to one gender, or, if so tied, requiring the other gender's perspective at every point, as "a helper, as if *alternative* to it." My main aim is to show that the fact that there are two genders who use language in both gender-specific and gender-common ways both documents and justifies the general idea of the double perspective.

I also have a few other purposes. Thinking back to Dorothy Dinnerstein's claim that there is a fundamental problem in human sexual arrangements, I want to claim that the failure of men and women to speak one another's language is an aspect of this problem. The way in which each gender uses language (today) is the result of the failure to share gender-specific styles. So I will try to disclose these styles, propose their political accents as well as their possible links to biological gender identity, and suggest the grounds of their complementarity.

Consider first the basis for not ruling out biology as a contributing factor to gender-specific language styles. Reasoning about the biological basis of both mental and physical phenomena has never been a straightforward matter. For example, certain diseases are gender-related or race-related; yet members of the other gender or another race also get the disease. Or, while baldness occurs primarily in men, some women become bald also. At a certain age, women can no longer bear children, but some men can continue to beget them into their old age. Certain antibiotics work on most people, but not on others; does this mean that there is no real understanding of how antibiotics work? And what is the basis of homosexuality? Some now believe that it is biological. In some instances, it seems clear that both psychosis and neurosis have physiological features. In all of the foregoing cases, it is customary to say that biological understanding of such things is incomplete; but it is nevertheless reasonable to suppose that *two* sorts of understanding are needed: the knowledge of a *generic* regularity and the knowledge of *an individual's* biological idiosyncrasies. Medical advice has been traditionally given on these grounds.

I think that the problem of gender differences in language use requires this less-than-certain, nonpredictive sort of understanding. When I teach a class, I often notice that men speak differently than women about the same works of literature, but that is in no way true of all men and all women: there are significant patterns but there are also significant exceptions. In the material that Robin Lakoff discusses,[2] there are strong gender differences in usage, but one gender can use the other's language yet remain in its own idiom in more general ways. We are therefore looking for contingent regularities: those which exist in large numbers of people, but which are also regulated by individual or other local factors of growth, taste, and culture. In medicine, "influenza" is generic, but "new strains" pop up, and new manifestations of the old strains look different in different people. In the study of literacy, the case is similar but much less certain. Because of the overwhelming influence of culture on language use, it is hard to see what counts, in each age or each

---

2. Robin Lakoff, *Language and Woman's Place* (New York: Harper & Row, 1975).

culture, as a biological influence on language. A great deal depends on how biology itself is conceptualized on the occasion of our research.

Psychoanalysis has had to cope with the unclear division between biology and culture from its beginnings. For example, in the early studies of hysteria and neurosis, the first guess was that they had a sexual origin, but this guess proved somewhat too simple. As psychoanalysis moved from hypnosis to the conscious use of language (free association by conscious patients) as its principal technique, the patient's ability to articulate the circumstances and history of his or her illness created a new perspective on the illness (not in every point sexual) which often ameliorated it. Sometimes, however, the illness remained and even worsened. But as with other medical problems, these failures did not mean that the successes were fraudulent or ascribable to chance, but only that some people were more amenable to treatment than others. I will understand psychoanalytic treatment, therefore, as a kind (genre) of medical treatment but with language as its principal mode of functioning. The therapeutic use of language is highly localized and individuated, and thus less uniform or fixed than the therapeutic use of penicillin. Nevertheless, there is something regular, repeatable, and, perhaps, generic, about the fact that, sometimes, the right articulation of one's personal history permanently ameliorates neurotic suffering.

The generic element, I think, is the presupposition that for each person, there is a path from the biological body, through his or her psychology, to the public language used in consequence of this psychology and the person's history of social relations. In particular, biology creates the social circumstance of there being two parents for each child. In all human societies the child of these parents develops psychosocially through interacting with them and their communities. This situation "mixes" the biological (say, the genetic personality predisposition) with the psychosocial so that it is difficult to distinguish one influence from the other. The child's development of language not only is influenced by a combination of biological and local psychosocial factors, but it also is influenced by the wider culture as soon as the child enters a peer group, and probably even sooner. Yet as later influences make themselves felt, the earlier influences remain; even though as adults we feel relatively independent from our parents, we nevertheless remain "their child." For this reason, it is a plausible strategy to reflect on how the combination of the biological, psychosocial, and cultural affects the language of each person. At every stage of development, language plays a central role in stabilizing stage-specific crises. Each stage requires a certain advance or an incremental growth in language for a person to retain his or her psychosocial stability. As a result, there are grounds for expecting a person's language to reflect, to one degree or another, the biological aspects of psychosocial development. With regard to gender, we should expect that one's *sense* of one's gender (the psychological issue of gender identity) follows, in part, from the fact of biological gender; as this sense is brought more deeply into society through growing up, the person's language will be a function of both the biological fact of gender and one's sense of it.[3] The sense of one's gender names one's gender, so that if your gender is "female" you might name your gender as either "old heterosexual woman" or "young homosexual woman," for example. Gender identity might be understood as the knowledge of the congruence (the double perspective) of biological gender and the psychosocial sense of it. In this way one is self-aware with regard to gender identity. Similarly, vocational identity adds another *name*, among others, through which one constitutes (names) oneself and is constituted by others.

The foregoing considerations were suggested to me, in part, by Leo Stone's 1961 monograph, *The Psychoanalytic Situation*,[4] in which he reflects on what interpersonal role language may be playing in psychoanalysis. Stone's aim is relatively modest. He investigates the classical psychoanalytic issues of transference and countertransference to justify a more flexible and negotiable posture for the orthodox psychoanalyst. He identifies his study as "a brief critique of the principle of unmodified 'anonymity' " and presents his "conviction that some experimental relaxation of stringency in this sphere can be carried out . . . with appreciably heightened effectiveness for the psychoanalytic situation." (pp. 110–111)

Stone bases his argument on the traditional role of the physician as one who has intimate access to the patient's body. He argues that it is reasonable to understand the patient's view of this special access as an analogue to the patient's mother's similar access in childhood. Before children even get to a doctor, they have made their bodies fully available to their parents, more often the mother, for examination. When the child grows up, the doctor retains this "parental" privilege. The psychoanalytic doctor, Stone observes, changed this practice in an interesting way: the analyst declared a strict taboo on bodily contact and demanded instead the same level of intimacy on a purely verbal and emotional level. Stone's main insight is that, although this shift occurred because of the needed change from hypnosis to free association, the new conversational situation actually recalls a basic

3. The sense of one's gender does not need to correspond in some obvious way to the fact of one's gender; for example, different men have different ideas of what counts as being a "man." Similarly, in cases of homosexuality, the senses of gender are mixed, while the fact of gender is the same as it is for the heterosexual person.

4. Leo Stone, *The Psychoanalytic Situation* (New York: International Universities Press, 1961); hereafter cited in text.

event in infantile development—change in the child's conception of mother as the "mother of intimate bodily care" to the "mother of separation." Stone's proposal for psychoanalysis is that the analyst would do well to be both sorts of doctors to the patient. This means not that analysts ought to examine their patients physically, but that they ought to reduce their doctorly anonymity by becoming a more open figure—to identify themselves interpersonally, as well as continue to be thoughtful listeners. The more open analyst will appear as the generous mother to the patient whose transference neurosis, which is what the analyst actually works with, is given more room to develop. With a more easily identifiable "mother of intimate care," the patient is more able to work through the separation needed to reachieve autonomy and release the neurosis.

Consider further the role of language in this situation. The maternal role of the analyst is created by the verbal intimacy of the analytic relationship. The verbal conventions of psychoanalysis—the "literacy" customs of analytic conversation—recreate the mother-child relationship. The process of cure— the patient's separation, individuation, and resocialization—is actually a process of "language acquisition" analogous to the original acquisition of language in infancy (as reviewed in chapter 4). The patient creates a new language, so to speak, for his or her present sense of self by individuating relative to the analyst. This new language is a new name for the patient's developmental history, where this history acquires a new meaning. If neurosis is understood as the paralysis of the growth of the sense of self, the new name enables the growth to resume by cancelling, through acts of verbal initiative, the exaggerated unconscious dependency on the "mother." This initiative usually takes place in the characteristic psychoanalytic "moment of insight," in which the patient simultaneously sees the "otherness" of the (maternal) analyst as well as the separateness of him or herself. This is the same process Helen Keller went through in coming into language with Anne Sullivan. The patient likewise releases the "old" self and comes into the "new" self by acquiring a decisive, salient new language. In principle, this process is the same regardless of the genders of patient or analyst.

The analyst is, therefore, a generic symbolic mother (though he or she may assume other roles too) in all cases. In life, every person speaks the "mother tongue," which is an idiomatic reflection of the fact that the overwhelming majority of people are brought into language through the first relationship with their mothers. Just as both sexes are born of mothers, the language foundation of both sexes is maternal (historically, but not, obviously, necessarily). The highly differentiated and socially shaped styles of language we find in adulthood are, in part, responses to, and development of and from, the intimate "literacy" of the mother-infant relationship. Psychoanalysis uses not simply language for its work, but language-within-relationship, which repeats the language acquisition circumstances of infancy.

Gender consciousness appears in the developmental phase[5] (ages two to five), which follows the phase of language acquisition. The child's ability to objectify things and persons—including him or herself—through naming is also the ability to establish kinds or classes (genres), the most certain of which are the "me-world" and the "not-me-world." Put another way, the self is in one class, and "others" in another. With the beginning of bodily sexual consciousness in the middle of the third year, a new affective and psychosocial situation requires new categories and (therefore) new names. Among people, to the child, there are now two kinds (genres, genders) of others, and the child sees him or herself as a "member" of one of those categories in addition to being a separate person altogether. There are two kinds of otherness: a general kind, applying to all other people, and a sexual kind, applying to only the other sex. There are also two senses of self: someone different from all others and someone different from the others of the other sex. From an affective and biological standpoint, a new kind of stereoscopy therefore sets in which complicates the sense of self. As we know, children in their third year begin to see connections between social authority, physical power, and bodily vulnerability. In this way sexual consciousness enhances social consciousness, which, in turn, stimulates all sorts of new identity elements that become permanently associated in the child's mind with the biological status at that time. Before going further with these thoughts, I want to present a few classroom experiences to help us detect a possible change in language use that reflects the change in psychology wrought by the gender-consciousness developmental stage. My claim is that yes, provisionally, we can find features of adult language that are consistent with the appearance of gender identity in early childhood. After presenting the account of the classroom experiences, I will take up the theoretical line of reasoning again. As a secondary but nevertheless important point, I hope and expect this material to further demonstrate the psychosocial integration of language, literacy, and literature.

In a 1979 graduate seminar at Indiana University, I and seven students studied what I called "comparative literary response patterns of men and women." We had no guesses as to what would be the outcome, but we tried to create circumstances which we thought might or could show differences in the perception and handling of language and literature according to gender. We read works by Emily Bronte, Emily Dickinson, Herman Melville, and

---

5. I am using here Erik Erikson's concept of a phased life cycle found in his *Childhood and Society* (New York: Norton, 1949).

William Wordsworth, and collected, from each of us, the kind of "response statements" I first described in my *Readings and Feelings* and subsequently demonstrated in *Subjective Criticism* (chapters 7 through 10).[6] We "asked" if reading or literary perception varies according to the gender of the author as well as of the reader, and if readers' perception and language use vary as a function of literary genre—in this case, fiction and lyric poetry. After collecting five response statements from each of the four men and four women, we found a significant gender-related difference in response only with regard to literary genre. We did not see that response varied significantly with the gender of the author, and we did not find any striking differences in the respondents' local use of language—though we did not do a detailed sentence-by-sentence analysis.[7] What we eight seminar members did generally agree on was that men read prose fiction differently than women did, while both sexes read lyric poetry similarly. The salient parameter was the perception of the "voice" in the literature. Men and women both perceived a strong lyric voice in the poetry, usually seeing it as the author's voice, while in the narrative the mean perceived a strong narrative voice but the women experienced it as a "world"—without a particularly strong sense that this world was narrated into existence. Perhaps in other words, women will more likely *enter* the world of the novel, take it as something "there" for that purpose, while men are more likely to *see* the novel as a unified result of someone's action, and construe its meaning or sense in those terms.

In presenting the differences in reading, I will not first present the work of all eight seminar members, as I have in the past, but only that of four, myself included. Second, and perhaps more important, I will quote only part of each response statement. Third, I will forgo a description of the character and atmosphere of the seminar and of the attitudes brought into it by the members.

Masculine response to fiction: Mr. C

Here is the opening of Mr. C's response to *Wuthering Heights*:

> Before re-reading WH for this response statement, I read a biography of Emily
> Bronte by Winifred Gerin, and looked forward to applying that new knowledge

6. Those of you who would like a full discussion of how and why these statements are prepared as they are should look into these books. Since this is perhaps a great deal to ask, it might be more efficient to read this chapter first, and then consult my descriptions according to what challenges your own senses of plausibility and intellectual decorum.

7. In the material I present after the main citations from my graduate seminar, I will note some preliminary differences in language use according to the gender of the respondents.

of the author in the attempt to understand precisely what emotional significance each part of the narrative held for Emily herself.[8] This attempt to discover and re-enact through my own emotions the configurations of emotions that Emily probably felt in composing WH reminds me of similar attempts of mine to "fully" understand and master the viewpoints and emotional responses of real-life friends and lovers. One girl-friend of mine in particular, R, continually awed me with her ferocious energy and baffled me with her kaleidoscopic changes of mood; quite often I felt uncomfortably off-balance in her presence, particularly when she attacked deep-seated traits of mine (e.g., fear of communicating) as instances of male chauvinism, when I had had no inkling that, nor could persuade her to explain to me how, those traits were typically sexist and not mutually shared by both men and women . . . The single person in my life with whom I most strongly identified the fantasy figure-of Emily Bronte was R; both of them possess a great strength of character and high original minds. . . .

Several of my responses to WH, then, proceed, I think, from this identification of Emily Bronte with R. I was both awed and irritated by several instances of Emily's behavior as documented in the Gerin biography: her outraged refusal to speak to her sister Charlotte for weeks after Charlotte's discovery of Emily's hidden cache of poetry, her willful, perhaps even willed, death after brother Branwell's funeral, her outbursts of rude unsociability. I can remember a three-day stretch when R would not speak to me while she nursed her anger, and several times when she picked a fight in public.

While Mr. C does not concentrate on the author throughout his response, his sense of her is a point of orientation, a perspective that defines his attitude and his sense of the reading. Mr. C prepares himself for his reading of the fiction by reading a biography. This is particularly connected with Mr. C's own aspirations—at the time of the response—of becoming an author himself. He sees Bronte as being in the same *class* with himself—one who creates fictions, but still clearly a different person.

By identifying Bronte with a former girlfriend, he marks the author as a well-defined other person: in this case, one who poses a serious challenge, emotionally and intellectually, to this responsive capacities, mainly through her unpredictable outbursts of hostility. In the rest of his statement, Mr. C portrays his reading as if there is a strong force in the text, and he is reacting to *it*, reflecting on it. A characteristic statement is, "At the moment she [Catherine Earnshaw] fakes a fit in order to upset Edgar, I lose any approval I felt before for her love relationship with Heathcliff and never give that approval again throughout the rest of the novel." A similar statement

8. Mr. C, like many men, had a habit of referring to female authors by their first name. It should take no deep analysis to understand this habit as the result of the usual masculine academic social psychology.

appears about Nelly Dean: "I strongly disapprove of her continuous lying and her withholding of information which could allow the people around her to carry out their responsibilities toward family members, kin, and friends." At another point, Mr. C does blame the author directly for the kind of characters she presents: he feels "irritated with Emily Bronte for her contradictory treatment of Edgar Linton," who at one time is portrayed as a "poor soft thing" and another as the " 'captain' who does not abandon ship." Mr. C's acts of "approval" apply not only to the characters themselves, but to them as products of the author's initiative. His presupposition must be that the author presented her figures to him (for some reason) and his role as the reader is to approve or disapprove of the author's presentation.

Even though there may be a certain animus against what he perceives to be the feminine accent in Bronte, this animus is not behind Mr. C's objectification of the author, only perhaps, on the *value* he places on that objectification. His isolation of Melville as an author is just as pronounced, but the value he places on him is higher:

> Melville is one of the few authors for whom I feel a detailed affinity. . . . If you have read my other responses this semester, you will no doubt recognize the recapitulation of concerns in the fantasy portrait of Melville: the identification with old age, the concern for financial responsibility, the feeling of being an underground man, etc. . . .
>
> I am resolved to go underground, as I imagine Melville also did in his mid-thirties, from which vantage point I could scrutinize the possibility of receptiveness in others or launch an unexpected assault that would strike dismay and fear in others (identification with Babo in *Benito Cereno* and partially with Claggart in *Billy Budd*). For all these reasons, I feel a fellowship with Melville, and sympathize with his sorrows, burdens, self-irony, scorn, and suppressed rage.

It did not make so much of a difference to the strength of his objectification of the author whether he felt affinities with her or him: the strong sense of otherness is the same for Mr. C for both authors.

A student in this seminar, Ms. D, also studied Mr. C's responses, and came to the following opinion about his response to *Wuthering Heights*:

> Mr. C seems to respond more strongly to the author than to the actual novel, or to put it differently, the response to the text is only secondary as it is mainly determined by his image of what he self-consciously calls "the fantasy figure of Emily Bronte" which he arrived at from reading Winifred Gerin's biography. He responds to the novel as to something Bronte thinks and says and which he objects to. Thus he is more involved in his comprehension of Emily Bronte's personality and constantly differentiates himself from the male figures in the novel. . . .

In objectifying the author he seems to enter into a dialogue, a controversy with her which allows him to present his own point of view, to define himself in his own terms, and thus assert a strength which would have been denied to him in a close identification with the male figures.

By characterizing Mr. C's involvement with Bronte as a "dialogue," Ms. D calls attention to how the reading has been first internalized and then resocialized. Mr. C might also be said to be in dialogue with Melville, though with no comparable feeling of opposition. Mr. C emphasizes, in Ms. D's view, his self-definition, but it would be fair to say that the dialogue shows that self-definition and other-definition proceed at once. In addition, Mr. C is defining himself for the other readers of his response, as is apparent from the opening of his Melville response. One begins to see Mr. C's strong sense of boundaries in his style of perceiving literature.

Masculine response to fiction: Mr. Bleich

Here is a passage from my response to *Wuthering Heights* which was analyzed by Ms. D:

> An especially striking scene for me was when Hindley finally decides to kill Heathcliff but is prevented by Isabella who also wishes him dead. Instead of allowing the murder, she gets in the choice remark, "Heathcliff, if I were you, I'd go stretch myself over her grave and die like a faithful dog." This is more or less what he does. He did what his wife told him to do. All the dogs that appeared at the outset of the novel annoying the hapless Lockwood began to make a little more sense, and they made even more sense as I read of Emily Bronte's fond attachment to her bulldog, "Keeper." These dogs are men—wild, hungry, and incomprehensibly loyal to their master—woman. The author of the tale is a woman, as is its principal narrator, Nell, presumably an effigy of a real servant in the Brontes' home. Lockwood is an inconsequential and peripheral listener, a mere foil, a contrivance so that the female principle can have its say.

This perception of the novel is placed between a whole series of my associations with my mother and her family, which, I report, was ruled by a "tough, caustic, and money-hoarding woman"—my grandmother. These associations emerge as I notice that "there are no mothers in this tale—just motherless men and passionate women." This missing "mother," therefore, is the author, my association with whom appears in response to the "especially striking scene." From the beginning and throughout, I "know" this is a novel presenting "feminine" thoughts. When I say that Lockwood is a "contrivance," I mean that Bronte contrived him into her work. While, in reading, I identify with Heathcliff in several salient ways, particularly when he says "So much the worse for me, that I am strong," my identification with him flags when I decide that "Heathcliff is swallowed up by the female principle and fritters away his own life acting it out." I perceive, in other words, Bronte as an external figure who controls the novel by the "female principle," stimulating my own feelings about the "paradoxical character of relations between the sexes."[9] Ms. D thinks that I try to escape from these feelings when she observes:

> In this objectification of Heathcliff, Mr. Bleich defines his present [1979] perception of himself. Through the power of reason he has found a way of dealing with his dependency on women which was threatening only in its inexplicability. He has come to accept the relations between mother and son as "the strongest of all" and thinks that only in the case of a motherless man the attachment of man and wife can attain a similar strength. In respect to *Wuthering Heights*, Mr. Bleich observes that "there are no mothers because the Catherines are the mothers and Heathcliff and Hareton the sons." I infer here that he perceives the power of women as the power of mothers, as every woman is potentially a mother. In responding to the novel Mr. Bleich seems to assert the power of his reason in opposition to the female power of procreation which, though strong in its unavailability to him, is not a faculty of intellect and reason. The author Emily Bronte is thus the symbolical mother of her creation, the fiction. Her power as author is the power of the mother. Identifying with Heathcliff therefore means not only identifying with a man dominated by women in the fictional context but also [dominated] by the author, a woman. In objectifying the author, Mr. Bleich related to her as a woman telling a story whose mode and content confirm his comprehension of the typical female.

Although I think Ms. D misses elements of irony, humor, and fun in my response, as well as a kind of enjoyment I get in pitting my "reason" against the "female principle," she is right in pointing to my political sense of gender relations. I also think that my attention to the author, while different in style from Mr. C's, is more or less as great as his. My seeing her so prominently, and my incipient opposition to her—through, perhaps, sarcasm more than "intellect and reason"—is the enabling logic of my reading. This logic releases me to respond freely. In the response, my various associations with my mother and grandmother disclosed my (gender-) political perspective on the author, which Ms. D then interpreted in her own idiom as my reliance on "intellect and reason."

In my response to Melville's three stories ("Cock-a-doodle-doo," "Bartleby the Scrivener," and "Billy Budd"), my focus on the author is just as strong:

---

9. I used the term "paradoxical" in describing how men and women relate to one another when I wrote this response in 1979, but my feeling now is that how men and women get along is about as unparadoxical and unmysterious as language phenomena—following the mood of my discussions in chapters 2 and 3.

This reading was a surprise to me, since I hadn't read Melville in many years at which time I remembered only the power of the stories, rather than the power of the language. . . . I became aware that the way things were said as if I had said them after long deliberation. . . . I looked at the picture of Melville at the front of the book and was glad to find, instead of a wise, grey-haired old man, a young man with a Mona Lisa like expression telling of a faint sneer behind the thoughtful pose.

I am beginning to suspect old Melville of hating himself for the very solution of becoming a writer, for standing by and observing, for joining the multitude of those with "rational" solutions to the undertow of natural depravity served by the structures of civilization. . . .

Is the man who cannot speak also the cock who can write? Like Bartleby, Billy, and the cock, all rolled into one? Does man-the-writer hate man-the-speaker? I begin to read the narrators as men, and the objects of their attention as women. I begin to think that, whether cultural or biological, this silent element is the woman in Melville—either a real woman or a part of himself he associates with women that he considers unavailable even to himself.

Here again, my sense of the author as having a comprehensible psychology orients my responses. The figure of the author is a reassurance, a password which unlocks any inhibitions I may have in becoming an active respondent. Although my specific speculations about Melville are germane as part of my overall reading experience, they are, in view of the pattern I want to document, secondary. For both Mr. C and me, the authors were necessary frameworks for our responses and how we were to present them to the class. We needed to consider and perhaps establish the "otherness" of the author.

Feminine response to fiction: Ms. B

Ms. B does not mention the author in her response to *Wuthering Heights*. Her attention is on the heroine, Catherine, but as analogue of her own (Ms. B's) mother, who died prematurely when Ms. B was in her teens. Ms. D explains Ms. B's response as follows:

The closeness to her mother was based on her identification which in its completeness approached self-obliteration. In identifying with her mother she could never be like her mother—strong and the main protagonist—but remained a helpless, dependent child.

In her response, Ms. B does not report that she actually identifies with her mother, but only that she admired her, particularly her "magnetic" personality and her physical beauty. The response shows that Ms. B sees Catherine as she sees her mother and then she identifies with those who also long for her, like Heathcliff, and one who longs for someone else—Isabella in her longing for Heathcliff:

> Because my father had a personality similar to Linton's, mother never knew a man like Heathcliff. Yet, I gathered from my reading that Heathcliff and Catherine were so close that they possessed the same identity. Although I didn't possess Heathcliff's strength, as a child, I was at times so close to my mother that I felt an extension of her identity. It took a few years after her death before I could distinguish my own opinions and feelings from hers. Like Catherine, my mother was a forceful and enigmatic woman. . . .
>
> Isabella's infatuation for Heathcliff resembles a crush that I had on a professor of English at another college. I idolized him to the point of idiocy. Like Isabella, I was shy and greatly embarrassed around the object of my misguided affections. When I discovered to my horror that he was marrying someone else, I cried for days and bitterly cursed the bitch he had chosen. Like Isabella viewed Heathcliff, I considered that jerk a real "monster."

Ms. B's identifications are fluid or flexible. In part, she identified with Catherine through Heathcliff because of his longing for her and his "identity" with her. At the same time, Catherine is an object of infatuation not unlike the English professor, but also like her mother. It is true that Ms. B's feelings for her mother are strongly presented in the response, but they translate not into the single perception of a single character, but into the tendency to feel affinities with several figures in the novel and several relationships.

In the foregoing excerpt, we should also consider its nonjudgmental style. Her last sentence says that she considered the English professor—or was it the woman he was marrying?—a "monster." She does not render a similar judgment of Heathcliff directly but instead shows the analogy between her feelings and Isabella's. I cite this in contrast to the "approval" Mr. C gives or withholds from the characters and to the interpretations I place on the narrators in Melville. Ms. B's response articulates the analogy of feeling without interpolating a judgment of the characters as in her response to the Melville stories:

> The character of Bartleby reminds me of my friend J. She used to sit in the secretarial lounge and constantly study. Her entire life was concerned with Russian linguistics. She rarely went out drinking. . . I have tried to understand her odd personality for six years. . . .
>
> I remember that as a child on Good Friday we would attend religious services at school. The preacher would exclaim that everyone should feel a sense of guilt because of Christ's crucifixion. We, depraved beings, were responsible for his death. (We weren't relieved of our guilt until his resurrection on Sunday.) While reading "Billy Budd" I felt a sense of guilt and futility from my relationship with J. Although I could not change the events leading to Billy's

execution and Christ's crucifixion, I felt a sense of guilt and responsibility. It's stupid to feel guilty for an act that you did not commit.

Here Ms. B gives two judgments, but each is about a real person—J's "odd personality," and her own stupidity of feeling guilty under the influence of preaching. There is no judgment of Bartleby directly, and it may not be correct to infer that her judgment of J applies to Bartleby, since in another part of the response, Ms. B explains what a valuable friend and influence J had been. In the second paragraph above, Ms. B's strong judgment is against religious doctrine for influencing her to feel guilty while reading the story, and against J for giving her the occasion to experience futility. What we see in this response seems quite different from what occurred in Mr. C's and my responses. The story or the author—items outside Ms. B's life—seem not to have borne on how Ms. B felt in response to it. Ms. B remarks: "Probably because I read the novella on Good Friday and had talked to J I responded to the religious aspects." She tries to explain her response situationally: the circumstance of her reading made her see the work in a certain way.

Ms. D used the term "self-obliteration" to characterize Ms. B's response to Catherine and her (Ms. B's) mother. In writing the second paragraph above, Ms. B reports feeling "guilt and futility" reading "Billy Budd." The last sentence of the paragraph says, "It's stupid to feel guilty for an act that you did not commit." When juxtaposed to one another, I think the two sentences suggest just how Ms. B gets "in" and "out of" the story. Her entry could be described (probably too severely by Ms. D) as "self-obliteration"; her getting out is her judgment about herself that it is "stupid" to feel guilty. This style of moving in and out of the story—her reading experience— appears in both of Ms. B's responses to the fiction, and it describes Ms. B's *relationships* with her mother and J *as presented in the responses*. Ms. B's development through the responses could be seen as "her own growth through several relationships." On the other hand, the masculine readers developed their readings by working out an orientation with regard to the author, with the relationships that were mentioned perhaps appearing to *serve* the spontaneously strong sense of the author.

Feminine response to fiction: Ms. D

Reflecting on her response, Ms. D observes,

My response is concerned exclusively with Catherine's life and death; it is her fate that I responded to most and that in the selective process of writing the response I chose to negotiate with the class.

In identifying with Catherine I have to confront the ambivalence I feel about myself. I sympathize with Cathy's power, her uncontrollable temper, yet, aware of the unacceptability of her extreme behavior, I feel that "I would not like to be together with a woman like Cathy." . . . In identifying, I too become the object of disapprobation and disrespect. Though troubled by my ambivalence toward Cathy I am more disconcerted by the criticism of her person and begin to fervently "take her part."

Like Ms. B, Ms. D's attention is on Catherine in a way that calls up in her conflicting values and feelings: the problem of self-definition is the orienting factor. Also, there is no mention at all of the author. Instead, Ms. D begins her response with the following thoughts:

The first time I read *Wuthering Heights* . . . I found the book in my father's room on his desk. What made me finally want to read it was a handwritten dedication to my father by an acquaintance of my parents—the wife of a colleague of my father's about the same age as my mother—which I read with curiosity because of its personal character. It had been one of those days when I was hunting around for something to read to get completely absorbed in and many times ended up reading a detective story or the like. I still remember being kind of frustrated by the novel because none of the women were agreeable to identify with.

The keynote here is the reader's own family, in particular, the family issue raised by the fact that a woman "about the same age as my mother" gave her father a book with a personal dedication. Ms. D suggests that she was in a mood to find things out—perhaps by reading a detective story—but reading the novel did not seem to answer this mood because of the difficulty of identifying with the women. It looks as if her curiosity about the book and about her father were combined, but that neither "question" was answered by the reading experience. The uncertainty of the external circumstances of the reading was continued in the actual reading experience (in which the author played no role). Notice now in the following remarks how the earlier material seems pertinent:

Catherine kisses her father good night and discovers that he is dead. I've never witnessed a death yet and the idea of only very suddenly noticing that death of a close person is really frightening—also very repelling. The only funeral I ever attended yet was the one of my aunt last summer. I had not seen her for at least ten years; my father avoided seeing her because of a serious controversy they had concerning the inheritance from my grandmother, but that's not the reason why I didn't see her any more. She was the mother of my favorite cousin but he has so much trouble with her and his stepfather and I never felt easy at their place. As I never met her on family meetings I just stopped seeing her. I never felt close to her yet I could not hide it from the astonished eyes of my brother. I feared that he thought me ridiculous just doing what everybody else did.

The idea of an ambivalent identification with Catherine puts at least some light on the material in this paragraph. In responding to Catherine suddenly seeing her father was dead, Ms. D shifts the attention to her own father's sister whose *son* was Ms. D's favorite cousin. Instead of surprise at seeing the aunt dead, there was surprise at *her own response* to the death. Thinking back to the implications of the earlier paragraph, the nature of the ambivalent identification with Catherine seems clearer. The questions about her father which the inscriptions may have raised in her are balanced by an identification with the aunt as being close to the favorite cousin, and by the natural identification of a young woman with her mother. I suggest this relatively complex explanation only because it seems consistent with how Ms. D presents her identification with Catherine: one which reflects partial stakes in several relationships in her (Ms. D's) real life and which is not concerned with the author. It is as if the reading itself began with the family rather than with the text or author; at the beginning of the response she alludes to her school experience, but only to say that she was already out of school when she read it the first time. Her "placement" of herself, rather than her awareness of the author, is the basis of her responses to and perception of *Wuthering Heights.*

Ms. D's response to the Melville stories alludes to the author only once—in her first paragraph. However, the purpose and style of the allusion is much different from mine and Mr. C's:

> Knowing that my roommate and friend N liked Melville a lot I felt that our recent frequent fights only added to my dislike of Melville. I read "Billy Budd" about one year ago in a course I liked a lot. And it is also due to this course that I started associating Melville with one of these "major writers" forever concerned with a universal truth, with mysterious mysticism, all so much more highly valued than the "trivial" occupation of so-called minor writers with domestic and regional concerns. In his admiration for Melville N seems to be as impressed as other men by what I like to call Melville's pretentious universal significance.

In the remainder of the response, N continues to occupy Ms. D; he, more than Melville, is the topic of the paragraph. In particular, Ms. D announces that her attitude toward the stories is partially determined by sexist men's admiration for Melville. But if we go through the whole response, we would not be able to identify Ms. D's strong feelings on this issue, or not as some kind of prejudice against the stories in any case. As she reports it, first a friend and then a course—two social experiences in real life— explain her sense of the author. But this sense does not remain a rigid perspective on the reading. Rather, N's attitude, and other attitudes like his she finds in her experience, appear as part of the reading response. She returns, in other words, to the personal context of her sense of the author, rather than to that sense itself. The masculine readers rely on their sense of the author itself.

In the responses to lyric poetry, the sense of the author seems more or less similar for both men and women. Each gender saw the author as the governing intelligence of the various works. While each respondent also reacted in detail to various parts of the poems—thoughts, lines, images, and so on—at one or more points in every response the readers show a direct concern for the historical figure of the author, usually presupposing that this figure is the speaker of the poems or that the speaker is a direct "representative" of the poet. The three works by Wordsworth we read were "Resolution and Independence," "Intimations of Immortality," and "Mutability." Some poems by Dickinson were suggested, but respondents felt free to choose others and respond to them, so there was no fixed list.

Masculine response to lyric poetry: Mr. C

About the Wordsworth readings, Mr. C observes,

> In general, I am left cold by Wordsworth's idealization of childhood and boyhood in "Resolution" and "Intimations." Perhaps that is because I did not enjoy the unusual freedom Wordsworth seems to have been allowed while a boy at Hawkshead Grammar School. . . .
>
> I rarely envision the future as a less happy time of life because, like the narrator of "Intimations" I celebrate the "falling from us" and find hope in the "blank misgivings of a Creature/Moving about in worlds not realized." . . .
>
> I often tend to share Wordsworth's fear that the inevitable end of poets is "despondency and madness," poverty, solitude, pain of heart, and distress. My knowledge of biographical facts seems to bear out the idea that poverty is a major care of great artists (look at Mozart, Beethoven, Schubert, Melville, Faulkner, and company). . . . I fear that my life as an artist will involve parasitism on others as unfortunate as my parents vicarious satisfactions in the careers of their children and will confirm that status of a child to which my parents have tried to confine me all my life.

Mr. C hopes to be a writer. He takes Wordsworth's reflections on the fate of poets very seriously and translates them into terms that he thinks will likely be in his life if he follows his aspiration. In spite of the fact that he sees real differences between himself and Wordsworth—that is, his identification is not thoughtless or vain—reading the poetry seems to be for him a positive occasion of identification. Mr. C's sense of the author is therefore a very active one, even to the point of consciously appropriating the poet's life history, and is more important than his identification with the poems' speakers.

About Emily Dickinson, Mr. C writes,

> I realize that I sometimes feel like a father to Emily, although in a majority
> of the poems in our selection I usually feel the older brother's indulgence
> toward a tomboy sister (e.g., in the poem "I never told the buried gold"). In
> "I never lost as much but twice" (49), I intermittently identify with Burglar-
> Banker-Father-God, looking through my door at the endearing little urchin on
> my doorstep. Again, in the poem "My life had stood—a Loaded Gun—" (754),
> I see Emily as a young girl fantasizing that she is a boy-child who is allowed to
> accompany his father on a hunting trip, although at times she reverts to the role
> of the devoted daughter: "And when at night—Our Good day done/I guard My
> Master's Head—". There is a slightly uncomfortable feeling about identifying
> with the Master in this poem, however, because I read in the scene at night
> after the hunt the possibility that Emily is incestuously attracted to me, and that
> I am not repelled, though made uneasy, by that knowledge. . . .
>
> I admire Emily's self-objectivity in being able to notate [*sic*] a variety of
> responses to this sense of rejection and to the integrity of the Other ["A Bird
> came down the Walk" (328)].

Although "Emily" becomes a relatively clear "other" for Mr. C, his attention
to her is similar to what he pays Wordsworth. Mr. C's sense of the poetry
involves a specific image of Dickinson that is self-consciously assimilated
to the satisfaction he may derive from the reading: he imagines Dickinson
wishing to be a boy, and he imagines her "incestuous attraction" to him as
Master/Father. But the psychology of such an involvement is less pertinent to
our concern than is the fact that Mr. C considers Dickinson to be the poems'
speakers, and sees himself as the reader in personal communication with the
author, just as he did with Wordsworth.

Masculine response to lyric poetry: Mr. Bleich

Here is a sample of my response to the Wordsworth poems:

> Reading Wordsworth makes me understand why he is a source of great fasci-
> nation for people I respect.[10] I first "understood" Wordsworth when I heard
> his poetry read by his descendant, Jonathan Wordsworth, some years ago. He
> had suitable British tones, the general atmosphere of understatement, and the
> overall enactment of the term "emotion recollected in tranquility." I understood
> at that time this characteristic action of mine—to rethink a feeling over a long
> perspective on the past and to come to terms with it by providing the memory
> with just the right vocabulary.

---

10. As I have rethought my attitude toward Wordsworth since 1979, I am more suspicious
of what it means to like his poetry. But I reached this "suspicious" point by doing just what
my 1979 response admires.

Most of the rest of my response goes through a series of identifications with the various speakers, and I compare my ways of coping with their ways. My comparison is motivated by my underlying sense that I am listening to and learning from the "real" Wordsworth, just as I felt I finally understood Wordsworth when I heard his poetry through the voice of his actual descendant. The need for, and sense of, the historical figure is heightened in me by the elliptical character of the lyric language: I do not merely confront interesting language; rather the language underscores ever more sharply the person originating it.

Here is one of my comments on Dickinson:

> Emily Dickinson is one of my favorite authors of all. Her words, I have found, repeatedly express feelings I have and always seem to present new slants on things I habitually think about. She represents what I consider a quintessentially womanly intelligence, of a kind I often seek and expect but rarely find. She seems to have an extraordinary power not just to say things but to think without a trace of baloney. Her economy of expression is seductive, leaving "pregnant" "gaps" in my perception of the thought, that gives me the feeling of being thus "loaded."[11]

My sense of Dickinson, and of how her language is directed toward me, is the same as my sense of Wordsworth. The language "means" the person, so to speak; it means that "quintessentially womanly intelligence" is meaning (as in "wanting to say") the language. The gender perceptions, for both poets and both Mr. C and myself, are subordinate to the perception we have in common—the otherness of the poets who are speaking to us. Since I identify with both poets, I infer that their gender is not a serious factor in my perception of their otherness. Ultimately, the effect of my response to Dickinson is that I assimilate her language—I cite it in conversations and in classrooms as something brought into my own language: I make her language my own. While I will return to this in the theoretical commentary at the end of the chapter, the point now is that the *poet's* language and not the language-by-itself is the main object of my attention.

Feminine response to lyric poetry: Ms. B

About halfway through her response to Wordsworth, Ms. B offers the following:

> Lionel Trilling's article "The Immortality Ode" considers the lines "Whither is fled the visionary dream?/Where is it now, the glory and the dream?" Trilling

---

11. The preoccupation Ms. D discerned in my reading that semester is borne out by this response, which also suggests my idealization of motherhood.

discusses Wordsworth's fear of his decline as a poet. His article helps me to apply other meanings. I remember when I belonged to a poetry group in my home town. We went around town reading our poetry. I remember thinking that I was the next great female poet, but when I came to Bloomington I began losing that "visionary gleam." Classes began to consume all my time and I began to suffer from writer's paranoia. Other poets past and present were better and their poetic vision greater. My fears caused me to lose that creative motivation. Now, for me to write a line of verse is almost impossible.

Although Ms. B's thoughts are put somewhat less directly than Mr. C's or mine, this passage shows that Ms. B also "sees" the poet in the poetry. Ms. B does say that she understands the lines in terms of Wordsworth's fear of his declining talent (I assume this because she does not dispute Trilling, but seems to see him as an explicator of the poetry). Her description of her "decline" as a poet in Bloomington presupposes an identification with Wordsworth: "I began losing that 'visionary gleam.' " While this is not a deep or complex identification, it is enough to show that her perception of the poetry is related to her imaginary perception of the poet, just as Mr. C and I had such an imaginary perception.

Ms. B also sees the poet in Dickinson, but her response is more complex in this case:

"this world is not conclusion/A sequel stands beyond/Invisible, as music . . . ." I can envision many of my Lutheran teachers or ministers saying these words. It reminds me of all the optimistic garbage I was told to believe in. The words "positive as sound" greatly irritate me, because I could never be positive about the next world. I was and still am naturally skeptical about everything, including religion. Perhaps I am one of those puzzled "scholars" Dickinson refers to.

Poem 448: "This was a poet—it is that/Distills amazing sense/From ordinary meanings." I remember two poetry readings I attended at IU. Two years ago I listened to Borges give a public reading of his poetry and last year I attended a reading given by a Russian poet. In both instances they read their poetry in their native language and then a local academic translated. I was usually disappointed when the individual poem was translated, because the academic lacked the fervor and insight of the poet. . . . The Russian poet was always greatly applauded, while the academic was given mild appreciation by the audience. I become bored by the academic.

Although Ms. B does not discuss Dickinson directly, the associations of teachers, ministers, reading poets, and academics are all impersonal, and Ms. B cites them as analogues to Dickinson as the speaking poet. In the first paragraph above, Ms. B sees the poet as an inauthentic speaker, but in the second, the poet acquires authenticity in contrast to the boring, self-deluded academic. Ms. B did not, in this response, think directly of the historical figure of Dickinson, yet she cites, in several instances, the situation of being spoken to privately in a public place, a circumstance not much different from reading lyric poetry in a published volume for one's own private edification, where the identity of the speaker matters a great deal and establishes, in the reader, a private authority.

Feminine response to lyric poetry: Ms. D

At the beginning of her response to Wordsworth, Ms. D remarks that his poetry "reminds me of my first semester in English" in college. The course was given in an old building where "the professors seemed old and the poets dealt within a lecture course on Romantic poetry seemed to be as old and dusty as the instructors." These remarks reveal a feeling of "distance from Wordsworth" that appears in the rest of the response. At the end of the response Ms. D observes,

> At this point I feel it would have been good to know something more about Wordsworth, some biographical information in order to get close to him as a person and to create a picture of him with which I could establish some kind of contact.
>
> In "Intimation of Immortality" I imagined the speaker to be a child; or, to put it another way, I could "understand" the childhood he looked back upon because I partly identified it with my brother's. In both other poems I lacked this contact, especially in "Mutability." The opening lines remind me of a physics laboratory: scales and numbers, dissolutions and chemical processes. The words of the poem only seem to disguise pure theory and the voice remains unsubstantial and impersonal to me.

If Ms. D felt that biographical information might reduce her sense of distance from Wordsworth, why did she not feel a similar need for Bronte and Melville, from each of whose works, her responses show, she felt some distance? Even though she felt an antagonism toward Melville (by name), biography was not brought up as a possible help. With Wordsworth, she is influenced by a pre-reading atmosphere (as she was with Bronte), which might be helped by some sort of "contact" with him "as a person." As I will discuss later in this chapter, I think the difference lies in how she approaches each genre—including how she (or any other reader) thinks the genre "should" be read—and not with the values she thinks each writer represents. Probably, lyric poetry has come to represent something more "personal" that is not given by narrative fiction.

Ms. D's response to Emily Dickinson also bears comparison to her response to Melville. Near the beginning of the Dickinson response, she observes,

Dickinson's name had been familiar to me for quite a while, but I had never read her poetry. About half a year ago a student mentioned her to me saying that she was crazy and hypersensitive and told me the story about her sitting in a separate room when visitors came and conversing with them through the scarcely opened door. The small book of her poetry I borrowed from the library . . . was edited by Ted Hughes, the husband of Sylvia Plath, which added another particle to an evolving picture—Emily Dickinson as one of those women always on the verge of suicide. Cody's biography (first chapter) only completed an image I had thought of already before; a depressed and egocentric woman hard to understand and to love.

As in the Melville response, Ms. D reports that her familiarity with Dickinson is helped along by the opinions of a friend, though the friend's own values do not seem to have been influential. More important is the "evolving picture" of Dickinson, helped along by a formal biography.

Toward the middle of her response, Ms. D writes,

Emily Dickinson's secluded life in the house of her family, her anxiety to meet people, this all seems like a nightmare which I have left behind; it reminds me of thoughts and anxieties I had when I was sixteen years old—the fear of never being able and never wanting to grow up and getting away from my parents.

Ms. D sees the poems in terms of themes she attributes to the poet herself, rather than to the body of the works or even to the works that she, Ms. D, read. Responding to poem 285 ("Because I see—New Englandly") Ms. D writes, "She conceives of herself as a product of the landscape of her birth, of its nature and climate. I feel the same about me, at least, I'm inclined to sentimentalize a part of my home city, a suburb where I spent my first four years." No comparable level of involvement with the authors appears in her responses to the fiction.

Although the foregoing eight responses do not amount to conclusive proof of my claims, it is unlikely that the pattern we found is accidental. To pursue the matter further, I would like to inspect the issue of response to narrative—the genre where gender differences in reading did seem to appear—from another perspective: how a narrative is retold by men and women. In the following material, we will be able to discern a difference in *retelling style* which, by itself, could correspond to the difference between the genders' language use in general. In addition, however, the retellings suggest gender differences in the perception of the text, the different senses of what is "in" the text, and the different senses of literality and interpretation.

The retold story is "Barn Burning" by William Faulkner. In 1981, from a class of 120 first-year students at Indiana University, I picked at random 100 retellings—fifty by men, fifty by women—for use in this inquiry. The exact instructions were: "Retell, as fully and as accurately as you can, Faulkner's 'Barn Burning.' " The essays were written in about thirty minutes in a large lecture hall and ranged in length from 200 to 600 words. The purpose of this exercise was to study, in class, individual reading differences; and the instructors (I and four assistants) treated the essays with this purpose in mind. However, students also knew that gender differences were part of our class's general interest, and some instructors raised that issue with their students in discussion sections after the essays were written. However, the finding that I will discuss now was not apparent to me until after the whole course was over and I had studied all of the essays again. As with the previous set of responses, I will only cite pertinent passages rather than complete essays.

Generally, the men retold the story as if the purpose was to deliver a clear, simple structure or chain of information: these are the main characters; this is the main action; this is how it turned out.[12] Details were included by many men, but usually as contributions toward this primary informational end— getting the "facts" of the story straight. The women tended to present the narrative more often by including judgments on its atmosphere or experiential effect. They seemed more ready to draw inferences without as strict a regard for the literal text, but with more regard (than the men) for the affective sense of the human relationships in the story.

Here are the first paragraphs of retellings by two men; the second is my own:

> The story begins as the boy and his father are in the courthouse of a small town where the father has been thrown out of town for allegedly burning down his boss's barn. The motive he had for burning the barn was that he and his boss had a disagreement over how much he owed him for the corn his pig had eaten while he roamed around unpenned. The family left town as they had so many times before. (Mr. J)

> Sarty was in a courtroom when his father Abner was accused of burning a barn. Abner, it was testified, had sent his black servant[13] to tell that the barn was

12. Recall James Baumann's "experiment" described in Chapter 1, this time with attention to thoughts like "main idea comprehension." It could be "socially masculine" merely to presuppose that any paragraph, or any text for that matter, "has" a "main idea."

13. My euphemism here has an interesting sidelight: The story did say "nigger," but my peremptory inhibition from writing this in my class changed it to "black servant." I am certain that today, only six years later, I would write "nigger" in the service of my "masculine" standard of "literal" accuracy—a term, by the way, which was in my "masculine" instruction to the class! At the time I wrote this retelling, I was still overly responsive, socially, to the unacceptability of "nigger," and I could not see upholding the standard I now claim is right: to retell the story "accurately."

flammable, and this testimony made it seem that Abner was guilty. Sarty, who seemed to know that Abner was guilty, did not testify against his father and so it was not proven that Abner burned the barn. The judge, however, told Abner to get out of town, which he did. (Mr. B)

I cite these together because, in spite of the fact that I was about twice Mr. J's age at the time, the narrative tone of the paragraphs seems similar. The detail of the pig enters for Mr. J as the dispute which brought them to court, while my detail of the "black servant" enters to explain why Abner was accused. I call these items "details" not because they are unimportant in any way but because other readers omitted them without seeming to distort the story. In both of the above cases, detail was used to explain rather than to characterize or to give a judgment. Neither of us introduced at this time the issue of loyalty or "blood" which was also a part of the story's first paragraph. Here now is the beginning of a retelling by Ms. S:

"Barn Burning" by William Faulkner was a story about a family, two daughters, two sons, a mother, a father, and an aunt. The story was based during the time when plantation owners owned farmers to work on their land. The father was a poor man and was obsessed with burning barns when he disliked the plantation owner. Burning barns was the only way the father could show retaliation. (Ms. S)

In this paragraph, there are several tendencies I found more frequently in the women's retellings than in the men's. Ms. S sees the story as something that happened to a family, not just to the "main character." At least seventeen of the fifty women took a sentence to enumerate all the family members, while only three or four of the fifty men did. When men alluded to the family, it was usually of the form: "Abner took his family to another place," or in one case, "The story begins with Abner, the father and head of the family, . . . " Mr. J's paragraph above shows something like this: "The family left town as they had so many times before." My opening paragraph says nothing about the family. Ms. S's second sentence was something not many readers alluded to altogether—the sociohistorical circumstances of the story—but there were perhaps six women and one or two men who did this.[14] For Ms. S, these circumstances are part of the story. Also for more women than men, Snopes' poverty was included in the retellings. In this connection, Ms. S gives an interpolated judgment: because the family was poor, Abner developed an obsession as his way of "showing retaliation." This issue is not named

---

14. I have found it to be a general cultural "rule" not to refer to issues of rich and poor in America: students just will not discuss the problem of how wealth is distributed. However, the few who are willing to are almost always women, even if there are men who, privately, are concerned or worried about this problem.

as such in the story, but it nevertheless seems reasonable to include it in a retelling (thus raising the issue of how men and women understand the meaning and purpose of "retelling" to begin with). However, I also made such inferences but did not think of them, in the retelling, as part of the story.

The distribution of comments about Abner's mental health and moral intention is significant. Only two of the fifty men seem to mention them. One said that Abner had "poor character," while another said he had "no sense and fewer patience." Similarly, the idea of revenge was virtually unmentioned among the men, although some did say he was "angry" or "defiant." At least eight women, however, wrote that Abner was "mentally unstable," or showed "a lot of emotional problems"; the women gave these judgments as part of their presentation of his behavior: "The father was crazy or had some kind of mental problem. He never told the family exactly where they were going." The latter sentence is a "fact" in the story; the first is this reader's explanation of the fact; but it also looks as if this reader sees the craziness of the father as the "main" fact, and his behavior as the evidence for it. By and large, the women who mentioned mental problems said they were the cause of Abner's desire for revenge:

> The story, "Barn Burning," dealt mainly with one man's struggles with society and the effect it has on his son and their relationship. The father is an outcast, which is established fairly clearly at the beginning. He has a disposition that possibly is mentally unstable and consists of revenge in the form of burning down the property of other people. (Ms. C)

As did Ms. S before, Ms. C brings in the idea of "society" and the "fact" that Abner is an "outcast." Also, it was more characteristic of the women to mention the relationship between father and son—as opposed to discussing each one individually.

Whatever negative comments the men had about Abner, they were not associated with his habit of taking vengeance, while the women related the vengeance to a psychological obsession (as well as being poor). We might pause here to reflect on whether we would, in our culture, understand the idea of vengeance as more masculine than feminine. We see plenty of "Mafia" stories, Westerns, police dramas, and vigilante movies, and the barely concealed ethic of vengeance among "tough" men is an acknowledged folk value. We might guess that on these cultural grounds men would "see" the vengeance in this story more often than women did. Yet, just the opposite happened. I don't believe enough men are embarrassed enough about this ethic to want to censor it in their work. I think, rather, that the men are *being more literal* in their renditions of the story; the story does not announce that

Abner is seeking vengeance. One must infer it from the narration of events. Because the women feel freer to include their inferences—both about the vengeance and about Abner's mental health—such inferences appear more often in their renditions of the story. Even though cultural values are definitely at work in the reading of both men and women, I think this is an instance where an underlying psychological tendency (but perhaps also culturally or ideologically determined) to render language in a certain way overrides the effect of apparent cultural values in the retellings.

A related case came up when I asked various groups to retell Hemingway's story "Hills Like White Elephants," which refers to an "operation" several times. Even though all readers were old and experienced enough to know about abortions, women regularly "see" an abortion much more quickly and with more certainty than men do. It is true, of course, that culturally, women are "closer" to thoughts of abortion than men are (and, they are biologically closer to the possibility of it). At the same time, men are frequently involved in conversations such as the one in the story and at least know about abortions from the standpoint of their own self-interest. Although it may be true in some cases, it would be hard to argue that in general men know less about abortion than women. (I remember one instance of an educated man over thirty identifying the "operation" as a prospective robbery being planned by the couple.) I think, therefore, that because the *word* "abortion" does not appear in the story, men tend not to want to insert it. They are cautious about "accuracy" and inhibited about saying things (that is, making public their thoughts) that may not be literally documented. It may also be the case that the masculine author of the story did not use the word "abortion" for self-protective reasons, thinking that for reasons of "verisimilitude" one would not use it—that is, one can give an aesthetic reason instead of a psychosocial reason for not using it. Since masculine readers of today may well share the values of the author, they *combine* the cultural value of not seeing the abortion with the language/reading tendency toward "accuracy" and tend to defer a decision on just what the "operation" is.

Because of their greater fluency of inference, women tended to "see" feelings in the "Barn Burning" story more quickly than the men did. In their retellings, both men and women gave most of their attention to Sarty, but we can discern differences in the *kinds* of attention each gender gave to him. As we recall, the story's opening introduces Sarty through his response to the cheese smell in the courtroom:

> The store in which the Justice of the Peace's court was sitting smelled of cheese. The boy, crouched on his nail keg at the back of the crowded room, knew he smelled cheese, and more: from where he sat he could see the ranked shelves

close-packed with the solid, squat dynamic shapes of tin cans whose labels his stomach read, but not from the lettering which meant nothing to his mind but from the scarlet devils and silver curve of fish—this, the cheese which he knew he smelled and the hermetic meat which his intestines believed he smelled coming in intermittent gusts momentary and brief between the other constant one, the smell and sense just a little of fear because mostly despair and grief, the old fierce pull of blood.

Here are three renditions of this opening:

The "Barn Burning" starts out in a courtroom that at one time by my guess, was a store or something. It smelled of cheese and meat to the boy whose father was on trial for allegedly burning down someone's barn. (Mr. B)

As the boy stood there watching, at a distance, his nose began to pick up the scent of cheese and fish. (Mr. D)

In the beginning there is a general store filled with people and a trial is going on. The author[15] focuses on the little boy. The boy's father is on trial for burning a man's barn down. The boy must be hungry because the smell of cheese and some kind of fish are capturing his attention. (Ms. A)

The "facts" for Mr. B are that the boy who was awaiting the trial smelled cheese; for Mr. D they are that the boy's "nose" began to pick up the smell. This latter is a plausible change since the text says that the boy's stomach and intestines sense the smells of cheese. But both of these contrast to Ms. A's observation that, first, the store was "filled with people" and that "the boy must be hungry" because the smells are "capturing his attention." Ms. A both alludes to the social scene while aiming to portray what is in Sarty's mind (rather than in his nose). Also, if we contrast Ms. A's "capturing his attention" with Mr. B's "smelled of cheese," we see that Mr. B repeats the words of the text, but Ms. A is *inferring* that the "boy must be hungry." Ms. A was the only one of the hundred respondents to draw this inference. I think she sees the language as already *aiming* to create (in the reader) the sense of Sarty's feelings and motives. To understand the language to begin with *means*, for Ms. A, to draw such inferences about feelings and motives from the metaphors in the original text. For the men, however, to understand the language *means* to repeat the "facts" and to avoid drawing "extra" inferences. Mr. B can only "guess" that "at one time" the courtroom was a store. Not only was Mr. B needlessly cautious in his own desire for accuracy, but he

15. A feminine allusion to the author is neither uncommon nor inconsistent with the claims I made earlier in this chapter. This particular instance is a good example, since the way Ms. A uses the author is as the agent bringing forth the world that she can enter, and not as the intelligence that is controlling her responses. To Ms. A, the author is subordinate or incidental to the "world" in which she is involved—he is a kind of delivery boy.

made the "fact" of there having been a court actually in a store (the second word of the story) into a guess. Ms. A's guess about the boy's being hungry seems completely likely and reasonable, perhaps even obvious.

In general, the women's retellings showed a greater willingness to reconstruct the boy's emotional condition. One woman wrote that Sarty was "fearfully awaiting to hear of his father's outcome." Another said that the boy was sitting in "quiet fear," and a third said that the "boy was glad" to learn he wouldn't have to speak in court. These seem to be fair renditions of the text's "just a little of fear" that Sarty "sensed," but the men do not render this affective circumstance at all. The following contrast is also pertinent. One woman describes Sarty as "thinking to himself that he had to lie about what his father had done." A man reporting the same idea wrote of Sarty's "uncertainty of whether to tell the truth or lie." Compare "thinking to himself," a private action, with "uncertainty," a fixed state; compare "whether to tell the truth or to lie"—the need to calculate a choice—with "he had to lie"—a feeling of being out of control. The woman describes an active subject feeling coerced; the man describes a person reflecting on which action to take. Although many men probably did feel fear, force, and pain in response to the story, such feelings stay out of the retellings, and this is just as true of my retellings, my years of experience in reading and responding notwithstanding.

Here is another pair of descriptions of Sarty which both use the word "torn" to name his situation. The man writes that the story is "about a small boy torn between lying and telling the truth." The woman writes, "A young boy is torn between what he knows is right and his ties with his father." The man's description (using the adjective "small") centers entirely on the boy and presents the problem as between two abstract courses of action, lying and telling the truth. The woman's description (using the adjective "young") emphasizes the active subject—"what he knows is right"—as well as the demands of the relationship with the father—"his ties with his father." I claim that because the men are more psychologically distant from the reading, abstractions emerge in their retellings more readily; the women, because they enter the human situations of the story more readily, retell it more in terms of motives, allegiances, and conflicts, and less in terms of the perspective of a single character or of the author.

Elizabeth Flynn has suggested, from her observations,[16] that men are generally more frustrated by the failure to understand the reading than are women. This tendency emerged in the present inquiry also. I attribute it to the condition that the need for complete literal comprehension is an essential

16. Elizabeth Flynn, "Gender and Reading," in *Gender and Reading*, ed. Elizabeth Glynn and Patrocinio Schweickart (Baltimore: Johns Hopkins University Press, 1986), pp. 267–88.

part of the distancing impulse: one cannot risk involvement without the security of topical mastery.[17] Because women are generally more willing to risk involvement, complete comprehension is not as urgent in their response; they will construe a general affective logic for the fiction even if they are not quite sure of what is "going on." In my samples, men will more often interrupt their retellings by saying that the story was "written in a confusing way" or that it had "many ambiguous parts to it." Only one woman wrote that the story was "somewhat confusing," and this was because "it was not totally clear in where exactly it took place." (The classroom situation is also a factor in how many risks the students are willing to take, an issue I will discuss in the next chapters.) One woman expressed no doubt at all in reporting that the story is about "a Negro and his family who are constantly moving from one place to another." This error may have been due to another judgment she also made, that "the father, presumably out of hatred for whites, has an obsession for burning their barns." It made so much sense to her that Abner's violence was racially motivated that she thought nothing more of it. Her strong preconceptions of the political situation in the South (as well as, possibly, an inflexible stereotype) created the affective logic that overrode details of her reading that may not have borne out *her sense of what would* lead someone to burn barns. To her, the only underdog in the South is the black, and she would have to be explicitly told that there are other underprivileged groups in that society. The men, rather than take the risks that this woman did (she acknowledges her risk with the word "presumably"), would sooner announce that they just don't know or can't tell, thereby keeping a safe distance.

When I review some of the received aesthetic theories in this light— Wordsworth's "emotion recollected in tranquillity" (a standard I cited in my own response to Wordsworth), the nineteenth-century concept of the "aesthetic emotion," or Bullough's handy idea of "aesthetic distance"—they seem to me to be culturally masculine ways in which men have related to works of art. We need not cancel these viewpoints forthwith nor reject the possibility of their existing in women's minds on occasion. However, the fact that these theories and perspectives are always offered as universal views—must all aesthetic readings "have" psychical distance, for example?—prevents us from recognizing how thoroughly masculine values and psychologies have created "objective" standards of literacy and language use. It may well *enhance* the importance of traditional theories to reunderstand them as interest-bound, especially when such interests are gender-related.

17. Another instance of this masculine tendency is found in chapter 7, in my discussion of Mr. R and Ms. J.

The foregoing thoughts support the general argument raised in the first four chapters that kinds (or genres) of writing—or categories of language use—have been created in part by genderized cultural values. Before reflecting on how cultural values may combine with biological influences, let me pick up the theoretical thread I suspended on page 127 by considering how the responses I have discussed may point to biologically related differences in language perception and use. The important finding that requires explanation is the uniformity among men and women in feeling the strong voice in lyric poetry, and the gender difference in their perception of the narrative voice.

The lyric trope is self-reflexive—"I sing of myself, I speak of my experience." It enacts the psychological schemata of self-objectification. The poet/speaker's self-objectification leads the reader through the same action, and the reader's action is at once figurative and real. In this trope, the act of reading entails recreating the original schemata of language acquisition, in which the child became capable of objectifying both self and the undifferentiated-with-respect-to-gender other. Men and women, as a result, read lyric poetry similarly, that is, with the same strong awareness of the poet/speaker. Self-other objectification occurs without respect to gender awareness and is the psychological achievement that makes language possible in both sexes, as each comes into language in relation to the same figure, the (m)other. The self-reflexive *convention* of lyric poetry—a cultural phenomenon that is, in different historical periods, not as self-emphasizing as in nineteenth-century poetry—*combines* with the established psychology of language acquisition and use in both sexes.

Lyric language can be understood as autonomous, expressive, and/or presocial speech. It is meant less to be spoken to someone than spoken *in the presence of* someone. It is most fully and most originally a speech act—speech which is important as much because it was performed as because of what it says. This is very similar to an infant's speech, whose development is encouraged by the parents' enthusiasm at its sheer performance. The infantile exercise of self-reflexivity is a cause for celebration, since it is taken by both mother and child to be a shared accomplishment, a common cause. Take Dickinson's line, "I heard a fly buzz when I died." This is a performance to be registered rather than a communication from which information is to be extracted. Its self-reflexivity is not narcissistic but *invitational*, just as the mother's use of language is always also an invitation for the child to "use language" and not just "say what I say." Although the child in some sense does imitate the mother (even if only in offering a vocalization), he or she eventually uses language by answering, responding, or reacting. In Dickinson's line, the false phrase "I died" calls attention to the pure performance of the speech. But the autonomy of such speech is meant to be shared as mother and infant share language. Each performance is an invitation to the other, and this gestural exchange creates the groundwork for all subsequent use of language in dialogue situations. That this psychology is common to boys and girls renders the fact that both men and women focus on the voice of the poet/speaker in lyric poetry plausible.

The adult reader of lyric poetry is not unlike the adult patient in psychoanalysis as described by Leo Stone. Regardless of gender, the analyst is a psychological (or generic) mother to the patient, who becomes verbally infantile by being verbally intimate. In salutary cases, the patient will "separate" from the mother-analyst and "individuate"—become a newly enfranchised person. The readers of lyric poetry, by noticing or *naming* the author in their response, by expressing concern and wanting to know more about this person, are, in the process, "separating" themselves from this voice, thus changing an identity with the author into an *identification* with him or her. Readers of either gender try to objectify the voice in conventional ways—by seeing its historical separateness, by inquiring after biographical information, and by conceptualizing the figure as a comprehensible person. This is, of course, not a clinical process but a natural one (it is not unlike the popular wish to know details of the private lives of public personalities). Readers spontaneously focus on the poet's voice and catch the singleness of its source in the way we started making original voice meaningful—by including them as part of our first ideas of an objective person. For the readers we studied, the characteristic form of objectification is biography, history, and so on, and by objectifying both the poet and ourselves in this way, we socialize the reading experience—present it in shareable ways, present the reading experience as *named* by naming our sense of the poet. The response-statement process permits a socially usable materialization of the "mental" reading events and, however provisionally, converts our thoughts into social legal tender by fixing them into a text that provides new grounds for collective growth.

The narrative voice, like the lyric voice, is still the voice of the generic mother (tongue), but instead of the characteristic trope being "I speak of myself," it is "I speak of this other item, this object, this 'third' person." The narrative voice brings a third item or party into the reading "conversation," then he, she, or they, and invites the reader *both* to identify *and* to contemplate the third parties. If we think of the first and second persons as mother and child, the third person would be the generic father—which actually means the other person who represents gender difference. Affectively, a child becomes a third person when he or she makes the gender distinction among people and sees his or her own implication in this distinction. Because gender identity is achieved relative to *two* different people, we would expect that the path toward this achievement is different for each gender. This difference in path is reflected by the different ways each gender perceives the narrative trope.

When little girls identify with their mothers (with regard to gender) they will have the greater tendency to *sense that* "my language is mother's language," or that "mother and I, because we are the same sex, speak the 'same' language." The little boy, seeing his similarity with father with respect to gender, will have the greater tendency to *sense that* "my language is other than mother's language" (even though it may actually be quite similar in many respects). The little boy has psychological grounds for seeing an otherness in the mother's language that is more radical than what the little girl sees. Because the narrator's voice remains the "mother tongue," and because this voice now invokes a "third person," the narrative action thus enacts the childhood action of gender identification. (I am *not* claiming that the child first learns to use the third person at this stage, but rather that he or she first grasps these sociogrammatical categories in a gender-affective way.) For the little boy, the speaker herself becomes an other in a way she was not, to him, in the language acquisition stage. Put another way, not only does the narrative point outward, to something or someone else, but the "narrator" herself is someone else in a different sense. For the boy, both the content of the narrative and the source of the narrative are other.

For little girls, this is obviously not the case. In an important way, the narrator herself remains the "same" figure she was in the language acquisition stage—just an other, but now somewhat *less* of an other by virtue of her being the same gender as the little girl. As we discussed in chapter 2, otherness in general for the little girl becomes less marked than it does for the little boy. This condition of "less otherness" explains why the women perceived the narratives as they did. The women, in a sense, automatically "blended in" with the narrators (thinking of them as "the speakers of the mother tongue") and/or they automatically blended in with the authors. The women "become" the tellers of tales they are reading, and they therefore tend not to notice or demand to notice the author. When the women enter the "world" of the tale it too loses its distinct otherness. The women tend to identify with more than one figure in the narrative, to have partial identifications, often with whole families or other groups, to identify with feelings and situations, and to experience the reading as a variety of emotions. Both the teller and the tale are not radically other for the women.

The men, however, draw boundaries much more decisively. For them to "see" the author is as spontaneous as it is for the women not to see the author. Being aware that an author is behind a narrative seems, for the men, to be a gender-specific form of orienting oneself toward the narrative.

Regardless of the author's gender, the status of being "behind" the narrative activates the men's sense of a referential use of the mother tongue as "other." Similarly, the tale itself is more other for the men. The novels were more self-consciously *appropriated* by the men than by the women who tended to "enter" the tales. Also, to retell a story, one must recreate "it" as it "is." The women seemed more ready to retell it as it was *experienced*, which would account for their greater fluency in interpolating their judgments into their retellings. The men were more prone to judge the individual characters while identifying with only one or two. The women were less likely to offer judgments of individual figures and more likely to describe differential allegiances to various figures and situations.

While I have suggested that developmental events going back to infantile life may in part account for these differences in the perception and use of language and literature, that does not demonstrate conclusively that biological differences are at work. However, the accounts of Dinnerstein, Chodorow, and Gilligan of psychological gender differences showed considerable respect for the instinctive, and therefore biological, status of mothering in women, for its strength and continuing social value, and for the historically repeated underestimation of its importance. But there is, of course, one unchangeable fact that links mothering with women—that women bear and nurse children. Women who take their bodies seriously (that is, who are alert to how bodies work) pay attention to these potentialities, whether or not they intend to use them. Most women that I have known who have carried children have paid intense attention to the pregnancy, to the living thing inside; many of these women have anticipated this experience since becoming aware of what a girl can do when they were two and three years old. Women's involvement with the child inside them is undeniably less boundary-defined in some sense than the involvement of the father with the child-to-be. If the "other" were ever actually "inside" men's bodies, I'm sure we could tell the difference between that experience and the more distant one we now have. Biologically, therefore, the physical closeness of women to children is the ground for entertaining, at least, a generically different sense of self in women, a sense that is likely to treat boundaries as less permanent or less rigid, a sense of pairs and groups of people as units rather than just a collection of individuals. If anything is implied by the "double perspective," it is that the single perspective which we all feel is functional in the experience of daily life, must be made up of two or more other perspectives—in this case, cultural and biological or feminine and masculine—and that no one perspective is finally or absolutely authoritative.

Earlier, I tried to explain how men tended not to see an abortion being discussed in Hemingway's story. I suggested that a combination of cultural and biopsychosocial values might explain this phenomenon. The cultural value might be men's tendency not to recognize what is of major importance to women, and the biopsychosocial value would be men's tendency not to violate the verbal "boundary" of the text, i.e., "if it doesn't literally say so, one can't assume it's there." This combination of values (along with others, no doubt) might also explain Hemingway's usage—or lack thereof—in the story. The combination would explain both language use and literature, reading and writing. If language itself is not considered essentially just one thing—just referential or just metaphorical—but the simultaneous presentation of several perspectives or potentialities, it is plausible to suppose that an explanation of language in language must need a similarly multiple perspective.

I had described the double perspective as doubly double—intrapsychically and intersubjectively double, and suggested that these two "doubles" are themselves combined in experience, thus giving conscious life its characteristic feelings of depth or dimension. Carrying over this style of explanation to gender differences, it becomes less of a riddle once we acknowledge the simultaneous presence of biology, psychology, society, and culture as features in our explanation. To use language in a certain way contributes to one's sense of biosexual well-being—that is, to one's sense of gender-specific social roles—and to one's sense of being just a person who counts in society—a citizen. Since we are already functioning with multiple interests and perspectives (economic, ethnic, geographic, religious), why would not a language act, which has traditionally been held to be separable from all of these interests, in fact serve them all, using any of the aforementioned perspectives on any one occasion? The occasion we studied—reading and writing about literature in a mixed gender classroom—comprised many perspectives, and it would be surprising if we did not come up with such a multiple explanation of it.

The literary material, as I implied at the end of chapter 4, and as I discuss in subsequent chapters, provides a psychosocial scope not usually found in inquiries into the problems of language. Literature is a repository of language tropes and genres that have accumulated in the history of culture. They are all "traces" of human initiatives in the past and starting points for present and future ones. Our interest in literacy has led us to claim that these initiatives have never come from one person or one kind of person, that all new language has already been used, that no language is free of other languages, and that no kind of writing does not use other kinds of writing. These genders, genres, kinds, names, and classes all materialize in the classroom.

6

Reauthorizing Classroom Membership

The Tiger is the weekly student newspaper of Clemson University. In its December 1, 1983, issue there was a brief story with the headline "Plus/Minus Grading Ratified by Senate," telling how the faculty senate had added seven new grades to the system. The senate president said that the "vote was so strongly in favor of the proposal that no one called for an actual count." The professor who introduced the proposal said that "it offers the teacher more flexibility in assigning grades, as well as more accuracy" and that "it would give the students more incentive to work for grades in one of the new categories."

At Indiana University, where I worked, there is an agency called the "Bureau of Evaluative Studies and Testing," which is known by its acronym, BEST. It recently issued a pamphlet entitled "How to Write Better Tests," which names no author or group of authors. Among other things, it says, "The research on essay tests, especially their scoring, must give pause to the serious scholar who is rethinking his/her testing procedures," and it then goes on to explain why multiple choice and true/false tests are much better. On the one hand, these developments are not very important. Plus/minus grading has been going on for generations, but there was some relaxation in the 1960s, which, in the 1980s, is being cancelled along with other accomplishments of the politically active student movement. Testing has also gone on for generations, and all those who have given tests know very well that it is more difficult to score an essay test than a multiple choice or true/false test, which now can be graded by machines. Thus, in a system that has already used grading and testing for so long, such returns to the past are relatively unimportant.

On the other hand, they do suggest something quite important. By and large, such initiatives are the only ones that university faculties and administrations are now taking under the heading of "improving teaching." Because of the political climate in this country right now, attention to teaching means reaction against the broadening of its styles and accents which took place in the sixties. In the present atmosphere, the professor rightly claims that more available grades increase the teacher's flexibility in grading. As for testing, the authors of the pamphlet rightly claim that the teacher will have an easier time grading digital examinations. The "new" refinements, therefore, are supposed to make life easier for the faculty and administration, while at the same time making the system more manageable for the students. With these initiatives, however, the faculty and the administration are acknowledging something that students have known throughout their school careers, but which teachers always deny when confronted with it: *the governing action of all classrooms and of the university degree programs in general is the assigning of grades to the students by the faculty; testing makes grading easier.* It is grading that permits the academy to keep an authoritarian policy toward the classroom, a policy that inhibits imaginative social initiatives for the class as a whole as well as risk-taking by individual students. Although students often complain about grading, they have no choice, finally, but to view it as something benign, something ultimately for their own good, something without which the system cannot function. As they get older, many come to believe this on their own, before even entering the university. Many college students, especially those hoping to be doctors and lawyers, for example, are already apprentice members of the academy and advocates of its interests. They help create a false sense of harmony in the university not because they work as partners of the academy, but *for* it. Their own aspiration to enter professions even more exclusive than the academy forms them into a fifth column that helps prevent any change in how classrooms use and distribute social authority. Because these preprofessional students "need" grades in order to comply with the competitive styles of medical and legal training, it comes to seem that all students who wish professional accreditation also "need" grades. In this way, the cultural values of individualism, competition, quantifiable knowledge (for testing), are recursively perpetuated in a system analogous to the one which perpetuates mother-exclusive childrearing as described by Nancy Chodorow.[1]

In the previous chapters I have tried to show that literacy and language use are inherently social rather than exclusively individual, and that several disciplinary perspectives are needed to understand the social character of

---

1. Although I will not make an extended argument here, it also seems clear to me that grading in schools is one of the *results* of mother-exclusive childrearing. Because there is only "one" parent, the child's own "oneness" is emphasized in the formation of identity, and individualism seems a "natural" paradigm of social functioning. From individualism it then "naturally" follows that competition is the way to distribute "from above" rewards for achievement, rather than collective achievement creating its own rewards.

literacy. However, my arguments will feel academic unless I can outline how that real phenomenon, the classroom, which also exists as an ubiquitous institution with a long history, can be reconceived, reused, reenlisted, and/or recast to work with this greatly enlarged sense of "English." In fact, the need of this subject matter for a different sense of the classroom, coincides, in the views of many, with the need for classrooms to do something other than "convey" knowledge, which is the activity created by testing and grading.

Paulo Freire, like Richard Ohmann, sees the abandonment of "transferrals of information"[2] as a first step toward recognizing and using the social potential of the classroom. His formulations suggest the connection between his political interest in enfranchising nonindustrialized poor societies and our own political interest of deindividualizing contemporary styles of thought and language:

> To exist, humanly, is to *name* the world, to change it. Once named, the world in its turn reappears to the namers as a problem and requires of them a new *naming.* . . .
>
> But while to say the true word—which is work, which is praxis—is to transform the world, saying that word is not the privilege of some few men, but the right of every man.[3] Consequently, no one can say a true word alone—nor can he say it *for* another, in a prescriptive act which robs others of their words.
>
> Dialogue is the encounter between men, mediated by the world, in order to name the world. Hence dialogue cannot occur between those who want to name the world and those who do not wish this naming—between those who deny other men the right to speak their word and those whose right to speak has been denied to them.[4]
>
> If it is in speaking their word that men, by naming the world, transform it, dialogue imposes itself as the way by which men achieve significance as men. Dialogue is thus an existential necessity. . . . this dialogue cannot be reduced

2. Paulo Freire, *The Pedagogy of the Oppressed* (1968), trans. Myra Bergman Ramos (New York: Continuum, 1983), p. 67; hereafter cited in text.

3. It is fair to be worried about the traditional sexist usage here, I think, as a possible indication of an unbalanced approach to how gender ideology enters into economic ideology. This is a point which applies to a great deal of, if not most, Marx-inspired thinking, and it is up to us now appropriating this thought to make the needed changes. However, the reader may observe the same sexist usage in my own work of ten years ago.

4. Those who wish to pursue the gender-political issue here might want to read Dale Spender's work on who speaks in classrooms. She shows convincingly that the whole set of classroom speaking customs—in traditional classrooms and whether or not the teacher is a woman—encourages boys to speak, overlooks their tendency to interrupt, and does not urge the girls to share the floor equally.

to the act of one person's "depositing" ideas in another, nor can it become a simple exchange of ideas to be "consumed" by the discussants. . . . Because dialogue is an encounter among men who name the world, it must not be a situation where some men name on behalf of others. It is an act of creation. (76–77)[5]

The act of naming, which we previously discussed in the contexts of analytic philosophy and infantile language acquisition in chapter 4, is presented here in its necessarily collective sense. In addition to naming being psychosocial and collective (as opposed to psychological and individual), as when two intimate people agree on a name and "fix" it, naming is a political act of one constituency in dialogue with others. This means that if a class of students, as a collective entity, reaches a consensus, its "audience" is not the teacher who gives a grade for it (but is actually a member of that collective), but is, or should be, other communities with whom this community relates. Just as a name matters in the narrow sense—because it is fixed it imposes a degree of responsibility on an individual—it is apparent that it matters in the collective sense since the effort to name at once reappears as a "problem" which "requires of [the namers] a new naming." As Freire renders it, the double perspective in his sense of naming is the congruence of the collective/creative act in the formation of the new name with the "problem-posing" act that naming also always is. As with individuals living among others, a class(room) is not self-contained. As acts of naming, the academy's giving of grades disenfranchises the classroom community by "deny[ing] other [people] [—the students—] the right to speak their word." Grades are recorded in permanent records, rather than being used as brief, informal judgments—by all class members on the work of others, perhaps—in a problem-posing attitude; permanent grades are not negotiable.[6] Because grading is the academy's unilateral act, it regularly stops dialogue that is opened by the periodic meetings of a group of people who all freely decided to study a given subject (take a certain course). Part of the academy's assumed justification for doing so is its belief that the function of a course to begin with is to "deposit" ideas into the classroom.

Freire calls this depositing the "banking" style of education, as much

5. Again, from a gender standpoint, and using the foregoing argument, it matters a great deal who speaks in class, who "identifies" things, and how the names of things are actually decided. If half the population is taught to defer, in speaking time, to the other half, how much "naming" can women actually contribute?

6. Since I advocate eliminating grades, I am not advocating negotiating them. But exchanging "informal" grades functions like sharing opinions of restaurants by assigning them an "A" or "B." Such grades are forms of discourse that mark a social scene different from the usual ones in which grades are fixed by "higher" authorities.

because it is primarily in the "interest" of the academy—the actual "bank"—
as because knowledge is treated as inert and depositable. The actual flow
of advantage in banking education is from the students to the teachers. His
revisionary idea of "problem-posing" education is meant to create the flow
of advantage in both directions. In this project, he offers his own act of
renaming:

> Through dialogue, the teacher of the students and the students of the teacher
> cease to exist and a new term emerges: teacher-student with students-teachers.
> The teacher is no longer merely the-one-who-teaches, but one who is him-
> [or her-]self taught in the dialogue with the students, who in turn while being
> taught also teach. They become jointly responsible for a process in which all
> grow. In this process, arguments based on "authority" are no longer valid. . . .
> Here, no one teaches another, nor is anyone self-taught. Men [people] teach
> each other, mediated by the world, by the cognizable objects which in banking
> education are "owned" by the teacher. (p. 67)[7]

By renaming the relationship of student and teacher in this reciprocal way,
Freire redefines the classroom community with the *teacher as a member*,
and redefines the academy *with students as members*. Pragmatically, all
arguments based on "authority" are those which are exempt from dialogic
examination. They appear in communities as if from outside the communities,
from those who are not members. If, in the classroom, however, no one is
not a member, no one can bring in a preauthorized piece of knowledge,
which means that no one can foreclose the act of naming in advance, nor
can anyone produce some "final" naming. Yet in the ordinary classroom,
this is just the role of the teacher.

In considering the idea of "banking education," it is hard to overlook both
the analogy and the real connections between a taken-for-granted economic
structure and the religious hierarchy that has provided most of the models for
how classrooms are usually run. The analogy is that the teacher is thought
of as a representative of yet higher authorities (but this time understood to be
"experts") whose role it is to render authoritative pronouncements on matters
of individual handling of knowledge, where this handling takes on ethical
force—a "good" student is not merely competent, but is morally certified
by virtue of this competence. A teacher offers a kind of "absolution" for
error and provides "guidance" on how to proceed next. There is quietly
believed to be an "ultimate" authority, "truth," which is found in books by
certified leaders, usually members of the academy who work at a few "elite"
institutions whose endowments and populations come from the ranks of the

---

7. Although this salutary situation does occur in classrooms from time to time, it is never
institutionalized and it is only a marginal part of any grade-governed scene.

well-to-do. The condition of "ignorance," which students are all understood to bring into the classroom, is a not-so-faint echo of "sin" or other sort of inner deficit or stain requiring the *personal* ministrations of the teacher. To overcome the failing, the student develops "faith" in the system and enacts this faith by systematic, and, it is hoped, imaginative compliance with a received program of thought.

Although Walter Ong does not advocate this conception of education, he describes and conceives of writing as an instrument that will promote this idea of education, with its emphasis on solitary individual effort aimed at mastering the private language of a select group of leaders. Historically, in addition, the Church had strong connections with the secular political and economic seats of authority. Its upper echelons were wealthy enough to build extravagant monuments to its own history and culture, which could never actually be used by the vast majority of the illiterate memberships. For centuries, the meaning of "education" was religious education and the purpose of literacy was either to learn Holy Writ or the "laws" of commerce and taxation. The growth of literacy as a widespread phenomenon is historically contemporaneous with the growth of political enlightenment and the emergence of an ever-growing middle class.

Today, however, we are still not alert to what it means, practically, for teachers and students to be members of the same (social, political, and/or school) class; we are still in a state of lethargy and compliance, which helped motivate the work of Freire and Ohmann. In subsequent chapters, I will present a few instances from my own classrooms that could help show what happens when common class(room) membership of teacher and student is assumed.

Now, I would like to take up an issue that I suspended in chapter 4 (where I discussed naming in its individual dimension) and explore in some detail what being a teacher meant in a social sense to Anne Sullivan as she undertook to teach, enlighten, and socialize Helen Keller. I have reflected on Helen Keller's psychology in her acquisition of language, focusing narrowly on the sheer presence and influence of the relationship between the two women during the month in which Helen changed into a social being. The background of this change, particularly Anne Sullivan's personal history in comparison with Helen's, is a full, rich instance of what it entails for a teacher to be in common membership with a student in the same community.

Moreover, the political/economic class issue behind Freire's arguments becomes particularly clear in this history, even more so because the teacher is from a lower "class" than the student, as well as being from an ethnic group that was considered then to be inferior to the student's. It is also the history of two women whose major early influences were other women, and who, even throughout their later lives, regularly had to cope with (largely masculine) efforts to exploit one or both of them. What comes from this picture, among other things, is a sense of involved teaching from a feminine (and perhaps, but not overtly or necessarily, feminist, in this case) perspective, one which further underscores the psychology of mutuality I discussed in connection with language acquisition. Finally, this history shows how, after the early stages of socialization in regard to the use of language, the use of literature plays an active role. While Helen Keller's early achievement may be localized as language alone, her full achievement through her development into adulthood cannot be thus localized, since her literacy, alongside and in interaction with Anne Sullivan's, was also derived from the same teacher-student situation which brought language. I am not claiming, of course, that what happened in this relationship could be repeated, miraculously, in classrooms today. But I am claiming that what the teacher brings to class in terms of gender, ethnic background, economic condition, and style of human involvement are all part of his or her membership in that class in just the same way that they are part of every student's membership. I am presenting this history to show what common membership in a (literacy or other) classroom can contribute to its change.

Anne Sullivan was the oldest of five children born to Irish immigrant parents, Thomas and Alice Sullivan, in Massachusetts in the late 1860s. Thomas was an extremely indigent farmhand and Alice a constantly pregnant housewife. Anne witnessed the death of three of the four other children. When she was seven, her five-year-old sister Ellen died of an unknown fever; when she was eight, a newborn sickly brother died at two months of age; and when she was eleven, her brother Jimmie died while the two children were in the almshouse—apparently of his chronic tubercular hip. After her father left her and her brother Jimmie in the almshouse in 1876 (when she was 10), he was not heard from again. Four months after she watched her infant brother die, she watched her mother die of tuberculosis. During Ellen's last illness, Anne developed trachoma, which inflamed and occluded her eyes; she was more than half-blind until she was operated on at age sixteen and regained most of her sight until well into adulthood. For the last two years of her life, Alice Sullivan walked on crutches because of an accident in which a stove fell on her; all the while she was coughing. She depended on friendly neighbors to do the laundry for the six people in her household. Thomas was regularly drunk.

Alice Sullivan, Nella Henney reports,[8] was a dignified and cheerful

---

8. Nella Braddy [Henney], *Anne Sullivan Macy: The Story Behind Helen Keller* (New York: Doubleday, 1933). Mrs. Henney was the first one to take the trouble to understand just

woman. She was alone in America and came here at age twenty on the bounty of her husband's family; her only family was Thomas and the children. The first four or five years of Anne's life were good—she had the benefit of her mother's strong character and good health and of her father's undiluted Irish imagination. She was also probably a privileged child in the sense of being especially loved, her mother's firstborn and first family in an alien country. It seems likely that Anne's first eight years of life with this loving and intelligent mother were essential to her subsequent survival, perseverance, and success. They also probably nurtured her instinctive sense that the mother alone and exclusively is responsible for the dependent child.[9] There was just no one else who cared.

As a child, Anne enjoyed the luxury of a perspicacious and vindictive temperament. A neighbor whose daughter wore white gloves brought red gloves as a gift for Anne. Interpreting the disparity in color as a disparity in value Anne threw the gloves into the fire. She was always particularly sensitive to the condescension from the rich and she very often did not hesitate to let such feelings be known. She envied the rich only their money, which, in adult life, was sometimes forthcoming to her and Helen, and she took it without guilt or shame.

The almshouse in Tewksbury, Massachussetts, where Anne and Jimmie were sent in 1876 was notoriously filthy and, though frequently investigated, conditions never improved. The two children were put up for the first night in a room called the "dead house," where inmates who died were taken before burial. The administration of the almshouse intended to separate the two siblings because of their different genders, but Anne made such a scene that they "compromised" and let Jimmie stay in the women's section if he wore girls' clothing. Anne reported that her civilized behavior was regularly enforced by threats to separate her from Jimmie.

---

how important Anne Sullivan was to Helen Keller. Previously, she was "just a teacher" who happened to have had "miraculous" success with this child. Until Mrs. Henney's book, there was no record or understanding of how Anne Sullivan was able to restore Helen Keller's life to normalcy. My account, which follows, is based almost completely on Henney's account, which, unfortunately, is no longer in print. In 1971, I had the good luck to meet with Mrs. Henney on several occasions and discuss Sullivan and Keller. Because of Mrs. Henney's personal generosity I was able to read many documents that were not yet publicly available, some of which were subsequently used in Joseph P. Lash's biography, *Helen and Teacher* (New York: Delacorte Press, 1980). I will cite material that first appeared in Lash's biography but which I had read previously in the archives of the American Foundation for the Blind in 1971.

9. I mention this because of Dinnerstein's and Chodorow's attempts to show how mother-exclusive parenting is rooted in social values and privileges automatically taken by men. In this case, the indigent father's behavior presupposed his own exclusion from the tasks of child-raising. Women learn not that it is their right or need to be the exclusive parent but that it is just a necessity to insure survival.

In the women's ward, the two children were surrounded by syphilis, cancer, and schizophrenia, among other things. The regular activity was the telling of the history of compounded misfortunes which brought each person to Tewksbury. There were unwed mothers of all ages, and dead babies; and there were people who had been there all their lives. A watershed experience for Anne was her brother's death less than a year after coming to the almshouse. After he had died, she wanted to see him but was not allowed:

> Then I crept to the side of the bed—and touched him! Under the sheet I felt the little cold body, and something in me broke. My screams waked everyone in the hospital. Someone rushed in and tried to pull me away; but I clutched the little body and held it with all my might. Another person came, and the two separated us. They dragged me back to the ward and tried to put me in bed; but I kicked and scratched and bit them until they dropped me upon the floor, and left me there, a heap of pain beyond words. After a while the first paroxysm subsided, and I lay quite still. One of the women—a poor cripple— hobbled to me, and bent down as far as she could to lift me up; but the effort hurt her so that she groaned. I got up and helped her back to her bed. She made me sit beside her and she petted me and spoke tender words of comfort to me. Then I knew the relief of passionate tears.

Some time later, Anne was allowed to view her dead brother:

> Before they could stop me, I jumped up and put my arms around him and kissed and kissed and kissed his face—the dearest thing in the world—the only thing I had ever loved. I heard a voice saying "Come away now. You can see him again after breakfast . . . " I believe I have hated that voice as I have not hated anything else in the world.[10]

These events became significant because the already painful grief of her brother's premature death was aggravated by the banal, routine detachment of the institutional overseers. The obsessive and uncaring rule-following administrators became the objects of her unrelenting rage. They were agents of separation who did not recognize ultimate sources of emotional sustenance. In adult life she reacted to such agents as "the enemy." As Helen grew through adolescence, there were repeated instances when "professionals"— teachers and philanthropists—decided that they knew what was best for Helen, and they initiated movements to care for her without regard for the long history of attachment she and Anne had developed. Anne, however, prepared for such enemies, was unusually resourceful in thwarting the efforts of the professional altruists.

10. Henney, *Anne Sullivan Macy*, pp. 25–27.

Another trait that played a role in her subsequent life as a teacher was the ability to help the helper at the moment of her own greatest pain. Having been a "mother" to her own crippled mother as well as to her younger siblings, she used her strength at once on behalf of herself and of the "poor cripple" who consoled her in her grief.

After Jimmie's death, Anne developed friendships with several of the younger women at Tewksbury; for the most part these women were her teachers, especially about womanhood, childbearing, and men. At the same time they kindled in her a great deal of imagination and aspiration; one of them told her that there were schools "on the outside" for the blind, and another introduced her to the library and its uses. From the first time she heard of them, she intended to get to one of those schools (Perkins was only about twenty miles from Tewksbury). When she was fourteen, she waylaid a visitor from Perkins and implored him to let her go to school—which is how she secured admission. Between twelve and fourteen, she cultivated her literary interests by persuading a mildly insane inmate to read books to her that she got from the library. Being illiterate and half blind, she remembered the stories and retold them to the other women; she became the "blind poet" that Homer and Milton might have been to their audiences. The price for getting the "crazy" girl to read to her was to help her plan half-gestural escapes from Tewksbury. But Anne actually used the literary opportunity to facilitate her real escape. She took the element of romance in escape and in literature seriously; romance for her was initiative in the service of idealism. She never let romantic impulses become illusory or fatuous; in later life it allowed her to take pleasure in what others saw as a suspicious marriage.

When Anne arrived at Perkins, illiterate and unable to spell her name, she was ridiculed by the other students. She left Perkins as its valedictorian and became its most celebrated alumna. Her success at Perkins, as at Tewksbury, was traceable to her ability to develop deep and significant relationships with two or three important people who took their pedagogical responsibility beyond what was formally expected. Perhaps the most important of these women was Miss Moore, Anne's English teacher at Perkins. Anne described her memories of Miss Moore for Nella Henney:[11]

> "A perfectly fearless champion of the oppressed and friendless is a perfectly helpless human being without knowledge and self-discipline. . . . I know," she said tenderly, "it is hard for rebellious natures like yours to understand that so little can be done for humanity by individual action. Perhaps the best way to helping the world is by teaching it to help itself . . . "

11. Ibid., p. 70.

I was almost defenseless before her gentle philosophy. I had never heard anyone talk like that—it was a revelation to me.

That one hour a week with Miss Moore and her Shakespeare class were Paradise to me. As I look back, it seems as if those hours contained all that was stimulating and fine in my school days. I used to leave the classroom in a trance . . . The impression that the plays made upon me was profound. I literally lived them. For the first time I felt the magic of great poetry, the beauty of words, the romance of life; kings and princesses and fairyfolk became my intimate associates. My absorption in this newly discovered beauty was elemental, passionate. It was as if my perception had gained intensity in the starved, stunted years of my childhood.

Although Anne well remembered the folktales of Ireland her father told her as a little girl, literacy early became dissociated from masculine things and assumed a more pragmatic and profound feature of her growing feminine identity. Men themselves were as distant as literary fantasies, but literary feelings were bound up with Miss Moore and her "gentle philosophy"; what had been in Tewksbury a compensatory skill of retelling heard stories became at Perkins the affirmative voice seeking its own themes.

The passages above also suggest that Miss Moore imparted two attitudes which ultimately became a part of Anne's teacherly self-understanding. She brought a rationale with which to deal with the instinct for help and mutual involvement in a world defined by the ideology of individualism, and she presented literature as a source of the power language can bring.[12] Although it's not certain just what "I never heard anyone talk like that" means, it probably refers to Miss Moore's ability to recognize a fundamental part of Anne's nature, her rebelliousness, and to declare a use for it in the real world: "to teach [the world] to help itself." Through both her literary and conversational "talk," Miss Moore "civilized" Anne with the idea of *teaching*.

Anne had a similar relationship with two other women at Perkins, one a teacher, Cora Newton, and the other the matron of the cottage where she lived, Mrs. Sophia Hopkins, who subsequently became the recipient of the now well-known letters Anne wrote describing her progress with Helen Keller. These were all relationships of active interdependency; for Mrs. Hopkins especially, Anne was a substitute for a lost daughter; there were many personal reasons why these women took an interest in Anne. All three women were similar to her mother in their quiet dignity and their

12. The rationale for helping others and the idea that literature is a source of power are really needed by women in the masculine "outside" culture. As I will discuss in my conclusion, the nineteenth century saw the founding of literary/political women's clubs which had, collectively, the purpose of enfranchising women through active cultivation of the use of language and literature.

admiration for Anne's courage to speak out and talk back to unreasonable and authoritarian demands. Miss Moore passed on to Anne access to what both thought was the real language of those who were not blind and poor. Because Anne had been blind for so long, literacy had unusual power for her; because she was poor, literary language became access to the knowledge of wealth and dignity. From these women, Anne learned what it meant to be a teacher—one who consciously uses all the instincts of the mother, the older sibling, the guardian, and the strong friend in the service of *other people's self-enlightenment*. When she identified herself to Helen Keller as "Teacher," which is what Helen continued to call her through adulthood, these women were the original referents that Anne now refixed on herself.

Helen Keller was born into an atmosphere that was in most essential ways the opposite of Anne Sullivan's. Captain Arthur Keller had a relatively productive farm in Tuscumbia, Alabama, though its fortunes gradually diminished after the Civil War. In the South, life was slow, leisurely, with enough room for all the children and enough of everything else to sustain life without worry. White women in such circumstances were pampered and not expected to work. "Spoiling" a girl was a means of acculturating her to the abundance of the past-life in the South, and these old customs continued even as the economy deteriorated. Helen was a healthy child and was raised in an atmosphere of health and well-being. She was physically strong and had never known want or privation. After she was ill and lost her eyesight and hearing, she was spoiled even more. If her demands were only slowly met, tantrums would speed the response, for who would resist the pathetic needs of a deaf and blind child of four years of age? Psychologically, to be spoiled is to be dependent and not to know it. For Helen, the occasions of dependency were met so quickly and with such ignorance of the problem's complexity, a nondependent relation between her and others had no room to develop. And, in any case, no one could speak to her. After four years of Helen's innocent tyranny, the Keller family took steps to educate her.

Although there were many things that made this opportunity attractive to Anne—the good weather, the abundance, the hope of good health, and the dignity of meaningful employment—her main concern was whether or not she could work with the child. This is Anne's description of Helen not long after she had met her for the first time:

> Somehow I had expected to see a pale, delicate child—I suppose I got the idea from Dr. Howe's description of Laura Bridgman when she came to the Institution. But there was nothing pale or delicate about Helen. She is large, strong, and ruddy, and as unrestrained in her movements as a young colt. She has none of those nervous habits that are so noticeable and so distressing in blind children. Her body is well-formed and vigorous, and Mrs. Keller says

she has not been ill a day since the illness that deprived her of her sight and hearing. She has a fine head, and it is set on her shoulders just right. Her face is hard to describe. It is intelligent, but lacks mobility, or soul, or something. Her mouth is large and finely shaped. You see at a glance that she is blind. One eye is larger than the other, and protrudes noticeably. She rarely smiles. . . . She is unresponsive and even impatient of caresses from anyone except her mother. She is very quicktempered and willful, and nobody, except her brother James, has attempted to control her. The greatest problem I shall have to solve is how to discipline and control her without breaking her spirit. I shall go rather slowly at first and try to win her love. I shall not attempt to conquer her by force alone; but I shall insist on reasonable obedience from the start.

It appears that Anne feared Helen would be an invalid of some sort—pale, nervous, or sickly. Her language can hardly suppress her excitement at the opportunity afforded by Helen's energy and health, and she rightly suspects that Helen is emotionally backward. While those who have subsequently told and retold the story of Anne Sullivan and Helen Keller have probably oversentimentalized it, it is very likely that the sense of this being a romantic adventure—and in the real world—was one of the things that mobilized Anne Sullivan's energy. For Anne there was something clean and unsullied about this work and this child, who had physical and emotional features that she even envied and continued to admire as Helen grew up. At the same time, in seeing Helen as a "restless spirit, untaught, unsatisfied," and destructive because of her frustrating ignorance, Anne undoubtedly saw herself again in this child, but now in the presence of the one person (herself) who might be able to help.

The significance of this opportunity in Anne's life can be seen in Anne's letter to Mrs. Hopkins written about two months after her first success with Helen:

And right here I want to say something that is for your ears alone. Something within me tells me that I shall succeed beyond my dreams. Were it not for some circumstances that make such an idea highly improbable, even absurd, I should think Helen's education would surpass in interest and wonder Dr. Howe's achievement. I know that she has remarkable powers, and I believe I shall be able to develop them. I cannot tell how I know these things. I had no idea a short time ago how to go to work; I was feeling about in the dark, but somehow I know now, and I know that I know. I cannot explain it, but when difficulties arise, I am not perplexed or doubtful. I know how to meet them; I seem to divine Helen's peculiar needs. It is wonderful.

As we know, Anne Sullivan's achievement did surpass Dr. Howe's. This ambition, however, seems secondary to the moment of "stereoscopic" knowledge: "I know now, and I know that I know."[13] This moment in Anne's life matches Helen's (when she caught on to the principle of naming) in its life-changing potential. The adult process of vocational self-development for Anne is seamlessly attached to Helen's juvenile tasks of self-development, and both are embedded in a variety of community forces both in Tuscumbia and back at Perkins, where Anne's progress is being monitored. At the same time, Anne's ambition is a response to the variety of antagonistic people and values of her youth; few things could better explain her championship of poor Irish immigrants, abandoned women, the handicapped and struggling children than to have achieved success more quickly and effectively than the established Protestant man who then set the standard of what could be done with the severely handicapped.

In retrospect, Anne's achievement seems more an outstanding act of courage than of genius, since she went into a Southern home and seized parental authority, first in the presence of the parents, and then by taking Helen to a private place nearby. Most in the home did not quite know what Anne was doing. Many years later, Mrs. Keller did seem to have understood it and observed that Anne was probably more Helen's mother than she was. Because of Anne's own history, however, motherhood was something much different to her than to Mrs. Keller. Motherhood was more collective in Anne's life, and thus much more bound up with caring adults' ordinary pedagogical function with younger people. Also, it was not associated with abundance and plenty, with the total effort by one person to care for another, but with a highly focused effort by someone with many personal responsibilities and burdens to salvage something from a situation in which normalcy is not possible. Toward the Keller family, Anne was a representative of reality, and she raided the family peace with impunity, knowing that the family's own despair would at least grudgingly permit her a certain latitude to produce results. She taught the family what the real cost of Helen's education would be, namely, that Helen would have to enter a "new" family. It is noteworthy that as Helen's and Anne's relationship grew, Helen's mother was the most understanding figure of the immediate family. She seemed to know that Helen could succeed only by leaving the family; she seemed glad to admit that if this is what it took to normalize or humanize the struggling child, that is what she too wanted for her.

Throughout her public life, Anne was repeatedly asked what her "method"

13. Without belaboring the issue, compare this sentence with the lines from Keats and Shakespeare I cited in chapter 4. The sentence has two parts, with the second part, after the "and," modifying the first. Both the declaration and the statement that "I know" the declaration are coordinate and, as I described previously, "reversible."

was, and people eagerly waited to hear the Great Secret which produced the
Great Miracle. Anne's ever-disappointing answer was that she treated Helen
normally and spoke of obedience and love, exactly as she had written to
Mrs. Hopkins. Many doubted her authenticity not only because of her bland
explanations, but because it was a poor Irish girl rather than a prominent
Protestant intellectual speaking. Anne could not put into her explanation the
sources of her understanding of Helen—her own history of struggle with the
charity of the privileged who could give without ever joining her causes.
Throughout her life with Helen, Anne continued to subvert such predatory
interests and gave in to no one who did not recognize the permanence and
integrity of her tie to Helen.

It is of interest to compare Anne's style of teaching with Samuel Gridley
Howe's method of teaching language to Laura Bridgman in 1837. Although
his effort should not be underestimated, the comparison shows the limitations
of a detached and "professional" teacher. In his first months with Laura,
Howe paid considerable attention to her, and the result was similar to Anne's
with Helen. This is one of Howe's early reports:

> Hitherto, the process had been mechanical, and the success about as great as
> teaching a very knowing dog a variety of tricks. The poor child had sat in mute
> amazement, and patiently imitated everything her teacher did; but now the truth
> began to flash upon her, her intellect began to work, she perceived that here
> was a way by which she could herself make up a sign of anything that was
> in her own mind, and say it to another mind, and at once her countenance
> lighted up with a human expression; it was no longer a dog or a parrot—it
> was an immortal spirit, eagerly seizing upon a new link of union with other
> spirits! I could almost fix upon the moment when this truth dawned upon her
> mind, and spread its light to her countenance; I saw that the great obstacle was
> overcome, and that henceforward nothing but patient and persevering, plain
> and straightforward efforts were to be used. [14]

The facts of this report are extremely similar to those reported in Anne Sullivan's letter of 5 April 1887, in which Helen's enlightenment is described. The
moment of human insight is preceded by a period of animal-like obedience.
Then the face acquires what it had lacked for years—the smile of knowledge
and the animation of initiative.

The main difference between Howe and Sullivan was that once Howe
decided that "the main obstacle was overcome," he delegated an increasing
number of teaching duties to other professionals. Laura lacked neither attention nor instruction. From most reports, she was just as intelligent as Helen

14. Fifty-Eighth Annual Report of the Trustees of the Perkins Institution (September 30,
1889) (Boston: Wright and Potter, 1890), pp. 163–64.

Keller and temperamentally more aggressive. But she remained for the duration of her life in the Perkins School, where she died in 1889. Howe did not come to his task with Anne Sullivan's depth of motivation, nor with the same passion for achievement. He did not himself have to overcome handicaps; he did not have to achieve in spite of blindness, poverty, gender, and ethnic background. His was the motivation of the conscientious charitable man for whom the project was one of many. Teaching Laura mattered to him, but not as Helen Keller mattered to Anne Sullivan. As a teacher, Anne had a stake in what happened to Helen; but if Samuel Howe had failed, it would barely have changed the course of his life.

Anne and Helen succeeded by forming *their own class*. They were always worried about support, yet they had rich friends and were known around the world. Anne came out of her original class just as Helen did. Their own "work," for better or for worse, was to help establish philanthropic organizations and to make help available to the blind and deaf. Both succeeded— insofar as they did—by creating a community of interest from their common situation as dependent members of the society at large. Anne's early attachment to a single "pupil" developed into her membership in a wide and important community. Because of her style of involvement—as contrasted with Howe's detachment—something new was actually achieved on a social scale. Anne persevered in her role *as a teacher*, not accepting the common expectation that the teacher must go on to a new student, especially since she continued to break so many collective barriers with this student, not the least of which was putting Helen (as well as herself, unofficially) through Radcliffe College. Those of us who have been teaching for some time know the value and interest of retaining relationships with former students and having them join us later as colleagues. This is the process of community formation. If a teacher is already a "member" of the class when it begins, these communities can be expected to continue—not, perhaps, with whole classes, but with those students able to grow along with their teachers, and those teachers able to change under the influence and, strange as it may sound, *guidance* of their students. This *reciprocity* is missing in the vast majority of today's classrooms, yet it is a habit, a style, a value, easily derivable from the orientation toward language and literacy we have been discussing thus far.

In narrating the history of Keller's and Sullivan's relationship in some detail, I have tried to show that Helen Keller contributed as much to Anne Sullivan's life as Anne did to Helen's, that their relationship, while not symmetrical, was reciprocal. Similarly, in discussing language in chapter 4, I characterized the relation of subject to predicate in any name or sentence as not symmetrical but nevertheless reversible. In both of these cases, the asymmetry is associated with the uniqueness of the sentence or relationship, while the reciprocity and reversibility is associated with its normal potential for change and growth. As classrooms are now structured, one finds asymmetry, but not reciprocity. One of my main claims is that *one cannot reconceive language and literacy without also making the corresponding change in the social relations of the classroom.*

Since the initial turbulence of the late 1960s there have been a variety of efforts to change the structure of the classroom, all stemming from the wish to treat it as a collective rather than a collection. One of the simpler changes was from audience seating to circular seating; encouraging each member of the class to look at and speak to other members directly, instead of filtering remarks through the teacher. While some students respond to this encouragement, however, most need to be urged and coaxed to do so, as they continue to address each of their remarks to the teacher and expect the turn-taking to proceed in class in the familiar student-speaks/teacher-speaks pattern. Another, less simple change is the periodic "break-into-groups" technique, in which the teacher poses a problem and asks the small, randomly chosen subgroups to discuss it among themselves. On subsequent occasions, with other problems, new groups are put together. Group work thus "happens," but it is suspended aimlessly in a traditionally structured classroom. The new relationships among students that may form have no chance to grow into a contributing unit. Because of a profound naiveté about the complexity and potential of groups altogether, teachers simply do not know what can and cannot be expected from group work in the first place. And in any event, because a grade has finally to be assigned, this social action by the teacher preempts any authority a student group may have developed.

In some quarters, particularly under the influence of a sudden surge of belief that "people can't write (well enough)," there have been some well-organized and sustained efforts to cultivate students' authority by teaching one another and relying on *continuing* membership in small writing groups for guidance and support. These efforts have been characterized by the *reduction*, but not the elimination, of grading, and the teacher's more deliberate effort to be less of a judge or evaluator and more of a resource person. Kenneth Bruffee's effort at Brooklyn College is one of the more important initiatives.

Bruffee first organized a program of "peer tutoring," in which students worked in pairs and each student judged and criticized the other's work. This dialogue was the principal activity in writing instruction, though teachers entered the process sometime near the end. Efforts were made by faculty to teach tutors themselves; since each student was a potential tutor, Bruffee succeeded in giving some meaningful form to Freire's idea of teacher-student/student-teacher. There was definitely a reciprocal activity—among students. Here is one of Bruffee's descriptions that gives a sense of what went on:

> In the tutor-training course, peer tutors work with each other in a way analogous to that in which they tutor students in the tutoring program. Tutors write short essays, then use the essays as raw material in learning to write progressively more complex, demanding, and tactfully helpful critiques of each other's work. Thus, the course is designed to make each step in the displaced social process of writing directly social again, so that the writing process can be refined in collaboration with others and then, in effect reinternalized. Tutors practice each step in learning groups. Usually, these groups have five or six members. Sometimes, they have only two; other times, the group is the whole class. . . . students learn how to solve many of their own writing problems as well as those of the students whom they will help.[15]

Of note here is the apprentice-style teaching technique that Bruffee uses: tutors learn their work by forming their own group and practicing on one another. Then, a variety of group situations are used to create different forms of interchange.

Behind Bruffee's thinking are two ideas: that writing is an internalized social process—"displaced," that is, from its social origin to the individual—and that any learning takes place through "conversation." In connection with Vygotsky and Mead in chapter 3, I discussed the internalization of language—not just written language. But Bruffee also introduces Michael Oakeshott's idea of the "conversation of mankind" (1962), something followed up at some length in Richard Rorty's *Philosophy and the Mirror of Nature* (1979). On one hand this idea participates in the previous one (internalization), in that thought is characterized as internalized conversation. On the other hand, however, conversation is offered as a description of an ultimate process of inquiry: the growth and development of culture is understood to be the outcome of various subcultures "speaking" to one another. Here is one of Rorty's uses of the idea of "conversation."

> The fact that we can continue the conversation Plato began without discussing the topics Plato wanted discussed, illustrates the difference between treating philosophy as a voice in a conversation and treating it as a subject, a *Fach*, a field of professional inquiry.[16]

15. Kenneth Bruffee, "Teaching Writing Through Collaboration," in *Learning in Groups*, ed. Clark Bouton and Russell Y. Garth (San Francisco: Jossey-Bass, 1983), p. 26.

16. Richard Rorty, *Philosophy and the Mirror of Nature* (Princeton: Princeton University Press, 1979), p. 391. A topic that I am only marginally raising in this book, but which I consider of first importance, is the presupposition, given by Rorty's statement, that *Plato* remains a starting point for conversation. I think that the value of Plato is questionable in the pursuit of collaborative and communitarian classrooms. Don't Plato's dialogues actually abuse conversational format?

Conversation as a social activity permits a change of subject; Rorty is thus able to loosen the boundaries of the subject while retaining respect for its history and value. Furthermore, many "voices" are permitted in a conversation, whereas participation in a "*Fach*" demands certification of particularly narrow sorts. Bruffee successfully carries over this spirit into the writing classroom and brings the process of learning or gaining insight into a distinctively human idiom—relaxed and noncoercive.

And yet, although Bruffee unambiguously advocates "collaborative learning," questions arise regarding just who is collaborating and on what. In the paragraph I quoted above, the missing part reads, "By working through such problems as defining topics, gaining focus, establishing unity and coherence, and writing effective introductions in learning groups, students learn . . . " The problems Bruffee refers to are the classic technical ones of the composition classroom. The complex machinery and psychology of intragroup activity are addressed to mastering certain formalisms in the technique of essay-writing. It is true that these formalisms are not unworthy of thought. What is disturbing to me is the remedial purpose that implicitly underlies this otherwise imaginative classroom proposal, that groups are formed and used in class in order to "solve problems."

Bruffee explains that one of the motivations for his initiatives was the widespread discovery that "Harvard M.B.A.'s, government officials, and university teachers" (Bruffee, p. 24), in addition to the nontraditional students, all found writing "difficult." The "writing crisis" that brought him and others to action was apparently one of *competence*: people doing certain jobs found themselves not competent enough when they had to write. While Bruffee's more abstract formulations definitely imply that writing as a school subject had been imbued with inappropriate *values*, his description of group interests as pointing to "solving problems" in writing suggests *no significant change in the subject matter* engaged by the various groups. Anyone who has written anything knows that there is no reducing its "difficulty"; there is no way to reduce the amount of time needed to prepare a piece of writing; there is no way to eliminate the struggle to find the most satisfying language; no computer can lessen the responsibility of *conceiving* a sequence of thought. From our perspective, the difficulty of writing cannot be the subject matter of collective studies of language.

One should allow that where remedial work is needed, tutorials and learning groups are excellent, as Bruffee's results show. But I assume that neither Bruffee nor others who have taken imaginative pedagogical risks think of language use as a subject in which "improvement" can be measured in any one person. If you are eager to present language use as a social process, you will not need any immediate reassurance through improved test scores.

The concern for improvement is inevitably tied not only to test scores, but to classroom grading. What those who have used groups in language classes all report is that the most palpable change from other classes is that of student and teacher *attitudes*. It would be disappointing if this new affective resource for the classroom were squandered on refining technical proficiency in the use of language. The change in subject matter ought to correspond with the change of classroom social relations.

Collaboration among the students alone is necessary, but not enough to change the classroom from what it is now. The most intractable feature of the classroom structure is the unchanging authority of the teacher who assigns grades. If Bruffee sees prospective peer tutors as needing to go through a course in which their work is scrutinized and criticized by their peers, why wouldn't the same principle hold for teachers and students sharing the same classroom? If some university teachers find writing difficult, why wouldn't their attitude be appropriate material for a classroom in which they work? As I will show in succeeding chapters, freshmen are able to read and criticize my work, contributing to my understanding of how I write and use language. (As Bruffee probably knows, students do not require permission to have insight into how a teacher speaks and writes.) If a teacher does not participate in collaborative learning, the collaboration takes on a somewhat subversive character, and can easily become collaboration *against* instead of cooperation *with* the teacher. Cooperation is itself an ambiguous idea. Many parents use the word to mean "follow my instructions." A child who does not follow instructions is "not cooperating." This usage could be appropriate for preschoolers, but, in the university, its literal, "fixed" meaning must apply. Ways can be found for teachers and students to "operate with" one another. If they do, a teacher cannot, at the end of a course, cancel his or her implication in the class project by recording a binding judgment on the student's permanent record.

Here is Bruffee's conception of the teacher's role:

> The teacher's role is neither that of a performer, nor oracle, nor facilitator. The teacher sets tasks that students undertake collaboratively: to write, to examine writing formally, and to evaluate writing. As such, the teacher is a representative of the community of literate, knowledgeable people appointed to help students to become full members of that community.[17]

In this statement Bruffee wants to oppose the narcissistic roles teachers often take: even when the teacher presents him or herself as a "facilitator," students

---

17. Bruffee, "Teaching Writing Through Collaboration," p. 27. In the conclusion, I comment further on the idea of people being "appointed to help students to become full members of that community."

will take the "follower" role. Although the teacher's setting of the task need not be coercive—and is not, when the topics are open-ended, such as "come up with a reading of so-and-so's text"—students will legitimately wonder whether and how their execution of the task will be evaluated and how binding this evaluation is, if done exclusively by the teacher. In this and in other work, Bruffee claims that teachers are rightly viewed by students as "representatives of literate communities," implying a pre-established pedagogical authority. But one cannot expect students to recognize it: the actual deportment of the teacher in the classroom must win "new" authority in that class, and those of us who have been teaching long enough realize that this "winning of authority" anew in each new class provides us with the grounds on which to judge our own relative success.

To win authority, we become members of the class by making cooperative contributions, including announcing and explaining just which communities we do consider ourselves to be members of already. The teacher's own writings (in class and out) could show such membership, and the students' analysis of this work could open up the subject of the teacher's self-conception for discussion. How a teacher speaks of him- or herself matters, and the teacher's hesitations about self-disclosure should be studied alongside the students' analogous uncertainties. Furthermore, the teacher's background and training are relevant. While students cannot evaluate how well a teacher has been trained, their familiarity with the educational process makes the teacher appear as how he or she really is—as a growing and developing person. When grown children discover this about their parents, parents seem more accessible, and a new sort of community is formed in the immediate family. The same type of community development is necessary in the classroom, and, while it requires a certain affective risk on the part of both students and teachers, there is no other way for teachers to mark their *membership* (not their authority) in that community. In place of authority to grade, the teacher must contribute in such a way as to show common interests of teachers and students.

When a task is set and done by the teacher, but only the student's work is graded, it appears to students that the teacher's work is exemplary, i.e., the "right" way to do it. But if the teacher does not grade the student's work, and if, instead, the analysis of the task is reciprocal, the teacher's work may or may not appear exemplary. Instead, many students will then judge the work of *other students* as exemplary. In principle, the expectation that there is a "right" way to do the task will be greatly reduced, and intuitions of what suits different occasions will be cultivated in both students and teachers.

It is hard to overestimate the disturbing psychological effect that grading has on group work. Dene Thomas's dissertation describes one of the many small group writing courses in the University of Minnesota's writing program. She describes the group leader, a graduate student, as one of the least intrusive of teachers, as he opens a series of six conferences that he conducted with four students:

> Mike starts this first conference, on prewriting, by taking himself out of the authoritative role and making himself one of the group: "The object is to work together toward resolving those kinds of problems we all face as writers." He establishes himself as a fellow writer who faces writing problems, too. He asks for cooperation and for willingness to risk and backs up his requests by temporarily removing the greatest risk: "I'm not looking for anything to grade yet, I'm not looking for a product, anything like that at all." The "yet" is enough of a reminder of what his position is—and students are only too willing to have him play the role of authority anyway.[18]

The program Thomas describes is one of the few in the country where viable groups meet long and often enough for the interaction among its members to have an effect. Thomas details the personalities of each member and how they respond to the group situation. Even though transcripts of these meetings are not easy to read, they show what is involved if collaborative learning is taken seriously.

But consider the problems raised by this brief description. Thomas claims that Mike includes himself as a group member—as a "fellow writer"—and "takes himself out of the authoritative role." Thomas also seems to know, however, that this does not really happen. She is careful to note that Mike's use of "yet" reminds the students that he is the authority and that *he is eventually going to grade their work.* By then adding that the students are "only too willing to have him in this role," she has announced to us that Mike's attempt to take himself out of the authoritative role has actually failed. The students, who are a majority of the group, immediately realize their collective interest and go along with whatever role is suggested by the person who gives the grades.[19] As Thomas's group transcripts show, in this as in any other group, there are those who care more about grades than others and those who care less. But it is not possible to see *any* student's efforts as somehow independent of the fact that Mike will finally grade their work. If collaborative learning as forcefully articulated by Bruffee is to have its intended result, the collaboration must change the way authority is used and distributed in the classroom. Until the authoritative figures

18. Dene Thomas, doctoral dissertation, Department of English, University of Minnesota, 1984, pp. 115–116.

19. My own classes are no exception to this effect, as I will document in my discussions of two different students in chapters 8 and 10.

change themselves, students will not be *willing* to go beyond a compliant role.

Many teachers are willing to take new paths toward changing the classroom structure, but they say that "the system won't let them," especially if they don't have tenure. The objective constraints of the university system are very great, but it is worth considering how deeply such constraints have infiltrated the *values* of even the most progressive prospective teachers. In an unusual experiment, Marilyn Sternglass and Sharon Pugh taught a research seminar for graduate students in English and in Reading at Indiana University. The topic of the seminar was "Introspective Accounts of the Reading and Writing Processes." Students were asked to do simple, self-explanatory assignments, and to provide a running commentary on how they went about doing them, including, especially, an account of their feelings and attitudes. Sternglass and Pugh "gave" all the "assignments." This was, of course, a graded course, and while this fact exerted its usual pressure, the age, experience, and interest of the seminar members may have reduced it somewhat. Here is a journal entry of an experienced teacher commenting on the experience of doing assignments herself:

> While I was doing this assignment [relating articles she was reading to her prior knowledge], I found myself speculating about this class, too, and how our responses to the assignments seemed to be directed by certain sets of expectations we have about particular assignments . . . and about graduate class behavior in general. It's sort of interesting that even attempts to get us to break out of rigid interpretations of assignments have resulted in responses that seem teacher-directed [such as] more creative responses after discussion about our lack of them, [and] at least one research paper after a comment [by one of the teachers] about how we didn't seem to frequent the library for this particular course. I've become aware of how my own responses have followed some recognized pattern of behavior in courses (I normally assume that assignments have a particular purpose and that teachers expect me to fulfill that purpose, and it's hard for me to break out of that—it seems interesting to try to look at what I'm doing, at the same time that I'm sort of analyzing what undergraduate students are doing.) In a lot of ways we're all doing the same thing, only the graduate students do it "better." (But then, is it better?)[20]

The nub of the matter is that "we're all doing the same thing." Undergraduates and graduates participate in the psychology of compliance with the teacher's "purpose" rather than using the assignment as an occasion for imaginative work and intellectual risk-taking. Presumably there are good reasons,

20. Marilyn Sternglass and Sharon Pugh, "Retrospective Accounts of Language and Learning," *Written Communication*, 3 (July 1986), 297–323.

throughout adult life, to comply, to aim to please, to go along. In general, such compliance is successful only when it is temporary and done with the *expectation of a subsequent reciprocal compliance.* But this is not what is being described above: this student writes of a habit, a value, and a common regular practice in the university. Even in this course, with mature students and teachers who announced the opportunity to "break out of rigid interpretations of assignments," most of the students could not develop the energy, courage, motivation, and imagination to behave as both independent individuals and group members. Of course, these students did not go through this course fearing a low grade at every point. It seems that the kind of behavior grading usually produces (in both graduate and undergraduate students) simply reappeared in this course and the students were at a loss to understand that the momentum of grading psychology reduces the opportunities of even a new pedagogy. The grade as a *naming* procedure fixes more than its own referent.

The naming community can, in principle, change deliberately. Under pressure of the "writing crisis" mentioned by Bruffee, the Humanities Department at Michigan Technological University took steps to change the deportment of the faculty, a change described by Art Young in his recent essay "Rebuilding Community in the English Department."[21] While such accounts always seem somewhat utopian, this one is plausible enough, given the special character of this university. Michigan Tech is mainly a science and engineering school, in a part of the country where two feet of snow cover the ground seven or eight months of the year. In a sense, the whole university is communalized from the outside, while the humanities faculty is communalized from "outside" itself. The possibility of radical monadization is a danger felt by all in such circumstances. (In an urban university, there is usually monadization relative to the university, but each person then lives in his or her own circle of associates.) There is, therefore, a good reason to create an active and growing communal life on several levels at once.

The initiating event was to hold writing workshops for faculty members in all disciplines: there was interest in writing and interest in getting together. Here is part of Young's description:

> Teachers who participated in the workshops experienced, in one way or another, collaborative writing exercises, small-group dynamics, oral and written peer feedback between successive drafts, writing anxiety, writer's block, writing for themselves, writing for others, writing for discovery, writing to communicate, and feeling good about writing. . . . We took back to our classrooms new

21. In *Profession 85* (New York: Modern Language Association, 1985).

and renewed strategies for teaching writing: conferences, peer groups, journal writing, prewriting, revision exercises, sharing our own writing with students. But perhaps more important for our departmental and professional lives, we began to duplicate within the department itself the supportive environment we strove for in our individual classrooms.

During the four-day faculty writing workshop we experienced intellectually and emotionally the power and possibilities of a community of scholars searching for knowledge through writing and the sharing of writing. We attempted to create certain aspects of the workshops in our classrooms and in our department, and what emerged blurred the traditional distributions between classrooms and departments. For one thing, students and teachers began writing to each other. (pp. 25–26)

The importance of these events is to show us how, *when the leadership begins to function collaboratively*, it is no longer difficult to promote collaborative work in classrooms, nor for teachers and students to collaborate with one another. Also important here is the purely local character of these changes. *This* community, working within its own constraints, found some ground for creating a collective identity.

One still may wish to dispute the way writing itself was treated or handled in this case. For example, suppose we substituted our more general sense of "writing" as "language use," thus suggesting other ways for such a community to function. But the point is that *this idea* of writing (as described by Young) was suitably germane in that community at that time. Once an underlying habit of mutuality and reciprocity is established in a community, it becomes much easier to take new initiatives, particularly in the way students and teachers work with one another. No one set of ideas can become a dogma because the natural process of change—faculty hiring, students graduating— always brings in new perspectives. Young reports that his department has a policy of "redundant hiring" and follows an unspoken attitudinal style of "healthy irreverence." New faculty are sought not to fill slots but to provide new voices, even if someone in their "field" is already on the faculty, and there is ongoing skepticism, interrogation, and probably a certain irony about any new project. One can not legislate such values, but they arise when collective interests and priorities are permitted a certain freedom of operation. Once all the department's key functions, including, as Young prominently mentions, tenure and salary, are responsive to the intersubjective atmosphere, the classroom is automatically a part of it.

The fact that consequential steps can be taken within a local area alone is a particular problem in our society. On the one hand, there is the wish to somehow generalize what has been done in one place to a variety of situations. One the other hand, there is the sense that local differences prevent any such transfer of achievement. Because of an historical naiveté about social functioning, only individual plans or mass plans tend to be understood; there is no machinery for communities in distant geographical areas to cooperate regularly in matters that involve mixing people rather than sharing technology.

Clifford Geertz's idea of "local knowledge" is, in part, a response to this problem. Modern anthropology has been studying distant and seemingly self-contained societies for several decades. As acquaintance with other societies or with subcultures in our own society grows, the question arises how to conceive of the integrity of such groups while nevertheless accounting for their relatedness to other groups and to our own. Geertz's first step is to admit that there is such a thing as local knowledge:

> To an ethnographer, sorting through the machinery of distant ideas, the shapes of knowledge are always ineluctably local, indivisible from their instruments and their encasements. One may veil this fact with ecumenical rhetoric or blur it with strenuous theory, but one cannot really make it go away. [22]

Geertz's point is that there is a sense in which no general theory or comprehensive view of "culture" will do justice to the way things are known in a culture already having a history and autonomy of its own. If the general subject of ethnographic inquiry is to "understand how it is we understand understandings not our own" (p. 5),

> We must . . . descend into detail, past the misleading tags, past the metaphysical types, past the empty similarities to grasp firmly the essential character of not only the various cultures but the various sorts of individuals within each culture, ... to encounter humanity face to face. [23]

This double task—that of examining both the culture *and* its individuals—is one of the new elements in Geertz's program, one that argues for a certain courage to accept separateness and distance as a prerequisite to making connections between ours and other cultures.

Shirley Heath's work, a small part of which we reviewed in chapter 3, exemplifies this attitude. We noted that in addition to the more patient respect she came with as an observer, she also brought something to contribute as a prospective *member* of the culture she was studying; in part she used her own birth in that part of the country as membership credentials. But she also needed to balance her obvious nonmembership with an ongoing function that could grow into membership. Her role as a *teacher* served this function for the many who needed and wished to be taught.

22. Clifford Geertz, *Local Knowledge* (New York: Basic Books, 1983), p. 4.
23. Clifford Geertz, *Interpretation of Cultures* (New York: Basic Books, 1973), p. 53.

In the study I cited, Heath taught literacy *and* ethnography. She created a situation in which T, the young mother, could write a great deal herself in the process of preparing for her infant son's improved access to literacy. At the same time, T understood that the letters, which were accounts of her son's behavior, were "field notes" or ethnographic texts. In a single relationship between Heath and T, T could be a mother, a teacher, a student, and an ethnographer, while deliberately cultivating her own and her son's literacy. T emulated Heath but also collaborated with her in a situation of mutual benefit.

In one of his earlier essays, Geertz characterized the basic job of the ethnographer as "writing": "What does the ethnographer do?" Geertz asks, "he writes."[24] He rejects the standard answer to the question: "observing, recording, and analyzing," because it suggests some permanent cultural map is being drawn to claim a fixed correspondence between the ethnographer's texts and Cultural Reality. "Writing" better portrays the hermeneutic qualities of ethnographic inquiry and urges a more flexible attitude toward the materials being presented. Geertz's renaming of his work encourages us to relate it to Derrida's general idea of writing, to Ohmann's political sense of it, and to Cohen's sense of the interaction between kinds of writing and social purpose. Heath's ethnographic studies of literacy become in this light writing about writing, a literate inquiry about the nature of literacy. If one of the major problems in the study of language has been the "paradox" of using language to explain language, Heath's studies propose this paradox does not exist: *each use of language is anchored in a generic social act, and it is not a paradox to use a new form of social initiative to change, enhance, or understand an existing social situation.* By understanding language in this thoroughly social sense, it no longer makes sense to approach it as if it were an abstract and infinitely variable code; it is considered instead as a feature of identifiable human interests. Access to language that is no longer purely formal in the mathematical sense promises both understanding and social results. From this standpoint, it is not an academic matter to study language, but an ethical, social, and political project which requires active collaboration among individuals, communities, and classes.

The language and literacy classroom is where this new kind of study can begin. A classroom includes people from all classes—social, ethnic, and economic. It also includes a collection of individuals with detailed, idiosyncratic psychosocial histories. This is the place where the "descent into detail" makes sense, where the debunking of the "misleading tags" and "metaphysical types" finds welcome and thoughtful response. A classroom

24. Ibid., p. 19.

starts without a collective identity, but the steady growth of familiarity and patient disclosure of both individual and shared traits among members, leads not to a consensual label, but to a complex series of "names" that shows the variety of human purposes and interests. Subcollectives may form small cliques (their pejorative role notwithstanding) of common concern and quiet kinship. It is essential that this process not be preempted by grading. No one really believes that growth and development in people will suddenly become invisible if it is not tested and graded. The real fear is that students and teachers will abandon their sense of responsibility toward one another unless fear itself is used as a deterrent.

The activity of writing disciplines the literacy classroom. What one writes is a "measure" of what one contributes. What each text says renames one's relations to a class once again and creates the occasion for a new collective effort. In most classrooms, the activity of "handing" takes place in only two directions, in and out: students hand work in and teachers hand things out. While speaking takes place in a variety of directions, it is unfortunately, most of the time in only two directions (teacher talking with class). In a variety of ways, texts, like talk, can go *across*, and can be created with certain subgroups and close relationships in mind. In the lower grades—junior high, for example—students do write "across" on topics of considerable importance and with considerable wit and irony. These little notes are then "intercepted" by the teacher in order to embarrass the writers and "restore order." But suppose these missives were taken seriously, collected, laughed about, and understood. How far would that go to reduce the exuberant opposition teenagers have to the coercive circumstances of the classroom. These notes are forms of writing, and they represent student interests, often sex or other forbidden topics, which have a legitimate place in the literacy classroom. They are spontaneous writing efforts and their value ought not be underestimated. Why shouldn't writing efforts in university classrooms be directed toward other individuals in that class? Why shouldn't texts be exchanged fluently, not just for "peer evaluation" but for interest and reflection on what they *say*. To have such sorts of writing activity implies taking students' relationships seriously by inviting them in as occasions for study. The study of language is quite dry unless one "descends" into these everyday contexts.

As I have said in a variety of ways, writing is a "double" subject: it is a moment of naming, and a moment of naming *something*. In the literacy classroom, that "something" is both the history of individual language use and class language use—the texts produced after the class has been convened. Each person enters the classroom with a history of language use, a history which most people have no reason for remembering in any formal way. Once it is allowed that how we speak and write is the product of how people speak in our homes, the speech customs in our native communities and early school years, in stores, on ball fields, in the movies, people will recognize these everyday language-use occasions. If one task of the literacy classroom is to try to reconstruct that history, then many hours can be spent thinking and asking friends and family about what one only partially remembers, and a surprising number of salient events of the past can be assembled. While it is never clear how "accurate" our memories are, the fact of having remembered *something* important always facilitates new reflection and analysis.

This inquiry creates the first texts for collective study. In the process of writing an "ethnography" of one's language-use strategies, one creates a new moment of language use and naming, a moment for the new community of interest, the class. These texts are, in a sense, the "property" and a property of the community. They are a way to secure several perspectives on one's own language, perspectives which are reciprocally studied themselves. They also begin the public accumulation of the materials that mark growth and development in class. Gradually, as relationships form, the texts begin to change in consequence of the writers knowing just who is going to read them, and these changes become more apparent as time goes on. Eventually, a significant corpus of texts makes it possible for those studying them to detect habitual usages, tendencies, regularities of language use that the user will not have seen. When such patterns are noticeable, the whole project takes on greater weight, since those studying the corpus begin making serious ethical, psychosocial, and political judgments about the language user. To put it another way, each person *feels* what others only noticed as language patterns, so that existing relationships in the class are "used" and sometimes even strained because of the sense that every judgment matters.

Throughout this process, as I have repeatedly implied, the "teacher" is producing texts in more or less the same way, making inquiries into his or her own language-use history, citing relationships, calling up moments of pain or consequence, reflecting on the apparent meaning and value of the past. In this respect, the teacher as a developing being is the "same" as the students. If the teacher is older than the students, one of course takes account of this fact just as one takes account of ethnic and economic differences among people. Most students are surprised to learn that teachers change their minds in the middle of a course, that they are not quite sure of how to say or do this or that. The accumulation of the teacher's texts discloses these ordinary eddies of thought, and perhaps more importantly, shows how language-use habits and strategies fluctuate. Often students are unaware how much of a struggle it is for a "professional language user" (an English teacher) just to be happy with his or her verbal handling of a situation, oral or written. In addition to this normalization of the teacher's "image," in a collective study of the teacher's work students can (and should) contribute to the teacher's growth. An important compensation for students' lack of experience in any class is their tendency to "close ranks" and collaborate in the search for what the teacher is not aware of. What might typically be a subversive impulse in the "mob" toward the "leader" is honored instead as a contribution to a common project. One indication of how authentic this procedure is is that even after having had this go on repeatedly in my classes, I am still slightly nervous each time because of the inevitability of the students' success. *When this success is habitual and ordinary in the class, it is the most important psychological substitute for whatever reassurance is given by the expectation of a grade.*

The structure of the literacy classroom I have been outlining makes it possible for literary response to create an essential opportunity. As the discussions in chapter 5 suggest, reading literature activates in different ways and degrees a person's sense that the literary language is *not one's own*, but is associated, in one way or another, with someone else. Let me now add the following consideration: *writing* the response statements, for all genres and both genders, objectifies both the literary material and one's own reading experience. The response statements show that readers, by virtue of their necessary social positioning, all see that literally, literature is always other — about someone or something else in language that is associated with others — that is, the not-me. When, in the response statements, personal memories and relationships are brought to bear as elaborative and explanatory analogies, they remain associated in the reader's mind with this "other" language world of the literature. In this way, our orientation around the literature permits us to conceal from ourselves our actual sense of implication in both the literary language and its referential statements. The materials that we report as associations to the literature tend to be those that we would censor if we were only trying to remember them as historical events.

Because of this special psychological role that literature plays in our minds, the response statements are able to disclose the *essential second perspective* which always contributes to our general repertoire of language-use strategies. In the same way that we are implicated in the language of those with whom we speak regularly, we are implicated in the language and reference of the imaginary matters and references of literature: *both areas of mental life are present in language use*. As I will try to show with specific instances in subsequent chapters, literary response statements disclose language-use strategies that are not found in texts whose main purpose is to consciously reconstruct one's past. These strategies emerge from the "unconscious" perspective we all have, though in everyday discourse our two perspectives always "merge"; those intimate with us, of course, can often tell how any of our statements entail two perspectives—say, an overt benign meaning and a covert aggressive one—but in impersonal conversation, their doubleness is very hard to detect.

These, then, are some of the principal features of a literacy classroom's function in view of the conception of language use I have been developing. Teachers and students are mutually implicated in one another's uses of language; the students' relationships with one another are more important than individual students' relationships with the teacher; collaborative group efforts among students and including the teacher are essential; individual histories of language-use strategies may be compiled to reveal present language-use strategies; literary experience and response statements are necessary to understand the stereoscopic experience and action of language; every one of the foregoing relationships and activities centers around disciplined writing by all parties. Finally, all forms of language use in the classroom, including the oral and the informal, should be understood as potential contributions to the general project of simultaneously studying and cultivating literacy.

In the next four chapters, I will "descend into detail" and try to show some results of trying to enact these principles. In these presentations, the loose ends and ragged edges of the classroom will be obvious, as will certain inconsistencies between what I claim ought to be done and what I actually did do. But if what I am proposing were without problems, it would be of no use to anyone else.

7

Disclosing and Using
the Double Perspective

In trying to make sense of the details of literacy in the Piedmont communities she studied, Shirley Heath defined a "literacy event" as a useful focus or unit for attention. In a 1983 essay, she explains it as "any occasion in which a piece of writing is integral to the nature of participants' interactions and their interpretive processes."[1] The event itself is some purposeful social occasion, such as a church group meeting to apply for a loan in which regulations have to be read, or a Girl Scout selling cookies and bringing a written folder announcing her identity and the program. As Heath describes them, the events each have an oral part and a written text which depend on one another. In viewing many of these events as they appeared in the communities, she comes to the following formulation:

> . . . there are more literacy events which call for appropriate knowledge of forms and uses of speech events than there are actual occasions for extended reading and writing.[2]

In people's actual experience, in other words, reading and writing are more often than not connected with some form of oral commentary, some spoken interaction or purposeful conversation. When Heath claims, in a general way, that orality and literacy cannot be separated, she means that when looking at specific cases one cannot fully understand the import and value of reading and writing without taking into account the oral circumstances which often accompany them.

As I intimated in chapter 3, in the discussion of Luria, oral activity (or "speech events") is always clearly interpersonal, whereas reading and writing is customarily assumed to be a private or individual activity. Thus, when

1. Heath, "Achievement of Preschool Literacy," p. 71.
2. Shirley Brice Heath, "Protean Shapes in Literacy Events: Ever-shifting Oral and Literate Traditions," in *Spoken and Written Language: Exploring Orality and Literacy*, ed. Deborah Tannen (Norwood, New Jersey: Ablex, 1982), p. 94 (in small caps in original).

Heath claims that the oral and the literate are intertwined with one another in "whole" communal events, she is also implying that in the study of literacy, the writer/speaker and the researcher/observer each require an individual and collective perspective: the literacy event is to be understood from the standpoint of the individual language user and from the standpoint of the collective purposes of the user's communities.

Heath is careful to say that in the communities she studied, where the literacy events predominate, there are still such things as "occasions for extended reading and writing." In the university classroom, and in academic practice in general, we would tend to say that the situation is reversed: there are such things as literacy events, such as the analysis of an individual's writing in the classroom, or a public forum in which certain texts are studied, but far more common is "extended reading and writing," such as research and writing a dissertation. Whereas the character of Heath's communities is defined by literacy events, the character of the classroom community is defined by the cultivation of individual literacy at various levels from routine technical competence to sophisticated hermeneutic skills. Many students, perhaps the majority, get through a course in which reading and writing are the major activities by simply doing the reading in private, following instructions on the preparation of essays and examinations, and then turning in good or even excellent work—where good work is expected to be thorough compliance to an announced standard. Even though "classroom participation" often "counts in the grade," it usually amounts to only a small fraction of that grade, and there are no means to make that participation interdependent with the private work which then becomes, as we all know, the main determinant of a student's performance. However, for many students, perhaps also a majority, participation with others is a significant part of their work, sometimes through competition, sometimes through cooperation outside the classroom, so that in an *unconscious* way, the private reading and writing are actually embedded in literacy events. But because such events are not considered to be the ordinary procedures and functions of the class, students and teachers will deliberately marginalize their total participation with others: they will not see their work in class as *already* being a part of a "literary event" situation. It is therefore possible to understand classroom communities as being "mostly" literacy events analogously to how Heath understood her communities. To understand the classroom as Heath understands Roadville and Trackton, a double perspective that combines awareness of oral and social factors with written and private ones is indispensable.

The work that I will examine in this and subsequent chapters comes from classrooms and other contexts that are, in one sense, traditional, and, in another, particularly redesigned to pursue the principles I have been discussing. The classrooms are traditional in that they are from a course

I taught in a whole system of traditional courses: students in my course can just as well meet the same requirements by taking other courses that are taught differently. They expect "training" in "good writing" as well as some introduction to the study of literature. They go to lectures once a week and they work in discussion sections of about twenty-four students, led by an associate instructor (a graduate student, apprentice teacher) who correctly appears to the students to be an "agent" of me, the principal instructor. The students expect to do more writing in this course than in most others and, finally, they expect a grade that will be recorded on their permanent transcript. In fact, grades are always assigned by the associate instructor and authorized by me. A great deal of work was written privately by the students and then "handed in" to their instructors, who returned the work to each student with "comments." Students correctly assumed that their grade was mainly determined through their one-to-one relationship with the associate instructor and usually behaved in class as if this were the case. These were the elements that I thought I had to retain to make any departures at all from the conventional classroom community.[3]

3. Anyone wanting to try new things in a system that is already working will have to make similar decisions about what can or cannot be changed in their particular school or university. My repeated requests at Indiana University to teach this course on a pass/withdraw basis, even for an experimental period of one year, were refused. Every possible technical rule was cited to declare that it was not a good idea. Most faculty members in other departments who had a chance to give an opinion on this matter conceived of writing as purely remedial and they therefore found no justification for suspending the custom, even for just a year, of requiring grades in the College of Arts and Sciences writing-requirement courses. These faculty members claimed they would not be able to tell who the good writers were and who the bad ones were. They claimed that the students' own records would be unclear, and that their careers would be jeopardized. From my point of view, the panic among these presumably informed colleagues was so great not because of their convictions about writing—they did not really understand what it meant to learn to write—but because they feared the likely consequences of an ungraded course being a success. If it clearly demonstrated that students do better in an ungraded course, leading to other requests by other faculty members, it would mean the gradual erosion of the grading system. I do not see any other explanation for refusing my request.

In most universities, the pass-fail system works in more or less the same way: students may take a small percentage of their elective courses pass-fail. Privately, when they register, it is noted that any passing grade will be recorded as a "pass." Instructors are not informed that this is the case, and they treat the student as if a normal grade will be assigned. The student may therefore "slack off," while the instructor has no idea why more effort isn't forthcoming. In proposing my course, I repeatedly told the relevant committees that I, the instructor, would establish the "pass" standard, which would not only be a departure from the usual pass-fail procedures, but would provide the needed insurance that students would continue to work hard. Because of the underlying panic about the mere idea of eliminating grading, however, my explanation was simply not heard, and the traditional rule about "pass-fail" courses not being allowed to count for writing credit was cited. I ask any reader who doubts that an unreasonable fear is behind the resistance to eliminating grading—even for one semester in writing courses— to try requesting the same thing in your own university and then to tell me what you find out.

In seeking to make the classroom host to literacy events instead of just "training" for individuals, I followed the grading practice I announced in my 1975 book, *Readings and Feelings*. The grade of "B" was considered a normative one, which required students to complete all work on time and in the right length or depth of treatment, and, generally, with a reasonable degree of conscientiousness and sincerity. It required students to attend all classes and to find suitable ways of contributing. Although this year-long course required about twenty-four essays, including two of three thousand words each, no essay was graded. At the end of each semester, the associate instructor gave a grade according to the aforementioned principles. If any student demonstrated some interesting initiative in thought, writing, or classroom participation over a long enough period of time, the grade was "A."[4] If any student failed to do two or more essays, or did not appear in class regularly, the grade was lower than B. Under these grading conditions, there was virtually no discussion about each student's technical competence, or, more generally, of the "how-well-am-I-doing" concerns that naturally accompany students' wishes to succeed.

A basic feature of this course, which required attendance as well as written and oral contributions from each class member (including associate instructors and me), was that students belonged to subgroups of three for the year. The title of my version of this generic "literature and composition" course was "Studying One's Own Language." One of the main reasons for meeting in these subgroups was for each student to hear the views of two other people about the student's own use of language. The principal task for each student was to write a comprehensive analytical commentary on his or her language use—as it appeared in essays and in any other germane circumstances during the year—at the end of each semester. At the same time, a subtask for each student was to master as far as possible the language-use habits and strategies of the two other students in the subgroup. Under these circumstances a student derelict in writing the essays—whether by not writing them or writing them without a serious effort—was impeding the work of other students, who needed a set of texts analogous to their own. Students who failed to read the work of their subgroup colleagues were also derelict, in that each student needed to have the perspective of his or her

---

4. In spite of my attempts to indoctrinate my assistants not to give plus and minus grading, most nevertheless could not seem to do without it, and, of course, I endorsed their final decision. I teased, prodded, whined, and constantly complained at the end of the semester during grading time, but it did not help. They just were unable to change their traditional styles of grading; they seemed to feel that a certain loyalty to the students required the more detailed grading style, even though, at every turn, they insisted that a completely ungraded course would be best.

colleagues for their final comprehensive commentaries. This restructuring of the usual classroom procedures enlarged the "audience" for all classroom writing from just the instructor to, first, the particular subgroup, and then to the discussion group as a whole. The diffusion of the audience for writing corresponded to the diffusion of the instructors' authority, so that all class members could see and perhaps experience the correspondence between the social relations of their work and the thoughts they recorded in their writing. Although this diffusion did not reach some ideal state, students did get into the habit of depending significantly on one another and of thinking of one another as the real audience for their work. The instructors retained authority as guides and contributors of advice and response, and as figures who urged continued discipline, but not as people whose definition of the issues determined the content, attitude, and stance of the students' work. Their essays, individually and as a collection, helped to render each subgroup meeting and each discussion section meeting more of a literacy event and less of an occasion for the display or performance of individual work.

In most courses in which "writing" is the subject and students are expected to practice and improve their "skills," students are frequently asked to write for imaginary or hypothetical audiences, some group that they are supposed to persuade or inform, upon a subject that has only an abstract connection to their everyday life. In this course, the audience is always real and relatively well known to each student, and the purpose of writing is, first, to record in some orderly fashion memories and experiences of language use that seemed to have remained important, and, second, to make these experiences meaningful to specific real people. While persuading and informing are parts of language use, the emphasis in this course is first on expressing, articulating, and sharing, and then on using one's own and others' insight to develop a more sophisticated analytical understanding of one's own and others' use of language. I have tried to translate some of the aims of ordinary but serious conversation among people who care about one another into a disciplined mode of collectively inquiring into language use and literacy. Put another way, I have tried to increase the role of everyone's daily experience of language in the study of writing, reading, and speaking, to teach students to "descend into the details" of their own lives as a path toward understanding what language is for other individuals and for larger and larger groups of people. In following this purpose, the "audience" is transformed from a group of listeners to a group of respondents, or, perhaps, more accurately, *correspondents*: people who respond to one's own work just as one responds to theirs.

In the rest of this chapter, I will examine how this different idea of audience can transform seemingly conventional student-essay texts into focal points of classroom literacy events that are best understood through the double perspectives of private and public, oral and written viewpoints. I will also explore how literary reading enters this self-conscious language study, a point I touched upon at the end of chapter 6. Then, in subsequent chapters, I will explore in detail three other aspects of the connection between literacy and social relations that this course involves: how an individual develops a comprehensive perspective on her own language (chapter 8), how the teacher interacts with students under these circumstances (chapter 9), and how students interact with one another (chapter 10). I will explain additional features of how this course worked as they pertain to the specific issue under discussion.

Consider first an essay written by Ms. V during the second week after our course first met:

Question

Think back to the first time in your life that a verbal or language event scared you. Name the person speaking, describe the full circumstances, and discuss the extent to which a purely verbal event (someone saying something) is fearful. Describe your fearful feelings as fully as possible, and explain the significance of this event today.

Ms. V

The first I recall of saying something that frightened me was when I was four years old and my grandmother told me that if I swallowed my bubble gum all my insides would stick together. My imagination then told me that one of two horrible fates would overtake me, either I would swell up and bust or I would die of starvation.

To this day I don't enjoy chewing gum and just the sight of someone else chewing it makes me queasy. During my first grade school years I, of course, told all my chums what chewing gum could do to them and one of them asked the teacher if it was true. A very concerned Mrs. W (3rd grade) drew me aside and told me that chewing or swallowing gum could not hurt you and would I please stop scaring the rest of the students.

To say the least, this confused me and caused me to distrust and not speak to my grandmother for about four months, but the enlightenment from the teacher never did quite cure me of my fear or slight phobia of chewing gum.

This may not be considered by some people a very big deal, but consider how many children and adults chew gum and what it would be like to be made sick by it.

Taken in the conventional way, as a freestanding, "handed-in" piece of work, this essay permits a number of judgments to be made about it. It seems to at least touch on every point in the question. In a relatively brief space, Ms. V was able to use an experience in her own life to translate the abstract elements of the question into a coherent anecdotal account. While there are elements of historical reporting, there is also a slightly ironic tone, as given in the phrases "one of two horrible fates" or "a very concerned Mrs. W." The phrase "to this day" in the second paragraph recalls perhaps the fable format which tells small stories to explain how the crow became black or how the leopard got its spots; in this case the implied riddle is: how I got to be slightly phobic at the sight of people chewing gum. The fluency of the account itself gives it a self-contained quality, a narrative unity that one might easily associate with fiction. Ms. V is herself one of the more articulate members of the class, who, throughout her year in class, showed a relatively higher level of cultivation in her language use than most of the others. In this essay, she used the skill, not in an analytical cause, but to characterize what she considers a more-than-trivial feeling. Even in its brevity, it is to me forceful and interesting.

But it would not be fair to this piece of work for me to have written such comments on her paper; Ms. V would then have read them, perhaps would have been pleased with the teacher's favorable response, and then continued to think of her work mainly in connection with what I like or consider good work. The context of the essay's "life" is then far too narrow, and in the terms I have been using, too "single in perspective" to understand the important meanings of this language act.

Instead of offering such comments, I duplicated the essay and distributed it to the class of twenty-three first-year students. Several students immediately said that they did not know if they believed this account, particularly Ms. V's claim that she still has a "slight phobia" of chewing-gum. I understand this skepticism to be a response both to the literal sense of the claim and to its having come across in the somewhat ironic and literary idiom of the essay. In any case, the students wished to know directly from Ms. V if she is really fearful when she sees people chewing gum today. In seriousness, she continued to say that yes she was somewhat fearful. Even though her further confirmation helped to persuade the class of her *sincerity*, the class still seemed to require further explanation of how such a fear could continue for so long. The task of understanding the essay became combined with the task of understanding something important about Ms. V, changing Ms. V's work from a text into a literacy event, in which Ms. V's presentation of herself becomes a deeper subject than an anecdote presenting information. To put it another way, the pertinent social meaning of her text required an answer to questions raised by the community to which it is presented.

After the class contemplated the situation for a while, a (female) student asked Ms. V to describe her relationship with her grandmother. Ms. V's new information then gave her essay a new context. She explained that her grandmother, her mother's mother, had dominated her mother, who, when Ms. V was five (a year after the grandmother's warning), was divorced from her father. As Ms. V stayed with her mother, the grandmother continued to be the significant authority figure, perhaps some apparent "ultimate" authority. In Ms. V's situation, in other words, what the grandmother said mattered much more than what most grandmothers say. About three years before Ms. V wrote the essay, her mother had died, and, her father being out of the picture entirely, her grandmother had actually become something of a parent. Thus, in view of the history of the grandmother's role in her family and her authority in Ms. V's life *at the time*, when Ms. V claims to have a slight phobia of anyone's gum-chewing, we may now understand the claim as a marker of her relationship with her grandmother, a marker which may very well have some literal force in her life. In addition to confirming her sincerity, Ms. V enhanced the authority and credibility of the claim itself.

Considering Ms. V by herself, there are two contexts for reading the essay: the original text and the additional material about her grandmother which we now associate with the text to help create a new reading of it and a new attitude toward it. We could now read the irony and "literary" features of Ms. V's essay as, perhaps, a certain distance she wishes to impose on the whole matter by casting a real experience in a mildly humorous genre, so that "the essay itself" has both a serious content and a way of revoking its seriousness. The essay is thus seen as the enactment of an affective dialectic in Ms. V's mind, and perhaps, the resolution of that dialectic, or even, a "dialogue" between herself and her grandmother.

But since the essay is a document meant for public presentation, we could not just consider Ms. V in isolation. Were there no collective engagement of the essay, the foregoing conception of the essay would be hard to see. The irony of the original essay derives, in part, from Ms. V's understanding that she is writing for or to her class, and it is this sense of prior social belonging that makes an ironic presentation possible, appropriate, and, perhaps in this instance, necessary. The class then takes up the irony as a question of Ms. V's sincerity and veracity—that is, as something having to do with her sense of membership in the group—and seeks to interpret the essay with these questions in mind. The point of the class's inquiry is: what would you have us believe about you; what about yourself are you actually contributing? Although the idea of personally "telling the truth" matters in this connection, it matters just as much to achieve a collective sense of Ms. V's particular words and language, phrases like "to this day," "two horrible fates," "slight phobia," and so on. The meaning of these phrases as well as the overall sense or purpose of the essay, is a function, of course, of her own individual history, but it is just as much a function of *her membership in the class*.

This membership, we see in this instance, made it possible for the purely individual sense of Ms. V to emerge in the first place. The "second," public context is, in a sense, no more secondary than the "first," private context is primary. No contextual perspective has priority, but there is a literacy event defined by both perspectives at once.

It could be argued that ordinarily the teacher's reading of a classroom essay provides a second perspective, and that students then reread their work in the light of their own and the teacher's perspective. Consequently, the cultivation of language use and writing in the university appears to be a stable institution. As stable as it may be, however, it shows what I previously have claimed, namely, that the social situation in which students work—the regular gathering, the steady physical formation of a collective body—is deliberately bypassed in favor of a more private, authority-heavy dyadic relationship in which the student is encouraged more to adapt to the teacher's perspective than to proceed in an authentic negotiation—since the teacher's final binding judgment is always anticipated. If the class were treated as a "thought collective," on the other hand, there could be no *a priori* sense of either the group's perspective or its judgment, and a genuine negotiation of meanings could proceed. The meaning and value—or the "reading" of an essay at one moment—depends on how the contributing individuals *choose among* several views, no one of which is privileged. By insuring that the "second" context is collective, the authority of each context is enlarged.

Many teachers, independently of the theoretical issues I have been discussing, also wish, at the prompting of their own aspirations for the classroom, to promote collective initiative among students but are inhibited by their sense of the historical inertia of the traditional pedagogical authority. In the terms I used in chapter 4, many teachers do wish for a "syntactic" relation between themselves and the class, a relation in which priorities are interchangeable, and the teaching and learning, in Freire's terms, move in both directions at once. Although any group or classroom event or process has to be started by some initial premise or question, such as the assignment which prompted Ms. V's essay, the subsequent result of class inquiry can then appear to be prior to, or even the cause of, the event which precipitated it. As the class reunderstood Ms. V's "slight phobia" in terms of her relation to her grandmother, the essay then appeared to be predicated on the "new" understanding. On the one hand the essay brought about the new understanding; on the other hand what is now understood brought about the essay. In this sense the premise and conclusion of the literacy event are interchangeable because they are syntactically interdependent on one another. The teachers want the "premises" they bring to class to collectively generate knowledge which then seems to be the premise for the initiating questions. What is not generally understood is that this reciprocal condition requires a fundamental change in the common conception of the teacher's authority.

I brought the topic of authority in the classroom to a summer workshop for English teachers in the following form: how can the use of literary response statements change the conventional sense of pedagogical authority? The "premise" or subject matter of my visit to this group could be simply stated as "The teacher's authority," while the "conclusion" or predicate for this subject could be understood as the several senses of this phrase that various group members came up with. If, to begin with, the "sentence" of knowledge can be stated as "The teacher's authority is what I think," interchanging the subject and the predicate brings, "What I (now) think is the teacher's authority." In the foregoing two sentences, the "is" is not the same as an "equal" sign: the structure of any sentence presupposes that the subject and predicate clauses have *unequal* status, even if the subject and predicate are the same word, as in "a rose is a rose." If this sense of the interchangeability of an inherently different subject and predicate, premise and conclusion, "sticks," then a double perspective will have promoted a change from a fixed sense of the teacher's authority and a single ("semantic") direction of its definition to a variable sense of it and a dialectic ("syntactic") context of its definition.

With the question of pedagogical authority "in the air," the first step is to create, through a writing event for the whole group, texts which present each individual's subjective sense of authority. But rather than soliciting this sense directly, in literal terms, I gave a "double" exercise that asked the teachers to speak about literature as they normally would, but in two different ways. The resulting "double" essays disclosed many of the language idioms they normally used in teaching, thereby giving a sense of their *enactment* of authority, and, in addition, the essays suggested ways in which the teachers *already* had a double sense of their authority.

The exercise consists of addressing two issues, consecutively, but the second question is not posed until work on the first has been completed. This technique permits an informal separation of perspectives whose relation to one another is then seen in retrospect. The assumption behind this technique is that the moment of writing always appears to be governed by *one* perspective (just as, in the well-known duck-rabbit drawing, one cannot see both the duck and the rabbit at once), but that when two or more moments of an individual's language use are examined, the "ingredients" of either perspective then become more apparent. In criticism, it is common to view the work of a single author as coming through one perspective, as in the title of Eugene Goodheart's study, "The Utopian Vision of D. H. Lawrence." But if one views each work or each theme in Lawrence's work separately, his work will then appear to be a combination of several disparate ideas and values which

Lawrence *rendered* dependent on one another by making them part of one story. If a work "lives" as a recurrent literacy event in a given community, it is regularly taken apart and reassembled in new ways as the community changes; the *work's* perspective cannot be fixed. (I will show this process in more detail in several of the instances I am discussing below.)

Members of this group read in advance Hemingway's "Hills Like White Elephants." When we all gathered, I first asked them to "retell the story as fully and as accurately as you can." After about thirty minutes, they were asked to "discuss what you think Hemingway was trying to do in writing the story." The two instructions suggested two different kinds of focus, one which calls for an account of the "facts" and centers on the text, and another which calls for a "judgment" and centers on the author. These perspectives are common enough in school situations, and, while they are not without their own problems,[5] they yielded differences in emphasis in the essays, which proved useful. In the discussion that follows I will examine the essay-pairs of two members of the group, a woman and a man. Here first are the essays of Ms. J, a secondary school teacher in her early thirties:

Ms. J 1

The man and woman who are the main characters are having drinks at a bar. They talk. Their sentences are short. He speaks of surgery. Their sentences are ambiguous; they speak of times gone by. Their conversation is light, yet the tone of the story revealed in the dialogue is dark. Deep undercurrents run through the spate of words. There must be an abortion, he says circumvently [sic]. Her depression frames the listlessness of her replies.

The woman would prefer to drift. She wishes life to continue as it exists— or perhaps even return to a time when this shadow had not yet covered the equatorial sun. The man's desire to urge her out of inertia is coupled with his own accustomed blandness. Together they gaze into the future and see it far removed, as though viewed through the wrong end of a telescope.

There is a vitality in the story, but it beats slowly and softly, muffled beneath the shallow surface, like the baby's heart beneath that of the woman who wants to be "amusing."

Ms. J 2

Hemingway was showing off in "Hills Like White Elephants." He was per-forming his particular type of literary pirouette with verve and style. Take the very bones of a story, a skeletal frame, and hang on it a few shreds of inci-dent—this is how the dance begins. Then take ten paces, twenty, thirty or more back and fire from the hip, whizzing dialogue, like bullets, through the

---

5. For example, the natural response of most readers who acknowledge that they do not know what the author was trying to do is that it makes no sense to guess.

narrative's skull. When the death dance ends, the reader's brain has also been pierced, and Hemingway, like a sweating Nureyev, waits in the wings for the applause.

Let me defer temporarily the question of Ms. J's relation to the group in order to see the relation between the two essays. It was immediately noticed that in the first essay, Ms. J's style seems to want to resemble Hemingway's, as when Ms. J writes, "Their sentences are short," It looks as if for Ms. J to "retell" the story means to recreate the *way* of telling as well as the "facts" or events "in" the story. She tries to make her language do what she thinks Hemingway's language did. In this process, she takes the initiative of translating the story's "operation" into "surgery" and "abortion," perhaps specifying something only implied by the story. She uses the metaphor of the "deep undercurrents" and the simile of the "wrong end of a telescope" to retell important complexes of feeling. Finally, she likens the story to the child's heart inside the woman's body, showing that the story's life is similarly "muffled." For Ms. J, to retell the story is to actively overtake the role of the author, using some of the author's own techniques and some of her own. From this standpoint, her sense of the story is of something understated, concealed, and perhaps, like the woman, depressed and resigned.

When she objectifies the author (with whom she has just fluently identified) in the second essay, a new picture emerges: a show-off inclined to violence. Ms. J, meanwhile, now writes in the imperative voice—"Take the very bones . . . , " "Take ten paces . . . "—and recreates the author's action as a "death dance," sees him with a gun which shoots its dialogue "like bullets" which penetrate the narrative's skull and the "reader's brain." This is her answer to the question of what she thinks the author is trying to do.

Ms. J was particularly adept at changing perspectives, from the storyteller to the critic, from the reader to the teacher. In both essays, Ms. J speaks with authority, as she views the initiating questions as empowering her to speak out and perhaps, in a good-intentioned sense, to show off. But if only one of these two essays were considered as her "response" or her "reading," it would be hard to discern the sense of authority in either reading. For example, in the first essay, is Ms. J conscientiously following instructions or is she, in a more independent act, seizing the opportunity to enact the story in her own way? Would it be enough to say that her sense of the story is one of concealment and quiet frustration, "like the baby's heart beneath that of the woman"? Would her attempt to imitate the author's voice seem frivolous or self-indulgent? In the second essay, which presents a judgment, is Ms. J merely invoking a stereotype of Hemingway and caricaturing it?

How serious is the simile of the "sweating Nureyev"? How are we to take the shooting imagery?

If the essays are seen as predicated on one another, however, one would have to take Ms. J's theme of performance seriously and understand it as an important feature of her sense of authority. For the group which she knew would read her work, the essays are definitely a performance: none of the others in this group of about thirty people took the metaphorical liberties she did. Although the performance may be slightly tongue in cheek, as if Ms. J were saying, "I am *not* taking myself so seriously," it also has a very serious pedagogical impact, since her presentations of her reading experience involves "getting into the part" in the theatrical sense: she wants to *show* the story to others, not just tell it or report her opinion of the author. If performance may be attributed to both essays, its function in each is different, yet the performances depend on each other at the same time. Perhaps indirectly, Ms. J in the first essay identifies with the woman and she sees the vitality of the story in terms of her situation—the need to conceal an important element in her life. The imitation of Hemingway's short sentences contributes to the task of concealment, the feeling that not much seems to be happening. But, in the second essay, where Ms. J openly judges, she characterizes the author's presentation of the story as violent, damaging, and lethal, and even sees the author's love of violence being enacted toward her, the reader. In both essays, Ms. J uses her authority to speak metaphorically to say something important to her audience, but we could not have understood from the first essay that her idea of frustrating concealment also meant that she felt literarily assaulted, nor could we have known that her judgment of Hemingway's violence meant that she was moved in a serious, meaningful way; reading the second essay alone we might read a thoughtless antagonism into her opinion of Hemingway. Ms. J takes a language strategy of her own—performance—translates both the reading and her judgment into its terms, and enacts her authority as a contribution to the common project on that occasion.

All the while, this common project (the question of the teacher's authority) has been functioning as a prior context. On the one hand, we will want to say that this context "influenced" how Ms. J wrote her essay, and on the other we will want to deliberately use our knowledge of the prior context to "read" the essays—to understand what they say for our post-essay interests, that is, without trying to discover a prior cause for the essays. By virtue of Ms. J's language having developed in a certain way, one can say that her essays manifest the direction of growth in her individual mental development; but one should also say that the essays cannot be removed from their immediate context of production: her work is as decisively bound to the interests of the present group as it is to her individual set of language-use strategies. Again, both of these perspectives on Ms. J's essays are necessary and syntactically dependent on one another; understanding the essays *means* reading them in this syntactic, dialogic, dialectical, or relational way.

Here now is an essay pair which suggests a different sense of authority, that of Mr. R, also a secondary school teacher in his middle or late thirties:

Mr. R 1

A man and a woman are sitting in the bar of a railroad station somewhere in Spain, waiting for a train. They are discussing a "simple operation" the woman is to have. The man assures her that there is nothing to it—just "letting a little air in." The couple goes back and forth throughout the entire story discussing whether or not the woman should have the operation. Although it seems like the man would rather she have the operation and the woman would rather not, it also seems that neither wants to impose his/her will on the other. The man wants it "just like it used to be." The woman wants the man to be happy. She "doesn't care about herself." The discussion is really tedious and repetitious— very much like it might be in real life. The story never makes clear what the "it"—the operation—really is, although I've heard people say that it was an abortion. The couple have several drinks while they are waiting—beer, the 2 specialties, Anis del Toro—which tastes like licorice—then more beers. The man goes back to check on the train and has one more anis. That's basically the story. One detail that sticks in my mind is the curtain over the door—stringed beads "to keep the flies out."

To recap the action, the couple sits down and the man orders "dos cervezas." Then the woman asks about the "Anis del Toro" and the man orders two. He assures her that the operation is simple. She asks, "Will everything be as before?" He says, "Certainly, it's just a simple airing—I want it to be just the two of us." The woman says that she doesn't care about herself. She just wants to please him. The man assures her that she doesn't *have* to have the operation. It's her decision. That pattern is repeated over and over again.

Mr. R 2

I haven't the slightest idea. But since I'm an English teacher, I can't say that so I'll make an educated guess. I'm going to believe those who say the operation is an abortion. Regardless, it's obviously *not* just a simple operation. Hemingway is showing the tension through the tedium of the conversation. Neither the man nor the woman is voicing his/her real concerns. The man wants her to have the operation but doesn't want to seem to be pressuring her. The woman is afraid of the operation and perhaps she would like to have the baby, but she doesn't want to risk offending or losing the man. But none of this is what they say. Instead they talk around the issue, trying to reassure themselves and each other—but accomplishing nothing. The world itself is disinterested—operating on schedule, serving drinks, keeping out the flies. The couple seeks diversion in their drinks, but really finds none. Around them are "hills like white elephants." Perhaps resembling a woman's pregnant belly. For not understanding the story, I think that's pretty good. But not for all the world would I have guessed that the operation was an abortion. Nothing in the story gives me that impression, although when I consider the subject, it all fits together.

A feature distinct in Mr. R's work and not found in anyone else's in this group is his second retelling, or "recap." While there is no announced reason for this move, it seems likely that Mr. R gives the second retelling to better authorize the first. Where, in the first paragraph, for example, Mr. R says that the *man* wants things "just like it used to be," in the second paragraph he mentions the *woman* asking if things will be as before. Also in his first paragraph, Mr. R makes a point of noting that the story does not identify the operation being discussed by the couple. Further, in both paragraphs, Mr. R gives descriptive comments: "That's basically the story" and "That pattern is repeated over and over again," phrases which contribute to the sense that, in his first essay, Mr. R took the instruction to retell the story accurately much more self-consciously than did Ms. J. But because there is the "recap," and because Mr. R did not comment on or clarify whether the man or woman or both wanted things to remain as they had been in the past, this first essay poses the *problem* of accuracy as a reading concern.

Although his second essay immediately takes up the issue of just what the "operation" was, its main concern suggests the sense in which it may be understood as a context for the first. The train of thought in the opening part of the essay suggests this conclusion: Mr. R does not know what Hemingway was trying to do; but because he is an English teacher he cannot be content with saying that he does not know; and in order to guess Hemingway's intentions, he reasons, he has to decide on what the operation is. There is, of course, no necessity to decide on what the operation is in order to answer the second question, which could very well be discussed without identifying the operation any further: the lack of further identification could itself be considered as part of the author's intention. For Mr. R, however, the fact that he could not find an exact textual confirmation for what the operation was is already involved in the context disclosed in his second essay, namely, his competence as an English teacher.

A measure of Mr. R's concern with his competence is suggested by his reaching for new insight at the end of the second essay. Contemplating the story's title, he observes that the hills "perhaps" resemble "a woman's pregnant belly." On seeing the plausibility of this thought, he congratulates himself—"For not understanding the story, I think that's pretty good." This move alleviates the concern that arose in the first essay about just what the operation was and his somewhat nervous attempt to "recap" the retelling. Mr. R took the provisional hypothesis about the operation's nature and related it to something else he did not understand—the title—and then made the two pieces of "data" work together: the title contributes to the idea of pregnancy and the idea of pregnancy illuminates the meaning of the title. In this process, Mr. R solves both the local problem in the first essay of what the operation was and the local problem in the second essay of recuperating his competence. As we view the two essays now, however, it is clear that the two "local" problems are predicated on one another, and that *the opportunity to begin thinking in a new context (given by the second essay assignment) also stabilized Mr. R's thinking about the story.*

Just as the common project of the question of the teacher's authority had been a prior context for Ms. J's work, it is in the exact same way the prior context for Mr. R's. In fact, Mr. R alludes to it more clearly when he says, "I've heard people say that it was an abortion." The "people" he is referring to are the rest of the members of this group, which, it should now be mentioned, was composed overwhelmingly of women. Among the thirty or so group members, only three were men. As I discussed toward the end of chapter 5, among those reading this story for the first time, women almost always "see" the abortion quickly and unequivocally, while men either don't see it or need considerable persuasion. In this group, Mr. R is in the minority. When he brings his standard of "accuracy" to the reading, which does not easily permit translating the text's "operation" into "abortion," his competence is challenged by the sheer majority opinion about the story (which was obviously informally discussed before the exercises were given), and he is made to *feel* the question of his authority in a new way—relative to a group of peers who seem unaccountably ahead of him in some way. When Mr. R comes up with his "insight" about the allusiveness of the title, it is his attempt to rejoin this community of peers with a suitable contribution of his own. In other words, he used the opportunity of the second essay to reintegrate himself into the community which existed even before the writing began.

This step calls, perhaps, for somewhat more attention, particularly because of the gender factor. On one hand, because Mr. R is a secondary school teacher, it is reasonable to think that he is already used to being in a minority. On the other hand, the fact that he actually brought into his retelling something that he's "heard people say," suggests a certain amount of discomfort with his minority status. No one else in this group alluded to what other people had said when they "retold" the story. His discomfort is probably also apparent in the "insight" itself—the alleged resemblance of the hills to a pregnant woman. Of course if a woman is considering an abortion, it is not likely that she "looks" pregnant. The way experienced readers often relate the title to the substance of the story is through the *metaphor* of the "white elephant"—something no one wants—rather than the visual image. My point is that Mr. R's "insight" is not just a simple measure of his competence as a reader or an English teacher, but is the expression of a certain exclusion from, and the wish for inclusion in, this group of "competent" women readers and teachers. The context in which Mr. R wrote his essays is not merely "English teachers" but, probably, "female English teachers."

The question of gender in Ms. J's work is much less related to how she belongs to this group and much more of a factor in her identifying aspects of the story and identifying *with* figures in the story and its author. It seems to me that it is generally less of a problem for Ms. J, even though neither she nor Mr. R explicitly mentions gender. The social value operating for Ms. J, as we discussed, is "performance," and her way of bringing this value out includes identifying with the masculine author in her first essay and then objectifying him in her second. We might want to say that Ms. J has a greater fluency in gender identification than Mr. R, so that the issue of gender is quite visible but not intrusive on the social tasks undertaken by Ms. J's work. In both of Mr. R's essays, there is no real sign of his identification with either of the characters or with the author, since his attention is almost completely on objectifying the couple in the service of accurately retelling the story. This strategy also succeeds in keeping the gender issue unconscious, so to speak, relative to his whole presentation, and, in my judgment, ultimately inhibits both his confidence in his perception as well as his capacity for response. His essay pair is ironically concerned more with his own performance as a member of the group, and this concern actually attenuates his performance. In contrast, Ms. J, who actually performed a great deal in this exercise by trying to imitate the author's style of writing, is much less self-involved and more successful in achieving a balance between her personal reading and values and her address to her coreaders.

My opinion, however, about whether an individual has achieved some desired balance is not of primary concern for us now. I want only to stress, thus far, two points: the "syntactic" dependency of each essay on the other, with each being helpfully considered "prior" to the other, and the similarly syntactic dependency of the essay pair on the social context in which they were written. This latter point implies that the opinions I presented just above should actually be posed as questions that should have been (and were to some extent) brought into the "prior context" of the plenary group discussion. When the two pairs of essays appear for discussion (after each member has written such a pair), they become the "subject" and the discussion of them becomes the "predicate." For Ms. J my question will then be, "Are you performing your reading experience for us, and if so, what does this mean?" And for Mr. R my question becomes, "Are you testing your competence for and through us?" In discussing such questions, each person's work is necessarily viewed *both* as a "reading" of a story and as a mark of their membership in the group. Needless to say, whatever opinions are finally given by other group members, whatever new judgments are given by Ms. J and Mr. R, they also are neither resolutions nor final truths, but starting points for the informal extension of the formal plenary discussions—that is, the "aftertalk" that customarily takes place when class is over. The important point is that, on one hand, there is no "last word" on the matter, and on the other, there is a last word in the formal functioning of the class, and it is *collective*.

In regard to Ms. V's essay, the collective (and provisional) "last word" was achieved when the class got a new commentary from Ms. V; it served as a temporary closure which made her work more eligible to link up with whatever work followed. I characterized this closure (page 194) as establishing a reciprocal relation between the essay and its critical reception, between Ms. V and the rest of the class, a relation which could not be cultivated, generally, in classrooms, without a fundamental change in the distribution of authority in the classroom. I then went on to discuss the two essay pairs that were produced and discussed in a group which was not organized according to the usual classroom model, trying to suggest, perhaps, how authority remains part of the pedagogical mentality. I would now like to discuss how the essay-pair technique functions when there is an authoritative teacher. I will try to show how the students' sense of the teacher's authority influences their work, and how the double perspectives created by the exercise negotiates this authority in a way that it is neither denied nor complied with in a perfunctory way.

The two essay pairs that follow were written toward the end of the course I described early in this chapter. The authors already had many weeks' experience working in groups and had acquired the confidence and style to challenge both me and their discussion instructor routinely. (Unlike Ms. V, Mr. S and Mr. G were not in my discussion section.) The reading for this exercise was Shirley Jackson's "The Lottery." The first question was:

> *Give your affective and associative responses to the story, your strongest feelings, your general feelings (as in previous exercises). Give relationship analogies to elaborate on these feelings; indicate if and to what extent you identified with those in the story.*

After about twenty-five minutes, I wrote the second question on the blackboard:

*This story is often understood as an allegory of the fact that every commu-
nity has a scapegoat whether they know it or not. Tell the extent to which
your response contributes to this interpretation, and the extent to which your
response leads to a new meaning for the story altogether.*

Here, first, is Mr. S's essay pair:

Mr. S 1

Before I begin to elaborate on my affective and associative responses to "The
Lottery," I feel it is most important to take into consideration the fact that I
read this story once before in ninth grade under the regime of a teacher who
somehow knew exactly what the author meant when he or she wrote a story.
Therefore, I feel I have already been programmed to see in the story what the
teacher wanted me to see.

My strongest feelings and associations with the story took place at that point
where Tessie Hutchinson was totally surrounded by all of her friends and the
inhabitants of the community. In the sixth grade, I experienced a similar ordeal.
I had stolen one of the biggest hothead's girlfriend from him and somehow he
had persuaded or coerced my friends into turning against me. I didn't make
any big deal over the situation and made no attempts towards a reconciliation.
One day on my way home, the emotions of the other boys came to a climax as
they followed me home from school. They took me to a backyard where at one
point I was totally surrounded by all of my friends just as Tessie was. At this
point, I had my strongest feelings of anxiety, fear, and anticipation. Although
this was my major association with Tessie, there are also a few minor details
that coincide with my "tragic event." On more than one occasion, Tessie tries
to talk her way out of her predicament. I also attempted this evasive strategy.
In another instance, all of Tessie's friends seemed glad to contribute to her
doom. In my experience, it seemed to me that my friends enjoyed seeing their
sharp-tongued leader, helpless, at their mercy, and without any following. All
of these points were stronger associations in the ninth grade than they are now.

Pursuing my last statement further, my affective responses were much
stronger in ninth grade than they are now also. As a matter of fact, I think
that I just have memories of how the story affected me in ninth grade and that
it really has no other effect on me now rather than a comical one. My memories of flashback feelings are ones of fear, weakness, and loneliness. Probably
because this was the first point (and the last) that I have felt alone without
friends (followers) or dominance (power and control). I had no control over
what course that event may have taken and that situation caused my feelings.

Mr. S 2

I really do not feel that my response has any correlation with the "Scapegoat
Allegory" hypothesis. I do believe that my response could have some point
where this scapegoat idea is extracted. As I said in the beginning of this essay,
my situation was caused by my so-called stealing of someone else's girlfriend.
Because he was jealous, due to the fact that his girlfriend liked me, he took out

his feelings of anger and jealousy on me. I was his scapegoat. Following this
train of thought, my friends may have been releasing their feelings of inferiority
to me by going along with the hothead in rebellion against me. Again, I was
the target (scapegoat) of their emotions. These are really the only significant
ties that I can make with the story at this time.

Jackson's "The Lottery" is a story that many students had read already,
usually early in high school, and Mr. S's report of his own reading comes
from our habit in this course of announcing if we had previously read a story.
A more distinctive feature of Mr. S's announcement is his description of the
situation in which he read the story—"under the regime of a teacher" who
already knew the "correct" interpretation. In consequence of this teacher's
authority, Mr. S reports, he felt "programmed" to see the story the way
the teacher wanted him to. He does not announce in this essay whether
the previous "program" is still in effect or whether he feels himself to be,
now, on his own. He suggests in the second paragraph of the first essay,
however, that the association he reports here may represent the "stronger"
ninth-grade feelings about the story, and it seems that the present reading
may have affected him mainly in having brought back the earlier experience,
which he now views with a certain comic irony. However, it remains unclear
from this essay exactly what the case is, because at the beginning of his
second paragraph he comes right out and says that "my strongest feelings and
association with the story took place at the point . . . ," which implies that
the events he narrates actually did come to mind on *this* reading, and he is
not *merely* reporting the previous reading. In a case like this, our interpretive
procedure is to take *both* views seriously, namely, to understand the essay
as an expression both of comic detachment and of the feelings he reports
having had back in the ninth grade and which returned on this reading. What
we still are not certain of, in reading this essay, however, is the significance
of his announcement that he had been "programmed" by his earlier teacher.
From the essay, it looks as if his response is his own and spontaneous—now
as well as then—so we would like to know why he thought it important to
make the preliminary announcement.

We get some help in this issue when we consider his second essay,
particularly the first sentence, in which he claims to feel that his response
does not have "any correlation with the 'Scapegoat Allegory' hypothesis."
Although he immediately qualifies this claim in ways that I will discuss
shortly, the claim itself should be understood as a reaction to the *source*
of the question which almost all students see similarly: Bleich, the teacher.
Like all the students in the course, Mr. S implicitly takes the phrase "is
often understood" (in the second question) to be an academic euphemism
for "the professor's view." Students do not, in some general way, think this

literally and consciously, but rather see its citation—in the passive voice—as the professor bringing to bear his own knowledge, his own reading of the criticism, his own way of resaying the "meaning" of the story. The students correctly see my attempt to propose some "official" meaning, some standard which implies a *test* of their own reading of the story. In other words, students read the meaning proposed in the second question as *authoritative*.

In the light of Mr. S's second essay, therefore, his remark about having been programmed by his teacher seems clearer. The first sentence of the second essay expresses a theme that the first paragraph of the first essay presented—the feeling on *this* occasion that he will not be coerced by an authoritative opinion. This sense of the classroom situation is then bound up with his perception of the meaning and content of the story, or, to use the terms I have been proposing, his sense of the story and his sense of the classroom situation are reversibly predicated on one another.

As a student and as a reader, Mr. S is claiming his role as a leader and as a dominant figure—one who has "power and control" and who cannot be rendered "helpless" either by weak friends or by a domineering teacher. In this cause, Mr. S presents his first sentence of the second essay in relatively extreme terms. However, he immediately appropriates the scapegoat "idea" as a useful description of how he felt in his associative analogy. From the story he told in the first essay, he became a scapegoat for reasons very different from those that made Tessie Hutchinson one; in particular, he shows how it was his own initiative—stealing the "hothead's" girlfriend—which led to his victimization. His second essay, however, presents a somewhat different accent. The "stealing" of the girlfriend becomes the "so-called stealing," and then he adds the information that the girlfriend liked him (instead of the other fellow): in the first telling it looked as if the girl's feelings had nothing to do with whether he could "steal" her away from someone else. Also in the second essay, Mr. S brings in the jealousy of his rival as well as his own friends' possible "feelings of inferiority" in order to build a case for the view that he, like Tessie, was an innocent victim—a *scapegoat*. He says, "I was the target (scapegoat) of their emotions."

What, then, has Mr. S achieved? Clearly, what Mr. S did not do was comply with or address the general issue that I raised of whether or not every community has a scapegoat. But he does reinterpret his own response in terms of the scapegoat idea and succeeds in presenting himself in a more favorable light. In a sense he makes good on his claim (in the first essay) that he will not be victimized again, and he does so by partially rejecting and partially appropriating the "authoritative" meaning of the story. In other words he now *negotiates* authority in the second essay, one form of which he ridiculed in the first essay. From one standpoint, Mr. S shows no great loss of narcissism as he moves from the first essay into the second. However, the point of this exercise is not to change people's character but to begin the process of negotiating other perspectives, to stimulate each person's natural resourcefulness to cope with the social challenges of the classroom. Obviously, Mr. S was already a young man who had a certain orientation toward authority and toward his peers, an orientation which, however we may wish to evaluate it, was perfectly serviceable and successful throughout the tenure of this course. Indeed he is not the only young man who comes to school with that turn of mind. In his case, he was able to achieve a new reading of the story—one with more comic detachment—and then he was able to negotiate my classroom authority in what I consider a relatively creative way: as selfish as it may make him seem, it rings true for him to describe his experience in sixth grade as that of having been scapegoated. In any event, his essay pair provides a useful proposition that his peers could then review and judge *without* his becoming a scapegoat.

Here now is the work of Mr. G, who coped with the "authoritative" question in a somewhat different way.

Mr. G 1

My overriding sentiment after reading "The Lottery" is one of sadistic joy. It appalls me, this feeling, but I got a very vivid mental picture of the events of this story and could really see Mrs. Hutchinson getting nailed in the head with a rock. Perhaps I feel this way because I have read the story previously, many years ago, and knew how it ended. Though I enjoyed the situation Jackson put us in, I am an impatient person and was anxious for the stones to be let loose.

Jackson manipulated me into this feeling in many respects. The extensive use of children in the story and down-to-earth people makes one feel like nothing this cold-blooded could be happening. Then as it develops, Tessie Hutchinson sets herself out as the (for lack of a better word) cry-baby—whining of the unfairness. Something very fair came across to me. Everyone of these people took a turn; it had hundreds of years of tradition behind it, and that's the way it is—accept it and die.

Mr. G 2

My response was not so much of one about a scapegoat. Rather I felt a strong sense of power, and at the same time, the helplessness this power created. I didn't go so far as seeing the victim being held responsible for anything, so much as her being a victim of fate. Many things in life don't make sense. We could ask ourselves why countless times. Why did those nice people stone the lady? Why does rain fall down? Why are we alive? I don't know. What are we going to do to change it? I don't know—why?

The difference between the first and second essays cannot be easily traced to the influence of the second question. Nevertheless there is a change in mood and tone in the second essay, and it is likely that the need to *consider* the second question had something to do with Mr. G's change in mood (just as the need to consider the second question produced an analogous change in Mr. R's views). Perhaps the least ambiguous difference to be noted is in the language. In the first essay the sentences are declarative and forceful in their meaning—"overriding sentiment . . . is one of sadistic joy"—and the essay ends in a figurative imperative—"accept it and die"—that is meant to represent Mr. G's imaginary conversation with the story's victim. Similarly strong is Mr. G's figure of "getting nailed in the head," a phrase which does not appear in the story, and which Mr. G uses to elaborate on the feeling of "sadistic joy." Mr. G uses the declarative tone to enhance his sense of justice as well as his spontaneous feeling of celebration when he says that "something very fair came across to me," or "that's the way it is." Mr. G's *response* to the reading, in other words, is clear both in its feelings and its conviction, and there is no way of predicting from this essay alone the kind of thoughts he presents in the second essay.

Like Mr. S, Mr. G begins the second essay suggesting that the issue my question presented does not bear on his response. He starts out in the declarative voice but ends the essay with a string of questions, reflecting the *double* declaration toward the beginning—the simultaneous feeling of power and helplessness, a feeling that perhaps contrasts with the unqualified sense of fairness that he expressed in the first essay. Although the questions Mr. G presents are, in part, rhetorical, they call attention to the fact that Mr. G is thinking *about* what he said in the first essay, and he is asking himself (as well as the readers) about the now-interrogatively experienced state of power and helplessness. He does not mention in this connection that anyone or anything *put* him into this position, or that the sense of *necessary scapegoating* proposed by my question encouraged the sense of quandary about the position he took in the first essay. At the same time, in the first essay, he seems to have no trouble stipulating that the author "manipulated" him into having his strong feelings and no trouble implying that he is collaborating with the author in this cause. We are led to think that Mr. G may be less critically aware of the social situation of his writing than is Mr. S, while being more aware of the problematic character of his thoughts. Specifically, Mr. G is less vigilant about the action of authoritative figures than is Mr. S and not inclined to consciously censor their influence. In his second essay, Mr. G seems less reluctant to question his earlier perspective than is Mr. S, even though each writer's change in perspective is decisive. However, while the two underlying approaches to authority are quite different, one sees how the second question elicited in each man a critical review of his perspective; in fact, each writer sees the change in the perspective of his first essay as his own effort, that is, something specifically *not* done in compliance with an assignment, but in negotiation with the terms proposed by the assignment.

In all of the preceding examples, I have been presupposing the principle of language analysis that I first discussed in chapter 3, namely, the belief that each person's language-use strategies are subjectively registered through a process that might be called *social insertion*. Self-awareness appears in each of us at the moment of language acquisition because both self-awareness and language require and "mean," in a sense, our implication in other people's lives and their implication in ours. In each of the instances of individual effort I just discussed, I tried to show that their status as "literacy events" is decisively marked in a variety of ways by language which can only refer to the individual's sense of social implication, and, particularly in the last two instances, the ways in which the individuals were implicated in the *authority* situation of their classroom. Each person's language use, in other words, has a simultaneous individual and social reference.

Toward the end of chapter 6, I proposed that people's responses to literature offer a particularly useful way to disclose this double reference because literary language always enters our minds, regardless of our gender, as *other* language, thus automatically creating an internalized dialogue. Reading literature creates a box in our minds of "provisional other language" which permits us to think about virtual social behavior, as we "listen" to the texts and "answer" them in various subjective ways. In most normal people, these answers, as they appear in literary "responses," show ways in which we have appropriated the other language and ways in which we are implicated in it. But because the literary language is only "imaginary," or is taken as not "counting" in the same way that referential language is taken, the categories of our thoughts which we normally consider "unfit" for social contribution usually enter into our responses peremptorily. In this way, the processes of literary response enable us to gain access to parts of our overall language-use capability, which we may not want to deliberately share, but which we nevertheless wish to recognize and perhaps bring under the aegis of conscious use. To demonstrate this process, I will use the case of a somewhat abnormal student, since the difference between his conscious and unconscious language-use strategies is much more distinct and radical than it is with most people. In subsequent chapters inquiring into the work of more ordinary students, we will see the same principle at work in a less extreme form.

The examples from Mr. B's work are in the two previously mentioned language categories. The first is three full essays in the "referential" mode. The sample here is longer, since it would be hard to get a sense of Mr. B's writing using only excerpts or fewer essays. The samples in the second category give a good cumulative picture. The first three essays were written during the first semester and the excerpts from the last five the second semester. Mr. B left school after his freshman year.

Question 1 [given in discussion section, the first day of class]

In the time remaining, tell something about yourself that you consider impor- tant—something you would like others to know. Be as detailed as possible and try to explain why you want people to know this particular thing.

Mr. B 1

I am from a small city in southern Indiana, and as one well knows, not much happens in a small farming community. The people are generally only concerned about their farms and have little interest in the rest of the world. I have all ways tried to be just the opposite of the people in my town, so life would have a meaning and be interesting for me. I have traveled to Europe hoping to get a better perspective of the world and the way people think. When one is away from people other than himself he has a different perspective about himself and others.

I believe that for one to enjoy and obtain satisfaction from the earth one must be able to go many places, the solid, liquid, and gases of the earth. I started flying so I could see the earth from above, and add a whole new perspective to the earth and myself. I started traveling so I could see the solid of the earth, its beauty and history. I am starting scuba diving so I can enjoy the liquid part of the earth and yet add another perspective to my mind. With these three tools one can observe the earth where we live and better understand ourselves and others. I believe that since I was so opposite of the people in my town I became lonely, and in search for something to do I traveled to meet other people more like myself.

I am very impatient, I have found no reason, so I must have been born with this trait. I am also full of contradictions.

Question 2

Try to recall a comment or judgment about yourself, said to you, or to someone else in your presence, which remains important to you today. Discuss the extent to which you think the remark is true, and describe just how important the speaker of this remark was to you.

Mr. B 2

When I was 15 an amazing ability seemed to find me. During that winter I invented 13 objects and didn't know what to do with them. I started asking people how to patent inventions. I went to atterney [*sic*] after attorney all advising to see another. I finally found one that didn't know the exact steps but would work with me until the job was compleated [*sic*]. Time after time he said, "How do you do this?" "You must be a genious [*sic*]." These words expressed his interest in me and I was extremely impressed with his persistence in helping me. To this day the adventure and judgment of him of me made us very close friends. . . .

I also told an owner of a firm in a big city of my invention and he was quite impressed with my enginuity [*sic*]. My respect for him had allways [*sic*] been extremely high and our friendship very close. When someone with such power tells you that you came up with some very brilliant ideas it "makes your day." To this day both are very impressed with me and I am very impressed with them.

Question 3

From the way your instructor speaks, writes, and conducts himself in class, describe and justify what you think might be behind *this public presentation. How close a "match" do you think there is between what you see on the outside and what you think is inside?*

Mr. B 3

I believe that when Mr. M speaks he speaks with confidence. I base this upon the fact that one can almost watch the gears in his brain turn through his eyes. When he speaks it sounds like what he is saying has been thought about before and recorded for a later time, sort of a mechanical voice. . . .

It should be clear from these samples just how unusual a student Mr. B was. However, it is not his departure from the norm that concerns us now, but some of the substantive themes in his work. Consider, therefore, what I am calling the "machine" theme in the foregoing samples. In the first essay there is the "solid, liquid, gas" description of the earth. The second essay cites the student's thirteen "inventions," none of which could he describe either to me or to his discussion instructor, Mr. M. In the third sample, there is his perception of "gears" in Mr. M's brain and his "mechanical voice." There is a less clear interpersonal theme: his distinguishing himself from those of narrow interests in his hometown, his being recognized by powerful men in a big city, and his perception of premeditation in his instructor's speech. The question is what to make of these thoughts, as well as of the other interesting details of his writing: the misspellings, the tendency to repeat words and phrases, and the vaguely melodramatic way of telling things. Before engaging these questions, consider the following excerpts from five of his essays written in response to five literary texts:

Mr. B L1 [response to barroom anecdote]

I can just picture this incident: two blacks, deep South, poor community, low intelligence. . . . If I were one of the neighbors I would have called the sanitarium and had those kids taken care off [*sic*].

Mr. B L2 [response to Faulkner's "Barn Burning"]

When you have something nice like Major de Spain's house you take care of it, keep it clean. Then when some scud comes barging in like he did, and doing damage, he should have been shot [*sic*] on his merry way. People like that shouldn't even be allowed near the house. The servant should have been armed to control such a person.

Mr. B L3 [response to O'Connor's "A Good Man Is Hard to Find"]

The old lady got on my nerves and I wished she would have a heart attack or stroke. . . . I think she got what she deserved at the end of the story. . . . I would not like being on a small, almost never traveled, unfamiliar road without a gun. If thickheaded Bailey would have carried a gun in the car he would have had no problem.

Mr. B L4 [response to Kafka's "A Hunger Artist"]

I thought that if I were the watcher of the artist and after days (30 or so) of watching him, making sure he did not eat anything, and I then saw him eat something that he had hidden, I would make sure that that was the very last thing he even would have the chance to eat again. . . . I thought to myself how much I would have liked to have been there while he was dying, it would have been very unpleasant for him . . . did the watcher get paid for his time [?] . . . I [*sic*] he did not get paid for the job I think I would have given him food and then shot him for payment.

Mr. B L5 [response to McCullers' "A Tree, A Rock, A Cloud"]

The drunk in the bar reminded me of the old drunks in downtown [big city]. One would just as soon run over them than look at them. They just seem like stumbling targets . . . for a car.

As I suggested previously, one essay alone can not tell whether a particular pattern or language feature is salient. For example, we may surmise a particular sense of the phrase "taken care off" (B L1) only when we see that there are four subsequent instances of a prospective murder, with Mr. B the clearly implied murderer. In presenting these strong images, Mr. B is taking advantage of the customary license, in discussing literature, that permits one to "kill" literary figures in conversation. At the same time, when such images appear in five consecutive essays, each separated by about two weeks, and with Mr. B's knowledge that they may be duplicated, read, and discussed by the whole class, Mr. B's use of the custom takes on more than casual authority.

The theme of murder in the response essays may be related to the unspecified relationships cited in the experience essays (the first series I cited). The phrases "opposite of the people in my town" and "I became lonely," interpreted in the light of the murder theme, obviously suggest an emotionally violent and radical isolation. Mr. B's ordinary language in the experience series refers, it is likely, to a painful ostracism that has an extreme "me versus them" quality. Reading the word "opposite," for example, as syntactically dependent on the idea of murder, will then name feelings of wanting to be loved as being related to wanting to kill when one is not loved. The sentence "I am full of contradictions" may also refer to this struggle. It is one of those language markers that, in a sense, *must* be telling the truth. On the one hand it expresses a *covert* sense of inconsistency and—probably in this case—a sense of mendacity, and on the other hand it is a perfectly ordinary and affably humble remark that people sometimes make about themselves. The response essays suggest the directions in which the meaning of such common phrases may be pluralized.

In the B2 essay, the attorney and the urban businessman, both "powerful," have recognized Mr. B's own transcendental power. They have (to him) converted the underlying ostracism into unique distinction, so that Mr. B is not merely loved, but admired, honored, and perhaps adored: "You must be a genious." Also, the phrase "I am very impressed with them" suggests his precocious accession to adulthood and maturity rather than the admiration of a young man for older ones. But, as we also see from the response essays, adults may be permitted to kill, while children are in the class of potential victims, along with blacks, nagging old ladies, drunks, and starving men. In describing his instructor, a real person he had to deal with from day to day, and who therefore could not be vaguely or unspecifically identified, Mr. B is more circumspect and confines himself to noting that Mr. M speaks with much premeditation. In fact, had we not read the response essays, there would be practically nothing unusual about the perception of Mr. M, and in some sense Mr. B knows this. He had noted Mr. M's own circumspection and care in speaking and expressed it in a metaphor which, by itself, implies only mild criticism rather than potentially strong feelings.

The description of Mr. M, however, defines the "theme of the machine" in the following sense. To control oneself with mechanical precision is a positive value for Mr. B, and his way of describing Mr. M may therefore imply an acknowledgment of Mr. M's power while tacitly converting him from a living to a nonliving thing. In this indirect, metaphorical sense, we read (in retrospect) that Mr. B "kills" his instructor and—at the same time—notes the instructor's potential for "killing" him with his "gears" and "mechanical voice." Mr. M is not a "machine" that can be operated by Mr. B.

In the response essays, the "machines" are the guns (or, the guns—and the car in B L5—are the machines; the syntax is reversible). But it would be wrong to interpret the guns and the shooting as the operation of machines. They are guns, instruments of murder and human purpose, and they are presented that way in every one of the essays: there is no ambiguity or vagueness about how the guns are used or when a shooting would occur, and there is no abstract admiration of their mechanical quality. In Mr. B's idiom, they are a natural part of a person's repertoire of behavior, and they appear in his language with just this fluency. Mr. B accepts the customary "literary" license and "rubs out" imaginary people without hesitation or misgiving. At the same time, the gun itself is important—it is the formula for self-protection, and it, like the car, is the means for enacting one's will with dispatch.

For Mr. B to present himself as the inventor of thirteen unnamed, though admired, objects is a *socialized form* or *translation* of his privatized will and its instruments. To report his life experience to the rest of the class is one social role, and the first three essays present the language of this role. To be a reader of literature is another social role, one which includes the license to "rub out," and so the language of the response essays represents this "literary" social role. The language of each role is a translation of the other, or, in the other terms I have been using, each role is predicated on the other.

If we reduce the subjective predication of social roles to a formula, it may be written as "tool (means/is) gun," and their reverse. Flying, traveling, and scuba diving are described as "tools" to "observe the earth." Mr. B's "amazing ability" to invent objects supplies his credentials for admission to society—one outside his hometown—but even that society "didn't know what to do with" the objects: Mr. B is the inventor of an object that did not fit in. But the guns have the opposite function: they are the natural instruments of the most authentic wishes. When Mr. B, in an apparent error in diction, writes "shot on his merry way" instead of "sent on his merry way," it represents one of his many *combinations* of his two different languages. It is noteworthy in this connection to report that we instructors could not quite discern what was up as we read only the first essays and observed the failures of diction, the careless spellings, and the lack of editing or rewriting. The "big picture," namely, that the first essays were *fantasies*, dawned on us only after we read the second semester's essays and saw the accumulation of "killings." It was only then that we became alert to the fact that we were dealing with a very disturbed young man. What is significant from the present perspective, however, is that we could not be certain of this until we saw the range of work in *both modes* that added up to a unified paranoid theme. Yet, this clinical suspicion notwithstanding, Mr. B's *use* of the two modes is actually no different from anyone else's, but for the extremity of the fantasies in the first group, and the extremity of the feelings in the second. The principle of the syntactic interdependence of the two languages is the same in Mr. B's work in the other students', some of which I will discuss in the coming chapters.

The foregoing instances of the double perspective, and in particular of the essay-pair technique I use to study and think about language use and literacy events, are meant principally to give some practical sense of the theoretical point I made in chapter 4. I also wanted to show why it is not idle to think of redistributing classroom authority while still improving individual discipline and cultivating the habits of collective and collaborative work (instances of which I will discuss in detail in chapters 9 and 10). However, the double perspective urges the view that changes will take place in how individuals think of themselves in consequence of the sustained attention they give to their own language use. For example, I implied that the local changes which took place in the second essays of Mr. S and Mr. G were related to overall changes in their thinking and approach to themselves, the class, the teacher, and, finally, their use of language. In this regard, therefore, it is important to study in some detail an individual student's development to see, on the one hand, that a double perspective is already a part of one's thinking and mental functioning and, on the other, just what paths an individual takes as she gradually becomes aware of her various perspectives and of how they are manifested in her habitual uses of language. In this process, we will be examining the connections between the abstract idea of the double perspective and the concrete facts of human growth and development in a university classroom. For a person to "take a course" is, in itself, a "literacy event," so that if we reconceptualize a student's experiences and achievements with Heath's term in mind, we will get a sense of how the written work, the casual conversations, and the student's overall sense of belonging in a variety of communities can be used to change the idea of taking a course from academic training to a more fully involved social experience.

8

Studying One's Own Language

Just as all language has already been used, one's own language is also "common property." In most instances of every day conversation we do not note or think about its uniqueness or allude to the fact that it is "ours" and not someone else's. We are, on the other hand, firmly aware of the difference between ourselves and our interlocutors: the difference between us and other couples, groups, or communities who are speaking among themselves. In keeping with our sense of the double perspective, the idea of "one's own" language cannot be understood as a definable "thing" in isolation but as a series of texts and other language uses—produced by one person (an author)—whose language must be understood as the feature, product, or accoutrement of its author's network of social relations. Put another way, to study our own texts as a unified collection is necessarily to invoke our history of relationships, our sense of self, and our sense of integration in our community. It is not possible to extract a language sample from such an environment and then claim knowledge of "the language itself" as being autonomously meaningful.

The course that I began to describe in chapter 7 was entitled "Studying One's Own Language," and the task each person faced was to produce a series of about twenty-four essays over two semesters, four of which were analyses of texts the person had already produced in the course. The last essay of each semester was a comprehensive analysis of the previous semester's and year's work, respectively. The instructions that I gave for these final essays (which are included in the appendix of this book) were issued to students on the first day of class as both guidelines to the course and as a reminder of how to begin thinking about the work as it was regularly produced. The essays that I will discuss in this chapter were all written by Ms. K, an eighteen-year-old freshman, and they will be understood to have two major contexts: Ms. K's memory of and sense of her principal relationships—with her parents and peers; and her membership in the class—the discussion section of about twenty-four students which I led. In pursuing this analysis, I will try to show how the distinctive features of Ms. K's "own" language have developed over the two-semester period under the influence of her recursive rearticulation of her out-of-class social relations and of her increasing involvement in the class.

The general pattern followed in the course is more or less the same one discussed in the previous chapter: the first semester's essays were mainly "experience" essays—recollections of language events in one's life before and outside of class, while the second semester's essays were largely literary responses which included the announcements of feelings and associative analogies, as alluded to in the questions written on by Mr. S and Mr. G in chapter 7. In my discussion, however, I will start with one of Ms. K's essays which raises the most salient issues of language use and psychosocial development in class and then cite other of her texts as they bear on these issues.

I am trying to show the value of a longitudinal analysis of an individual's work and to disclose the general organization of Ms. K's literacy psychology in order to emphasize that *development* is a fundamental factor in language use, and that this concept ought to be substituted for the present standard of *remediation* in the teaching and study of writing. It would be a distortion to think of changes in Ms. K's work, as the course continued, as improvement in some technical sense, when what actually took place was a gradual increase of self-awareness observable in the interesting changes and complications in her use of language.

Toward the end of the first semester, I distributed the following text, taken from *The Intimate Enemy: How to Fight Fair in Love and Marriage*, by George Bach and Peter Wyden (1968, p. 280):

> Father (*disgusted*): You're a lousy mother.
> Mother (*unbelieving*): You're out of your head!
> Father (*insistent*): Come on! You're never even around to *be* a mother!
> Mother (*primly*): Dr. Spock says it's important to get away from your child. At least Jimmy isn't going to be overprotected like you were.
> Father (*accusing*): How many days in the last six months were you gone and how many nights did the baby wake up and I had to take him into our bed?
> Mother (*nettled*): Don't you call a four-year-old a baby! He knows about my job. He knows I always come back. He loves to come to the airport to pick me up. And how about all the times when I took him along?
> Father (*stubborn*): I don't like it.
> Mother (*triumphant*): Now you're talking! It's *you* who resents my career. I'm not going to give up all my fun. And there's no fun around here!

The question for this text was: "Based on your experience of conversations such as this, tell who is right, who won, and *how you know* both of these things." The students knew the source of this text and that it could be either a real or imaginary dialogue. They were free to answer the question on the basis of whichever assumption they thought most appropriate. Here, now, is Ms. K's essay:

(1) The mother won the argument. Although she won by "unfair tactics" she did get her own points across and restrained her husband from explaining what he meant. The father was originally concerned about the baby's welfare when he started the argument (although his feelings of what he was missing were in the back of his mind). The mother was able to "turn the tables" on him by placing the blame of the argument on her husbands [*sic*] resentful feelings and *not* on the concern for the baby. She doesn't even consider her four-year-old a baby—she acts as if the child were much older than he is. The mother tries to get back at the dad by talking about his situation instead of the childs [*sic*]. The wife even cuts down her husband. She makes a comment as to his "overprotection." This has *nothing* to do with the fact that the comment was made as to her being a lousy mother. The father was right. The mother is trying to avoid her responsibilities. She talks of not giving up all her fun—no one said she had to. She *does* have a child to care for—and she should be around to do it. Even when the mother brings up Dr. Spock she is not supporting her point. Sure its important to get away from your kid but *not* to the extent that she was away. The dad asks how many times she has been gone in the past 6 months—which lead us to believe that she is hardly *ever* around. The father *does* miss the wife but also feels that she is avoiding her obligations. He has a heavy burden of care for the child and probably working too. When he begins talking you *know* there is going to be an argument. It seems like he doesn't even want to discuss it rationally—and how would you expect his wife to react to this comment—of course she is going to take the defensive.

(2) Although the mans [*sic*] whole point of argument was to show what a bad mom she was, she was successful at turning things around to make it seem as if the father was concerned *only* for himself—says *he* is selfish. She gets in the last words of the argument. Although she doesn't persuade him as to his real intentions of the argument, she does get to some of his feelings which *are* the way he feels and is able to sustain her end of the argument, which he is not able to do.

(3) The father *is* right in this argument, though. Although he does not "win" the argument I'm sure that his wife will think a little bit about what he said. I think it is OK for her to work and have fun and maintain her freedom—as long as she doesn't avoid her obligations. Since her husband seems to think that she *is* avoiding her responsibilities—there must be some truth to the comment and things need to be discussed (not argued about).

(4) I think that if the father would have started the argument in a more subtle way the argument *could* have been a constructive conversation. By saying what he did he immediately put his wife on the defensive. Whereas if he could have said something different at first, she may have accepted his criticism (because

it would have been constructive) and they may have been able to talk about a solution and maybe even come up with one.

(5) The wife won the argument mostly because she was put on the defensive. She used a lot of different techniques to put her point across and never ran out of things to say. The father was not as intense as his wife was and didn't really back himself up enough. I know that when my partents fight—if my mom says something to cut down my dad and start an argument he might say to her that if she will speak civilly to him he will be happy to *discuss* whatever is bothering ~~him~~ her.

Ms. K knew that our class's interest in this essay was both in the "reading" of the text and in what contexts and values each person brings to bear in an essay. Considerations of technical proficiency were relevant, Ms. K understood, not as something that would be formally evaluated but as something to be analyzed descriptively and ultimately integrated in her sense of her use of language. She further understood that there were no "right or wrong" answers, and that her task was to share her thoughts as fully and candidly as possible. In other words, Ms. K wrote the essay knowing that its substance and the *kinds* of usages it revealed were the main items of interest.

With this in mind, let me first raise a few questions about the technical character of the essay. We note, for example, that Ms. K omits apostrophes in possessives but keeps them in for contractions, the one exception being "baby's" in the third line of the first paragraph. Her spelling, however, is generally flawless, so how is her unusual use of apostrophes to be understood? Ms. K uses many parentheses and dashes: are these liberties she takes with what she was taught? Are they an irrepressible need to comment on her work; an inability to say what she has to say without self-interruption; an advanced level of self-awareness? She uses quotation marks a great deal in ways that seem to make sense. Is this usage redundant? Does it belong in the same category as the parentheses and dashes: that is, is Ms. K the sort of language user who likes to insert many diacritical roadsigns? Or is she just doing something that all people want to do but are trained not to, and she has simply resisted the training better? Should the phrase, "the father was/is right," which appears twice in the essay, be taken as careless redundancy or a sign that two different emphases are being proposed, and that she expects the italics and the present tense [in the second usage, in paragraph (3)] to show the difference? Should such redundancies be a sign to us that she actually means to have more explanation but did not get it in? There are many declarative sentences with the decisive verbs "to do" and "to be" and many conditional sentences with "ifs" and "althoughs"; shall we consider these usages in the light of the relative absence of "maybe" and "seems"? Are there other of her essays in which the latter usages are more prominent? What are we to make of the habitual use of "I think," "I'm sure," and "I know"? These phrases are so conventionalized that it is hard to assign a stable literal meaning to them. Do they represent something important in Ms. K's linguistic self-representation?

In seeking to disclose the factors that could describe coherently these technical features of the essay, let me list several inferences that Ms. K made about the dialogue: the mother and father are also husband and wife; the mother "restrained" the father from explaining what he meant; the father was "originally concerned" with the child's welfare; the mother "turned the tables" on the father; the mother "acts as if the child were older than he is"; the mother is trying to "avoid her responsibilities"; the mother was away from the child too often; the father's "missing" his wife is "at the back of his mind"; the father is "probably working too"; the mother "says" the father "is" selfish; the mother gets to feelings which "are" the way the father feels; the mother "never ran out of things to say"; the father was "not as intense" as the mother. Some might rightly call several of these judgments and inferences "errors," putting them on the same list as the technical ragged edges I listed, and then urge Ms. K (and help her, no doubt) to produce a smoother statement. Let us stipulate, however, that we only wish to *understand* why the essay was written as it was, and to consider the ways in which the technical idiosyncrasies and the substantive inferences and judgments are part of an underlying language-use strategy.

Consider the grammatical feature of the essay. There are five subordinate clauses beginning with "although"; in three of them the mother is the subject of the main clause, and in a fourth Ms. K is the subject of the main clause, to which the mother clause is subordinate. Each of these sentences names some accomplishment of the mother, which was achieved "although" she failed in some other way. This group of clauses can be related to several other sentences, two of which appear consecutively following the "although" sentences in paragraph (3). The main clauses of these two sentences give Ms. K's judgments that it is okay for the mother to work and that there is truth to the father's comment. "Avoidance of obligations" comes in the conditional clause of both sentences. Ms. K shows that she believes the father's claims. All of the believed premises appear in the subordinate clauses; the mother won by unfair tactics, the father misses the mother, the mother doesn't persuade him, the father doesn't win. The grammatical pattern places the believed propositions into the *premises* of key sentences. Premises are not offered for discussion, since they appear in the language slot which conventionally behaves as a "taken for granted" condition. This does not seem to be a calculated usage by Ms. K but a peremptory one coming from a predisposition to understand the dialogue in a certain way.

The last sentence of the essay gives an idea of how she was predisposed: "I know that when my parents fight—if my mom says something to cut down my dad and start an argument he might say to her that if she will speak civilly to him he will be happy to *discuss* whatever is bothering ~~him~~ her." This sentence suggests that the schema of "parents arguing" in her family is that mother says something to "cut down" father, and father responds in the less intense way. Notice that this also implies the situation described in the essay of the mother "winning" the argument but the father being "right." Ms. K uses the verb "cut down" to characterize both the dialogue-mother's behavior and her own mother's behavior. In addition, the superficial error of her having first written "him" for "her" suggests that, in her opinion, it is the father who *should* be bothered. This is how I would boil down Ms. K's sense of the dialogue: the father, irrational but less intense than the mother, has a legitimate grievance of being neglected due to the mother's "avoidance of obligation." He is in no condition to talk things over because he is hurt. The mother, sensing the father's reduced condition, "wins" the argument by unfair tactics—she "restrained" him while she herself "never ran out of things to say." She "even cuts down" her husband and "even denies" the babyhood of her four-year-old son. In the light of this reading, the list of interpretive inferences becomes coherent. It would not be stretching anyone's imagination to claim that the substance of this essay is tightly bound up with Ms. K's sense of her relationship to her parents, how they use language themselves, how their relationship affects her as an independent person— in paragraph (4) she counsels the father on how to behave better—and how much she is willing to share with her colleagues. Later on, I will return to the technical usages I cited and suggest how they are a part of this coherent reading.

Ms. K's perception and interpretation of the dialogue cannot be considered as entities independent of what is written in her essay. She did not "get" some meaning, hold it, and then "translate" it into the essay. The writing of the essay is both her creation and presentation of the reading at once. It is a language or literacy *event* whose public form, the essay text, alludes to both past and present, family meaning and current perceptions, private thoughts and strategies of public self-presentation. What is new and unique about the essay is its special *combination* of language forms and thoughts and attitudes, all occasioned by the similarly combinatorial novelty of the moment in class when the text was distributed and the essay written. Her essay should be seen as an incremental change in her sense of self, and we are exploring this change by noting both the technical and interpretive features of the essay's language.

In regard to the interdependency of language use and social belonging, consider this comment given by Ms. K in her final analytical retrospective essay in the first semester:

> I use conventional language when speaking with most strangers. Especially when I talk to any older person or someone who has a lot of authority. When I dealt with the customers where I used to work (the steady customers, that is) I could joke around with them and ask them the trite questions that most people ask of each other. If I'm sitting next to a stranger I usually won't start a conversation. If I were sitting next to a little kid, though, I'm sure I would say something. I will only start a conversation with someone I feel comfortable around. What determines if I would be comfortable around them is their age, sex, and outward appearance.

This routine statement has several allusions to the important criteria involved in making a choice which, gradually, we will see as playing roles in Ms. K's language. Two of these items are her observation that she will use "conventional" language when talking to someone with "a lot of authority" and that she would *start* a conversation with a child-stranger but not someone else. The connection between these two items is the issue of *authority*, which, she implies, has a great deal to do with when she speaks. Familiarity is also a strong factor, according to this comment, but, as we will see, familiarity has an authorizing function. Here is an essay which brings out this point in its particular dimensions for Ms. K:

Question

Tell of an incident in which a verbal action by either you or the other person in a relationship with you produced a mutual understanding, but where the words themselves do not show what that understanding was.

One important incident where there was a mutual understanding took place between my father and myself. I don't remember the first part too well—but I do know it was Father's Day maybe three years ago. My brother and sister and I, with the help of our mom, had gotten my dad a really nice gift we knew he would love—a barbecue grill I think. We kids were really excited. That day we helped mom to fix a really nice dinner and tried to wrap his present. We ate outside on the picnic table. All during our meal I remember my mom being in one of her "moods." There was a lot of tension. I didn't have any idea why she was teed off this time. After the meal it was time to open the present. My mom suddenly blew up and stormed off into the house, saying that she wasn't going to be around when the presents were opened. I was so upset. How could she just get up and leave? What were we supposed to do? Fetch her back to the table and apologize for whatever (or was it my dad who had to do the apologizing?)

Well—my brother and sister went their own ways to play or something. I just sat at the table half-stunned and furious. My dad and I were at the table and I just started bawling. That was one of the few times I cried in front of my dad—let alone by myself. He said c'mon and put his arm around my shoulder as we walked around the back yard and I sobbed. When I finally spoke I said, "She ruined your Father's Day!" My dad understood exactly what I meant, what I was implying, and how I felt about saying what I did. He understood how much hate I was feeling towards my mom—because that day meant so much to me and she had ruined it. My dad said to me, "I understand how you feel, but she *is* your mother." This was how I felt about saying what I did. I was mad as hell at her but also feeling guilty for saying (implying) that I hated her so much. My dad always said how much we were alike and I found this was very true when he understood the way I felt so completely without my having to say very much. It made me feel better just to know that my dad understood the way I felt and that it was O.K. for me to come to him whenever I needed to talk.

This essay tells something about what it means for Ms. K to "have authority," though the essay itself is not about authority. Of interest is a family condition intimated by Ms. K's having written that her mother was in "one of" her moods. As this incident suggests, mother's moods are connected with her parents' arguments, which she alluded to in the dialogue essay, but the essay did not spell out how she felt implicated in her parents' relationship; in this essay her involvement is the subject. In the second paragraph Ms. K reports that her father "always said how much we were alike," which implies a certain degree of common opposition to the mother. But this fundamental matter did not actually emerge into language on the occasion she wrote *about*. The phrase "saying (implying) that I hated her so much" in the second paragraph tells us that Ms. K at the time *felt as though* she had said she hated her mother without actually having said it, and, she claims, *this is what her father understood anyway*. The situation did emerge into language *in the writing of this essay*, which came at a moment in the development of the class that had been "prepared for" by the writing of the previous essay, which I will discuss shortly. Ms. K writes that her father's understanding was signaled when he said "she *is* your mother," which Ms. K interprets as a mild admonishment for her unspoken feeling. Thus, she felt this was an occasion of solidarity with her father, when their common opposition to her mother had emerged. The physical situation at the picnic table also contributed to the moment. Out of concern for her father, Ms. K stayed at the table, unable to accept the "ruined" occasion, and in frustration started to cry; while her siblings, like the mother, left, putting her and her father in the same place literally and metaphorically. Her father then went for a walk with her and announced that he understood how she felt. One of the subsequent practical results of this little communion was a new option in her use of language: "I felt that it was OK for me to come to him whenever I needed to talk." She felt *authorized* by her father to speak, a feeling important mainly in that it had been absent before.

Ms. K did not think to put the matter in these terms, however, until the final essay of the first semester when she wrote the following commentary:

> I wrote about the relationships within my family, especially with my dad, when asked to write about an understanding. I found this interesting since my family is really not on an understanding basis. If there are arguments between kids and parents—parents are always right and don't want to hear any "back talk." I felt that "back talk" was a way of explaining my thoughts and feelings. By not being allowed to explain myself, there were a lot of covered up feelings. In this one particular incident dad allowed me to say what I felt (even though it was speaking badly about the parent) and there was actually an understanding between parent vs. child. It meant a lot to me to have my dad understand me and let me talk to him as an individual.

In this comment Ms. K discloses the terms of children's arguing with parents—the no "back talk" rule. In the Father's Day incident, Ms. K is "allowed" to move from "back talk" to just "talk"—a change from the adversary use of language to a negotiative use—to a situation where the same rules of conversation more nearly applied to both parties. In the first paragraph of the essay, Ms. K noted that her father may have been the one who needed to do the apologizing, which suggests that a part of her did not prejudge which of her parents was at fault. At the same time, she felt her own relationship with her father had been damaged by what looked like the mother's poor behavior—leaving the table. The talk with her father accomplished two things: it let out the "covered up feelings" toward her mother on that occasion and gave her access to the adult rules of language use in her family— the license to register oppositional feelings—without having been already "institutionally" deauthorized by the rule of "no back talk."

When Ms. K wrote her retrospective commentary, the principle of the double perspective worked as she assimilated her experience of writing the mutual understanding essay to the moment of analytical reflection in which she wrote the retrospective essay, thus producing the comprehensive insight about talk and back talk we just discussed. In the same way, she wrote the mutual understanding essay having assimilated the perspective gained from the preceding essay (and its class discussion). In particular, the previous essay had raised the matter of "authorized language use" as it pertained to *this class*. Here, then, is the essay immediately preceding the "mutual understanding" essay:

Question

Describe at least one feature of your instructor's language (spoken and/or written) that he/she might not know about and that you think he/she should be aware of. How does this feature contribute to your understanding of the instructor as a person, and why should he/she be made aware of it? Be as candid and as imaginative as you can.

One of the things I have noticed about Mr. Bleich's language is his ability to cut down others. Whether he does this intentionally or just out of habit—I don't know. I do know that when someone arrives to class late—you *know* there will be *some* comment made as to their tardiness. Even in his writings there are some of the same feelings that you would get if he were cutting someone down. His writing reflects his argumentative and aggressive style. By cutting others down I think he can let these feelings out. By also cutting others down he can show that he is in control. I mean—not many people would try to defend themselves in front of a whole classroom! Maybe subconsciously his cutting down of others only builds up his ego? I have heard that if a person cuts others down a lot they do it because they themselves feel insecure—?

Cutting down others is just a part of your style, Mr. Bleich. I don't think you build your ego up by cutting them down. I also don't think you are insecure. I think this way because of the way you speak—your spoken language.

Another thing I find interesting is your use of profanity vs. your use of big words. It seems that by using profanity we (the class) will be able to identify with you (you think). Maybe by speaking this way you think you are more on our level and will be accepted more readily. At the same time you use big words. This shows your high education. I think of these two language features as opposite and wouldn't expect to find them together in the same essay. It just seems as if there is an incongruity.

I think you should be aware that some people feel threatened when you cut them or others down. I'm not sure why you use profanity and big words together. Probably just to remain on our level but at the same time gain respect from us.

The topic of this essay, which was written about six weeks into the semester, was a surprise to most students, who were not used to getting writing tasks which involve criticizing the teacher. Nevertheless, for most students, this essay establishes one of the important purposes of this course, namely, that we are really interested in studying how all of us actually use language.

Ms. K's essay made me pay closer attention to her work (as well as my own, of course, as I will discuss in chapter 9). It seemed more bold and daring than most of the others, less circumspect about registering a complaint. It also seemed true to me, in that it alerted me to an effect I was having on some students that I did not wish to have—producing a sense of danger with my habit of teasing. But what caught my attention most was that Ms. K's attitude *seemed to change while writing the essay*, and that her language marked this change very suggestively. It seemed to me that as she moved from the first to the second paragraph she realized something important, changing from the third to the second person and finishing her essay in direct address, as in a letter. This change appeared to me to be a solution to the problems she was raising in the form of declarative questions at the end of the first paragraph. When her essay came up for discussion in class, I asked if she could not have written the following sentence, so that she would not have had to change "person": "Although it is probably not true of Mr. Bleich, I have heard that people cut down others because they are themselves insecure and thus cut down others to build their egos up." Ms. K said that my sentence would not have represented what she wanted to say, and the ensuing class discussion was recorded by a student minutes-taker as follows:

> Ms. A pointed out that there were more direct things in the first sentence [i.e., the last sentence of Ms. K's first paragraph]. Ms. D said that maybe Ms. K was not real sure of how she felt. Ms. R added that maybe she wrote it and then thought Mr. Bleich might think something bad. Ms. K agreed. Ms. S mentioned that she would write it and not worry about what Mr. Bleich thought.

In a general way, Ms. S's comment raises the issue with which the students are concerned—whether or not to worry about what the teacher thinks as long as one is sincere. The class also saw, however, that the ethical issue and the hermeneutic one of how to understand why Ms. K changed "persons" are tied up in one another. In class, Ms. K "agreed" that she changed usages because she suddenly realized that I might "think something bad"—not a very informative phrase. Still, we learn from this that it mattered to Ms. K that the essay remain faithful to her feelings while writing and that my phrasing of a similar thought would not have been faithful.

What could "think something bad" have actually meant on that occasion? If it meant that Ms. K thought it was wrong to say the things she did in her first paragraph, or that she had inadvertently jeopardized herself, she probably would have deleted the dangerous material altogether. It seems more likely, therefore, that Ms. K really thought what she said was the truth in a general way, but she did not sufficiently take into account that when I *speak* in a certain way it is *stylistic* rather than premeditatedly aggressive. As a result she deemed her last thoughts of the first paragraph *not true to the relationship she wished to maintain with me*. This gradually dawning confidence in herself is reflected in the *declarative questions* at the end of the first paragraph. She realizes that in one sense she is asking *me* the questions, but that because this seemed so inappropriate and untrue to her own sense

of how to take on a difficult interpersonal task, she addresses her actual
point *directly* to me and even adds a few more in subsequent paragraphs.
She adopted a stance which "said" something like, "if I can tell you these
thoughts directly, they don't quite mean the same thing either to you or to
me." The use of the second person, therefore, may be construed as a switch
to an "oral" mode (to be compared with the "speaking" mode which gave
her the thought that she might be dealing with my style), and perhaps also
a more private mode, which has more authenticity and more authority. Her
ethical concerns are served when, in transcending the vague questions of the
previous paragraph, she takes direct responsibility for what she only thinks
might be the case, and in this process finds the language (direct address) to
include her sense of our relationship, a sense that was suppressed while she
was writing in the third person.

This essay and its classroom discussion (the full literacy event) enabled
the strong and candid essays which followed it for several reasons. First,
Ms. K saw that her risk was well-taken, since her work was treated seriously
by other class members, in no small part because her views expressed some
of their thoughts which were not so boldly presented. Second, it was an
occasion for me to make good on my early claims that such kinds of writing
were encouraged in this class. I was not hurt by her thoughts, and I showed
how the expression of feelings that matter would enhance the classroom
atmosphere. Third, we showed how such work is an important part of the
class's subject matter, how such personal expressions need not be "taken to
heart" but only acknowledged as true and then used as part of our overall
collective inquiry. And finally, for Ms. K, her own sense of authoritative
language was brought out and honored by our discussion in the same process
that showed how my authority as the teacher was negotiable. The total event
became an important advance for the whole class.

This event, then, became a pertinent influence on, or prior context for
Ms. K's "mutual understanding" essay because "establishing authority by
direct address" had become part of her vocabulary of language use. What
Ms. K had reported in that essay—achieving conversational parity with her
father—helped make it possible for her to "find" the direct-address path for
the problem posed to her by the classroom assignment. The two essay-events
are thus predicated on one another; initially, the essay on my language was
predicted on the historical reality of the event with her father (in part), while
the candid "mutual understanding" essay could not have been written had
her authority not been so well-established in the class. In Ms. K's subjective
mobilization to write both essays, the family context and the classroom
context were substantively but spontaneously coordinated with one another.
When we, her audience, receive her work, we cannot understand Ms.

K's language in this significant way without having taken into account its contextual sources, and without invoking our own historical and communal perspectives. As we have already seen, and as we will see again in Ms. K's final essay of the second semester, she had to identify the pertinent double perspective through her own effort at historical reconstruction. Had our class taken the more traditional remedial path and spent our energy streamlining Ms. K's prose, we would have lost our opportunity to encourage her to find out for herself, with the participation of the class, one of the more important interpersonal motivating circumstances of her language use.

Earlier, I mentioned that the verb "to cut down" had an interesting role in Ms. K's set of usages. Discussing the dialogue she says that the wife "even cuts down" the husband. She then immediately writes (in the first paragraph) "She makes a comment as to his 'overprotection.' This has *nothing* to do with the fact that the comment was made as to her being a lousy mother. The father was right." We note, first, Ms. K's emphatic statement that the mother's "cut-down" is completely unrelated to the father's comment that the mother is a "lousy mother," which started the dialogue. Ms. K uncharacteristically uses the passive voice to acknowledge that the father used the accusative "lousy mother" epithet; that is, she *omits* mention (in that sentence) of the father's responsibility for having made that remark, does not see his remark as itself a "cut-down" and claims that the mother's alleged "cut-down" is unrelated to the father's opening remark! Yet in other parts of the essay, she "counsels" the father to behave differently and, more substantively, observes that the mother had been put on the defensive. The explanation for this apparent inconsistency derives from her little sentence, "The father was right," which immediately follows her strong claim of the unrelatedness of the mother's cut-down to the father's. Her siding with the father—possibly a typical alliance in her family—caused her not to categorize the "lousy mother" comment as a cut-down and even to see the mother as the principal user of cut-downs.

Before considering how her sense of this term comes into play in her essay on my language, let us inspect another essay which has a bearing on how Ms. K understand the term.

Question

In a relationship you consider(ed) important recall a time you said or wrote something, and your intention, motive, or purpose for saying or writing it was misunderstood or "taken the wrong way." Tell what you said, tell the response, and tell your actual purpose. Explain how you corrected the misunderstanding and the extent to which you were able to make yourself understood verbally. Bring in as much about this relationship as necessary to make your instance clear.

Mike and I had been dating maybe three weeks. He asked me to his Christmas Dance—he went to a different high school than me. This was my first formal dance and I was really excited. I planned the night out in my head *so* many times—what I was going to say to him when he came to the door, what I was going to eat, etc. I still felt a little uncomfortable around Mike and was overly anxious for the "big night." You see Mike and I worked together (that's how we met) and were kind of like the new gossip there.

Well finally the "big night" came. Of course, the weather was *terrible*— practically a blizzard outside. We went to dinner at this nice restaurant out in the country—a long drive through bad roads. On the way back from the restaurant it started snowing & blowing *really* hard. We came to a stoplight and Mike just couldn't stop the car. He started to skid and the only thing that stopped us from going off the road was another car. Both of our heads hit the windshield—but no blood. Well Mike got out of the car—after asking me if I was alright—and shakily went to check out the damage. They exchanged licenses etc., and the guy in the other car said he would call Mike's house the next day about damages (he ended up calling Mike's that night). Well Mike and I drove around for a while—he was *so* shook up. All he kept saying was that the last thing his dad told him was to be careful with his car and whatever he did not get in an accident. I tried to calm Mike down. I said something to the effect of "Your dad will understand. He's not going to punish you for the rest of your life." When I said that Mike got really upset—his anger was aimed at me at this moment. Mike said that his dad wouldn't understand and there would be *no* excuse for what happened. He went on to say that he *would* be grounded for at least another six months (he was already grounded before that night for something else). He went on and on about how I didn't understand his dad (when I knew what he was like) and that I was taking this all so light-hearted. Well—I tried to interrupt Mike a few times and clarify what I had meant. I said what I did mostly to calm him down because he was overreacting. His dad would (and did) understand that things like that *do* happen. He even let Mike go out after the accident. (You see we went back to his house later on that night— and told his dad). His dad said whatever & and told us to go have a good time & then would worry about it the next day. I think Mike *was* punished. But the reason I said what I did was to help him think straight. His misunderstanding of what I meant to do when I said it—I don't think he even stopped to listen to me try to explain what I meant. Which kind of got to me too.

On reading this essay, I asked Ms. K about her hyperbolic remark to Mike, "He's not going to punish you the rest of your life," because it sounded like the kind of remark I am likely to make—intending to help, but with a slightly sarcastic edge. She allowed in that conversation that, yes, this could be classified as a "cut-down." Why, then, would Ms. K use such language on this occasion? The ostensible reason is, as she explains, that Mike overreacted and she is helpfully trying to make him see that this was the case. However, other parts of her narrative suggest that other feelings also are coming into play. For example, in her first paragraph she takes some pains to characterize her excited anticipation of the dance and details her repeated imaginary planning of how she would behave. She twice refers to the evening as the "big night," a phrase, we now see, she is using with a certain irony. She then introduces the main part of the narrative with a somewhat ironic "return to reality": "Of course, the weather was *terrible*. The phrase "of course" here is not necessary to describe the events but does express, probably, both her present attitude toward her past feelings and the sense of disappointment she *then* had because of the weather's potentially bad effect on the adventure of the evening. The phrase suggests the *vulnerability* of her anticipatory feelings, as if she already had the thought in her mind that the occasion was going to be ruined somehow. As the narrative proceeds, we see that the weather itself did not ruin the evening, but that the accident had such a negative effect on Mike it looked as if he would ruin the evening. Thus, trying to rescue the evening by calming Mike down, but also expressing her irritation at the potential loss of the evening, Ms. K inadvertently "cuts Mike down" by making his fears seem exaggerated; that is, she uses "cut-down" language out of a sense of vulnerability and disappointment with a particular person, which corresponds relatively well with her point about insecure feelings leading people to cut down others.

Returning now to her perception of this feature in my language, it is probably safe to say that, in view of her sense of kinship with her father, Ms. K sees "cut-downs" as something one should not be particularly proud of, that she is somewhat aware that she has a tendency to make them, and that her mother *really* has it. In this way she is "primed" to understand my above-average level of teasing and joking—often of specific people in the "public" of the classroom—as the not-so-nice habit of cutting others down. However, the anomaly in this case is that I am a man in an authoritative position, someone who, in her sense of things, should not be given to this behavior. "Cutting down" is the trait of the underdog, of those who were not permitted "back talk," those who had to cover up their feelings or who got into "moods" inexplicably. Why, she considers, would one who has all the privileges to speak behave this way? This is the problem that caused the conflict which she solved by shifting to direct address in her essay on my language use. She "risked" identifying me as in the father "genre" (in her language system)—that is, someone approachable, with whom her concerns are negotiable instead of suppressed, as they were when she wrote in the third person. She peremptorily shifted into the "adult" mode (in her language system). In this light we could read her fear of my "thinking something bad" as her fear of being perceived as childish or as a less-than-forthright complainer. It would then be important for Ms. K to have recorded the rejection of this role and the assumption of the stronger and, to her, more reasonable role. This would be another reason my proposed conflation of the end of the first and the beginning of the second paragraphs was not acceptable to her. The significance of the latter part of the essay, all written in the second person, where she portrays me as wanting to be both "of" the class and "not of" the class, is that it represents a relatively clear and stable view of me. It is especially winning not just because I agree with it, but because it recognizes the doubleness of my role in class as it appears in two of my habitual uses of language. I did not consciously try to be in those two roles, but when Ms. K uses my language to show that this could be the case, it seems reasonable to me, and I now see my behavior in class in that additional light.

The underlying psychosocial circumstance of a young person of this age is that of adolescent self-definition—the search for adult "identity" as Erik Erikson describes it, which requires an extended negotiation of role-model choices in order to integrate one's gender and vocational identities. In both of these areas, Ms. K should be described as completely stable—the processes are taking place with a normal or typical level of energy, success, and conflict. However, it seemed to me that more of Ms. K's mental energy was being spent on gender identity, since her vocational plans were settled and they almost never entered into her essays. As the work that we have already seen intimated, Ms. K was in the midst of trying to find the right "mix" of identity elements from both parents, given the particular situation between her parents. Thus far, we have seen something of the role that her father played and how, in a circumspect way, she was able to cultivate and make use of her identification with him. But we might now remember that while a child takes over key identity elements from both parents, the identification with the parent of the same sex is more intimate. As we will see shortly, Ms. K's literary responses begin to disclose this (expectable) concern while also suggesting reasons why it would not emerge in the earlier, nonliterary phases of her writing experiences in this course.

Before crediting the literary response process with what I think it accomplished, let me mention a few other factors that worked toward the same result. By the time the second semester began, the whole class felt quite comfortable and ready to share important thoughts with one another. Conversation before and after class frequently alluded to the personal subject matter of the essays. There was a sense of cohesiveness as a whole class as a collection of loosely related colleague-friends, and there was a sense of individual belonging in the work-groups of three. In addition, by the time the first semester ended, the class had a good sample of my own writing, thoughts, and personal history, a sense for the kind of censorship that I exercised on myself, of how it felt to answer for one's work and to inquire into others' work, including my own. Most of the students, and definitely Ms. K, had a fairly well-established set of habits of how to disclose oneself and how to deal with the subsequent commentaries from other class members. These achievements of the common classroom socialization process helped make it possible for the literary responses to begin at a substantive level with a much shorter period of collective caution than might otherwise be needed.

As it has appeared in this material, Ms. K's underlying strategy of language use was related to how and when each parent spoke and what that meant regarding when and how she should speak (and write). Ms. K had reported having learned a certain rule of circumspection in her comment on how the "no back talk" rule led to "covered up feelings." But gradually Ms. K began to perceive that suppressed feelings often come out in indirect ways. In looking back on her work at the end of the first semester, Ms. K made the following comment on the "dialogue" essay I cited at the beginning of this chapter:

> In [the dialogue essay] there are a lot of sentences which consist of more than one clause. In every case, the mother is the subject of the main clause. I think that by putting the emphasis on the mother in this essay—in more ways than just the sentence type—I have drawn attention to her. This may be a way of pointing towards my feelings. By using sentence types I was able to put the emphasis on the mother without actually coming out and saying that the mother was the main point (or problem, if you may) in this essay.

In her final essay of the year, the analysis which studied the literary response essays as well as the experience essays, Ms. K made the following observations:

> In almost all of my papers, I use what has been written (in the stories) to my advantage. What I mean is that when I make identifications with a certain character's reactions I am somehow reading my own thoughts and feelings into what they actually do and say. A good example is in essay #7 [on Porter's "The Grave"]. When Miranda sees the dead baby rabbits she "admiringly" watches her brother skin the rabbit and is "excited" but not "frightened" (as the story describes it). In my essay I say that "Miranda was pretty much surprised. She didn't get sick or anything but she was taken aback." This is not how the story explains Miranda's feelings. It is, however, the way I explain my own feelings, through identification with Miranda. In essay #8 [on Joyce's "Araby"] I also do the same thing. I use the boy, who I identify with, as an instrument to show my own feelings without coming right out and saying them. In essay #10 [on Faulkner's "Barn Burning"] I even use the author as an instrument

in explaining my thoughts. I see that I may change around what the characters
say or put emphasis on what is said differently than how it has been intended.
Is this another way of mine of wanting others to comply to my viewpoints and
therefore putting them under my authority?

The last sentence of the second paragraph recalls a theme that we have
already seen was important to Ms. K in her family—the acquisition of
authority. But these two passages imply that Ms. K has a verbal way of
authorizing herself that is quite opposite from what we saw in her other
work—the move to direct address. In the former passage (above), Ms. K
describes how she is putting emphasis on the mother "without actually coming
out and saying" that that was what she was doing. In the second passage,
Ms. K says that she uses a character to show her feelings "without coming
right out and saying them," and she follows this by observing that she "put
emphasis on what is said differently than how it has been intended." The
term "put emphasis," which appears in both essays, means, approximately,
"express, tell, or show my feelings (about)"; so that Ms. K is, in both
passages, *announcing feelings without actually naming them*. The above two
passages are comments Ms. K made on literary material. When responding to literature, feelings emerge in her work *indirectly*, and Ms. K sees
this happening. As I will now discuss, Ms. K relates indirect "saying"
with her mother and her *lack* of authority, and in the final essay (from
which the second passage above comes) Ms. K puts this whole picture
together. To see how her comprehensive insight developed, I will first cite
her complete essay 9, a response to O'Connor's "A Good Man Is Hard to
Find":

Question

*Consider your reading experience of the O'Connor story. Decide on how much
you identified with one, or with more than one, figure in the story. Describe
the feelings which go along with your identification(s). What relationships in
your own history do these identifications bring to mind?*

(1) I can identify with a few of the characters in the story in different ways.
First of all I can see and understand the mothers position. She just seems like
the typical housewife—always tired and still she keeps on going. I can see her
position with the grandmother too. It isn't her mother and she really can't do
much to change her husbands attitude toward his mother. She must live with
someone else in "charge" of her life—his mother.

(2) I can also identify with the children's attitude toward their grandma. Since
they are kids they do tend to say what's on their mind (although June Star and
John Wesley are a little obnoxious and spoiled). It is hard to have an older
member living with your family. The kids make it clear that sometimes their
grandma is just a pain in the ass, which is very understandable. I'm sure that

they both love her but it's just that she gets on their nerves. As June Star says, "She has to go everywhere we go."

(3) I can also identify with the grandmother. She just wants to be loved and needed by her family. She wants to try to do what's best for everybody without realizing that she might be causing problems.

(4) I can identify with the mom in that I have felt tired & have had to keep on going. I have also been in positions where what I say really doesn't matter—things are done anyway. I feel like cutting down someone who bothers me, just as the kids do. I hate the feeling of someone always being there that you can't get rid of who just bugs the hell out of you. I can also feel the loneliness and need for love that the grandma feels. And when having these feelings wanting to help out and feel needed—just like the grandma.

(5) I have a "grandma" who is *just* like the one in the story. I call her my "grandma" because she is my best friends grandma and she calls all of us kids her grandchildren. In their family situation their grandma also lives with them. I can see all the attitudes of their family towards the grandma as well as the grandma's own position. Their grandma is continuously talking and trying to say what it would be better to do. She feels as if no one loves her—but she has nowhere to go because this is her only family and she wants to be with them. I can understand her feelings of loneliness because her husband just died and she is trying to get it together. In their family it is the mom's mom. The dad is driven crazy by her and has even dropped hints after living with her for a while that she should be moving out because she does cramp their life style. The kids all try to be patient with her but find it difficult. The oldest girl doesn't even bother to hold back her feelings any more. When the grandma bugs her she lets her know it—just as the kids in the story did.

(6) Mostly I think I can identify with the similarities in the families' situations. There is tension and unhappiness in both. I can feel for most of these characters because I know what they are going through. I can identify with their feelings.

It is noteworthy that Ms. K does not mention the Misfit and the murders in this story. It looks as if she did not identify with the murderer. Her emphasis is, rather, on the family relationships and her (imaginary) implications in them. This omission is an example of a response-trait that Ms. K showed through the second semester—the tendency to bypass the bizarre and unusual in stories and to concentrate on the human relations, to humanize or ratio- nalize, in a sense, stories which might seem extreme, radical, and fantastic.[1] The emphasis on the variety of human relations may be a gender-specific tendency, but I think the tendency to rationalize is just Ms. K's.[2] In fact, it

1. In essay 12, cited in the appendix, Ms. K prefers to reflect on the phenomenon of verbal scapegoating, which is much more common than the murderous events depicted in the story.

2. Whereas more women than men will respond to the relationships in a story, I have observed no special gender distribution of those who respond or do not respond to the bizarre in the literature we read.

looks as if such omissions are part of the "without-actually-saying" motif in her work, since she shows, indirectly, that her feelings are quite strong, and that she therefore may have some spontaneous reluctance to bring in story elements may disclose these feelings more directly. Her fifth paragraph may illustrate this point. She is speaking about *someone else's* grandmother and *another* girl who "doesn't even bother to hold back her feelings any more." To bring the Misfit into this situation might imply, as it appears directly in other students' essays, that strong feelings about the grandmother entail identifying with wanting to kill her, a thought which, even in its metaphorical dimension, Ms. K does not wish to bring into her statement. Notice how, in the second paragraph, her identification with the children is relatively mild and circumspect as well as qualified by the observation that they are "obnoxious and spoiled." While I think all the foregoing considerations obtain, however, probably the most important reason for her omission of this part of the story has to do with the consideration that the sentiment to be associated with each of her identifications is connected with her stage-specific identification with her mother.

The key items in the response essay are Ms. K's identifications with the children, the mother, and the grandmother and her formulations in paragraph (4). She views the three characters in similar ways—as people frustrated because they "can't do much to change"[3] their circumstances: the mother has an unremitting responsibility and has no authority over her husband's mother; the grandmother is dependent on others just to be loved and to get attention; and the children can only lash out antisocially if adults intrude in their lives. In paragraph (4) Ms. K suggests that she associates a feeling of reduced self-esteem with being a woman and a child (and as an adolescent, Ms. K is both), a feeling characterized by "what I say really doesn't matter— things are done anyway." Her response to these feelings is given in the very next sentence: "I feel like cutting down someone who bothers me, just as the kids do." This sentence begins to tell why the idea of "cutting down" plays a significant role in Ms. K's language and her sense of others' language. When backed into a corner in which saying things no longer helps, the response is to "cut down," a term which Ms. K unambiguously uses in its verbal sense but which also may imply the meaning "to kill."[4] Where the story presents literal instances of murder—imaginary instances of violence—Ms. K confines her presentation of antagonistic and aggressive feelings to the

---

3. Again, observe this same theme in essay 12, where she reflects on how people's attitudes cannot be changed.

4. Compare the metaphorical implication of Ms. K's usage with the literal and habitual murder usages of Mr. B in chapter 6.

relationships among the family members. Her not responding to the murders is a rejection of that solution to family problems on the grounds that she herself is implicated on both sides of the various disputes: the murders, in her way of thinking, take her out of the picture. But in her final essay of the first semester (cited above) she allows that her "cutting down" feelings are much stronger than she usually lets on. In the sentence following "under my authority" (page 234) she wrote the following thought: "In my essay #4 I get upset because Mike doesn't listen to me try to explain what I mean. I say 'which kind of got to me.' Well, here is the understatement, . . . I really do have much stronger feelings." Essay 4 itself shows how Mike should have accepted her authority; she narrates how her judgment of what Mike's father would do turned out to be correct. The essay announced the authority that she actually had, an authority which justified her "stronger feelings" at having been discounted. These stronger feelings were intimated in her essay on the dialogue (essay 6), but the shape of these feelings and, in particular, the conflicts they pose first emerge in essay 9 where their implication in her family situation at home is suggested.

In essay 9, Ms. K created an intersection of the problems of ethical and speaking authority, the problems of being in a reduced position due to being both a child and a young woman, and a set of language uses that have been appearing regularly in her work. Ms. K gradually comes to understand this intersection, and, in her final essay of the second semester, she puts the pieces together and relates this main insight to some of her other usages. Here is the relatively long excerpt in which this development occurred:

(1) With essay #9 my work starts to change. It still isn't as "free" as some of my essays from last semester but it isn't like the first three essays of this semester. It contains more than just "surface" thoughts.

(2) When I used the word "identified" I think a better word may have been "understood." The directions asked for identifications, though, so that's what was written. I never realized how much I really do comply in these essays. I found the fourth paragraph of this paper especially interesting. (Am I going back to my formal style?) Do I see my mom in the position of the mother in the story? Or as the grandmother? I start off with "I can identify" which I also used to start the preceding three paragraphs. The subject of the paragraph is the identification with the mother and the grandma. The subject of each sentence in the paragraph is "I"—and it also is the first word of each sentence. Hmmm. Right after I mention being in a position where what I say really doesn't matter—I talk about my feelings of wanting to cut down someone. This appears in *this* paragraph about my mother. I guess a couple of these sentences can be applied to my mom. I bet you don't have to guess which two I am referring to, Mr. Bleich. The thing is, the story refers to the grandmother as the "problem," not the mother. I give my mom some of the grandma's qualities

and the grandma seems to have what some of my mother's feelings would be. So I see my mother as a combination of both the mother and the grandma that are in the story. I see myself as the mother in the story— being in a position where what I say doesn't matter and when I'm in this position I feel like cutting others down—just as the kids do. When I say "I hate the feelings of someone always being there that you can't get rid of [5]—who just bugs the hell out of you," this is how I see the mother's attitude in the story towards the grandma. Since I just said that I am like the mom in the story and my mom is like the grandma—I guess my attitude is the same as the mother's. The next sentence then talks about how I can feel for the grandmother in the story. Or, in real life, how I can understand my moms feelings. But looking back at the beginning of this paragraph, I said I see my mom as a combination of the grandma and the mom in the story. Has the mother's qualities of being in a reduced position and the grandma's qualities of loneliness and need of love been applied to my mom? And if I see my mom like the mom in the story in some ways—and I see myself as the mom in the story in some ways—that means I identify with my mom? I say I can feel the loneliness and need for love that the grandma feels (my mom feels). In the next sentence I say that when I have these feelings I want to help out and feel needed— just like the grandma." I understand how my mom feels because this is the way I feel too.

(3) This is it: when my mom puts me in a "reduced" position I want to cut her down. I can understand her need for love and her feelings of loneliness just as I understand my own feelings of these same two emotions. When she puts me in this reduced position I know that she does it because she feels as if she were in the same position and the only way for her to feel in control is to reduce someone else. Maybe this is where my dad comes in also. With dad being in a more (what's the word I want to use?)—oh my God—*authoritative* position she feels reduced and the only way for her to feel as if she has more control is to cut down others. So my mom therefore sees *me* as authoritative?

(4) Where do I go from here? I thought things were different when I came to school with my family situation—I mean being away from home and all. But I guess my attitudes really haven't changed as much as I thought they had.

(5) It is interesting that all through this paper I have been talking about how much I have complied in my lecture essays and in my longer papers. Now I bring up the subject of "authority." I think the usage of "I'm sure," "I know," and "I think" have something to do with how I write and feel about authority. I use these usages when I am trying to show or be authoritative. Even if I am *not* sure and do not *know*—I might use it so that I appear more sure of myself. The use of this phrase appears only once or twice throughout the essays in the first semester—except in the essay about an understanding [cited above, page 223]. By using this phrase I am asserting my beliefs.

. . .

5. Here, again, is a phrase that may imply murderous feelings that Ms. K does not explore in this essay.

(6) What is also interesting is my usage of "I *guess*" as opposed to "I'm *sure*." I think I switch their meanings around. Look—I just did it in the sentence before this one. When I am not too sure about something I will say, "I know" as a way of justifying or proving what I have said—to make it look as if I do have some knowledge or authority about what I have said. When I use "I guess" I almost all of the time know that what I am saying is true. By saying "I guess" I am kind of slipping in my real feelings without actually coming out and saying what I mean.

. . .

(7) Now, I use "I'm sure" when I'm taking authority. When looking at my essay #3 [cited above, page 226, on my language,] I use second person when writing about your work, Mr. Bleich (Yes, I am aware that every time I have written something referring to you I have put your name behind the comma, Mr. Bleich). By doing this I can speak one-on-one. Does this mean that it is easier for me to take authority when speaking directly to a person, seen through the usage of "I'm sure"?

(8) In all of my lecture essays I complied. I didn't really take authority. Is this because these essays were not written specifically to someone but rather are going to be read by others?

(9) I guess in this final essay I have decided to speak (or write) on a one-to-one basis with you alone Mr. Bleich. By doing this then am I taking a position of authority? And then in taking this position does this mean I can be more honest and open? Where do I get the ideas of being more honest and open when in an authoritative position? Is it because I feel in control of situations and therefore my own emotions—I think so. Earlier I said that I wrote like my dad—therefore implying that we were alike—or on the same level.[6] By also sharing this authoritative position (like with my father) I can be more truthful because of this shared position.

(10) This is pretty neat finding out all this stuff just from the way I use language.

The main drift of this excerpt is that Ms. K begins her analysis with response material from the second semester, relates it to the "authority" theme that began in the first, and then comments on other language features

6. Ms. K is alluding to the following paragraph, which she wrote in her final essay of the first semester:

I have already talked about the ways in which I feel my family has contributed to my language. There was another thing I found out that I thought was pretty interesting. While looking at a letter from my dad I noticed that he also uses— [dashes]. I wasn't aware of this—but maybe I saw him do it and just picked it up. I also noticed underlining in his letter—to emphasize words. I also do both of these things. When I underline it makes it sound more like I was talking.

Notice how Ms. K relates the traits she shares with her father with talking, thus identifying her writing as *combination* of the oral and written "perspectives."

as they may relate to the whole picture. Furthermore, in commenting on her language use as it pertains to the various relationships she discusses, she *enacts* her principal achievement of reaching analytical insight by combining her sense of the oral and the written, as she observes at the beginning of paragraph (9): "I guess in this final essay I have decided to speak (or write) on a one-to-one basis with you alone Mr. Bleich."[7]

Essay 3 established the starting point for the development that ended in the above essay. The total event of her writing it and the class discussion which followed had ratified the trust she was seeking with me (and indirectly, in the classroom atmosphere). A one-on-one discussion was shown to be viable in this class, and she herself contributed to this achievement by reducing her claims against me by observing that the way I *speak* [paragraph (2), page 226] may qualify the observation that I cut down others because I am insecure. As we can now see, this early perception of the continuity between speaking and writing emerged in the above essay as an elaborate stylistic feature, decisively related to her assimilation of her relation to her father and her relation to me, and whose many dimensions I will discuss shortly.

The central insight of the foregoing excerpt appears in paragraphs (2) and (3), where Ms. K struggles for quite a while to sort out the meaning of her various identifications or, as she first wants to put it, her "understandings." The length of her reflection is probably related to the fact that the implied conclusion—and the one she finally reaches—is a more difficult and painful one than those regarding her relation to her father. At several different points in the second paragraph, Ms. K notes her own similarity to her mother, though it is first announced with the term "understand." She starts by saying "I see myself as the mother in the story" in regard to being in a reduced position. Then she says "I guess my attitude is the same as the mother's." Two sentences later she writes, "Or, in real life, how I can understand my moms feelings." Then she asks, "that means I identify with my mom?" as she observes the experiential difference between understanding and identification. In the paragraph's last sentence she writes, "I understand how my mom feels because this is the way I feel too," so that the whole process of identification, which began with a rejection of my term (in the question for the essay), is spelled out step by step in this analytical reflection, *yet without giving up her own term of "understanding."* This retention of her own term must be a factor in the confidence with which the third paragraph begins, "This is it." Undoubtedly, the force of this term derives from the fact that she *understands herself* in understanding the mother. Once she

7. We may wish to interpret the "I guess" in this sentence as she instructs us to earlier, as meaning "I'm sure." Notice also her identification of speaking and writing in the context of her relationship with me.

establishes the sense of her relation to her mother, the path has been cleared for the earlier thought about her father to enter the picture, and it does so with a sense of surprise at her finding the *right word* for this entrance. Previously, she portrayed her relationship to her father as privileged in some way and decidedly in opposition to her mother. Now, however, in seeing that her "reduced" position in the family is related to her identification with and, in part, her being in the same boat as, her mother, the sense of having a privileged relation with her father is not quite as safe. Because of this sense, the brief note of disillusionment is struck in paragraph (4). When she observes that her "attitudes really haven't changed as much as I thought they had," she is alluding to the depressing thought that her family problems had more staying power in her life than she had previously realized when enjoying the emancipation and authority she had gained from being in college and in the class. This realization explains the thought, at the beginning of paragraph (2), "I never realized how much I really do comply in these essays," which, from my standpoint, seemed to show relatively *less* compliance than most students'. Ms. K sees all of her work, and probably even this decidedly independent essay as being compliant. On the other hand, paragraph (8) suggests that the essay is somewhat less compliant because it is deliberately presented in the conversational mode in which she feels freer to speak/write. The important point is that she feels this sense in some significant degree, yet is able to place it in the context of her family, this course, and, most important, her habitual uses of language.

In the subsequent paragraphs, there is evidence that this is the case. She cites her routine uses of "I guess," "I'm sure," and "I know," with her observation that the more certain terms "sure" and "know" are used in circumstances of *reduced* certainty in order to "take authority." At the end of paragraph (6) she characterizes her use of "I guess" as a way of "slipping in my real feelings without actually coming out and saying what I mean." As we recall, Ms. K had previously used this phrase "without actually coming out . . . " to describe instances when her feelings were stronger than her language suggested, specifically, feelings about real people expressed indirectly in discussing fictional characters. In her final essay, she discovers the same trait in her habitual usage. However, her essay shows that the habitual usage and the use of literary effigies are both associated in her language system with her technique of (not letting on that she is) claiming, expressing, and showing authority. As I mentioned briefly earlier, the "I guess" in paragraph (9) probably does express certainty, documented by her comments on how being in control of her emotions is related to being "on the same level" as her dad in a "shared position." As we recall, in essay 3, Ms. K attributed my use of obscenity to a desire on my part to be "more on [their] level" and as a way of getting the class to "identify with" me. While this was a true observation at the time, we now see it is *also* true of Ms. K, who wishes to "identify with" (not understand) father and me as the teacher.[8] Ms. K learned to distinguish between when her language corresponded to her feelings, and when it was used to obfuscate them. It is a valuable insight about language use to know that one is more "truthful" when authority is "shared" in conversation.

Ms. K's understanding of the connection between sharing authority and using language more freely and imaginatively supports the principle, discussed in chapter 3, that an individual's use of language ought to be understood as an internalized conversation. Ordinary expository writing, with its characteristic third-person declarative usages, suppresses the writer's sense of having an imaginary conversation with the audience, and, insofar as an "audience" rather than particular individuals are the presumed readers, conversational exchange is suppressed in favor of abstract thought. Although Ms. K had her own reasons for preferring this conversational style in her classroom writing, everyone has at their disposal the same variety of uses and language choices. Of course, her usages are not cultivated or refined in the academic sense, but, by all measures, her work has a combination of emotional vitality and analytical force that is rarely found in essays written by first-year students.

One of the best examples of this special combination is Ms. K's use of rhetorical questions. In her ninth paragraph, which she opens by conflating the activities of speaking and writing, Ms. K poses the key questions about how and when she gets authority. Only her last question about being in control of her emotions is answered. The other questions remain final, so to speak, in their interrogative form. In the same sense, the various questions at the beginning and end of paragraph (2) are left open. Early in that paragraph the questions are relatively simple—"Do I see my mom in the position of the mother in the story?"; but at the end of the paragraph they are quite complicated—"And if I see my mom like the mom in the story in some ways . . . ?" All of these questions pose analytical points of substance— they present *ideas* about the psychology of her reading. Their complexity represents, in part, the unresolved status of these issues in her mind at the time; but the fact that she was able to articulate this complexity at all means that she was able to use the essay as an instrument of self-enlightenment. She is the audience for her own questions—she is asking herself these things, but lacks definite answers.

8. This is not to say that Ms. K uses obscene language and big words—quite the opposite, she uses ordinary language and, most of the time, small words—but that she interpreted my language habits by peremptorily using a wish of her own, which, I emphasize, correctly described my desires.

However, the interrogative form must also mean that she is asking *me* the questions, especially in view of her announcement that she has decided to speak to me on a one-to-one basis. This is also why there are no definite answers but only suggestions of answers. I am invited to answer these questions and consider their import. The questions thereby represent Ms. K's leaving room for me in her "conversation" about her work, "room" that is as complicated as the questions themselves: I might even be hearing the hidden question, "Do you expect me to believe that because I see the mother and grandmother in the story in certain ways that I must be identifying with my own mother?" Given Ms. K's concern with her compliance, and given the way I have discussed her and other students' work in class, there is every reason for Ms. K to think that I expect her to believe certain things. In this way, Ms. K's sense of sharing authority permits her to express these implied doubts about how I analyze her work, even as she views many of my thoughts as true. In any case, what finally matters is the richness of idea and feeling that Ms. K was able to produce in her essay as a result of her sense of sharing thoughts with me in conversation.

Questions and self-reflexive comments appear in almost every paragraph in the foregoing sequence. In the second paragraph Ms. K asks if she is "going back to my formal style"; in the third paragraph there is the parenthetical but climactic question, "What's the word I want to use?"; in the fourth paragraph, she wonders, "Where do I go from here?"; in the second, sixth, and seventh paragraphs we find the reflexive comments, "Hmmm," "Look—I just did it in the sentence before this one," and "Yes, I am aware that every time I have written something referring to you I have put your name behind the comma, Mr. Bleich." Ms. K has deliberately and self-consciously established an idiom of self-reflexiveness, placing the analytical task of the essay in the appealing form of human dialogue, which has the tone of "ordinary conversation" but which is not ordinary in the seriousness of the subjects of the essay. Ms. K had written three other essays on her own work, but it was only in this last essay that she felt ready to violate the rules of "formal style" and comment on her work *as it was being produced and then leave the comments in*. This may have happened because she assumed that only I would read it in private. On the other hand, her sentence in paragraph six beginning "Look" comes after the key insight in paragraph (3): it is very likely that that insight is a turning point in the essay itself which *authorizes* her to take the liberty of disrupting the formal presentation of thoughts with self-reflexive comments and other spontaneous remarks.

Ms. K's informal commentary and interrogative reflection changes the concept of "formal style" or "formal presentation" that we usually associate with "expository prose." As soon as such forms are permitted in essays in the university classroom, writing takes on a new meaning and purpose. Part of this new purpose is actually quite "old," as Ms. K's case suggests: the student's seeking an authorized private dialogue with the teacher. At the same time, Ms. K's own motives of wanting to share *authority* and then her actually finding ways to do it represent something new and rare in today's students' behavior in the academy. The key idea is *that the change in relation to the teacher entails a change in what kind of writing is done*. The extremely high level of self-awareness Ms. K shows in this essay derives from her being able to admit that her relation to the teacher is fundamental in her performance in the classroom, as well as her being able to see this relationship not in isolation but stereoscopically in the context of authority relations in her own family. I could not have instructed Ms. K or any other student to write this way; I cannot present this essay as a model that others may emulate directly. Other students may not, in fact, need to reach this point, since there cannot be fixed rules for sociosyntonic language-use strategies. Rather, Ms. K's work represents the culmination of her own history in this class, her *derivation* of a suitable mode of discourse for herself in this context.

Part of Ms. K's interest in authority is related to the concern all students have about their grades. Although I made a strong argument in chapter 6 that a course like this ought not be graded, the course Ms. K took was. Ms. K was an ambitious student and clearly eager to excel. She understood that grades would not be a topic of discussion in this course so that students could concentrate on the subject matter. As a result, Ms. K never discussed with me, either in public or in private, how she was doing in the course "gradewise," or what it would take to get an "A" rather than a "B." Before assigning the final essay in the second semester, I scheduled a conference with each student to review their plans for the essay, which I emphasized was very important. In the conference with Ms. K, I told her that I did not think she needed to discuss with me how to approach the final essay and she agreed that she understood the course well enough to proceed on her own. In this context, consider her comments at the very end of her final essay:

> Just one last thing. This final paper was important because I was told that I didn't have to comply. This then means that I could take the authoritative position—where I am most comfortable. In sharing this position with you I was able to talk one-on-one and therefore more openly.
>
> Well, I'm finished with this paper. If you will notice, Mr. Bleich, the folder I am handing this essay in is doodle-free. My grade-point average is not calculated on the back—like it was last semester.

In the first paragraph Ms. K alludes to what I have already discussed at some length—the issue of sharing—and I include it here to demonstrate its close juxtaposition with the material in the second paragraph. The doodle on her first semester essay-folder that Ms. K refers to included the "A" she expected. I doubt she did this for my benefit and I found it amusing regardless. It would probably have gone without comment from her, I think, if I had not, on the first day of the second semester, announced to the class that Ms. K had calculated her grade-point average on the essay-folder she turned in. She was somewhat embarrassed, of course, by my teasing since she had successfully maintained discipline in not discussing her grade with me. At the time, I read her "public" calculation as, perhaps, a way of saying something but "without actually saying what I mean." During the second semester, she maintained the same discipline about discussing her grade only to end her essay with the comment!

Its apparent purpose was to inform me that this semester, unlike the last, she was not suggesting to me what grade she ought to get. The conventional logic of any university grading system is that the teacher is the sole judge of a student's performance, as all students learn in elementary school. But now I come along and claim that authority is to be shared in the classroom and I actually succeed in doing so in several ways. But Ms. K is in this class and she is particularly interested in questions of authority.[9] She observes that if a grade is to be given—even if it is in the narrow range of "A" and "B"—it is the exercise of unshared pedagogical authority. Since Ms. K understood that my grading authority will not yield to a challenge, but nevertheless believed in the idea of shared authority—and also thought that I believed in it—her resourceful strategy was, as it was with regard to other issues of emotional consequence to her, indirection. In the first semester, the strategy was unconscious. The ending of the second semester's essay, however, was undoubtedly much more conscious. It was also rather witty. There is an implied critique of my taking doodles seriously, as well as an ironic calling attention to the fact that she is "not" calling attention to her grade-point average. But behind all this friendly and complicated joking, I heard a very serious point being made, namely, that if grades are given in a course at all, then they will remain important to her no matter what I say or what else I may do to change the classroom's authority structure. And if I am taking the authority to give grades, then I have no authority to oppose, diminish, reject, or censor her interest in her grade. Because I was persuaded by this view of the question of grading, I decided to make the serious effort to abandon grading in this course, an effort, which, as I explain in note 3 of chapter 7, has still not succeeded.

---

9. Perhaps this is an appropriate moment to say that Ms. K's choice of vocation was law enforcement, a choice that was settled when she was a freshman. She eventually became a police officer. In other words, her interest in authority was beyond the ordinary, and one can therefore perhaps attribute to her an above-average sensitivity to the subtleties of how authority is exercised.

In view of some of the issues and language-use strategies we have seen in Ms. K's work, I would now like to return to three of her earliest essays and study them in the light of what subsequently became clear about her work. I would like to show that many of the language features that were obvious in her later work had actually appeared immediately, but in a muted form. In addition, I would like to suggest how one might be able to detect the "seeds" of development in *anyone's* work from the beginning. In this way, I am trying to emphasize the necessity of introducing students to the subject of literacy only in this extended, patient way, a way which accommodates their pace of growth and their need to have the time for classroom socialization to develop naturally toward a point where it can contribute to the full exercise of mental capabilities. Here, then, is the very first essay she wrote in this course:

Question

Tell, in as much detail as you can, something important about yourself that you think would be helpful and/or interesting for everyone else to know. Be as candid and as clear as your normal sense of decorum permits.

I feel that by having a lot of outside activities you can learn a lot about people and they can teach you a lot. I have always been involved in activities outside of the classroom, I love to play soccer and have done so on various teams for three years. I also like drama and have been in plays. I like to ski, dance, walk in the woods, swim in the ocean, and be with close friends. In every activity there are many new people to meet. By sharing an interest with them, many close feelings are revealed and a friendship is easy to come by.

By way of outside activities, you can become friends with others quite easily. I value true friendship. When something as unique as a true friendship does exist, I feel as if there really is someone who will always be there. No matter how rotten you can be to someone (your friend) they don't turn on you—they put up with you and try to understand you. It is hard for me to open up to people. Even close friends sometimes feel as if there was more to me than I allow them to see. By sharing an interest with them I feel I can be more open and they can learn things about me, and in turn I may learn about them.

When I first read this, I thought it was a "classic" first essay—one which volunteered practically nothing of interest and would not be helpful to other students, i.e., she reported that you get to meet people in outside activities and presented the "I'm reserved and don't open up too easily" theme. It took some effort on my part not to judge this as a trite essay. The next two essays did not do much to change my opinion, and it was not until the essay on the instructor's language that I began to reread the earlier essays in a different light. Here is Ms. K's second essay in the course:

Question

Think back to the first time in your life that a verbal or language event scared you. Name the person speaking, describe the full circumstances, and discuss the extent to which a purely verbal event (someone saying something) is fearful. Describe your fearful feelings as fully as possible, and explain the significance of this event today.

I can still remember the first time that I was scared by what someone had said to me. I was about six years old—no I was younger—I hadn't started school yet. My older brother and I were going to walk a block away to buy some goodies at the dime store with money that our dad had given us. I was waiting in the front yard for him so we could leave. The neighbor boy was out waxing his car (or something). I remember him saying my name. I had never met the boy before so I was a little wary. Just the way he said my name was enough to get me a little uptight. Then he kept talking to me. I don't even remember what he said to me. I just stood in my front yard and I was scared by the way in which he was speaking to me. It must have been the tone or manner in which he spoke and not what he said—otherwise I would have remembered—right?

As I was standing in my yard I felt alone. I was aware of the fact that I was the only one around. I wanted to get away from him—yet I didn't move. He asked me questions but I couldn't answer him. I guess you could say the feeling was like when you have a bad dream and want to yell for help—but you can't. As I look back I seem to feel how it was to be young and frightened. I don't think that this even has any significance in my life today. I'm not afraid to stand in my front lawn and talk to the neighbor boy. I know that I am hesitant in giving someone directions when they pull up beside me—but I think that is just a fear instilled in me by my mom.

Although this essay also seems relatively bland, it does introduce Ms. K's immediate family, in particular the father first, who had made the trip for "goodies" possible, and the mother, who "instilled" the fear of giving directions to strangers. Before considering these presentations, as well as the interesting feeling of not being able to call for help, let me cite the third of Ms. K's first essays.

Question

Recall a conversation that took place between you and someone else, in a relationship of mutual dislike. Discuss at least one thing said about you by the other person that you consider true. Explain the remark(s) and your reaction to them as fully as possible. Say if this remark is still true today.

The only conversation I can remember having which involved feelings of dislike was with one of my very good friends, N. For some reason or another we were upset with each other and not *even* on speaking terms (which is really strange because N never shuts up—she *always* has something to say). Well during our disagreement two of my other friends became mad at her also. We joined together in the "silent treatment." I felt bad about everyone ganging up on her like that—but what could I do? I mean I *was* the first person to get mad with her. Well—this treatment had gone on for a pretty long time (one week). One day I was in my driveway and N was walking down the street. I wondered if she would come and talk to me—she looked *so* bummed out—but I knew I wouldn't be the first to speak. Well anyway—N walked up to me and as usual was defensive. I knew she wasn't going to apologize and this made me a little edgy. What did she want? She started telling me in her rather matter-of-fact way how stupid this whole thing was and how immature I had been. She continued to say that I was always in the middle of things. This made me stop and think. I actually asked her what she meant by that. She said that I would always have to be the compromiser—and that I would never turn against one person (which was weird of her to say because I *had* turned against her). N said that I would defend both sides and see the good & bad of both. (Was that what I was doing?) She finally came to the point and said she was "goddamn tired" of me being in the middle of everything. I guess I saw the truth in her statement even as she said it. But what was so bad about being in the middle? I would always defend my friends if they weren't around. I guess she thought I was two-faced. This made me angry—yet made me think. I didn't want to be like that. Today I still find myself "in the middle." I still don't consider myself two-faced. I still feel comfortable in that position (in the middle).

In this initial sequence of work, there is a gradual loosening of Ms. K's language-use style. The first essay is written with declarative sentences only, and the repeated thoughts of sharing and friendship seem somewhat redundant. In the first sentence of the second paragraph, however, where she writes "you can become friends with others quite easily," Ms. K introduces what will later become a significant usage—the second person. Although we may wish to say that this essay is written in her "formal style," the use of "you" instead of "one" in that sentence may suggest the artificiality of the "formal style" in Ms. K's language. In their conventional senses, "you" and "one" both mean something like "all of us" or "any of us"; for Ms. K to choose "you" implies a peremptory or natural move toward the personal and conversational pronoun. This small departure from formal usage now seems to have been a sign of things to come. It was the single colloquialism in the essay, and that is reason enough to take note of it for possible future reference.

The second essay introduces another sign: the interrogative in the last sentence of the first paragraph—"otherwise I would have remembered—right?" This sentence may be an allusion to one of my early lectures in this course in which I discussed the idea that really important emotional events in one's life have a way of staying in one's memory; Ms. K is saying that what was important was the neighbor's tone, since, according to my lecture, one remembers the important items, "right?" This interrogative usage is another example of direct address, first implied by the "you" in the first essay. This second essay also suggests that Ms. K's narratives become more fluent and complicated when they become personal. Although the incident she reports does not seem really significant, Ms. K seems relatively articulate in announcing her feelings—"enough to get me a little uptight" or "I seem to feel how it was to be young and frightened." As I mentioned earlier, this essay also introduces her parents. However, it is an introduction which prefigures, in ever so faint a way, how Ms. K sees herself in relation to them—the father in the more generous light and the mother who "instilled" a fear which Ms. K seems to think she does not need ("just a fear" implies that it did not spontaneously develop but was acquired because of her mother's fears).[10]

The third essay introduces Ms. K's analytical ability and, something we have not discussed in detail yet, her sense of herself among her peers. (I will discuss Ms. K's peer relationships further in chapters 9 and 10.) As Ms. K advances her analysis, she repeatedly uses both parenthetical and interrogative commentary. Questions such as "What could I do?," "What did she want?," and "What was so bad about being in the middle?" suggest that Ms. K came to this class with a relatively well-established habit of internalized conversation and a sense of its legitimacy in written work. This habit presents itself in the kind of situation in which she feels both psychologically safe and in control: recall how she first thought that coming to school, and thus placing herself in what is primarily a peer society, she would be free of the struggles of dealing with her parents. I conclude in retrospect of her later work that her natural tendency to integrate the oral and the written could emerge fluently and for the first time in describing a kind of relationship that is more or less stable in her life. This essay helped set the stage for the one immediately following, on my use of language, in which she transferred the value of a conversational writing style from the less urgent relationship to the more urgent one: because she "conversed" in the "mutual dislike" essay, conversation became a step toward her forceful

10. In view of Ms. K's vocation of law enforcement, however, it would be reasonable to argue that Ms. K took seriously her intuition that it is dangerous to speak to strangers in cars. The statement at the end of the second essay could then be interpreted as a kind of bravado, given that in the first semester Ms. K felt herself freer of her mother's influence than she subsequently found out she was, partially through her analysis of her literary responses in the second semester.

use of direct address in the next essay, which, in turn, provided a major key to her development in the course.[11]

In view of the development, other features of her first essay seem more significant. First there is the matter of "friendship." Although there is a sense in which her concern is ordinary and trite, we can now see friendship as a counterpoint to her interest in authority relationships and as an element in *her concern to normalize authority relationships in the direction of friendship.* Her repeated use of the phrase "sharing an interest" at the end of each paragraph prefigures her subsequent use of "sharing the position of authority" in her work toward the end of the course. In those last essays, as we recall, she spoke of being more "open and honest" when she felt she shared authority; yet this idea was introduced in the very first essay when she wrote that "many close feelings are revealed" and "I can be more open" as a consequence of "sharing an interest." We see that these seemingly conventional thoughts are actually quite meaningful in specific ways once we see a fuller picture of Ms. K's language use and social relations.

We might well read the phrase "teach you a lot" in her first sentence as an allusion to being in school, though the sentence is so vague it does not really say anything to a stranger reading it. In particular, the phrase "outside activities," some of which she lists, now seems to refer to activities "outside" the family rather than outside of school—the meaning one would usually assign to the phrase. In view of her own disclosure that family was a place where there were many "covered up feelings," it is not surprising that friendship and other peer activities offered a context in which "many close feelings are revealed." For Ms. K, the revelation of such feelings is intimately connected with teaching and learning, a theme she strikes in the last sentence of the essay as well as the first.

In addition to the key value of sharing, the idea of caution and indirection also appears in her first essay when she observes that "even close friends sometimes feel as if there was more to me than I allow them to see." I now read this as an allusion to her relatively well-developed strategies of indirection in which she says "I guess" when she is sure, and she speaks of her own feelings through discussing literary characters. Her "mutual dislike" essay also suggested that she likes seeming to appear "in the middle" when

11. It may also be worth noting that Ms. K describes N as "always having something to say," a trait she later attributes to the mother in the dialogue essay. In spite of her sympathy with the father in that essay, Ms. K remains, in a sense, "in the middle" of the two quarreling parents. It seems that N's remark "made her think" not only because it was at odds with her own initiating role in the dispute she describes in the essay, but also because she considers herself in the middle of their parents' disputes at home and she therefore may not have been so surprised to find her friend observing that social trait in her.

she knows that she has stronger feelings. We could even now read the essay as an achievement of concealment! While the essay is informative in one sense, we see how adept Ms. K is at conventionalizing what we now know to be two complex situations in her life and the complex strategies of language use. Yet in this regard Ms. K is not terribly different from other students. What distinguishes her from many others is that she found a very successful means and motive for disclosing what lies behind the universal ability to conventionalize oneself in social situations that are unfamiliar and potentially dangerous. I cannot see how it can fail to be the case that *behind every conventional essay we find in the classroom, there is the same richness and complexity we have seen in Ms. K's work, and that the language of those conventional essays somehow signals the depth of feeling, thought, and relationships beyond it.* In this class, perhaps half the other students were able to make comparable disclosures, though not that many showed the reflective or analytical skill that Ms. K showed. My point now is that any student is potentially able to achieve the self-awareness that Ms. K achieved of how she or he uses language, provided that the classroom structure is hospitable to such an inquiry.

Although growth cannot be measured, it is observable in Ms. K's work in the marked fluency, complexity, and subtlety of her writing. However, I would not want to claim that Ms. K has become a "better writer." It is hard to say that Ms. K will "use" what she knows about her language when she starts to write police reports. Yet, it is clear that Ms. K has acquired the ability to observe her language and has refined and cultivated her habits and styles of language use. For example, it seems clear that Ms. K understands some of the ways she adapts her use of language according to the authority situations in which she finds herself; that she has worked up her natural habit of self-observation and self-interrogation; that she is significantly alert to the influence of her gender identity on her uses of language; that she is systematically conscious of when to assert, when to suppress, and when to hedge in her literate activities. Such categories of knowledge are obviously not purely linguistic, since they are bound up with ethical, political, psychological, and practical choices for action. Ms. K became alert to how she shares her language in specific ways—her senses of what she may have in common with her father and mother and her sense of being able to observe others' language uses because she shares them.

The overview of Ms. K's work documents, in part, something all teachers wish to see—how one piece of work leads to the next, how each one accumulates in the student's mind as a *potential* source for the next effort, how growth proceeds incrementally, imperceptibly, yet nevertheless builds toward new habits and new initiatives. At the same time we have seen at least one aspect of how Ms. K became socialized in the classroom, somehow engaging my authority yet offering a persistent and useful challenge to it through her interrogative style, her wit, and her quiet insistence that grades matter to her as long as they are a feature of the class. With these thoughts in mind, let us now take a closer look at the social relations in the classroom from more than just one student's point of view.

9

Mutuality Between Student and Teacher

In chapter 6, where I discussed Freire's view on redistributing authority in the classroom, I said that teachers and students should be considered members of the *same class*. When Freire proposed changing the terminology of "students of the teacher" and "teacher of the students" to "student-teachers" and "teacher-students," I interpreted this name-change to refer to a class or genre change for classrooms. Instead of considering the classroom and the academy as two classes, I viewed all members of a classroom as members of a single class or genre, "classroom members." This conception of the classroom admits into it the reciprocity of pedagogical function—a reversible "syntax" of mutual teaching. The activity of students learning continues to be predicated on teachers teaching, but "students learning" also comes to mean "students teaching," and "teachers teaching" comes to mean "teachers learning." The reversals of subject and predicate refer to new social relations which can enable a new access to authority for all classroom members.

Attempts to change the classroom in the foregoing directions have not succeeded. Even the most progressive initiatives have continued on the assumption that the teacher should serve as a standard or model of individual knowing and thinking and therefore should be the ultimate judge of students' performance. It has been virtually impossible to dislodge the ethic of the primacy of the individual even in those efforts which recognize that mutuality is as primary as individuality, and which understand that leadership does not have to be authoritarian. For example, Shirley Heath's approaches to communities, classrooms, and individuals in her Piedmont work all show a significant degree of collective consciousness on her part and a spirit of generosity that is relatively uncharacteristic of educational thinking. She has introduced techniques of acquiring literacy that depend on exchange between individuals and on collective effort. Yet there remains an element in her work that implies a certain exemption of the individual leader from the processes and proposals that this leader brings. Heath is not to be faulted or criticized in

253

this regard, since this trope of exemption—which one might call the Moses-in-the-desert[1] effect—is present in much of what we consider revolutionary thought in our time. Marx remained a bourgeois intellectual working in a library; Freud insisted on the detachment and "objectivity" of the analyst[2]; and teachers and researchers retain a rigid boundary between how they "learn" and how students work in the classroom. So when we study the work of Kenneth Bruffee, who, unlike Heath, actually began making changes in his own classrooms, we see that when he speaks of communalizing the classroom by fostering regular and disciplined peer interaction, he continues to presuppose that the students are to be *brought into* the teacher's communities, that the relation of teachers to students remains hierarchical; he continues to presuppose that the purpose of peer interaction is remedial (in regard to the teaching and study of writing) rather than investigatory or epistemological.[3] From a social standpoint, I have argued that grading represents a major inhibition of our progressive desires for classroom mutuality; but it would be wrong to imagine that if, miraculously, grading were eliminated, that the intrapsychic habits of mutuality would emerge forthwith. In part, grading is now a social substitute for an ideal of pedagogy that itself unconsciously rules out collective work—the belief that the one-on-one relation of teacher and student is the ultimate unit of learning. As the common thought goes, "of course, if we could reduce the teacher student ratio to one to one, that would be ideal, but we ought not hope for that since it can't be done." Most teachers, myself included, have regularly relied on the individual private conference with the student to do what cannot be done in the classroom— to communicate to the student what I (the teacher) "really" want and expect the student to "get out of" this course, and, as a corollary, "what it takes to get an A." I am not, of course, advocating the abandonment of private conferences, but only that they be predicated on the ideal that pedagogy is the effective communication by an individual teacher to each of the individual students of what it takes to master the subject matter. If, within a relationship between one teacher and one student, I can describe a structure of interaction that does not require the teacher to retain a sense of exemption, a feeling of being the unmoved mover, but instead discloses both the teacher's own path of growth and change and how it interacts with the student's,

1. In the desert, Moses disobeys God, leading to his ultimate exclusion from the Promised Land. His sense of exemption was punished with a more climactic exclusion from the fruits of his other heroism.

2. Notice, in chapter 5, how circumspect Leo Stone's critique of psychoanalytic detachment is. It is generally believed that to abandon the custom of the psychoanalyst's own detachment is to alter the practice of psychoanalysis fundamentally.

3. I have further comment on this feature of Bruffee's work in the conclusion.

this will render the customary role of the authoritarian teacher[4] less plausible.

Many will think it foolish and perhaps idle to pursue a standard of reciprocity in classrooms where there are twenty odd students and one teacher. It is in fact impossible for what I describe in this chapter to take place between a teacher and each of the students in the class. Nevertheless, several things should be kept in mind. First, the interaction between Ms. K and me that I comment on in detail originally took place because of certain spontaneous events in that class; I did not single Ms. K out in advance as an "experimental" student and then "interact" with her self-consciously. The class was divided into subgroups of three, and, since I had decided to be a member of one of the subgroups,[5] it was a matter of coincidence that we were in the same subgroup: the subgroups were established arbitrarily on the second day of class as I went down the roster alphabetically; because there were twenty-three students, two were "left over," and I said I would join to form eight groups of three. Second, although, as I discussed in chapter 8, I did have several private conferences with Ms. K, the substance of the "interaction" that I will discuss is based on two sets of texts that were public documents: the essays that I wrote in the class at the same time the students wrote theirs, and Ms. K's essays which commented on my written work.[6] In other words, what might appear to have been a relatively private relationship was actually in large part observable by the rest of the class. Third, my purpose in the present discussion is to demonstrate, on the one hand, that an "authoritative" teacher can share substantial parts of his or her subjectivity, thereby disclosing my common participation with the students in the universal processes of growth and change, and, on the other hand, to disclose *for* the present discussion issues in my own mental and pedagogical development that bear on the claims of this book. Fourth, and finally, I want to show that author-

4. In case anyone should find this too strong a term, I consider a teacher authoritarian whenever students' records and careers can be permanently marked by his or her nonnegotiable judgment (assuming the good will and honesty of both students and teachers). Almost every teacher I know, myself included, is authoritarian in this sense, because that is how our "system" works. However, very many are authoritarian in the more familiar sense—tyrannical, arbitrary, antisocial, and dictatorial—making use of centuries of tradition which encouraged such pedagogical behavior.

5. In retrospect, there is reason to think that this was not such a good idea; it was very difficult for me to be both a responsible group member and the teacher for the whole class, even though no serious damage resulted.

6. I did not produce a written commentary on Ms. K's work but made my comments to Ms. K during subgroup meetings, where Ms. M, the other group member, was present. Sometimes I offered comments on her work in the plenary meetings of the class: the grade discussion alluded to in the previous chapter is one of those occasions.

itative action on the part of the teacher can and should consist in proposing to students and teachers alike how both can learn from *all* members of the class. Since I am claiming that habits of mutuality are missing both from pedagogical practices and from society at large, I am trying to render a plausible context for establishing such habits and for integrating them into the investigation of language use and literacy.

Perhaps the most difficult part of establishing the right context of mutuality is persuading students that they have something important to contribute to the teacher's development. The heart of this problem, in turn, is that students believe not that they have nothing of value to offer, but that teachers are, by virtue of their institutional role, age, and psychology, ineligible to become genuine students in the classes they teach. Students feel that the social teleology of all classrooms combines with the psychological habits— developed over many years and even over many generations—of both themselves and the teachers to create a clear consensus about their purpose in school: that the teacher is there to help them do something for themselves. That the school experience may also include their active contribution to the minds and lives of the teacher and of the other students is understood to be completely irrelevant.

In discussing the growth of mutuality between Ms. K and me, therefore, my attention will be on just how available I made myself seem to her prospective contributions, how she was able to take advantage of my availability and responsiveness to her thoughts, how I was then able to change some of my habits and styles of work in class, how these changes were reflected in my language, and how, finally, her perception of my having been thus influenced was a factor in her own growing ability to understand and work with her uses of language. Toward the end of the chapter, I will again reflect on the more general purposes of this process and how and why I think it is necessary to make any meaningful advances in cultivating universal literacy.

In trying to explain Ms. K's essay 3 in chapter 8, I put considerable weight on how her subsequent work, from the home-written "mutual understanding" essay on, disclosed both language and interpersonal issues which had already existed in her mind when she wrote essay 3. I would now like to entertain how her reading of the first three essays I had written in this course[7] may have enabled her to write that essay. Here they are in sequence:

7. In the course, there were two sorts of essay assignments: lecture essays and home-written essays. Lecture essays were written in a large lecture hall and took perhaps thirty-five or forty minutes; the students saw the questions for the first time at the time of writing. The four associate instructors (graduate students who were teaching other discussion sections of this course) and I composed the questions together and wrote lecture essays in class, along with the students. Only the students wrote home-written essays.

Question 1

Tell, in as much detail as you can, something important about yourself that you think would be helpful and/or interesting for everyone else to know. Be as candid and as clear as your normal sense of decorum permits. [8]

As is very clear to you, I enjoy talking. What you probably don't know is that I try to find ways to limit my talking. I sort of automatically respond to anything that is said, often interrupting others and taking special pleasure in engaging other people through conversation. It is also no coincidence that I became a college teacher since I knew when I was younger that that was a good way to talk a lot and have other people take you seriously. Of course, one has to have something to say—so, many of the things I say are actually about how we go about saying things.

I also like to argue, spar, and tease. These all involve the verbal exercise of aggressive feelings. Many people think, in hearing my aggressive language, that I feel angry at them, but this is only sometimes true. It is just as often the case that I am angry at something else, or at myself, or I am just speaking aggressively for the hell of it.

Argument is often like a kind of sport for me. I remember liking the "one on one" sports like ping pong or handball as a kid because they afforded me the chance to use psychology as well as physical skill. The same is true today in arguing with one or more people—it is not just a problem of advancing my own point of view to the other person, but of saying the things that can *change* the views of the other. Sometimes, when I fail to persuade others—like auto manufacturers and store managers and types like them—I get very angry and abusive and I concentrate on ways to piss the bastards off or otherwise aim for their points of vulnerability. I don't usually get such strong feelings when arguing with my colleagues—other teachers and students, that is.

In class, this semester, I will be concentrating on controlling and limiting my talking in productive ways. This should be easy to do with so many well-motivated students, but for me it isn't. I will be counting on help from you!

Question 2

Think back to the first time in your life that a verbal or language event scared you. Name the person speaking, describe the full circumstance, and discuss the extent to which a purely verbal event (someone saying something) is fearful. Describe your fearful feelings as fully as possible, and explain the significance of this event today.

The earliest time I remember being scared was during an argument between my parents when I was perhaps 8 or 9. It was morning and I was scheduled to go somewhere. My older brother was sleeping in our bedroom. My mother wanted to leave the house with me and my father tried to prevent her from taking me.

---

8. Ms. K's essay in response to this question is cited in chapter 8, page 247.

As I think back, I just cannot remember why there was a dispute, but I recall my father was quite enraged, while my mother as usual during arguments, was violently sarcastic—though in a relatively low voice—and brutal with epithets— obviously she knew certain things would enrage my father and she sometimes did [meaning, "said"] them if she felt enough frustration.

I recall that my fear had to do with my observation that words would not solve the problem and that my father looked as if he would *physically* prevent my mother and me from leaving the house. Needless to say, I did not know who to side with. I wanted to go to, I think, my piano lesson, but I was feeling angry that my mother used unfair tactics[9] to get her and my way.

I went into the bedroom into my brother's bed with him and I cried because I did not know what to do. In retrospect, I think my brother was listening to the actual words of the argument, but he was reassuring to me in a somewhat perfunctory way. I remember not being too reassured by him. Since he was ten years older than me, I know he understood the quarrel better than I.

My father's form of argument (though I don't remember the actual words on those occasions) was to say something like "You are not leaving this house with him" ("him" meaning me). My mother would usually say something like "We'll see" and move right for the door, coat on, telling me to come with her.

I can recall preferring my mother's way of arguing (as a child). But now I see that when I argue I have all the advantages of my father's rage and my mother's sarcasm. As an adult I see that my father was more direct and less mean and I think I prefer that, since I know if I am enraged, I'm not really going to hurt anyone.

It is interesting to note that out of this fearful scene, I did *not* learn to avoid argument, but to develop a wider repertoire of ways of arguing and to emulate the *tones* of my parents. As I think further, I actually feel frustrated at not remembering the actual words because I would very much like to know. Why?

Question 3

Recall a conversation that took place between you and someone else, in a relationship of mutual dislike. Discuss at least one thing said about you by the other person that you consider true. Explain the remark(s) and your reaction to them as fully as possible. Say if this remark is still true today.

What I remember is not just a conversation but a remark that took place in many conversations with a friend that I had been friends with since third

9. In Ms. K's essay 6, on the argument between two parents, she describes the mother as using "unfair tactics." I cannot say whether my essay was a conscious or unconscious influence, or whether it is a genuine coincidence that Ms. K used the same term for a very similar purpose—to describe a mother's behavior in an argument between parents. Her work suggests that she thought *her* mother used unfair tactics in arguing with her father. I therefore think that my usage had something to do with her later usage insofar as she unconsciously (but perhaps consciously) noted a similarity between my relation to my parents and her relation to hers.

grade but which ended about six years ago. Although we were "friends," I was always a little suspicious of this fellow's role in our relationship. There were several periods of no contact with him—mainly on my part, but after a while we were "friends" again.

The remark always had to do with my nose. At moments of stress in our relationship, some remark would come from him regarding its size, or he would just call me "nose." Of course the description of my nose being "long" was true then and it is true today, but years back it took effort for me to eradicate the effect this remark had on me. My friend, of course, did not have a long nose, but a normal sized one (I thought) and thus felt at a permanent disadvantage at the boyhood games of mutual derision.

The times when this remark was seriously damaging were during early adolescence when I thought the only thing on my face was a nose. It did not matter that others had long noses, that others did not notice or say anything about my nose. It was just this fellow's remark that got to me.

I believe the "truth" of this remark must be that my own behavior got to him in such a way that he had to strike back at me in this (to me) unfair way. I remember him thinking that I was selfish because I wanted to sell, and not give, him the electric trains I no longer wanted. It may be that other remarks I made to him prompted him to want to take revenge in this decisive way.

Although I don't consider it a problem today, I know that I have made remarks to people, where they heard mainly a derisive intention on my part and they want to strike back in some way they consider equally damaging.

On the other hand, I decided I would no longer correspond with this fellow (he lives in another city) because, in the final analysis, I did not like him enough to stand for his verbal manners, which on one occasion were used to embarrass his wife in my presence, just as, I felt, he once embarrassed me in hers.

The foregoing three essays suggest in a specific way just how Ms. K's essay 3 was, in part, an *answer*—or a response—to what I had already *written* in this course. If the risk-taking feature of her essay is based on her recognition that I sometimes cut others down, thereby jeopardizing my own pedagogical purposes, part of the justification for her taking this risk appears in all three of my essays above. In paragraph (2) of my first essay I observe that others sometimes think that my aggressive language is expressing my anger toward them; in paragraph (3) I tell how I sometimes deliberately try to irritate certain people. In paragraph (5) of my second essay I write that as a boy I "preferred" my mother's sarcasm (actually, cut-down arguing strategy), and I then suggest that even though I don't "prefer" this strategy now, I still use it. In paragraph (4) of my third essay, I suggest that I made certain remarks to my former friend that may have prompted him to "take revenge" by being derisive toward me; and in the fifth paragraph I observe that sometimes my own remarks are interpreted as being derisive by people other than my former friend.

Ms. K, like the others in this course, understands that my essays, as contributions to the class, are meant to be used in the extended project of studying my use of language, not as a confession, revelation, or contrite exposure of my faults or problems. Because of this understanding, she is able to "add up" my remarks in a productive way: that is, she uses them to comment on my *classroom* use of language, in particular, the instances in which I have teased students for coming late to class. When she raises the psychological issue of whether I use aggressive language because of larger problems of self-esteem, it is not only because she is reflecting intelligently on the issue itself and on her familiarity with cut-downs in her own family; it is because I have provided the class with some of my own history and revealed that my classroom habits and behavior also occur in other areas of my life. Her implicit larger perceptions of my language use permit her to take over my use of the adjective "aggressive" (which appears three times in the second paragraph of my first essay) and create a *new term* (which I did not use to describe myself), "aggressive style": The sentence in which it appears is general and important: "His writing reflects his argumentative and aggressive style." It is an instance of naming in the senses I discussed in chapter 4. The word "aggressive" is analogous to Piaget's "stuffing the handkerchief" schema; Ms. K takes the schema from its previous context—my essays—and puts it into the new context— her essay with its own purpose—thereby making "new language" out of it. I want to stress the importance of our recognizing that this *is* new language as opposed to a perfunctory or unthinking "borrowing." When Ms. K moves into her second paragraph in essay 3, where "the light goes on" and she shifts into the second person, she writes, "Cutting down others is just part of your *style*, Mr. Bleich." It is her own idiom, the second person, that changes her term, "aggressive style" into "your style." The liberating effect of this completely new term is that it permits a partial withdrawal of her strong psychological speculations—when she explains what she does *not* think. The whole emphasis of her essay changes with her second use of the term "style," marking the achievement of the *essay's* stereoscopy. She as a person has entered the essay as she moves into the conversational idiom. The new phrase, "your style," is predicated on her previous term, "aggressive style," which, in turn, was predicated on my term, "aggressive language." These terms mark a psychologically necessary movement of Ms. K's sense of me as someone outside her conversational purview to someone inside of it. Her "seeing" me in this new position is her combined "insight" into me the language-user. Her seeing into me is also her simultaneous bringing me into her *conversational* "sight," where she is now able to "see" the two of us at once. In this way, Ms. K's "new language," "your style," is the means and occasion of her new *relationship* with me. At the same time, my reading of the essay made me experience this new relationship with her, the experience which prompted me to share the essay with the full class, explore it further, and, as I discussed in chapter 8, create a wider social authorization for Ms. K's work. The mutuality between Ms. K and me became a moment of participation for all members of the class.

Other features of my first three essays also played a role in how Ms. K and I interacted in this course, which I will return to after describing our development more comprehensively. In this development the idea of "style" continued as a key idea. In Ms. K's last essay of the course, which I discussed at some length in chapter 8, she asked, "Am I going back to my formal style?" The idea of style became, from essay 3 on, a point of comparison *within* her own sense of her language as well as *between* her language and mine. Perhaps two weeks after essay 3, there was a home-written assignment which asked all group members to write about the language-use habits, strategies, and features of the other two group members. Here is part of Ms. K's commentary on my written essays:

> I have noticed in Bleich's essays that he will repeat one certain word throughout a particular paper. The word that is repeated is very important. It is the key to his main feelings on the topic he is writing about. Such words as "nose," "argument," and "talking" can be found over and over again. . . .
>
> Bleich's stories describe his thoughts and feelings. He writes his essays as if he were speaking—not in the formal written style. He will tell how he feels about what is going on around him or happening to him. He even asked a question on one of his papers. He was frustrated at not remembering the actual words of an argument and asked of himself as well as the reader "why" this was so. Bleich will also make comments which are self-reflexive. By doing this he puts emphasis on who is telling the story—himself.
>
> In Bleich's [third] essay, a certain remark having to do with his "nose" was made which bothered him. In his [second] essay, he is bothered by not being able to remember the actual words that were spoken. In all of his papers some type of argument is talked about. This shows how much *what* people say is important to him. With as much emphasis as he places on spoken language of others it is not surprising that he might be a sensitive person.

In Ms. K's second paragraph, she observes that my essays are "not in the formal written style" to make a point about me—that I am "putting emphasis" on myself. Her point is that the oral or speaking mode I am using calls attention to me more than would the "formal written style." Questions and self-reflexive comments contribute to this purpose. My informal style is my way of making my personal self more prominent. In Ms. K's third paragraph, she reflects on whether my "emphasis" on spoken language is related to my being a "sensitive" person. Her implication is that someone responsive to spoken language *must be* sensitive. Furthermore, her second use of the word "emphasis" in relation to "spoken language," after she has used it to describe what I am doing for myself, also brings out her perception of me as presenting myself in class mainly through an oral "style."

From my perspective, Ms. K's point is true: I definitely do use oral or conversational strategies to promote a more "personal" mode of behavior, as opposed to an impersonal mode that I consider to be given by formal written language. Her point about my "sensitivity" is also true, in that I think I respond to minute details of how a person speaks. It is also true, I think, although Ms. K does not make the connection, that my habit of repeating words in the essays is a liberty that one takes in spoken language much sooner than in formal written language: in an oral conversation, we expect and/or overlook repetition of words much more readily than we do when reading a formal text. Finally, while I know that I am in some sense deliberately informal and conversational in these essays, Ms. K's point about my "emphasizing" myself is something I do not feel myself doing, and it is helpful to learn that she sees this motive for my language style.

The grounds on which Ms. K perceives my work, however, existed already in her own set of language-use strategies. As I discussed in detail in chapter 8, Ms. K feels increased language authority in the personal or "oral" mode when she writes in the second person. Her early essays, we saw, also tended to include a rhetorical question or two, and she regularly repeats important words, slightly changing their meaning and emphasis with each new use. Finally, she too is sensitive to how words are used and is alert to the "cut-downs" and other language habits in her own family.

But the point here is not that Ms. K, or any observer, is capable of seeing in others only what already exists in herself, but that pre-existing language habits enable one to consciously perceive someone else's use of language in ways *appropriate to the new situation*. It is possible for any student, or other observer, because they necessarily have such language-use strategies, to make new, meaningful, and helpful comments on anyone else's language. Furthermore, it is particularly important to note that Ms. K, as a student, reaches a point of genuine mutuality with me the teacher because her perceptions are, on one hand, preauthorized by her history of language use, and, on the other, pertinent to my interest in my own language since the samples I presented to this class were "new" to this class—this new situation—and therefore susceptible of germane interpretive commentary. I am using this "case" to show why any student's commentary on a teacher's work is potentially binding and useful and therefore a path toward mutuality in the classroom.

I had mentioned earlier that students' comments are binding also because teachers are growing through each classroom experience in the same way that students are. In order to see more exactly the ways in which I am growing, let me now cite my next two essays and then Ms. K's home-written commentary on all five:

Question

In a relationship you consider(ed) important, recall a time you said or wrote something and your intention, motive, or purpose for saying or writing it was misunderstood or "taken the wrong way." Tell what you said, tell the response, tell your actual purpose. Explain how you corrected the misunderstanding and the extent to which you were able to make yourself understood verbally. Bring in as much about this relationship as necessary to make your instance clear.

When I was about 8 or 9, I said to my father, "You know, you're about as smart as Martha" (the woman who cleaned our house at the time). My father looked at me quietly, contemplating what I said, and then said in disbelief, "What? How can you say such a thing?" I said, "Well, you stopped school after the eighth grade and so did she," and my father walked away from the conversation unbelievingly and dumbfounded.

At the time, I could not understand what had happened and it is not really until much much later that I had any insight into what *really* went on. What is interesting, as I look back on this conversation, is how long it took me to discern what I think now are the "real" intentions of both my father and me.

Now I knew then just as I do now, that my father was no snob and in general did not set any store in condescending to others. In fact I had never seen him condescend on any score and he was always decent and deferential—so this made the mystery greater.

What I remember, now that I think of it, was that my father tried to point out what the difference was between him and Martha, namely, that he had spent a lifetime in cultural activity (acting and stage directing) and Martha had not and *I could not tell the difference*. It was my lack of discernment, I figured out, then with his help, I believe, that dumbfounded him so, that I did not *see*, that I made a value judgment on a calculation of *numbers of years* of school.

But as I further see, this was not the whole story. My father was very hurt by my aggressive callousness (a trait he had too, I think) and the revelation of my distance from him: I just had no appreciation of his career, his whole place in society, his accomplishments, the familiarity of his name among thousands of people.

It took me many years to discover how to relate productively with my father but I did finally succeed when I got to college and grew out of my boyish impetuousness. My intention at the time seems now definitely to try to reduce my father with some remark that I *knew* wasn't so. He recognized this intention and tried to be patient—he reasoned rather than flew off the handle. And, since I tell this story now today, this means he was successful to some degree, though obviously not right away.

My remark had nothing to do with Martha; it had only to do with my intentionality toward my father. In a sense, I behaved with restraint too, even in my original remark, considering that I was so pugnacious toward him at the time while he was trying to "bring me along" with more patience than he had had toward my older brother.

Question

Think of something said habitually *(by either you or the other person) in an important relationship. Tell what it is and describe how it is regularly used. Then tell of an occasion in which this usage took on a different or new meaning, and describe the circumstances of this meaning change. Discuss if and/or how your perception of the new meaning changed your perception of the relationship.*

My father always retold how, when he was thirteen, he had to work in a kitchen in Vienna for 80 cents a day to "bring home to his mother" while his father was a soldier in World War I. When I was young, he retold this fact of his life a number of times, though not too often as to sound strange. I don't really remember the contexts but I think they had something to do with my being spoiled and not knowing what hardship really was. In my home in general the idea of "support" in the sense of earning a living on someone else's behalf was mentioned often. As long as I can remember, my father had to support his parents, and since he was an only child the responsibility was his and no one else's.

When I was 20 and had just graduated from college, he said to me, "Some day you will have to support *me*." We had been discussing my graduate school plans, the cost, how much he could contribute, and what I would contribute. I had been sitting around the house feeling sorry for myself (because I had not yet gotten a summer job). My father was understandably irritated and impatient when he made this remark.

At first I thought it was an absurdity. "I am only a child" was something like what I thought to myself. *Me, support* my parents? Even though I had heard it from my father so many times, I did not understand its "real" meaning just because I thought it *did not* and *could not* apply to me. Then my father repeated this "support" idea and *at least* half seriously meant it to apply to me—what I would one day *really* have to do.

The meaning of what he communicated was that *now* I will have to think in terms of being responsible for someone else (and at least for myself). I think I actually understood for the first time that all the energy I had devoted to taking courses or reading or meeting friends would have to be redirected toward a way of life that at least "some day" *could* "support" someone else, and maybe my parents. Support meant really responsibility rather than income.

I perceived my father much differently and much more compassionately than I had before and I felt peaceful because a reality seemed to settle into my head.

Here is Ms. K's commentary:

Bleich's later essays seem to be less argumentative and aggressive. They now seem to be telling a story instead of arguing a point or trying to justify his feelings to others. The decrease in the number of cuss words he uses shows that he is *not* being as aggressive as he was in his earlier papers. They seem to be more subtle. . . .

I noticed a change in attitude in Bleich's work. In his second essay, he talks in a general somewhat joking matter-of-fact tone. His later essays reflect a more serious personal tone. His earlier papers are aggressive and argumentative and the subject matter is sometimes used to reflect this. In his earlier essays the subject matter dealt with arguments. I think he found it easier to talk about arguments because he understood when he wrote about them how he felt about them and the effect they had on himself and the other people involved. In the first and third essays as well as the second (though not as much as the other two) the feelings seem to have been already sorted out and probably even talked about before. He is aware and familiar with these thoughts. In his later essays, though, the feelings that are reflected seem to be more spontaneous. It seems in the later papers that he draws his conclusions when writing about the relationships that are involved. He kind of figures out what was meant by the things that were said as he reached the end of his paper. In earlier papers the conclusions were already there and he just expanded on this thoughts. For example, in Bleich's fourth essay he uses such phrases as "at the time," "as I look back," "what I remember," "I figured out," and "but as I further see" to progress step by step through this paper until he is able to draw a conclusion. By figuring out the meaning of what was said, Bleich's fourth and fifth essays seem to be very in-depth concerning a whole relationship. They seem to be more personal and have a greater impact on him. This is reflected in the amount of underlining when he is emphasizing important points. This backs up the point that in later essays he talks about things that may mean a lot more to him than other topics did.

I found it interesting that Bleich didn't talk about his wife or daughter in any of his later papers (or in any papers at all—for that matter). Considering that his papers did get more personal I thought that something would be written about this subject. I know it was easier for me to write about things that took place when I was younger (even though they were harder to remember) because they didn't seem to involve as strong and personal thoughts that come about when writing about things within the past few years. Even though Bleich does discuss personal topics he only wrote one essay about something that happened part-way in the present (six years ago). This is the third essay. I don't know why he doesn't mention his family. Maybe he feels that we can't relate to that aspect of his life since we have never experienced it ourselves.

Bleich's fifth essay recalls an awareness where a lot of maturing took place in his life. Through the efforts of his father he realized the true meaning of support and responsibility. This is the only essay in which Bleich talks about this age period in his life and the only time he deals with the subject matter. He became aware of the change in him and the way he thought of his role in life.

Bleich says in the fifth essay that he felt "peaceful" because a reality seemed to settle into his head. In the second essay Bleich mentions still being frustrated and in the third essay there is a feeling that not everything has been said at the end of the essay. These feelings of uneasiness or frustration take place in the essays which are argumentative or more aggressive. There is a change though when the narrative is switched from argumentative to one of narration. Instead of being preoccupied with the aggressive aspect, real conclusions concerning what went on were made. It seems that something has been accomplished or clarified through the writing of the paper.

I know that in adolescence kids tend to resent their parents—especially the parent of the same sex. As time goes on they tend to appreciate them more. I found this to be true in Bleich's work. One important change in Bleich's works was the manner in which he spoke of his father. In the second essay he speaks of an argument between his parents but he doesn't really go into details about the feelings or actions of either one. However, in the fourth and fifth essays his father is talked about in detail. Even within these two essays there is a change in attitude toward his dad. Essay five seems to be a continuation of the fourth essay, [which] deals with Bleich's "pugnacious" feelings towards his father when he was 8 or 9 and how he was later able to relate to his father after he grew out of his "boyish impetuousness." The fifth essay tells a story of when he was 20 and just graduated from college. He says that he "perceived his father much differently and much more compassionately" than he had before. In this essay he is becoming mature and aware of responsibilities. He views his dad differently than in the earlier works. He tells more of his dad's views and feelings than just the surface.

There are features of Bleich's language that do change with the relationship being discussed. With his increased understanding of his father I notice a less aggressive tone, an increase in underlining, and a reduction in the use of cuss words.

Ms. K views my latter two essays as a pair dealing with more or less the same topic and feels that in writing the fifth essay I "accomplished or clarified" something important to me. Ms. K seems to be saying that because the essay itself accomplished something, I am showing how the "student" part of me is also "working." However, I don't think it is clear from Ms. K's commentary just how I settled something and just what its significance was, relative to the class. Ms. K does discuss my apparent change in attitude, a less aggressive tone, a reduction in the use of obscenity,[10] and a greater

10. Ms. K is probably including my spoken language here, since there is no obscenity in my written work from my fourth essay on.

tendency to stress certain terms. While she seems certain that the changes are related to what I wrote about my relationship with my father, and that all of these changes have something to do with how I behave in class, she does not speculate on why or how these changes took place just at that point in class. However, I believe Ms. K achieved real insight into my development in this course, and it is useful for the present discussion to show why.

At the end of her sixth paragraph, Ms. K observes that "He tells more of his dad's views and feelings than just the surface." This sentence winds up her general point that my father appears in my essays more as an independent person and less as a passive function of my own sense of self. I think that my essays show how this happened. In the fourth essay, the point of misunderstanding was that I had no idea of what it meant, in the world at large, that my father had been an actor whose achievements many people had enjoyed, and who worked for many years to earn such recognition. Of course, before writing that essay, I already had known enough to understand my father's achievements, but to have presented this narrative at that point in the course was itself meaningful. The essay was written after the discussion of Ms. K's essay 3 which criticized my classroom deportment. While Ms. K had her own interpretation of my behavior, I had come to understand it as an instance of *showmanship*, a pedagogical habit of mine which appears in almost every class I teach. Ms. K had referred to this habit as "putting emphasis" on myself, while in her third essay she said that my obscene language and big words had to do with how I was treating the class as a kind of audience to be both impressed and won over. In one of the class meetings in which I had discussed my father's profession, I had also wondered out loud why, since both my parents had been actors, I did not seem to have any talent for this vocation and my efforts at acting in college had been utterly unsuccessful. I had explained to the class something I had known for a while, namely, that I was able to "act" in a classroom, but not in a "real" acting situation. Essentially, then, I was able to translate Ms. K's terms into my own—that my behavior was showmanship and that its potential offensiveness was related to the narcissistic aspects of showmanship.[11] For purposes of her own and the class's welfare, Ms. K had elicited from me a part of my language strategy that I had not consciously thought about as I conducted the class.

The disclosure of this language strategy in public made it possible, necessary (perhaps), and important, that I write the fourth and fifth essays the way I did. My essays were predicated on the class's knowledge of my

11. Compare, perhaps, Ms. J's "performance narcissism" that I discussed in chapter 7. Most teachers have some love of "performance"; in my case it is tied up with my father's profession.

showmanship. However, I did not deliberately write the essays with this in mind. On the contrary, my essay writing continued to be spontaneous—I wrote about what came to mind as I sat down before the question along with the rest of the class. But because Ms. K and others in the class brought out *their* perception as they did, it cleared the air in a sense for me to leave the argument topic and the aggressive style behind for, on the one hand, a more personal and deeper style, and, on the other hand, a greater willingness to recognize the "other," who, in most of the first semester, was my father.

In her second commentary, Ms. K implies that what I had written about was an "adolescent" issue. This is definitely true, and it is also true that I moved in my fourth and fifth essays out of an adolescent idiom—which usually does have obscene and aggressive language—into a more adult style. The fifth essay "accomplishes something" relative to the class in that its use of language (writing/speaking) seems to have been better adjusted to that particular classroom membership. It is likely that the class experienced moments of discomfort with my showmanship. But instead of having to bring this perception out as an informal or out-of-class observation, the way we approached the whole subject matter made it possible to include it in our regular course of study, under the assumption that the teacher's language is as much a part of the subject matter as the students'. My writing *about* a feeling of peace settling into my mind in the past relationship with my father was also, as Ms. K observes, a moment of resolution in the relationship with the class.

While I consider Ms. K's characterization of my fourth and fifth essays as having resolved a classroom issue in an adolescent idiom to be true, I also think that the way was prepared for this perception by what Ms. K had presented in her "mutual understanding" essay (chapter 8) where she discussed how she "hated" her mother (for her behavior on Father's Day), and how she won her father's understanding and his authorization to speak, and, partly, to speak badly of her mother. The presentation of this essay followed the class discussion of essay 3, and it also helped resolve, for her, the problem of when she was authorized to speak *in the class*. Speaking to her father and speaking to me in class were mutually predicated acts. Thus, the "mutual understanding" essay was a resolution in the sense that it *disclosed the other part of the predication that was to enfranchise Ms. K in this course*. This new independence was immediately put to use when she analyzed my first five essays, dividing them up into two sets—the first three and the last two—; seeing the second set as a resolution (based on my own reports and claims)—and then rounding out her insight with the idea that what had gone on between my father and me was an adolescent event. It would be correct to say, based on our essays, that we shared certain adolescent schemata in those first weeks of class, and we each constructed new schemata appropriate to our fulfilling our classroom roles in comfort, security, and with a sense of progress. Most important, perhaps, it was the public and private dialectics of interaction that enabled us to do this, and it was the careful analysis of our changes in language use that disclosed the whole process.

In her second commentary, Ms. K observes that I had not written about my (then) wife and my daughter. This point is noteworthy for several reasons. First, and perhaps most obviously, it announces Ms. K's curiosity about my important relationships. While it is true that most students would simply like to know about such things in a teacher's life, most would not (and did not) take the opportunity to announce this interest. But, as was the case with the students' feelings that I had been behaving too aggressively, the subject matter of the course made it possible for Ms. K to introduce for formal study what might otherwise have remained suppressed. Second, Ms. K's reports had discussed a variety of different relationships, including those with peers, a boy she had dated, and both of her parents. My own reports had discussed fewer relationships; only in my fourth essay did I discuss my mother, and then not really as I related to her but as she seemed to behave. Although Ms. K diplomatically guesses that perhaps I thought the class would not be able to relate to narratives of marriage and parenting, her implication that this is a significant omission on my part is nevertheless valid, in my view. Third, in making her observation, Ms. K shows her established sense of the course's purpose, namely, that *whatever* an individual presents for discussion is significant both in itself and because of what was *not* said. But more important, her mention of my omission bespeaks her understanding that the *same standard of language analysis* applies to my work as to hers and that of the other students.

One final point about Ms. K's second commentary. In an awkward sentence, Ms. K writes, "There is a change though when the narrative is switched from argumentative to one of narration." In her first paragraph, Ms. K correctly relates my argumentation to my underlying tendency toward self-justification in those first essays. In contrast, in my more narrative last two essays, I not only justify myself less, but I more fully recognize the others in my narrative. It might seem that an argumentative mode implies a greater consciousness of the other—the audience—than the narrative does. But as Ms. K observes, the reverse is the case. To explain this, consider the following. In chapter 5, I suggested that the implied social "format" of the lyric was related to the infantile phase of development in which there was a dyadic closeness between speaker and hearer, an assumption of sameness and identity, and, because in this phase gender consciousness had not yet set in, both men and women "read" the lyric in the same way. In the narrative mode, however, three parties are involved: the narrator, the audience, and the other figures in the narration. Because men and women acquire their gender identity through different forms of socialization, narration is "read" differently by men and women. When Ms. K read my early essays as self-justification, it surprised me since I had not been aware of what I was doing, though I now agree with her judgment. As a theoretical matter, Ms. K's differentiation of the two "modes" of my essays is a perception that my later essays, because more fully narrated, are more fully socialized. If we understand Ms. K as having nearly achieved her adult feminine gender identity, then we might specifically credit her feminine perspective with urging her to "see" my increased openness to others in my later essays, both in their content and in their narrative style. A masculine reader might be more prone to interpret the argumentative mode as being as "adult" as the narrative—that is how I thought of my own early essays, and so I required both the general otherness of Ms. K as well as her specific feminine otherness for me to recast my objectification of my essays. To put this point in pedagogical terms, had I stuck to the traditional self-concept of the teacher, that of the "banking educator," I would have conceived of my essays as having been written in a variety of different modes, and I would have disregarded the fact that my being in class *as a class member* was influencing my development. But since I now expect developmental change and growth on my own part, and since I understand that changes in my sense of gender identity may be a necessary part of this growth, the explanation of the differences in my essays is much more convincing and more inclusive because the interpersonal (pedagogical and psychosocial) contexts of my writing have been taken into account. I see that I am responding to Ms. K in ways analogous to how she is responding to me, and my machinery of response accounts for how I am learning as a teacher.

At the very end of the first semester, when the course shifted its attention to the study of language use in literary response essays, Ms. K's emphasis seemed to switch to her mother, as I discussed in chapter 8. My own psychological focus also changed. To disclose these changes, I will now cite three of my response essays, followed by Ms. K's third commentary on my work:

Question 1

Based on your own experience of conversations such as this, tell who is right, who won, and how you know *both of these things.*[12]

---

12. Ms. K's essay on this question, along with the text to which the question refers, was cited and discussed in chapter 8, pp. 218–223.

My experience of conversations such as this tells me that each person is wrong and that each person has a legitimate point of view. I know because when I was *in* conversations *such as* this, I also knew that the other person had a legitimate complaint, except that it takes a very long time to find out what that complaint is.

For example, if the conversation starts with the father, as shown, you can say it is all his fault because his remark demeans the mother. But an opening remark doesn't have to be the source of blame. The situation may have built up and rather than doing something more drastic than this, the father just says something to hurt the mother verbally. The mother's response is of the same sort because she is evening the score. So she is wrong because instead of diffusing the situation she answers in kind.

It is fairly hard to detect why the parents are *really* arguing, except that the father seems to resent the mother's absence, which the mother thinks is really a resentment of her career. The latter is a different issue—less justifiable than being upset by the wife's absence. So the two issues are mixed up by the two parents.

In this conversation I do not see the child as an important element—only what the two parents say to one another strikes me as important.

So my basis for understanding this conversation is my experience with marital arguments which I think take place more or less like this one, sometimes worse. When arguing with my wife I see myself exaggerating small things into features of character rather than local events. An argument sometimes feels like a war, in which fundamental values of mine are threatened, where I feel I must survive. I know my wife feels the same way and that is why things are said that are not "really" meant. So a statement like "you're a lousy mother" really means, "I feel badly about you doing this *particular* thing and I'm worried about its consequences." "Now you're talking" means "I think you really resent my career and that is why you disguise your resentment in accusations." In my home, we are much better now than before at getting to the *translation* of what was said, but I think it is very hard, even for smart people like us, to learn to discipline ourselves to translate before responding.

Question 2

Pick out the part or aspect of "Araby" where you found yourself having your strongest feelings. Describe these feelings as fully as you can. Give an analogy or association from your own life where you think you had similar feelings. Tell if and/or how a relationship with another person was connected with these feelings.[13]

The sentence at the beginning " . . . yet her name was like a summons to all my foolish blood" had a strong effect and reminded me of adolescent frustration experiences of my own and discussion with other boys who reported the same

---

13. In chapter 8, I did not include Ms. K's essay on this question.

feeling. This feeling is of excitement, giddiness, eagerness, and fear. The idea of "summons" is so right. I remember feeling compelled at the mere mention of certain girls' names to indulge in certain fantasies. It was very helpful to find another fellow with similar thoughts and with whom I could share these fantasies. Sometimes the girl was distant enough that the sharing was common or expected. But if the girl was a "real possibility" I sort of did not want to share my thoughts. My blood only felt foolish if my intentions failed or were rejected, however. I did not feel foolish being "summoned" to begin with. Yet it is so true that the mere mention of certain girls' names created such excitement.

The thought that came to mind in association with this is my mother's general dislike of gifts. Often I would want to give her a gift—Mother's Day or something,[14] or sometimes I would bring them home and her firm and vaguely angry answer was how expensive it was and that she did not need it anyway, thus making me feel unwanted and angry because I felt her behavior was unreasonable.

The frustration of the narrator throughout the story is like the frustration I felt on such occasions—the worst feeling being, perhaps, that I was not shrewd enough to anticipate my mother's response and thus just not give her a gift. As I think of it, I recall my brother often taking the initiative and proposing that we give mother a gift of some sort—and so the project was greater than just my initiative and so I thought, I think, that there was a greater chance of success.

I recall with some satisfaction having mastered the sort of temptation that this sentence brings to mind—the temptation to give my fantasy some actual authority in my behavior. I recall how long it took to truly understand that when a "name" "summons" my blood, this is probably a juvenile event and its apparent implication ought to be rejected.[15] This is one of the important compensations for getting a little older.

Question 3

Consider your reading experience of the O'Connor story. Decide on how much you identified with one, or with more than one, figure in the story. Describe the feelings which go along with your identification(s). What relationships in your own history do these identifications bring to mind?[16]

14. While I was definitely not conscious (when I wrote this essay) of Ms. K's "mutual understanding" essay, which referred to a Father's Day, it is probably not coincidental that I am now citing Mother's Day as a moment of comparable frustration in my own life.

15. This second use of the term "rejected" in this essay reverses (rejects?) in a psychological way my first usage, where I spoke about the possibility of my overtures toward girls being rejected. The end of this essay seems to want to rescue me from the beginning. The two uses of the term "rejected" are predicated on one another and thus form a "complete" and psychologically therapeutic thought.

16. Ms. K's essay on this question is in chapter 8, p. 234, followed by my discussion of it.

I identified with the Misfit. The family made me angrier and angrier—the bickering, the weakness, the grandmother's manipulation, the bratty behavior of the children. It is all awful and should be set straight. The Misfit says he doesn't want help and he's doing all right by himself. When the Misfit says that the grandmother would have been a good woman if someone had been there to shoot her every minute, I understand this as metaphorical, even though he is a real murderer. He says it's not a "real pleasure" in life (to murder, presumably). I wish I could put an end to such bickering as decisively, but of course, without murdering anyone.

I am reminded of identifications with both my parents—on occasions when I was full of hesitations and they got impatient with me and sort of embarrassed me into *acting* and from then on I felt I knew how to "take action." Once my father embarrassed me into getting a summer job when I was sulking around the house the summer after I graduated from college. He shouted at me to go out and get *myself* a job. He didn't threaten me but he shamed me and made me ashamed of my babyish self-pity. On another occasion my mother accomplished the same thing but in a different way—by doing herself what I should have done—getting a taxi at the bus station. We had come back from a trip and we needed the taxi to get home (I was about the same age as when my father embarrassed me). I was standing around trying to figure out how the taxi succession worked—where you stood, and who you asked, etc.— when my mother asked me why we can't get a taxi. I explained what I was thinking and she got extremely impatient, went over to the nearest taxi and got in or something. I then realized how one gets a taxi in New York City. I also understood, however, that on occasions such as this, when others are depending on me, I don't need to indulge myself by thinking everything out in advance so slowly—maybe trial and error is good too.

I don't think I understood before how similar my parents were to one another in this need and ability to act with dispatch. In spite of the unpleasant feeling it caused me on both occasions, ultimately I felt strength in identifying with the same aspect in each one.

The Misfit seems remarkably sane for such a perverse person—the only insane thing about him is that he is a murderer. So in a sense I ignore this aspect of him (I know I *wanted* to kill any number of people!) and identify with the fact that he takes action.

The purpose of Ms. K's third commentary was essentially the same as the first two—to relate any changes in language use to what I had brought into the essays of my history. To reiterate the analytical strategy: the new set of essays was to be compared to the full set of previous essays, that is, the first five taken as a group, to see if the literary response essays brought out different language-use habits and moves. Also, students (actually, Ms. K and Ms. M, the other subgroup member) were asked to take account of what they had previously written about my work and to see if their earlier conclusions still obtained or if and how they may have to change. Here, then, is Ms. K's third (and final) commentary on my work:

> Bleich seems to be more interested in explaining his own thoughts as well as those of the other person involved in the relationship, instead of writing aggressively. His papers from the first semester all deal with arguments or misunderstandings and those from the second semester seem to get into "deeper" thoughts on relationships. One of the ways I can tell Bleich's papers are less aggressive is because of his use of key words, underlining, and cuss words. Bleich no longer uses key words in order to keep emphasizing over and over again his main point. By no longer underlining it seems also that he is not trying to be as forceful in presenting his opinions. Obviously, the absence of cuss words show a less aggressive attitude.
>
> Even though there is less aggression in Bleich's later papers, I noticed feelings of frustration in both this semester's and last semester's work. The frustrations that are written about are aimed at different sources, though. In his fifth essay[17] Bleich writes about being frustrated because he has been embarrassed into taking action. In his eighth essay Bleich identifies with the Misfit because he *is* able to take action. . . . Also in the eighth essay, he mentions an embarrassing situation which took place with his mother in New York City while trying to hail a cab. Bleich is frustrated with himself and says in this essay that when others are depending on him he doesn't need to take such a long time to think through his alternatives, when a decision by trial and error may have been better and quicker. In the instances with both his mother and father he was frustrated because he was not taking action or that he was not taking action quickly enough. Concerning the incident with his father in the fifth essay, Bleich's frustration seems to be directed towards his own lack in taking action whereas in the eighth essay, the frustration deals with the embarrassment which was caused while no action was taking place (I really hope this is all making sense so far!)[18]
>
> In his third essay Bleich tells of his frustrations with being called "nose" (a form of rejection) and therefore being embarrassed[19] (for other reasons also). In the seventh essay Bleich talks of being frustrated (a combination of feeling unwanted, foolish, and angry) because he has been rejected by his mother and

17. Ms. K is referring to the fact, which I mentioned in class in response to students' observation, that, yes, the citations in the fifth and eighth essays refer to the same event: in the fifth essay, I did not actually say that I was embarrassed into taking action. "Embarrassed" first enters my description of the event in the eighth essay.

18. Although Ms. K is herself worrying about whether she is making sense, it is clear that she noticed the different vocabulary I introduced in the later essay while presenting the "same" event.

19. Notice how here, and on two previous occasions in her commentary, Ms. K automatically, but correctly, projects *back* the vocabulary of the later essay onto an issue of the earlier one, thereby further showing how a new *feeling* emerged in the later essay that was probably suppressed (repressed?) in the third essay.

by girls he used to have crushes on. In both essays Bleich is frustrated because of rejection, but in the third essay he takes a vengeful aggressive attitude and in the seventh essay he does not direct his aggression outwardly, but rather towards himself for not being able to anticipate his mother's actions.

Another example of the frustrations which are aimed at different sources are those resulting from arguments. In each semester different things were revealed. In the first essay Bleich wrote that frustration resulted if he did not have the upper hand in an argument. In the eighth essay he wrote of being frustrated if he is unable to take action in efforts to solve the argument.

I also noticed a difference in the way in which Bleich writes about marital argument in the first and second semesters. In the sixth essay Bleich is able to remove himself from the argument (emotionally) and see it like an outsider. He talks of the couple's argument in terms of what he had experienced—making him somewhat of an authority. In the second essay, though, he writes about a marital argument through his eyes as a child and not a partner in marriage. He was all wrapped up in the argument himself and therefore could not really be too analytical about the whole situation. Bleich refers to marital argument as a sort of "war" (in the sixth essay) and as a "scary event" (in the second essay).

Ms. K's main theme in this commentary is given in her opening sentence where she distinguishes between my "aggressive writing" and my explaining the thoughts of both parties in the relationships I discuss. It is true that I do not use obscene language, somewhat true that "key words" don't appear as often, but not significantly true that my "underlinings" don't appear as often: there are three stressed words in the sixth and eighth essays, though none in the seventh.[20] I think, rather, that these features appear somewhat attenuated because there is more narrative and a generally more conciliatory tone. Ms. K's analysis is mainly concerned with changes in the way I deal with the frustrations in the literary response essays.

In her discussion, Ms. K uses key words herself, "frustration" and "embarrassment," both of which she found in my essay and then reflected on at some length. Her main thought, which reappears in different forms, is that in the response essays my "aggressive" feelings are turned more on myself than on others. The most direct expression of this thought is when she observes, "he does not direct his aggression outwardly, but rather towards himself for not being able to anticipate his mother's actions." In the second paragraph she writes, "Bleich's frustration seems to be directed towards his own lack in taking action," immediately after which she introduces my "second-semester" term, "embarrassment," to describe my treatment of the same issue the second time. In her fourth paragraph she contrasts the frustration of not having

---

20. Those reading the present text might note the significant frequency of stressed words, a habit that I think continues in full force in almost any writing I do.

the upper hand in an argument—a thought from my first essay—with the frustration of being "unable to take action in efforts to solve the argument." (I will return to her thoughts in the fifth paragraph shortly.)

In reading this commentary, I wondered why Ms. K did not consider my identification with the Misfit and my parenthetical thought about wanting to murder certain people "aggressive," or why my characterization of marital argument as "war" would not seem aggressive. I know that the feelings I had reading the stories were stronger or more urgent than the ones I had first reported toward store managers or my erstwhile friend. For example, my irritation at the bickering family in the O'Connor story is more pertinent to my life than my impatience with auto manufacturers. Ms. K's point, however, is not that my feelings were less aggressive, but that I *presented* my sense of implication in these feelings, and especially my sense of responsibility for dealing with them. Her opening judgment in this commentary distinguishes not between kinds of feelings, but between kinds of *writing*. She thus implies that even though my essays do refer to certain feelings and show how the feelings changed, there is a correspondence between the change in the reported feelings and the change in the *effect* that my use of language has on her, and perhaps on the rest of the class. Ms. K again notes my inclusion of both myself and others in my discussion of the different relationships: "explaining his own thoughts as well as those of the other person involved in the relationship." "Explaining" thoughts considers the listener or reader more generously than if one is engaged in self-justification. Ms. K is observing that in the process of bringing others into my discussion in this fuller way, I am also more considerate to the classroom readers of my work. In this way Ms. K characterizes both my second semester's work and my membership in the class as more socially integrated.

Ms. K had originally helped to "authorize" herself in this class when she wrote in essay 3 that she felt that my aggressive use of language was directed toward the class, and, potentially, toward her. The fact that now my "aggressive" statements and judgments are directed toward myself was a result of her own "speaking out," which I gradually assimilated. Of course, I was influenced by other factors as well—the greatly increased mutual familiarity of all class members, for example—but it is nevertheless the case that my "inward" turn was my answer to Ms. K's earlier observations about my use of language.

My sixth essay introduces my experiences of married life. In part, this is a direct response to Ms. K's second commentary; however, I had intended to include the text from the Bach and Wyden volume when I was planning the course. Although Ms. K does not allude to the possibility that she might have influenced me, the way she contrasts my early and late comments on marital arguments continues our interaction. I was surprised at first by her judgment that in my sixth essay I see the marital argument more like an "outsider," while in my second essay I am "more wrapped up in the argument." I probably would have given the opposite judgment, namely that I was "more subjective" about an argument in which I had participated than about one in which I was only the occasion of the argument. I have to say, however, that on closer inspection Ms. K's judgment is correct. In Ms. K's own essay on this topic, the child alluded to by the arguing couple was important, and she spent some time reflecting on how each parent may have viewed the child. At the end of her essay, she wrote how things were when her parents argued, and we know from her other work how strongly she felt implicated in these arguments. As a result, she judges that I felt more implicated in the argument between my parents than in the arguments I actually participated in with my wife. Although this judgment may be reasonably seen as her own projection, the fact is that psychologically I felt much more helpless in the face of my parents' argument than in my own marital arguments. Ms. K is obviously responding to *the way* I wrote about my marital arguments. The "analytical" character of the sixth essay, along with the thought that, in principle, one is more *authoritative* when one is *a part* of the relationship, as opposed to being passively implicated in it, led Ms. K to judge that I was more "emotionally removed" in writing about my own marital arguments. This judgment, I think, also follows from the experience she described of being able to speak directly to her father, which helped to remove her emotionally (she was able to stop crying) from her parents' quarrel, and enabled her to see them more authoritatively as well as to be more authoritative in her relationship with them. Because I feel I understood the marital argument as well as the concerns of my former wife, I felt more authoritative in writing about the argument I had myself had participated in. Therefore, I am "somewhat of an authority" on marital arguments and my characterization of them as "war" is less aggressive than my characterization of my parents' argument as a "scary event": the term "war" seems to her obviously a metaphor, while "scary event" is more purely descriptive.

The same reasoning would hold true for Ms. K's not seeing the other "aggressive" expressions in my response essays as aggressive writing or use of language. The material that follows my announced identification with the Misfit associates my desire to "take action" with certain family standards so strongly that my saying that sometimes I wished to murder certain people seems relatively light-hearted, and, in any event, an obviously conventionalized report of routine temporary "tantrum" hostility. Ms. K's own reading of the story and her response essay also may have played a role in her interpretation of my essay. As we recall, she did not "see" the Misfit at all in the story, and, since her response concentrated on her identifications with the various family members, the fact that the family was finally murdered was of less importance. Ms. K seemed to rule out of her reading the comic and the eccentric aspects of the story, instead wanting to account for the discord within the family. Approaching my essay with this orientation, she likewise overlooks the more extreme formulations in my essay and concentrates on what my associations seem to promote: the idea of the Misfit as someone who takes action. Twice in the essay I disclaim any intention of "really" killing anyone: these statements permit Ms. K her own relatively realistic perspective, particularly in that it, like mine, deals with how to identify with one's parents.

There is, therefore, a certain similarity between Ms. K's development in the course and my own. Both of us, in the second semester, brought in our mothers in more prominent roles in our essays after having discussed our fathers in the first semester. Ms. K's achievement was to recognize how her uses of language were related to her sense of how authority is distributed; my achievement was to develop a more inviting and inclusive style of speaking to the class. While our achievements were individual, that we followed a similar path through our sense of our families' histories suggests that our interaction was instrumental in what we accomplished. While Ms. K was observing that I had developed a greater sense of the other people in my life, she was in the process of reunderstanding her "original" other, her mother. At the same time, while I was trying to tone down my masculine adolescent self-presentation (my "performance narcissism"), I was able to appropriate some of Ms. K's style of authority and find ways to share it with the rest of the class. The partial success of this redistribution of authority, along with the fact that I, like Ms. K, was becoming involved in the "literary" frame of mind, then led me to write my "deeper" and "less aggressive" essays of the second semester, when I presented my father in a more "compassionate" light, with a more adult understanding of the meaning and value of his vocation. At the same time, when the course shifted its attention to literature, the process of literary response also moved us, in certain unconscious ways, from psychologically obvious preoccupations toward issues that these preoccupations presupposed, thus bringing out language use that had not been apparent—or only marginally apparent—in our earlier work, such as Ms. K's use of the interrogative and my own use of narrative.

As my essay on the O'Connor story suggested, my principal achievement in this course was learning how to take the appropriate pedagogical action for the course I was teaching. I was somewhat cautious at first and entered the course with the goal of learning to regulate my impulse to speak a great deal and too often in an argumentative mode. As my work shows, this desire came from having had argumentation and performance too much on my mind, perhaps because of some unconscious insecurity about performance that Ms. K delicately suggested in her third essay. By alluding to my unconscious concern and making it a part of the course's subject matter, Ms. K succeeded in gaining classroom authority, which contributed to my increased sense of authority in having provided a situation that proved beneficial to most members of the class. This in turn led to a gradual softening of my own tone, away from self-justification and performance toward self-presentation and sharing. My seventh and eighth essays then directly suggest that during this change or shift, my idea of "acting" changed from a literal link and correspondence with my father's work toward a more general link and correspondence with a feature of *both* my parents' characters—their taste and desire for decisive action in everyday life. My changing the reference of "acting" from the stage to the class is perhaps my individualized version of seeing students and teachers (actors) as members of the *same class*. Because of the new perspective on my parents I renew some of my theater-related vocabulary— acting, the stage, dialogue—as part of my contribution to the redistribution of authority in the classroom.

It was not, of course, my experience in this course alone, nor my interaction with Ms. K, that caused me to write this book or to experiment with bringing group work into my classroom. Yet, as a result of my work with Ms. K, I learned a great deal about what it meant to interact *reciprocally* with an individual student; I also learned how to integrate this interaction with the work of other students and thus help them to participate in this redistribution of pedagogical authority. Specifically, I began to understand how traits that we (Ms. K and I) already shared—the use of underlining, key words, dashes to interpolate thoughts, and the interrogative, for example—led to a series of mutual perceptions and disciplined statements about one another's work, changing the traditional roles of student and teacher. As I write this chapter, I have not seen Ms. K for perhaps a year. While she was in my course, however, we also kept our distance. Ms. K was not chummy, expressive, or personally demonstrative, and felt no special access to my attention. She had a naturally "professional" attitude and seemed reassured that these difficult personal issues could be treated in the fundamental "work" mode needed for university life. Unlike other serious relationships we have—with parents, siblings, and spouses, for example—an undergraduate's relationship with each teacher is short and is not expected to grow or continue. As Ms. K began to see the more socially integrated changes in my writing, she naturally began to objectify me more, to see me as less of a function of her needs as a student and more as an equivalent counterpart in the study of language.

In elementary school, many of us recall thinking that the teacher "lived" in school and did not go home to her own kitchen table and bedroom closet. When we finally recognized the teacher's individuality, it was a pleasant and reassuring surprise. I believe this kind of recognition took place for Ms. K, as she saw in the complicated and sophisticated matter of language use that she and I went through analogous struggles, and that we each had tables to clear and closets to clean. I came out of class feeling that we made our private language histories serve public purposes and that we made our public interactions serve our own two selves and others who worked with us.

10

Collaboration Among Students

One of the fundamental problems for those of us seeking to encourage regular, habitual collaboration among students is our lack of knowledge of how groups work. In part, we have failed to learn more about groups because of a cultural adherence to individualism (as I discussed in chapters 2, 3, and 6): the purpose of a group is customarily thought of as the enhancement of individual life. Except in the most general sense, we do not understand how individuals interact with one another in groups, and we generally do not know how to textualize group interaction in order to study it in depth. Conventional wisdom about group work, particularly with regard to students, is that it always requires a leader to maintain discipline and to guide it toward a clear, predefined goal. Sometimes in classrooms and in smaller groups leaders "naturally" emerge because certain individuals wish to take such roles, while others, usually the majority, are pleased to let them. But we also know that when a group functions together for a long enough period of time, peer leadership changes, influenced by the daily politics of interaction. If we knew more about this interaction, particularly about what sorts of changes we might expect over what period of time, it would be easier for us to establish groupwork in the classroom and to devise tasks that would allow it to develop.

With these purposes in mind, I divided my discussion section of twenty-three students into eight groups of three.[1] Several considerations led to this procedure. Working in pairs might have been easier, but it would have lacked an essential political feature of a group—the presence of a majority and a minority. Two people might either agree or disagree on what matters in any one person's work. Double perspectives would develop in agreed-upon items, but they would be much harder to develop for disputed points.

1. The other five discussion sections in this course were similarly divided, but most of the other instructors did not become group members, as they judged (rightly, it turned out), that it would be too difficult for them, as apprentice teachers, to manage both their subgroups and oversee the other subgroups as well. As I discussed in chapter 9, it was not easy for me to play both roles either, though I found it enlightening to try.

Rather, I guessed, such disputes would have no *social* source for possible resolution, and it would be too easy for individual positions to become fixed in a stalemate; they would almost certainly become more rigid if personality conflicts emerged. With three in a group, I thought it more likely that on any one point two people could reach a similar perspective and thereby exercise a credible social influence—that of the "majority"—on the minority view. The challenge to the minority view would then have more validity and could not as easily be written off as "just an opinion." At the same time, it would be easier to detect differences in the "majority" views, since people rarely agree in such circumstances for identical reasons: each person's somewhat different variation on "that" view is then authorized by its membership in an "alliance" rather than by just its "essential" truth. In this way, political "interest" becomes an important factor in what counts as knowledge. The group of three is a structure which, because of its own political character, makes it possible to introduce political considerations of a larger order. Issues of gender, race, and class, for example, might not be confined to the subject matter of students' study of language, but might also find expression in the deliberations of the group itself. As I discussed in chapter 1, Richard Ohmann's argument that corporate economic interests often infiltrate textbooks on competent writing may be the kind of proposition that can also emerge as students examine how their own work may express such larger interests. Later in this chapter, I will discuss the manifestation of gender interest as it appears in the students' uses of language. Three, I thought, was the smallest group capable both of having meaningful internal politics and, therefore, of relating to the larger political forces in our culture.

As I suggested in chapter 5, the group of three has a meaningful history in each person's childhood development. Before and during the acquisition of language, the child relates to a generalized other until, with language, the other(s) become securely objectified, and the child "recognizes," so to speak, the group of two. During the subsequent stage of development, in which gender consciousness plays a key role, the basic idea of the group of three as two two-versus-one configurations develops: the child's relation to two parents, each marked by a gender identity, and the child's membership in a group of two same-sex people juxtaposed to the parent of the other sex. In this way, membership in a group of three is "stereoscopic" in that there are necessarily at least two senses in which one is the member of a group of three. Potentially, there are actually four modes of membership—two in which one is in the majority, one in which one is a minority, one in which there is consensus among all members. This political condition of earliest formation of gender identity creates the child's first ideas of what authority is, who has it, how to get it, and how to negotiate it when one doesn't have it. Because of this connection between gender identity and authority in childhood, I tried to insure that each group of three was gender-heterogeneous. On the other hand, regardless of the actual gender of the student group members, there is a tendency for each member to relate to the other two, on occasion, *as if* they were parents or *as if* they were of the same gender. The group of three is a distant but nevertheless meaningful psychological model of each person's first family situation.

Finally, the group of three is the smallest unit in which peer-group psychology can come into play.[2] For many young people, the peer group is affirmative, a set of others who can be trusted more easily than parents, teachers, and other authority figures. Students usually enter the classroom already prepared to act as mild insurgents against the teacher. A pair is perhaps not quite enough to create this feeling of "gang" psychology. But if enough psychological homogeneity can be found among three peers in virtue of their student "condition," and if they do not feel in serious competition with one another, they will have their own credible authority to interpret assignments and to establish work standards that will meaningfully influence the teacher's response, and that can, therefore, affect how things are done in the class. A small group functions in part as a "safe haven," a place where one's doubts about authority can find a sympathetic response to begin with; perhaps an even more permanent set of views can be cultivated and nurtured with less compliance to the teacher than if one had these views by oneself. Belonging to a group thus helps to validate differences between students and teachers and creates more authority for each class member to find common ground with teachers.

In examining the collaboration among students, I will use two instances—the first from the group in which Ms. K, Ms. M, and I were members and the second from a group in which I did not participate directly but which functioned well and autonomously throughout the year. I will try to show how each of the foregoing considerations was important, and particularly how the psychology of each group made significant contributions to some students' study of their own and other people's literacy styles.

Ms. M, the third member of my subgroup, was one of a number of students

2. Since working with this class, I have tried out larger groups of student collaborators with four, five, and six members. These larger groups intensify adolescent peer-group consciousness, particularly the sense of competition among members, in-group/out-group forces, and peer-leadership situations. However, these larger groups work better with older students—such as advanced undergraduates and graduate students—since peer group values are less urgent for them: they treat such values with somewhat more irony than do the younger students. In principle, however, there is no reason the larger groups shouldn't work well for first-year students, provided the group continues for at least a year.

whose sense of peer group membership played a significant role in how they worked in class. In this regard her work will contrast with Ms. K's, for whom this value is less important. To introduce Ms. M's psychosocial perspective, here are her first two essays:

Question 1

Tell, in as much detail as you can, something important about yourself that you think would be helpful and/or interesting for everyone else to know. Be as candid and as clear as your normal sense of decorum permits.

Something that is important to me, but may not be interesting to others is what I want to do after college. Right now, I'd like to become an elementary school teacher. I've always liked children and this past year I was a teacher's assistant for a second grade teacher at my old grade school. All I did was help the kids write in cursive and graded papers, but it was fun. I started babysitting in my neighborhood when I was 9 and I still sat for one family last summer on a weekly basis.

I know that teaching doesn't pay much, but that doesn't matter. I plan on marrying a rich lawyer or doctor anyways so money doesn't matter!

Actually I want to teach the children, not just make money. I just hope I can find a job after I graduate.

Question 2

Think back to the first name in your life that a verbal or language event scared you. Name the person speaking, describe the full circumstance, and discuss the extent to which a purely verbal event (someone saying something) is fearful. Describe your fearful feelings as fully as possible, and explain the significance of this event today.

The first time I can remember being scared of what someone said was when I was about 3 years old. My family and I were visiting my grandparents. We lived far away, so it was a big deal for my brother and sister and I [sic]. I don't remember much about my grandfather before that visit, but I guess I had always been scared of him because my mother said I used to cry when he held me. Anyway, when we got to my grandparents' house, I remember that my grandfather came out of the house and started yelling at my father. I remember I ran and hid behind my mother and it took me some time before I wasn't scared of him. I think the reason I was so frightened was that my parents only raised their voices at my brother and sister and I [sic] when we had done something bad. When my grandfather raised his voice, I thought he was going to punish someone. I didn't understand that he was joking. Now, my father had a deep, loud voice that scares my sister's son. I used to get a sort of scared feeling when my father raised his voice, but I remembered the event with my grandfather and I realized why I was scared. My nephew will start crying right away. I think when he gets old he'll realize what he's afraid of, and he won't be scared anymore.

My first frightening verbal event was only my grandfather's loud and deep voice, that made me cry because I thought I was in trouble.

Before getting to my analysis, consider first Ms. K's written commentary on Ms. M's work, six weeks into the first semester:

One thing I've noticed about Ms. M's written work is that there are always scratch-outs. In her first and third essays, entire paragraphs are scratched. Within these papers and also in her second essay entire sentences as well as words are scratched out. This may not necessarily mean anything but I also noticed that some of the phrases she uses don't reflect too much self-confidence. In her first essay she says that something which is important to her is what she wants to do after college but this "may not be interesting to others." Also in her first essay she talks about what she did as a teacher's aide by saying "all I did was . . . " In her third essay [not cited here] Ms. M says that Sally and she never really got along when, in fact, she knows they didn't.[3] With the considerable amount of cross-outs and the way in which some of her phrases are worded I think that Ms. M may be a bit unsure of herself, [may] be lacking in self-confidence, and [may] underestimate her capabilities at times.

One contradiction I found within Ms. M's papers was the way she felt about money. In her first essay she said "I plan on marrying a rich lawyer or doctor anyway so money doesn't matter!" which is contradictory in itself. In her third essay she tells of when she was little she used to brag about all of the nice things she had. This, I'm sure, has something to do with the way she feels about money today. It doesn't make sense for her to say that "money doesn't matter" when, in fact, she wants to marry a rich man.

The points Ms. K advanced in this commentary came out of an early group discussion in which we all three participated. I had characterized some of the material cited in Ms. K's first paragraph as Ms. M's "apologetic" style, but Ms. K had noted these items independently and added her view that Ms. M may lack self-confidence.[4] Similarly, in that discussion, Ms. K and I both made the same point about the apparent contradiction in the second paragraph of her first essay. Since this was early in the semester, and the relationship among the three of us had not relaxed yet, the pressure on Ms. M must have been considerable. Yet she insisted that the second paragraph was not contradictory and she could not understand why we thought so. On the other

3. Although this is not the topic in this chapter, notice how Ms. K is observing a trait of Ms. M's language use that she ultimately learns is true of her own—the use of "I guess" when in fact she is sure. Ms. K, however, did not decide that she had this trait, until she *first* observed it in Ms. M. This observation set the stage for the comprehensive view of her uses of such phrases that I cited in her final essay in the course. See chapter 8, page 234.

4. We may recall that Ms. K speculated that some of the features of my own language use could reflect insecurity. While her observations of Ms. M and of me have some truth to them, it is noteworthy that she "finds" similar things in both of our language styles.

hand, Ms. M seemed to have no trouble agreeing that many of her usages early on did show a lack of confidence—that is, she easily accepted Ms. K's almost clinical conclusion. But she stuck to her point that if money really mattered to her, she would enter a profession that would earn her money, and that wanting to marry a rich man does not contradict saying that money doesn't matter. This early and somewhat oppositional exchange did find a satisfying resolution but not until the end of the course.

Those reading Ms. K's commentaries, and perhaps my own for that matter, may think that we are making clinical judgments. I don't think I can deny that it is *possible* to read our remarks in this way. Because I make and encourage others to make such judgments, there is sometimes a note of discomfort in the group discussion of them. Our regular means of coping with the discomfort is to see how the judgments are analytical rather than clinical. We are still thinking in a psychosocial idiom, but we aim for judgments that disclose stylistic differences between people rather than differences in the level of mental health each brings to the course. Ms. M's tenacity in holding her point of view was an excellent basis for us to pursue analytical distinctions in language-use strategies as the course continued. I mention this now because it looks as if we could hurt Ms. M's feelings, and it is essential to see how and why this is not the conclusion to be drawn.

As the course continued, it became clear that there was an essential difference between Ms. K's and Ms. M's approach to the class. Ms. K's instinctive sense of belonging was founded on her ability and her desire to negotiate the teacher; Ms. M's instinctive sense of belonging was founded on her comfort and confidence in her peer-group membership. The great majority of Ms. M's essays and her behavior in the classroom strongly imply that she sees the peer group as a natural classroom habitat, and that her sense of stability in class comes from her feeling that what she does in class will generally or usually serve her status as a responsible group member. This underlying perspective permitted Ms. M to accede easily to Ms. K's judgment that some of her usages showed a lack of confidence. As we will see shortly, Ms. M agrees with Ms. K's judgment that her lack of confidence is related to her *relationship with her parents* and that the peer group was a place where she could share such thoughts. For Ms. M, Ms. K's judgment confirmed a feeling she already had on starting school: that friends are supposed to recognize such things, thereby saying "I understand how you feel." But on the matter of her ultimate values—whether money was so important to her—Ms. M felt quite confident in standing her ground against Ms. K, and particularly because I, the authority figure, also held Ms. K's view. In our first discussion, Ms. M accepted the seemingly harsh judgment of her peer (recall that I had not made any judgment about Ms. M's confidence) and was steadfast in her opposition to the apparently authoritative opinion.

My feeling is that Ms. M's first essay was actually more substantive personally than Ms. K's first essay, which was more routine and generally reserved. Ms. M's essay is about her vocational plans and some of the background to them. One of her key statements is, "I've always liked children," something we may contrast with Ms. K's less personal list of hobbies and love of sports.[5] One can contrast the conditional moods of two of Ms. K's sentences, "I feel that by having a lot of outside activities you can learn a lot about people and they can teach you a lot"; or, "When something as unique as true friendship does exist, I feel as if there really is someone who will always be there," with the narrative quality of Ms. M's whole first paragraph and its concrete historical information about herself. Furthermore, Ms. M brings in the weighty matter of whether one's chosen vocation pays enough and risks announcing her wishes to marry, thus making her vulnerable to the very response given by Ms. K, whose presentation of herself in that first essay was cautious if nevertheless sincere. Generally, Ms. M's work shows hopes and facts, while Ms. K's offers more abstract thoughts and principles.

A review of their second essays suggests that Ms. K associates fear more with peers and Ms. M associates fear more with parents. In writing about a fearful verbal event, Ms. K described how a strange boy on the street spoke to her when she was about six years old.[6] She described that she felt frightened and alone and then observed that her wariness probably derived from "a fear instilled in me by my mom." Ms. M's essay, on the other hand, described how when she was only three she had a fear of the loud voice of her grandfather, relating it to the fact that her parents raised their voices "when we had done something bad." The respective events reported by Ms. K and Ms. M are paradigmatic of their then-present perspective, in that Ms. K showed caution about an unknown peer, while Ms. M reported a fear of an authoritative parent—a fear of being "in trouble" with (probably) him. I suspect that because individualism is more highly valued in our culture than belonging to a group, and because Ms. K and I both unconsciously have this "majority" value, Ms. M might have appeared to us to be "lacking in confidence." On the other hand, Ms. K's original judgment that Ms. M seemed to lack confidence might be understood as true only when measured by the standard that requires self-assertive language, self-promotion, and other stylistic habits generally required of job applicants and "good students." Judged by a standard, say, of the primacy of group-belonging, Ms. M's essay might seem respectful of and deferential to her peers, acknowledging, for instance, that what is important to her "may not be interesting to others," and that, while her work as an assistant teacher may not count as a great

5. Ms. K's first essay is cited in chapter 8, page 246.
6. This essay is cited in chapter 8, page 247.

achievement from an individual point of view, it was still "fun" to help the second grade teacher and come into contact with the children whom she "always liked."

When Ms. M reached her final essay at the end of the second semester, she did not say "aha, now I see what I have been doing all year," a feeling that Ms. K expressed in her final essay; rather, she presented thoughts and observations in an unprecedented form that strongly implied a change in awareness on her part. Here are the opening sentences of her final essay:

> When I first started to write this essay, I tried to come up with some kind of outline or organization so that I would be able to include all of my ideas. I started out by following the outline that I had come up with, but as usual I got off the track about a million times. I rewrote almost half of this paper because I wasn't happy with it. I hope this paper doesn't come out too confusing.

This paragraph alludes to the "scratch-outs" that Ms. K commented on earlier, and it further demonstrates her tendency to be apologetic. However, the differences between this statement and her early ones are decisive. Throughout the year, undoubtedly in response to Ms. K's remarks, Ms. M crossed out many fewer words. In the above passage, however, she *reports* that she revised her essay and gives *a reason*—"because I was not happy with it." Of course, we understand that such a reason exists when we see erasures or other editing in a spontaneous essay, but when the author announces the reason, it marks a different state of mind altogether: Ms. M's dissatisfaction with her work is now *part of the work* being analyzed, and therefore under greater control. She was able to get to this stage because of her respect for Ms. K's opinion and admiration of Ms. K's style of self-reflexive writing. The sentence "I hope this paper doesn't come out too confusing" is also a significant change from her apologetic tendency. Rather than the "all I did was . . . but it was fun" usage, which has a note of rationalization in it, the later sentence is a direct, first-person statement of self-awareness, probably comparable to her statement, in her first essay, "I just hope I can find a job after I graduate." I can't say how conscious Ms. M was of this change, but the missing "just" in the later sentence suggests to me a greater degree of confidence when she expresses her hopes. A further subtle change could be construed from the contrast between the phrase "but it was fun" in the first essay and the phrase "but as usual" in the last citation. Even though the latter phrase is self-deprecating, it is not a negative clause, in that it cites a habitual aspect of her work rather than a compensation for what she fears others (her parents?) will think a more fundamental failure. The sentence which begins "I rewrote" then explains that she persevered in trying to maintain discipline. The overall difference in style between this passage and her early essays is that at first she acted apologetically, but here she reports her uncertainties directly. Notice that this change in style contributes to a *strengthened* sense of the primacy of the peer group for her. She is now, in her sense, a "better peer" rather than someone more conversant with authority, as Ms. K became.

Throughout the year, Ms. M, as a rule, did not report about relationships with her parents, though she did mention her siblings and boyfriends several times. With this fact in mind consider the following excerpt from her last essay:

> Donald [her brother] and I have a different relationship [than the one with Pam, her sister] and I think this is a big reason for the differences [in the way she spoke about each relationship]. Donald rarely gets angry at anyone; he's very easygoing and he just doesn't lose his temper like Pam and I do. So I haven't had very many "awkward" situations with him. Our relationship was also easier to write about. Especially since I was writing about when we were kids and back then none of us got into serious arguments or misunderstandings. Pam and I never did much together when we were youngsters. She was always so much "older." She had her own crowd of friends. I don't think Donald and I are any closer than Pam and I; we just have a different relationship. Pam and I will get angry at each other for things like someone saying the wrong thing; usually I say something stupid, but it doesn't last long. Donald won't get angry with me or me with him; we just correct ourselves and leave it at that. There have been a lot of changes in my family relationships during this school year. When I go home now, I feel like my parents give me less privileges than when I was in high school. In high school I could usually get a car whenever I needed it. Then when I go home it's a big deal for me to use the car. It's like I forgot how to drive or something. I know that my parents are used to me not needing the car since I've been away, but it still annoys me. My dad thinks I should work my way through school, which is fine. But I just hate looking for jobs because I'm afraid I'll hate the job I get. I ran out of my savings a lot earlier than I thought I would and so I've had to borrow from my parents a couple of times. They always lecture me about planning ahead and not spending a lot of money. This had created a lot of tension between my dad and I, and I think that's part of the reason why I feel like I don't have the same privileges I used to have.
>
> Mr. Bleich says I have become a smart-ass lately. I like to think of it as being cynical. I don't think that this is a change in me. I've always been that way; it's just that it's usually inside of me and lately I've been voicing my opinions more. This semester has not been a good time for me. I've had a lot of family problems and problems with my personal life also. My parents were considering a divorce and this caused a lot of problems between my sister and I. I don't really want to talk about it all, but it does seem like almost everything has been going worng [sic] in my life. When I get upset I take it out on others in the way of sarcastic remarks and have as my dad calls it a "snotty attitude."

Until she wrote about it in this passage, I did not know that discord between her parents was a major influence on Ms. M's state of mind during the course (though it is likely that Ms. K knew). In retrospect, however, it explains a great deal about Ms. M's language-use style. For Ms. M, the usual adolescent difficulties of rebellion and individuation are exacerbated by the issue of loyalty to her parents: any dispute with one of the parents contributes to the discord between them; such disputes would stimulate Ms. M to wash her hands of her parents and concentrate more than she ordinarily might on the salutary experience of dealing with those her own age, with her own sort of problems. This perhaps best explains why Ms. M saw no contradiction between wanting to be a teacher—money not being important—and saying that she would marry a rich man. In her early "contradictory" sentence, the "meaning" of marriage was that it was a peer-group act, and, at the time, Ms. M's wish to marry a successful man reflected not a desire for money, but for emancipation from her parents. It meant using her peer group to answer the concerns of her parents. Notice how in describing the car situation at home, she uses typical adolescent sarcasm: "It's like I forgot how to drive or something." She sees her parents forcing her into a less mature frame of mind. Similarly, her parents' lectures about planning ahead also push her not to plan ahead but to find a situation in which the lecturing will stop. Thus, when she announces that she wants to be a teacher (although it doesn't pay much) and to marry a rich man, she is invoking peer-characteristic ideals to remove herself from the unmanageable standards proffered by her parents, and probably more emphatically by her father. The money itself is clearly less "important" than Ms. M's desire for a more acceptable relationship, and it is therefore not a contradiction for her to say that money is not important and that she plans to marry a rich man.

Briefly, let me review what happened to Ms. M with an eye on her interaction with others. She wrote an essay the beginning of the course announcing something important about herself. The "answer" to this essay came from the two other members of her group who seemed to hold a "majority" opinion. Ms. M then accepted one part of the answer and rejected the other. This negotiation led to a provisional sort of knowledge which it then took the rest of the course to validate. Here is how I think this took place.

In the first paragraph cited above, Ms. M gave some idea of the peer/authority contrast as it appeared in her own home, adding to her sketch of the situation in her second essay. She describes relatively smooth relationships with her two siblings. Then when she abruptly shifts to the "changes" at home, the emphasis is on her reduced status—"less privileges than when I was in high school"—and changes in the relationship with her parents.

This psychosocial condition of her family life is what Ms. M brought to this course. In her second paragraph, she then alludes to what has actually been happening in the course during the second semester as she mentions my having called her a "smart-ass" recently. My comment referred to her bold behavior in class, such as holding up her watch if it was near closing time, or actually suggesting that we dismiss class. These, of course, were harmless asides on her part, which "went over" well because I too was a "smart-ass" who offered analogous remarks aimed at entertaining the class. However, her explanation of this behavior should be taken seriously—she is voicing her opinions more. That is to say, she is now using the peer group in a very definite adolescent way—what her father called the "snotty attitude"—but with irony and the knowledge of its ultimate acceptability in the class. In the second paragraph above, she claimed that this was her "real self" all along which had only now emerged. Here is one of her comments on this general strengthening of her peer relationships in this class:

> Some of the other changes [in her work this semester] were in how I write about relationships and how I make less corrections in my hand-written essays. Lots of changes in factors that affect my writing occurred too. Not only major changes with my family but with my friends too. Ms. K and I are a lot closer now, so we were able to have pretty good discussions about each others' work even though Mr. Bleich wasn't usually there with us. I don't think that Mr. Bleich not being there really hurt us. In fact it was probably better because we had to really think deeply to come up with points about essays.

Ms. M appreciates my frequent absence from subgroup meeting partly because of her confidence in the peer group, but also because individual action for her requires a more "purely" peer context. My absence made it easier for Ms. M to normalize her relationship with Ms. K, which had started out on an oppositional note, as I described. The process of peer-normalization included their mutual discovery of each other's sarcastic usages—Ms. K's "cut-downs" and Ms. M's classroom wisecracking. In the classroom—where Ms. K generally confined herself to a few serious comments on the work at hand—Ms. M tended toward "ringleader" behavior, showing a consciousness of other students' level of decorum and good taste. Here is Ms. M's comment on this phenomenon from her last essay:

> In my first semester final essay I said that I have little patience with some people, especially some girls. That still is true, but not as bad as before. Now I sort of ignore a person who bugs me rather than say something to them. Sometimes it's really hard though. Especially in our discussion. Every time I would come out of class, Ms. S, Ms. A, and I would walk back to the dormitory and eat lunch together. The whole time we would talk about the

discussion we had that day. We talked about all the things people said. We have just about everyone in that class pegged. It's pretty funny. I got so frustrated during the discussion that when I got out of there I just bitched about it for an hour. I talked about this in my other essay and I still think this is true. I do think that sometimes people make a mountain out of a molehill but I'm not sure about the deep conversation boring me though. Like I said in the other essay, I could talk for hours to some people on a deep level. In class I don't get bored at all, just frustrated.

Ms. M here discloses the importance of a spontaneous "subgroup" in her sense of belonging in the class. The two students to which she refers were, like Ms. M, both circumspect in the classroom, all three having an instinctive sense of when to stop speaking in class when their point was made, thereby leaving room for others to contribute. Ms. M is complaining about those who did not have this sense, but the way she describes the gripe session is significant: "We had just about everyone in that class pegged." Here, in this "rump" subgroup, the three friends share their sense of social authority in the class by analyzing the public behavior of all the others, a common activity of cliques of people of all ages. It is not that Ms. M is reporting anything unusual for an undergraduate class, but that she, more than any other student in the class, thought it important to include these thoughts about peer-group politics as part of how her authentic sense of self emerged in this class.

The frustration that Ms. M reports may also be related to my behavior and to a more private or subjective feeling. Here is a citation that appeared toward the end of her final essay:

This class has really forced me to look inward and really think about things that I do and say. Writing about situations that I am unsure about really has helped me to set them straight in my mind. I wonder if I had worn the brown suit more than just once, if I would have changed my writing, especially some of the more personal essays that I wrote, like about Mr. M and Mr. P [friends of hers, not in this class]. I never once thought of putting "do not copy" on any of my essays.[7] That would have been interesting to look for a change in my style. It's really strange to have someone your own age talk about your essays and their opinions of you. I like reading Ms. K's essays about me because every time I did I found out something about myself that I had never even thought of before. The best example of that is when Ms. K wrote about my lack of self-confidence. I never really thought of myself in that way, but I knew she was right.

7. Students had the option of indicating that they did not wish their work to be reproduced for the whole class to see by writing "do not copy" at the top of their essay when they gave it to me. The subgroup did have to see it.

"Wearing the brown suit" was a phrase I used to mean having essays discussed by the whole class. It was meant to call attention to the likely feelings of discomfort that the essay's author would have and to relieve some of this discomfort by making jokes about the "brown suit." In the passage above, Ms. M, in a mild self-reflexive mood, announces that she probably wanted the collective attention of the class more than just once. Although sometimes I asked for volunteers to have their work discussed publicly, it was I who chose among the volunteers, trying to make sure that all students had a chance.[8] Therefore, Ms. M may be saying that she wished I had been more attentive to her and her involvement with the rest of the class. I also had not noted that she had not withheld any of her essays from public scrutiny, as she now says in this last essay. It is possible that she is saying that if her work had been discussed more frequently in the plenary meeting, she would have had a public forum to "answer" some of those in the class who, she reported privately, "bugged" her. At the same time, Ms. M significantly appreciates that "someone your own age" paid attention to her work in an extended way, and she recognized the value of Ms. K's steady analytical comments, even more so as they became "closer." However, Ms. M considered this situation "strange" probably because in her experience it is not the usual role the peer group plays. She had not yet thought of the peer group playing an active role in serious schoolwork but rather as an arena for releasing the pressure of authoritarian classroom demands. However, another strange feature of this group was Ms. M's having to "see" peer elements in me, something else that Ms. K's boldness toward me helped to bring about. It seems certain to me that Ms. K and I, early in the course, were in some sense parents for her, Ms. K probably appearing to her more privileged (by my attention) than a student ought to be. For Ms. M, normalization of our group meant deparentizing us, probably me in particular, through her gradual understanding that our judgments about her work were not didactic or homiletic. As this did happen, Ms. M became more of a "smart-ass" in the plenary class meetings, which meant that she felt more authority to judge what behavior does and does not belong in class, and that I, finally, would not think that she had done "something bad." Finally, Ms. M reports that the class forced her to "look inward," which I think is more of an achievement for her than

8. It turns out that I was guilty of a serious failure in this course; I learned at the end that one student did not have her work discussed at all. The obvious solution is to keep track of whose work is discussed in each class so that such an omission cannot happen. I also did not know for most of the course that Ms. M actively wished for her work to be discussed, while there were other students whose work was discussed who did not need or want it as much as Ms. M did. I now think the best policy would be to poll the class periodically to see who would like to wear the brown suit, who would not like to, and to find out why in each case.

for many other students. Because of her personality and her family situation at the time, looking inward was not what she wanted to do. Her group experience answered to her first need for social comfort, but it also brought about attention to what in her was a suppressed need—to see herself as an individual in relation to peers as well as authority figures. As a result, what first looked like an apology in her writing came to look more and more like deference and consideration for others. This is not a sensational change in style, but it is nevertheless a decisive one, and one made possible by her collaboration with Ms. K and me.

Perhaps the most difficult part of trying to understand collaboration among students is gaining access to the collaboration without directly influencing it. Of course, all of the student work that I discuss in this book was done in my own course, so obviously I have already exerted a significant influence just by proposing assignments and speaking about them in the subgroup, discussion sections, and lectures. When the students are left alone to carry out tasks that I proposed, they are all in some sense seeking to meet a standard that I established, and, as we have seen in Ms. K's case, working to achieve that standard in the hopes of getting a high grade. Nevertheless, there are fundamental ways in which the language all of us used—students and teachers—is *not determined* by my influence or the course's, but only perhaps colored or constrained by them. Ultimately, there are no "free" uses of language; any context in which language is used is going to have to be taken into account as we attempt to gain insight into this use. In investigating the work produced in this next group of three, I am viewing it as more independent than that of the group in which I was a member. The issue is, how does an "independent" group function in my course, as opposed to a group in which I participated directly. I would like to show that how students influence one another is generic in that other groups in other courses can expect similar effects because the language and literacy processes I am considering are "deeper" in the minds of the individuals than what emerges in the topical conversations of the classroom.

One further caution. It might serve my purpose to present in brief form just what each of the eight groups of three achieved, which would give a sense of the range of thought and insight one could expect in a similar class. However, I will instead once again try to characterize the quantity and complexity of the work I think we teachers need to have before us to make responsible judgments about language use and literacy style. I continue to want to exhibit the "ordinariness" of the students' work as well as to give some impression of the time and the patience it requires to see the pace and degree of such "ordinary" development.

Finally, I will not even present a "complete" picture of the mutual influences of this subgroup, which would entail showing how the work of each student changed in response to the analytical commentaries of the other students. Rather, I will discuss how one student's work developed and compare how he views his work with how his two colleagues view it. In this small "segment" of a case, we will be noting not only differences between a majority and minority opinion, but ways in which the "minority" of one accepts, adapts, and rejects the majority opinion, as well as subtle differences between the two opinions that form the majority. In this case, the larger political issue is gender identity as it is manifested in the common details of language use and literacy style. Of particular importance in the achievement of this subgroup is the *disclosure of how the matter of gender and pedagogical authority— two of the central concerns of this book—emerge in the everyday life and politics of the students' work yet obviously affect their underlying strategies of language use.*

The three students in this group are Ms. A, Mr. D, and Ms. E. Our attention will be on Mr. D's work and how it changed during the course in response to his two female colleagues. Although I had individual conferences with each of the students, my discussion is based mainly on the texts they wrote and which each of the other two read. (On one or two occasions, which I will note as they appear, the individual conferences are germane. As in the case of all the group work in this course, the texts written by students about other students' work were usually the *result* of a discussion between the pair of students writing on a third's work, and they also often resulted from discussions among all three, as will be clear from the citations below. Here are two citations of Ms. A's commentary on Mr. D's work, the first from about seven weeks into the first semester, the second from the middle of the second semester:

Ms. A's first commentary on Mr. D

Mr. D's[9] style of writing demonstrates that he is very confident and sure of himself along with the fact that he is proud of his achievements. This poised attitude is reflected in the very first essay he wrote where he said, "I've also owned and sold three cars before I even turned eighteen."

From Mr. D's language it is also apparent that he is professional in his work. For instance in dealing with an irate customer, Mr. D kept his cool by saying, "Sir, I was just trying to explain to you that I have to take care of the full-service customers first." His high sense of self-worth is demonstrated when in essay #2, he called up the manager to settle a salary discrepancy. Mr. D

9. In her essay, Ms. A always referred to Mr. D by his given name. I changed this usage for the purposes of this discussion.

knew he was a good asset to the restaurant and felt that he deserved what was entitled to him.

Mr. D is also straightforward in his use of the English language. This feature is apparent in his last essay [essay 3, on my uses of language], where he indicated, point blank, that Mr. Bleich mumbled rather than saying something to the effect that he sometimes mumbles or at times he mumbles. As also stated before, usage of words like "pissed off" and "asshole" exemplify a straightforward[10] manner of writing.

The last notable feature of Mr. D's writing that I am going to analyze is his use of number determiners. This use of one, two, first, second, etc. shows that he is very conscious of chronological order and exactness. This follows along with his straightforwardness.

Ms. A's second commentary on Mr. D

It was evident last semester that work was of major importance to Mr. D; therefore, it was the topic of many of his essays. Then Mr. D made the transition from work to his friends and then briefly mentioned his girlfriend. But, the topic of his family had still not been dealt with in a significant way. Mr. D mentioned T, his girlfriend, in two of his essays so far this semester and they have been on a more personal level. Whereas in the other essay about T, it was complimentary but did not have that touch or hint of personal involvement like Mr. D's most recent essays do . . .

In accordance with Mr. D's change in topics and his greater expression of emotion, his specific use of vocabulary had changed to accommodate and exemplify the other changes. An example of this is that it is apparent that Mr. D uses the word "success" in several of his essays now—maybe taking the place of the word "work." Mr. D mentioned the word "success" in two of his recent papers, on "The Grave" and on "The Rocking Horse Winner." Mr. D writes "I still have a great desire to become successful and I know I will but I also know that success is not everything." This idea correlates with Mr. D's use of the word "work" last semester. It seems to me that in Mr. D's eye hard work will pave the road to success. The change from the use of work to success follows along the lines that Mr. D used more physical language last semester involving work. Now with his more emotional writings, Mr. D uses "success" because it is more of an emotional and individual state than a physical one.

These two excerpts give the general lines of discussion among the three students in this group when focusing on Mr. D's literacy style. Mr. D's early essays dealt mainly with work relationships, their politics, and his thoughts on how he handled things on the job. His thoughts were distinct

10. Although we are not discussing Ms. A's own work in any detail, her use of the term "straightforward" to describe obscene language almost certainly is explained by the fact that Ms. A was also given to using obscene language, as much as, and perhaps even more than, Mr. D, Ms. K was not given to using obscene language and so "sees" it more prominently.

and vigorously mobilized, and his strong attitudes came out in his casual use of obscene language—what Ms. A calls "straightforward" writing. His work gave the impression that that he was in command of all the situations he wrote about, and his personal bearing added to this feeling that he was confident and thought well of himself.

Ms. A's second commentary raises the basic themes of the discussions of Mr. D's work during the second semester—a greater willingness to express feelings and to comment on his relationships with his family and girlfriend. Also, however, Ms. A notes a fundamental conversion of vocabulary that marks the main repeated idea in his essays—the move from "work" to "success." As I will discuss when I cite Ms. E's second commentary and Mr. D's own views of himself, this turned out to be the key "name change" the second semester, and one demonstrably related to his sense of himself as a student in this course. Now, however, here is Ms. A's presentation, from her second commentary, of the key political issue in the group's investigation of Mr. D's language:

> I have also become aware of Mr. D's gender this semester by his use of vocabulary and his other language features. I think his gender pertaining to his writing has become more evident because we are now doing interpretation of written work and the only way we have to do this is by using our own experiences as comparisons. This means that everything that Mr. D has experienced has been through the eye of a male which will naturally have some effect on how he interprets things.
>
> An example of Mr. D's gender showing through is his word choice in essay #6 [on the arguing parents] where Mr. D writes. "He feels that he is doing the majority of the *work around the house* [these and subsequent emphases in this citation were all added by Ms. A] and he just can't handle *his wife having a career*. The father should have to take some responsibility for the child *but his liberated wife* must also sacrifice some of her time also to be with the child."
>
> Another example of where a reader could pick out Mr. D's gender without knowing that he was the author is when he identifies with the father in the story, "A Good Man is Hard to Find." In the beginning of the essay Mr. D writes, "When reading Flannery O'Connor two people that I probably identified with the most was the *mother and the father*." However, throughout the entire essay Mr. D describes the father and never really mentions the mother.
>
> A passage which illustrates Mr. D's identification with the father is when he writes, "So *here is the father who is trying to take his family on a nice vacation* and all of a sudden *everything has gone against him* and nobody wants to go. It was all because the grandmother opened her mouth and *tried to change the family decision which she had no right doing.*"
>
> . . . I did have the chance to question Mr. D about the gender question and the male chauvinism and he agreed with the basic concepts of my ideas.

It would not have been enough to conclude from Mr. D's first-semester work that because he writes about work relationships in which only men were involved there was a gender bias: these homosocial relations are important and common among both men and women, especially in adolescence. However, the response essays brought out *discrepancies* such as the one mentioned by Ms. A in paragraph (3) above, where it becomes clear that his "gut" sympathy lies with the father in the story even though he says he identified with the "mother and the father." Such observations, along with phrases like "liberated wife," imply Mr. D's culturally rooted gender bias. Although Ms. A reports that Mr. D agreed orally with "the basic concepts of my ideas," we will see as we look into Mr. D's comments on himself that his agreement was more of a diplomatic move in the group and that he is not ready to accept that his gender bias is *political*. First, however, consider Ms. E's two commentaries:

Ms. E's first commentary on Mr. D

. . . Mr. D writes on . . . a physical level. "Working" is his theme in all of his essays. From working on cars in his first essay, working in a gas station, and in a steak house, subjects for his second and third essays, to his last essay, having Mr. Bleich work on his mumbling, he seems very conscious of jobs. I think we can carry this a step further to say that he values an occupation as an essential and important part of his life. This attitude shows he is very mature and business oriented.

Working gave Mr. D extreme confidence when writing. He seemed detailed and direct. He knew he was good at what he did, as he tells us in his second essay, "He just had to wait until he had someone to replace me (which wasn't easy because I was relatively good and most of the other cooks were on drugs most of the time)." But when writing about something other than work he lost his confidence, and become passive in his writing. This is shown in his last essay when writing about Mr. Bleich's mumbling. It is the only time his language trait occurs in any of his essays; here are some examples: "I don't know maybe . . . " "I think that most of the time . . . " "it seems to me . . . " "Maybe . . . "

Mr. D is more concerned with the accuracy of his facts than with the mechanics of writing. He told me, "It doesn't bother me to spell the words wrong."

When at times Ms. A would vocalize her anger, Mr. D kept it inside. When talking with the customer at the gas station, he appeared calm, but inside he was boiling. He wrote, "Now I was mad . . . " and when he wrote about the steak house, although he was again upset, "very pissed off," he, instead of releasing them, kept them inside.

Ms. E's second commentary on Mr. D

When comparing Mr. D's works on literature in contrast to his works on personal relationships and experiences, there was a new feature that surfaced. This feature was an attitude he never really expressed first semester; wanting to succeed—and badly. In Mr. D's final analysis of himself [first semester] he writes about his father's influence on people. "He is a very powerful man and many people in the business world have a great deal of respect for him." He goes on to write, "I want to also become a respected business man and reap all of the benefits that go along with the influence . . . my determination will finally pay off when I graduate from college." This quote from the paper was the first time Mr. D had ever used the word "determination." I never knew he felt so strongly about success. Also in that paper he concludes with these two sentences: "It seems that I try to use my language to help me along the road to success. I only hope I was correct in thinking this way." This drive for success is brought out again in Mr. D's outside essay on "The Rocking Horse Winner." He was explaining the word money and how it played an important role in his life. Mr. D stated he could never be satisfied; he always wanted more and better things: "I would put my mind to it that I was going to have one and then I would go work my ass off for it." This attitude was not brought out first semester. In his first essay of the year he talked about his job at a gas station and said, " . . . I was employed there since I was fifteen-and-a-half years old and up until a couple of days before I left for school, I still worked there." He also says "I still plan to work there . . . to make a little extra money." The closest clue I could have gotten to his money-hungry, determined, and success-oriented mind was in his third essay, when he was not "going to cook any more that night until he got a raise." But that did not give me the impression in which he concluded his "Rocking Horse Winner" essay, in which he concluded with, "I had it in my mind that the only way that I would ever be happy was if I would always be able to get whatever I wanted, no matter what."

Why all of a sudden the attitude change? Or why did his determination to succeed surface at this time? I think Mr. D did not feel he succeeded to get the grade he wanted first semester and he is determined to get the grade he wants this semester. And this determination is possibly showing in his writing. Talking with Mr. D gave me this idea, and even though I never connected it together until now, I believe it makes logical sense.

Something that has come out in this semester is his definite gender association. Being male, Mr. D identifies in every literary work with a male character. His chauvinism also appears. In essay #6 on the conversation between a husband and wife, Mr. D is quick to defend the man: "The father has a legitimate complaint"; "The father should have to take some responsibility for his child but his liberated wife must also sacrifice some of her time." The word "liberated" stood out to me. It gave me the impression that Mr. D would be jealous if his wife had a successful career. When I asked him about this he said he would feel that way. Another instance that proves this is his closing remark: " . . . that he is resentful of the fact that his wife is doing so good, that he just doesn't like it." I think this is more an opinion of his than of the man in the story. In essay #7 on "The Grave" his whole essay is told relating to Paul. The fact that Mr. D dwells on is a man's sport of hunting. The essay #8 Mr. D related to to the boy in "Araby." But it is in essay #9 when the male chauvinist comes out in him. Mr. D states that "two of the people that I probably identified with the most was the mother and father." That is the first and last mention of the mother in the whole essay. From that point on he always refers to the family as "his (Bailey's) family." Mr. D says, "It's like he had no choice; he had to do what the grandmother said." Again brushing the blame off the male figure. Mr. D also takes the chauvinist attitude about women and the idea that they should be "seen and not heard" when he writes, "if it wasn't for the grandmother opening her mouth and starting something . . . "

The other new material released this semester is his obsession with being taken advantage of. There was a mention of this first semester but it never stood out until the second semester. In his paper on Perkins Cake and Steak he talks of not getting a raise when the other guys doing less than him were getting paid more. At the end he writes, "Thinking back on this I guess I would do the same today as I did back then. Just because I don't like being taken advantage of." In essay #9 he got very upset when Bailey was being "forced" (as Mr. D put it) to drive to see a plantation. Mr. D wrote "I could just get madder and madder every time something like this happened"; "I can't think of any relationship that I've had where I've felt this way." As you read before, there was just such a relationship cited. In a talk with Mr. D he said he couldn't stand being taken advantage of. He wants to be in control of every situation. "I was always impressed with the influence my father had over people. He is a very powerful man and many people in the business world have a great deal of respect for him." This is a quote from Mr. D's final analysis of himself (first semester). I think it speaks for itself and expresses how much Mr. D wants to be like that and not like Bailey. This is an important point. It is the first time that Mr. D has related that he wants to identify with an aspect that he admires in his father.

In this set of commentaries by Ms. A and Ms. E, each had at least three purposes in writing: (1) to collaborate with one another to get a coherent account of Mr. D's language, (2) to respect Mr. D's views of himself, and (3) to write essays on their own by presenting individually the fruits of their collaborative work. Each of these purposes is a commitment *both* to a principle of understanding language and to an interpersonal relationship. All students in the course are learning to present "accounts of a person's language use." Ms. A and Ms. E, in their approach to Mr. D's language, are an institutionally established subcollective whose aim is to produce social authority for the opinions of each. Part of this authority, which is at the same time ethical and epistemological, is their effort to have their opinions *regulated* by Mr. D's opinion of their observations. Since this was a principle the students knew in advance, we find, in both commentaries, but particularly in Ms. E's, considerable reporting of her having asked Mr. D what he thinks of their judgments. All the while, each person's commentary is individual; each is not speaking for others or presenting a consensus. Yet each individual, by virtue of the multiple perspectives they consciously seek and invoke, is enacting his or her belonging to the work-community of three.

The pair of first commentaries shows that Ms. A and Ms. E had several observations in common. In her first commentary Ms. A writes, "Mr. D's style of writing demonstrates that he is very confident and sure of himself along with the fact that he is proud of his achievement." She explains that he seems "professional in his work" and that he "kept his cool" in speaking to an angry customer. Ms. E writes that he is "very mature and business oriented" and that "Working gave [him] extreme confidence when writing." Also, Ms. E notes, Mr. D kept his anger "inside." Thus Ms. A and Ms. E generally agree that Mr. D shows strong interest in work, jobs, and profession, that he is in control of hostile feelings, and, most germane to this discussion, that his emotional bearing toward his work helps to explain how he writes: "Working gave Mr. D extreme confidence when writing." I mention again that the foregoing are not clinical judgments abut Mr. D, but ordinary judgments of his *psychology of language use*. The way Mr. D's essays turn out, their feel, so to speak, is connected with his orientation toward work. That it makes a difference to think this way is suggested by Ms. A's observation that Mr. D said "point blank" that I mumbled. This is an interesting observation because it seems to be an error. Mr. D actually wrote, "The one thing that comes to mind about Mr. Bleich's speech pattern is his tendency to mumble." Ms. E wrote that when Mr. D was writing about my mumbling "he lost his confidence, and became passive in his writing." However, Ms. A's observation is not an error, because to Ms. A simply *saying* such a thing is a bold statement. Ms. A viewed the mere mention of my mumbling as a "point blank" statement, while to Ms. E, Mr. D's use of words like "tendency" was more prominent. Ms. E, however, might be in error in saying that Mr. D's writing became "passive." Rather, it became more qualified than his other essays had been. These two different observations by Ms. A and Ms. E triangulate toward what emerged more strongly at the end of the first semester and at the beginning of the second: his involvement in work is part of his stage-specific developmental task of achieving the masculine ideal he was establishing for himself. Mr. D did not suddenly lose his "high sense of self worth" in speaking of my tendency to mumble, but Ms. E is right in noting that there was a change: his relationship with me elicited a more cautious use of language: this relationship, to him, had a direct bearing on his sense of identity as a "successful" man.

The second commentaries of both Ms. A and Ms. E help to bring out this issue of Mr. D's identity. They both note that "success" seems to have replaced "work" as the central theme; they both see the appearance of more emotional material—the more distinct expression of feelings and desires and the discussion of his relationship with his girlfriend; finally, each gives a strong statement of Mr. D's sense of gender identity based on several of his usages and thoughts in his literary response essays. Ms. A says that "success" is more "emotional and individual" and "physical," meaning that "success" is the name for a value, while "work" the name for a physical activity. Actually, the "new" word fills out the picture of Mr. D rather than changes it. The value of success belongs with his eagerness to work. The change in his writing, therefore, is a change in the emphasis within what may already have been "there," in much the same way as Ms. K elaborated on language-use traits that were already in evidence first semester. This change to "success" is also the introduction of a new topic because different things were announced under its aegis, different writing was produced, and different group discussions took place. From Ms. E's second commentary, however, the change may also be construed as his response to developments in the classroom.

Ms. E writes that she noticed an attitude "he never really expressed first semester: wanting to succeed—and badly." She then alludes to Mr. D's citation of the salient relationship with his father: the wish for success seems to be a wish to be like his father. One cannot say with certainty whether one sort of wish precedes the other, but we can easily say that for Mr. D each wish presupposes the other. Furthermore, Ms. E sees values other than success; she sees determination, a touch of avarice ("money-hungry . . . mind"), and a drive for personal power—his desire to "get whatever I wanted no matter what." Finally, Ms. E stipulates, with a certain daring, that the new attitude has a local source: "I think Mr. D did not feel he succeeded to get the grade he wanted first semester and he is determined to get the grade he wants this semester. And this determination is possibly showing in his writing." Notice how in formulating this sentence Ms. E managed to use the words "success," "determine," and "wants" as if to suggest that Mr. D assembled all his other wishes and motives into this cause of getting the right grade. What she says "makes logical sense" is that a certain degree of failure in this course motivated him to actually write about what he "really" wants in general, to bring out something deeper about himself. If Ms. E is right, Mr. D achieved a double perspective of expressing both long-range desires and wishes for achievement in this class. As we will discuss shortly, this was definitely a moment of growth since the second semester found Mr. D much less certain of how to work in class. His heretofore confident sense of "work" was challenged in this course.

First, however, consider how the gender issue enters into his attitude change. From the sentences cited by both Ms. A and Ms. E we see that their collaboration yielded some evidence in common—they each cite some of the same sentences from Mr. D's literary response essays. On the other hand, Ms. E presents her opinion of Mr. D more forcefully, perhaps even with a certain edge. She is somewhat more articulate than Ms. A, but she also seems to feel more strongly about Mr. D's forms of identification with his own gender. Ms. E seems to see a larger or more important fact that Ms. A sees, even though, in another sense, they see the "same" fact. Where Ms. E is ready to see Mr. D's pattern of identification in the literature as an instance of male chauvinism, Ms. A says that because "everything Mr. D has experienced has been through the eye of a male," that will "naturally have some effect on how he interprets things." From our standpoint, it might be helpful to say that both views obtain. Yes, he is chauvinistic in that he fails to credit, perceptually, the actual gender balance in the stories and shows certain usages that imply that he resents feminine independence; but on the other hand he is also involved in a phase-specific developmental process that requires him to understand the salient elements of masculine identity, and he therefore "looks for" such elements more intently. As we will see shortly, Mr. D's own view of himself does seem to reflect both of these views.

Ms. E's second commentary shows that the literary response essays brought out the most "chauvinistic" formulations in Mr. D's work. In two of the essays, his gender loyalty did not seem exaggerated—identifying with the hero in "Araby" and becoming fascinated with the hunting material in "The Grave." But his characterization of the arguing parents and his writing "parents" when he only meant "father" in the O'Connor story amounted, to both Ms. A and Ms. E, to a disregard of women. Ms. E then makes a further noteworthy point: Mr. D is highly sensitive to being "taken advantage of." In this connection, we note that the father in the dialogue and Bailey in the O'Connor story are both seen by Mr. D as underdog figures for whom he becomes a vicarious champion. In her second commentary Ms. E makes this very important connection and reports that Mr. D confirmed her view in a conversation with her. At the end of her last paragraph she returns to the theme she raised in the first paragraph—Mr. D's admiration of his father— and says that Mr. D's announcement of his admiration (in his final essay of the first semester) "speaks for itself." To Ms. E, Mr. D's announcement of his admiration of his father is in part a documentation of his exaggerated masculine loyalty.

The traits Ms. A and Ms. E brought out in their first commentary—the confidence, businesslike behavior, obscene language, and the tendency to seriation in presenting an argument—can (should?) be included in the idea of Mr. D's language as an expression of masculine/success values. Although Mr. D made local choices in writing his essays, it seems clear in retrospect that these choices were determined by a certain cultural ethic, the intensity of which emerged in his essays: the "forceful" writing of the early essays was created by his overall drive for achievement, part of which manifested itself as the intention to get an "A." On their own, Mr. D's two colleagues were able to put these pieces together and inform him of what they found.

Mr. D finally did not achieve with his work what Ms. K achieved with hers—that comprehensive sense of his language that might give him pause. Yet he was able to isolate several issues which all three group members agreed were part of his basic language/value system. I will reflect on what he did achieve, and consider why, perhaps, he did not achieve more.

In this course, Mr. D was more certain at the beginning than at the end of what needed to be done. He attributed this mainly to the different sorts of questions asked in the second semester. In his view, the early questions were very direct, so that it was no problem to reply in very direct language:

> "For instance, 'Recall a conversation that took place between you and someone else, in a relationship of mutual dislike . . . Explain the remarks and your reaction to them as fully as possible.' In reply to this question I wrote sentences such as 'Being very angry we stopped cooking and made a phone call to his house and told him we were very pissed off and that we weren't going to cook anymore that night unless he gave us a raise.'"

In other words the questions of the first semester seemed to make it easy for Mr. D to write historical narratives[11] with plenty of "facts." About the second semester's work, Mr. D wrote:

> Early into the second semester the style of writing gave way to a more cautious, less assertive type of writing. This was because suddenly the questions asked were much more abstract and were dealing with fictional experiences incurred in literature. Now the questions asked were like, "Based on your experiences of conversations such as this, tell who was right, who won, and how you know both of these things." My writing changed to sentences such as "I think they are both partially right" and "But if he also has a career I'm sure he also probably has been away a lot too." Now here in the last sentence I did not interpret the

---

11. Note the different role "narrative" plays in Mr. D's work and my own, or, better, the different meaning narrative has for each of us. For Mr. D, narrative is contrasted with something like "expression of feeling"; for me, narrative is contrasted with "argumentativeness."

situation as fact like I did in the first semester. Here I used the word "probably" because it gave me more flexibility about being right or wrong.

In this interesting contrast, Mr. D wants to claim that his writing changed mainly in response to the questions asked, something true in a sense not meant by him, however. For example, is a phrase like "Tell who was right" more "abstract" than "explain the remarks . . . as fully as possible"? If Mr. D is referring to the *problems posed* by the questions when he uses the term "questions asked," then he correctly sees the difference in each semester's questions: those in the first semester seemed to demand citation of historical facts, and Mr. D can report only on those he remembers clearly. Those questions in the second semester ask for judgments about things Mr. D knows there is no pre-determined right answer. Because Mr. D requires clarity and certitude as an element in the "success" ethic, he explains— or perhaps even apologizes for—his use of "probably" because it gave him "more flexibility about being right or wrong." In other words, if he can't be sure he is right, at least he might avoid being wrong. He does not feel that an intelligent answer which is neither right nor wrong is available to him. He seems to put more value on a sentence made up of a string of clauses variously linked by four "ands" cited earlier than on sentences in the subjunctive and conditional moods, expressing a direction but without certainty. He summarizes: "Because of the change in questions and the factor of interpreting the stories, I changed my writing style, using less forceful and direct words. This gave my second semester essays a feeling of uncertainty."

The fact is that as time went on in this course, Mr. D worked harder and harder and became less and less certain that his work was "right." Before writing his final essay, he requested and got at least three different conferences with me to go over his outline, his drafts, and everything in general. In leaving my office for the last time he still was not sure of what to do. This was at least part of the reason he took up serially, in his final essay, each of the points previously raised by his two partners and made a short essay out of each of them. The passages I cited above were written in response to one of those points—their observation that Mr. D expressed more uncertainty during the second semester. His own explanation gives none of the reasons his partners offered for his "less assertive" style. He prefers to attribute the change to the *different nature of the questions*, which suggests that all along he was only trying to follow instructions; the change in his work was due not to a different attitude toward the subject matter but to a different strategy in response to different questions.

Mr. D acknowledged that because "it was becoming harder to write on the topics given in class" a new feature appeared in his second-semester essay;

he would introduce them with a "cushion" such as, "Before I get into the discussion of the changes of Ms. A's and Ms. E's writing styles and habits . . . " or "Some papers such as this one become very difficult . . . " He explains:

> . . . it was as if I was afraid of going right into the paper for fear I had the wrong ideas. So I used this technique of softening the blow of the paper by setting the paper up in a defensive way. This feature was continued on into the paper, also showing up in my work mainly because of the absence of my teacher for prolonged periods of time. When I am working or studying I like to know exactly what I have to do and when I have to have it finished. So when the instructor was away for so long I felt as if I did not know what was going on. I did not know what I should be looking for and how I should be looking for it. So this feeling of not knowing showed up in my work in the form that I was trying to explain any mistakes in my work before I even made any.

In writing about a specific feature of his essays, Mr. D offers an important reason for his discomfiture during the second semester—my absence from class for about three weeks. Mr. D seems to have had two reactions—the uneasiness he describes in his essay about my not being there to present exact instructions, due dates, and standards of performance, and a more general feeling that the course was unled. This latter feeling suggests to me that he requires a strong masculine pace-setter in order to work ("When I am working . . . I like to know exactly what I have to do."), similar to the psychosocial guidance he derives from his father. Yet because he fears having the "wrong ideas," he interprets his "preliminaries" as defenses ("setting the paper up in a defensive way") thereby attributing his discomfort strictly to my absence, and not to his masculine work ethic. To the end, Mr. D sought to believe that the technical aspects of the course had more influence on his style than the relationships and values he brought into the class and the value judgments of his partners.

Ms. E observed that something important which showed up second semester was Mr. D's "obsession with being taken advantage of." Mr. D says his "identification with the victim" appeared in the first semester as well, citing his reports of how work supervisors were exploiting him and his coworkers. Here is his comment:

> At this point [the end of the course] it seems I wrote the essay to tell everyone about this horrible incident that happened to me, but at the time [early in the first semester] I wrote it out of anger at the manager. Even so, by looking at the language it is evident that I felt I was the victim on this occasion.

This passage could be read to mean that he was angry at the manager because he felt victimized. However, Mr. D actually separates his anger from the victim's feelings by saying that he *first* wrote of the incident out of anger *now* one could construe the essay as a victim-story. In other words Mr. D does not himself relate feeling victimized with his anger at the manager. In the fourth paragraph of Ms. E's second commentary, she notes that Mr. D says that "he can't think of" a relationship in which he was getting angry at being a victim and then shows that the Perkins story tells of just such a relationship. In his final essay, Mr. D overlooks this point by keeping his feelings of being a victim separate from his anger. Ms. E's commentary continued by bringing in Mr. D's admiration of his father for being "in control of every situation." If, therefore, Mr. D lives up to his father-ideal, he would want to stress the anger and the action he took and not the victimization, so as to appear to remain in control. In class, however, he could not become openly angry with me for being absent, but he could see himself as the victim of my absence. This is just what made him uncomfortable for most of the second semester. Mr. D was less successful in understanding his work in terms of his need to identify with his father, second semester, than Ms. K was in understanding her need to identify with her mother.

When Mr. D discusses his literary response, he does notice that he identifies with victims, but he tries to qualify this identification by defining a clear distance between him and them. Commenting on his response to Faulkner's "Barn Burning," he wrote,

> I identified with the little boy. I wrote "I also think he (Faulkner) wanted us to take pity on the little boy," and "It's like you just can't help but feel sorry for him, a 10-year-old boy whose father is an asshole." Here I was identifying with the little boy, not because he was like me in any way, but that I felt sorry for him and therefore saw the story through his eyes in a sense."

In this citation, Mr. D moves back and forth saying that he identified with Sarty, saw the story "through his eyes," yet was not like him "in any way." Notice how difficult it is for him to say that he identified with a victim. He may be wishing to keep his own sense of his father apart, since identifying with a boy whose father was an "asshole" may call it into question. He uses what may perhaps be called the "good father," Faulkner, to authorize his distance from Sarty by advancing his view that Faulkner "wanted" him to take pity on Sarty. Mr. D goes on to cite two other instances in which he apparently identifies with victimized sons—Bailey in the O'Connor story and Davy Hutchinson in "The Lottery." In identifying with Bailey, it is not as a victim of the Misfit but of his mother: "I thought Bailey was the victim here because his mother was always continually nagging him." Although Davy Hutchinson's mother was the actual victim of the stoning, he identifies with the son because "it was the meanest thing that could have been done to the little boy, that someone would actually give him rocks to kill his mother with." These cases resemble the identification with Sarty in which Mr. D is also the champion of those victims, thereby not implicating himself in their fate. However, his identifications lend a certain masculine color to his responses, in that, on the one hand, he sees Bailey as the victim of a woman (he obviously does not see this woman, the grandmother, as a victim of any sort), and he overlooks the main female victim in "The Lottery." Undoubtedly, part of the reason Mr. D failed to really engage the substance of his partners' political commentary was that they were women. Particularly, to accept Ms. E's critique would have exacerbated his already uncomfortable sense of being a victim in this course.

Mr. D does have a noteworthy response to this critique, however. He agrees that his work shows a masculine gender bias. "Even all my identifications with victims were with males, so this category has a lot of strength." As further evidence he points to his "fascination with mechanical type objects," with having "owned and sold three cars," and to his main identification with "the image of the businessman, buying and selling assets." However, he regularly read the term "bias" in its pejorative sense, and arrives at the following view:

> For instance, in "The Grave," when we were asked to retell it as best we could, I seem to have been biased in my retelling. I spent at least half[12] the paper talking about the hunt itself, and then another quarter of the paper was about Paul's experience while skinning and cleaning the rabbit. I almost totally wrote about the story from Paul's point of view hardly spending any time writing about Miranda, even at the end of the story when she was the main character. I followed this pattern by writing, "It reminds her of the day she and her brother were out hunting and they killed a rabbit about to give birth." In this sentence the most important part was that the rabbit was about to give birth, yet you can see I was more interested in the masculine traits of hunting and killing, skimming over the feminine trait of birth. I did this again in essay #9 when I spent three fourths of the time writing about the father such as "So here is the father trying to take his family on a nice vacation," instead of talking about how the grandmother got the family in trouble, which eventually led to their deaths . . . In essay #8 (on "Araby") I identified with the male again when I wrote about how this young man wanted to get to know this young lady in the story. When I wrote about his attempts at meeting her I identified him directly to myself, stating,"When I think about this it reminds me of myself when I wanted to ask out my girlfriend T for the first time." Here I was directly relating the masculine trait of courtship of this boy and girl to myself and T, which proves

---

12. In this passage there are three uses of numerical fractional estimates. This is the last essay of the course. Recall that Ms. A had cited this sort of trait in her first commentary. Mr. D had given no thought to it throughout the year.

that my underlying identification was with the boy, even though I could have just as easily identified with the girl, correlating her with my girlfriend.

A salient feature of this passage is Mr. D's vague sense that his various masculine identifications were erroneous, that it was some sort of error to have identified with so many men. A clear suggestion of this is when he changes his own correct sense of what identification is in writing about "Araby" to suggest that he was biased after all in identifying with the hero. He failed to realize that he had already "correlated the girl with his girlfriend" with his original identification. The actual error occurred because he was trying to respond to his partners' observation that he ought to have *paid more attention* to the female characters. Ironically, because *he took the comments of his partners to be criticisms of his competence rather than of his values,* he actually offered a less competent judgment. The case is similar when he observes that he was "biased" in his retelling of "The Grave." In this course, the term "gender bias" was not actually used to describe a failure of objectivity due to gender but an addition of gender-identified value to any reading or perception of language. While this meaning partially applies to Mr. D's usage, the more important meaning for him is that having a bias is the same as being incompetent. It is not at all clear that the sentence he cites from his essay retelling "The Grave" emphasizes hunting over the pregnancy of the rabbit; furthermore, Mr. D was one of the few readers who actually did notice Miranda's moment of enlightenment as she and Paul discover that the slain rabbit was pregnant. But under the influence of his partners' critique he again does not see the substance of their point and instead admits to an imagined failure—not paying more attention to the "feminine trait of birth."

Although the concluding parts of his final essay come to the issue of success, it appears as the fourth or fifth item on the list of language features which he presents. Because he continues to rely on the seriation of his issues as his principle of organization, rather than on their thematic relatedness to one another, it looks as if neither this nor any other theme plays any special role in his work. His search was more for the "right" language features than for an integrated explanation of his various language-use strategies. He shows no inclination to discuss his relationship with his father, even though his partners saw it as pertinent, when he engages the matter of "success" in his writing. Here is the beginning of his "success" discussion:

> The next feature I will bring up is that of how my papers throughout the first and second semesters were affected by my drive for success. All my life I have been told by my family how you should try to do the best you can, never giving in for second best. So this attitude has given me a drive to be as successful as I can, both monetarily and in love.

Although this statement could be readily dismissed as sentimental, it is important to take it seriously and interpret it in connection with the success that Mr. D did achieve in this course. First, placing the success theme at the end of his last essay suggests his tacit acceptance of the importance placed on it by his two partners. Second, the use of the word "family" in this paragraph does generalize what his partners—and even he, in previous work—reported as an ideal of his father and not necessarily of the family as a whole. Third, the idea of being successful in love makes its first appearance here in Mr. D's work. His introduction of "love" thus extends his idea of success to cover all of life and raises new questions, though he also blurs it through overgeneralization. His despecifying move here is probably a response to the strong comments of his partners, who were quite bold in their willingness to name details—for example his desire to raise his grade second semester. The foregoing paragraph, therefore, is probably less an obfuscation than a self-justifying response to judgments that were less nice than true. It is as if he were saying (with some justification, in my view, given that grades really matter if they are going to be given), "What is wrong with going for the highest grade? It is a family ideal. What is wrong with wanting to be rich and successful? Doesn't everybody? And, the masculine perspective really does need criticism if it interferes with my competence in this course." Here, now, is the bulk of his discussion of "success," which immediately follows the paragraph cited above:

> This theme showed continually in the first semester. For instance, in essay #1 the question was, "Tell, in as much detail as you can, something important about yourself that you think would be helpful for everyone else to know." When I started to write this essay naturally I wrote about where I worked and what I had done, trying to show the class my accomplishments so far. I wrote, "When I was sixteen I was forced to rebuild the engine and in doing so prepared it for racing." In this quote I tried to do a couple of things. For one, I was telling them that I had owned more than one car, which I thought was impressive. Secondly, I was saying that at sixteen I was already successful at building racing engines for bracket cars. I also wrote, "the one thing which helped me learn about my hobby with cars was my job working at a local gas station." Here again I was letting everyone know that my work experience was already helping me in life."
>
> The same theme of my emphasis on success showed up in the second semester in a different way. Now when I was writing on literature, I was thinking and writing about other people's careers and accomplishments instead of my own, but nevertheless, I still thought it was important.
>
> Take essay #6 for example. When we were asked to write about a family argument, I wrote a great deal about their jobs, even though they were fighting over who should take care of their child. I brought in comments such as "But

if he also has a career I'm sure he also probably has been away a lot too"; "he just can't handle his wife having a career"; and "if they both have careers than they are going to have to share the work at home also." These are just a few of the examples in this essay which showed my concern about their jobs. I used the words "career," "jobs," and "work" a total of seven or eight times in this short essay, which proved that I probably lost out on the main idea about the child because I was too caught up in their work experience.

Also, in "The Rocking Horse Winner," I again looked into the story, picking out the facts about jobs, success, and money. I wrote about the mother: "She is always looking for another higher paying job even if it means being away from her children. We can take this as meaning she and her children's lives take a back seat to anything dealing with money." Here I was bringing up the idea that the mother was taking the idea of success to the limit, further than I ever hope to go, until it was messing up her life. I also look at Paul in the story in terms of determination for power. I wrote, "day and night he continually forced himself to come up with the next winner at the horse races, for this was his way of making money." Here I was stating that I thought the most important aspect of this character was his drive to be a winner, when I could have talked about how he was unfortunately deprived of love as a child, which led to his early death.

All of the topics I have talked about seem to deal with my determination for happiness. Happiness in the sense of being successful in my career and in love. And being able to achieve this goal through direct and certain obstacles . . . I feel these are the most important and controlling features of my language . . .

The last paragraph resumes the sentimental tone with which he began his discussion of success. However, here too certain terms seem important, namely "determination for happiness" and "controlling features." Ms. E had emphasized this feeling of "determination" to describe Mr. D's more intense attitude second semester, but here he alters the idea of "determination for success" to read "determination for happiness," happiness being a somewhat more universal wish than success. In the process, however, he creates a rather bizarre expression, perhaps somewhat oxymoronic, since there is something psychologically unrealistic about a person "determined" to be happy. In his attempt to incorporate his partners' views, he inadvertently enacts the awkwardness he is trying so hard to overcome in the cause of improving his work. "Controlling features" also alludes to the previously important idea of his wanting to "be in control" like he thinks his father is. To name controlling features probably means to him to be in control of the material in this course, something he was not quite able to feel he was. These phrases suggest how Mr. D is attempting new syntheses of language and idea, yet they are somewhat artificial in themselves and their sentimental context tends to undermine them.

In paragraph (2), Mr. D claims that his first lecture essay of the year shows the theme of success. While, in retrospect, it seems true that he really was trying to "show the class my accomplishments," his partners felt his emphasis was on his concern for work and the workplace and on his confidence. Mr. D assimilated the second-semester insight of his partners, and projected it back on the first semester in this last essay. In a sense, Mr. D is trying to claim that his attitude did not change. In this way he *reduces the ethical force* of his partners' point, which is to highlight his growth and change by relating his *verbal* use of "success" to the loss of confidence in his ability to work successfully in this course.

Each student in the course was able to discern some difference between the character of their literary response essays and that of the historical/experience essays written first semester. Mr. D's claim in this regard is that his response essays are "writing about other people's careers and accomplishments instead of my own." Though this seems plausible enough, compare it to Ms. K's perception that she was writing about herself *through the literature*. The otherness of literature is more distinct for Mr. D than it was for Ms. K, a difference in approach which, as I discussed in chapter 5, could be due to gender difference.[13] Because Mr. D objectifies the literature more decisively, he is unable to assimilate his feminine partners' judgment [given in paragraph (3) of Ms. E's second commentary] about how he handled the dialogue in essay 6. This judgment did not mention anything about Mr. D having omitted the child from his discussion of the argument (Mr. D actually did include attention to the child, perhaps more than I had in my own essay), but claimed that Mr. D simply took the man's part and showed a certain intolerance for feminine professional commitment. Mr. D instead remembered that both Ms. A and Ms. E discussed the child more prominently in their essays, and he showed in his deference to their opinion not as it appeared in their judgment of his essay on the dialogue but in the way they perceived the dialogue themselves. This is why he writes in his final essay, "I probably lost out on the main idea about the child because I was too caught up in their work experience." Mr. D is acknowledging the wrong thing; his partners

---

13. Mr. D's emphasis on the otherness of the literary figures is reasonable. He seems not to recognize, however, that when he writes about their "work," he is, like Ms. K, writing about himself "through" them. Ms. K also omitted important elements of the stories—the violence, usually—in discussing her response to them, but she did not seem to think this mattered, even when I, the teacher and her partner in subgroup, asked her about this feature of her response. I take this difference between Ms. K and Mr. D to speak in favor of the "deep" gender differences with regard to concern for objectification. Incidentally, Ms. K's not paying attention to the violence in the stories is even more significant in view of the fact that her career choice was law-enforcement.

did not criticize his interest in work, but the way he valued it and perhaps viewed it as something exclusively masculine. In this instance Mr. D's masculine values got in his own way in two senses—the excessive concern for objectivity in representing the dialogue, and the inability to perceive the critique of his socially masculine values.

His concern for objectivity also supervenes on his discussion of his essay on Lawrence's story. Whereas he actually fully discussed the story in terms of success, power, and being a winner—paying good attention to both mother and son—in reviewing his essay, he writes, "I could have talked about how he [Paul] was unfortunately deprived of love as a child which led to Q his early death." In their essays his partners did bring up the "need for love" theme, a thought only briefly given at the very beginning of the story, and viewed it as the story's underlying motive. Yet Mr. D's own reading is perfectly workable. Instead of reflecting on the difference in values between his and his partners' readings, he apologized for his own loss of accuracy, thereby exercising his membership in the collective by trying to maximize objectivity in reading rather than by testing new perspectives.

The relationship between Mr. D and his partners helps to show how peer colleagues become authority figures. While they presented similar observations, it made a difference that Ms. A's tone was milder and Ms. E's stronger. Mr. D undoubtedly felt pressure from them, but Ms. A's greater sympathy with him, as well as, probably, her use of obscene language, helped reassure him that he was among friends and thus helped him keep up his discipline in actually doing the work. I also think that the difference between Ms. A and Ms. E made them seem more like parents who are urging on their child similar values, but with different emphasis and styles. Their emphasis on love and family matters in both semesters' essays had a definite effect on what Mr. D thought he should be seeing in the literature and thinking about in his own life. Although he was generally reluctant to be specific about his family—I don't think he discussed his relationship with his mother at all—he seemed to want to credit his family with instilling in him the values of ambition, discipline, and hard work. In addition, because I was absent for that three-week period and offered no grade on any piece of work, he sensed a hiatus of authority in the class, and his somewhat exaggerated deference to his partners' perceptions of the stories was probably his attempt to fill this gap in authoritative guidance.

On the other hand, he was obviously ambivalent about crediting two feminine peers with pedagogical authority, and he showed little inclination to engage their ethical and political critiques. That is, he was unable to recognize the authority his partners derived from being representatives of a larger political movement. However, his strategy was not to challenge their views but to redouble his emphasis on the value of success, perhaps humanizing it with thoughts of love and happiness, values he knew his partners held. The regular and close meetings among the three of them helped to create an atmosphere of familiarity which enlarged the standard peer-group option of rejecting others' opinions, and so Mr. D felt he was not forced to follow their views, and instead worked out linguistic formulations—such as "determination for happiness"—that he thought accommodated both his own and their points of view. In respect to my own purposes as the teacher, it does not matter all that much that Mr. D could not take up the political critique or was unable to create an integrated analysis of his language use. While this definitely would have been a welcome development, it was just as important that Mr. D had the experience of feeling uneasy under the influence of the class and his peers, and that his relatively rigid strategies of doing schoolwork were criticized and challenged by his peers. It may also be the case that more highlighting of the connection between "subgroup gender politics" and cultural gender politics by us teachers may have made it more incumbent on Mr. D to answer his partners' political critique directly.

You may be wondering if this is a language process at all. In entertaining this question, imagine what the group discussions might have achieved had there been no regular and disciplined writing by the group. At best, the discussions themselves would be remembered for having produced in each person some sort of illumination. Perhaps specific verbal formulations by individuals might also have proved memorable. The missing element in such a procedure would be the *record of the ethical role* played by each person. The complicated array of mutual responsibilities would be utterly diffused, since no one would be able to go back and check what someone actually said, how someone put things and under what circumstances. Although writing is not all of the ethical action in a group, it transforms the otherwise elusive mutual intentionalities into a set of texts which can be publicly judged. Because *in every instance the use of language is a social act of ethical self-presentation,* the writing of essays disciplines the social process of coming to understandings.

The psychological material which gradually emerges, this short history of a person's relationships, family commitments, hopes and fears, is not a secret that has been dug out. It comprises the "ingredients" of language use for each person, things that could have different meanings and values in other contexts such as job applications or psychotherapy. The commonly defined subject of interest, our present-time language use, unifies these disparate psychological materials and memories into an ethical posture which names the contemporary growth stage of each person. No one element in this posture can be tagged as defining. It would be just as wrong to say that the "defining" ingredient in pizza is cheese as it would be to say that Mr. D's language is determined mainly by his desire to emulate and challenge his father or teacher.

We should not try to separate an ethical posture from language use, which necessarily always belongs to some public, some mutuality, some shared interest. Language is a form of ethical behavior, to be contrasted with violence, for example, which is the failure of language, or sex, which suggests the superfluity of language. In our culture, the more "ethical" name for "having sex" is "making love," a term which marks a common tendency among people to socialize sexual experience with ethically responsible talk. Similarly, the talk of language in this course is a step toward the *simultaneous ethical and epistemological handling of language*. As a result, the issues of authority and compliance enter prominently, as we have seen with Ms. K. But also, in this purely peer-group interaction, authority and compliance shared the stage with other matters like confidence, success, and gender, all of which became strong elements in the understanding of Mr. D's literacy style.

Admittedly, the use of the group of three in which to exercise, learn, and teach language is an especially difficult proceeding. However, I think the subject of language use requires it and can no longer be taught using individualistic classroom practices. Furthermore, our need is not to isolate language, but to see it as a form of intraspecies action, not unlike grooming in apes or singing in birds, which are tied to social and ecological features of the species' existence. Grooming is related to authority structures in ape communities. Singing is related to nest-building, flying, and surviving for birds. By the same token, language use is related to every social instinct in human beings, and to disregard this fact would be to transform language— the name and the thing—into something else.

Conclusion:
Literacy and Citizenship

In elementary school I was told that by doing well I would become a good citizen. My grandfather, who I remember as not being able to speak English, referred to his status here in America as a "citiness," as if confirming the claims of my teachers. I even felt myself to be more of a citizen than my father (who spoke English with an accent), whose claims to citizenship were even shakier to me because not only did he not understand baseball, he didn't consider it important. What I did not notice as a child was that both my grandfather and father were fully literate in Yiddish, so that my point of view was similar to those in California today trying to enact an "official language" law as a way of claiming hegemony over the far-flung Spanish-speaking community there. Unlike myself, my parents were bilingual (at least), and therefore had capacities for cultural and political participation that I am not likely ever to acquire. Their double-literacy perspective, I now see, added a certain depth of perception to their view of things analogous to the kinds of mental stereoscopy I have discussed in this book, and their citizenship, therefore, was no different from my own.

In spite of today's interest in literacy, however, there has been very little change since my childhood in what people think citizenship is. If anything, the ideal of citizenship has become even more anchored in individualism. In large part, the pursuit of literacy studies is moving forward (and being funded) as a potential contribution to the better functioning of "the business world." Ong's ideology (as discussed in chapter 3) and its basic distinction between orality and literacy represents the motives and purposes of establishmentarian support of literacy programs. Somewhat more troubling, perhaps, is that this way of thinking still inhabits and inhibits some of the more progressive ideas I discussed in this book. In these concluding remarks, I would like to give some sense of how this is the case, and then discuss a few other ideas and proposals that I think give some hope of teaching a genuine, socially grounded combination of literacy and citizenship in the classroom and in the academy.

316

Two items that I cited as being especially promising in the study of literacy are conversation as a fundamental element of language use and ethnography as a technique of research. First, take conversation.

As I discussed in chapter 6, Kenneth Bruffee has been one of those who, through his leadership in the use of peer collaboration, has helped breathe new life into our subject and our profession. He is one of those few scholars who has helped make community-belonging and group membership topics that are part of the public exchange of ideas about literacy. However, a closer look at his concept of community suggests he is perhaps partly influenced by Ong's social ideology.

A recent essay of his, "Critical Thinking as a Social Construct: A Critique of Basic Premises in Teaching Higher Order Reasoning Skills," cites M. L. J. Abercrombie's 1959 study *The Anatomy of Judgment* and describes one of her conclusions about how medical students diagnose: "what she found was that students who learned diagnosis collaboratively in this way acquired better medical judgment faster than individual students working alone." Bruffee then observes that Abercrombie did not have the language to explain this fact and that she left unanswered the question of "how human relationships influence the receipt of information about apparently nonpersonal events."[1] He considers, however, that she "drops an invaluable hint" when she writes "that the social process of learning judgment that she observed seems to have something to do with language and with interpretation.' " He observes that she "came tantalizingly close" to Rorty's understanding of knowledge as "socially justified belief": knowledge, that is, Bruffee continues, as an "internalized form of conversations carried on in the language of the relevant community." In this way, Bruffee sees conversation and interpretation—two fundamental language acts—as being bound up with community membership, where community interests determine conversation and conversational styles define the community, reciprocally. As an abstract statement of the connection between language use and community membership, it is consistent with the argument of this book.

Look at what happens, however, when he carries over the idea to the literacy classroom communities. In the same essay, he writes,

> What our students don't know (naturally) is how to converse in a language that is adequate and appropriate to *our* community's conventions, values, traditions, interests, and goals. That community, our community, is the one we want them to join and suppose it is in their best interest to join. Our job as teaching members of that community is to help those nonmembers, our students, become full-fledged, committed members of the knowledge community we represent.

1. Bruffee, "Critical Thinking" (cited in text), p. 9.

Talking this way about teaching thinking, then, changes the questions we ask as teachers. We no longer ask questions about getting into other people's heads or teaching how vs. teaching what. Instead we ask questions like, "How do I convince my students to want to soften their loyalty to and dependence upon membership in the communities they are now members of?" and "how can I make joining a new community as comfortable and fail-safe as possible?"[2]

In spite of his obviously generous intentions, the conversations Bruffee has in mind seem to be between members of a privileged community—the teachers—and members of underprivileged communities—students. The social task of teachers is to "convince" students to be less loyal to their own already established set of communities and, presumably, increase their loyalty to the teachers' communities. While these statements represent a clear and specific sense of the connections between social relations and conversation, the substance of what Bruffee is saying is unsettling.

First, the basic idea of conversation seems to have been overridden by the presupposition that it is better to be in the teachers' community than in whatever community the students are already in. If someone comes in my door and wants to engage in "conversation" about why I should become a member of the community of "born-again" Christians, I close the door, since I have no reciprocal wish to convince this person to become a Jew. Insofar as teachers wish to "convince" students of anything, it is our responsibility to understand what it is that our students want to "convince" us of. The conversation must go in two directions at once; otherwise it is a lecture, and the classroom remains just as Ong wishes it to remain—the scene where the privileged speakers speak and the unprivileged are silent, as when we hear a sermon.

Which leads to the second problem: the implied conception of what a community is impoverished. Although in medicine a consensus may be needed for a diagnosis, since at any one time only one treatment strategy is possible, a classroom does not require a consensus to function, and in fact probably functions better without one, since it is more important to identify the variety of viewpoints and pre-existing community memberships of both students and teachers than it is to achieve some unified opinion about the subject matter. Once the real memberships do emerge through announcements or different kinds of writing and sharing, then the different styles of knowing, including the teachers', may be identified in terms of memberships and citizenships, in which cases a few consensuses may very well be reached.

Finally, I'm not sure it does anyone any good to assume that students

2. Ibid., p. 31.

ought to be members of our community. Even those who may actually wish to become teachers will work in communities far different from ours and will have different purposes and be confronted by different problems. It is still an open question for students how they will create their social identities, and it would be quite a success for us simply to disclose the degree of openness of that question for each individual.

The legacy of Ong's ideology is a fundamentally abstract and diminished sense of what a community is, a sense found in more or less the same reduced form in Stanley Fish's idea of an "interpretive community.[3] As Ludwick Fleck described it, it is not the knowledge that defines the community, but that, simultaneously and in a "double" way, communities develop knowledge *and* knowledge takes in community members. To speak of communities, one has to have in mind a group of specific real people and not an abstract category such as "those who believe in New Criticism." One must be able to locate communities as they are actually living and functioning—writing, teaching, getting paid, creating relationships, and achieving public identities. Neither Fish nor Bruffee considers these essential aspects of communities, and both, I fear, presuppose the traditional hierarchical arrangement in their discussions of what a classroom can actually become.

The interest in and use of ethnography does present some kind of response of this ideological inertia. As I discussed in chapters 3 and 6, anthropologists and other researchers studying how real people actually live from day to day have discovered that they can't really learn anything about other people until, in a sense, they are actually "in their shoes." Those following Shirley Heath have made some direct efforts to introduce ethnography in the literacy classroom,[4] to view writing itself as an ethnographic process, and therefore to teach literacy as a subject through which "mere" students can have an impact on the processes of formal research.

But I'm wondering if something more isn't needed. In Heath and Branscombe's 1985 essay, " 'Intelligent Writing' in an Audience Community: Teacher, Students, and Researcher,"[5] they cite a letter to Heath by a student, Eugene:

3. If you are familiar with Fish's work, you know that he spends considerable time arguing that each individual critic arrives at his or her reading of a text under the influence of whatever "interpretive community" he or she happens to be in. Although this argument has merit, it is also true that Fish never names an actual "interpretive community" nor even gives an example of how to find one. In fact, in Fish's work, the term does not name anything that exists in this, the one and only real world, but does name an idea whose only purpose, in Fish's argument, is to deauthorize any single individual's opinion, his own included.

4. See "Ethnography and the English Classroom," *English Record* (1983), for example.

5. In Sarah Freedman, ed., *The Acquisition of Written Language* (Norwood, New Jersey: Ablex, 1985), pp. 3–32.

I may be wrong but I don't think so. You see Ms. Branscombe is having all of us write to you. But in your last letter you said that you would only write to some of us and I think that you should write to all of us. Because all of us are writing to you. If you don't want to write to me than [sic] I want [won't] write to you or take any field notes. I think you will agree with me if you dont then put yourself in our shoes and if you still don't then let me know.

In commenting on this letter Heath and Branscombe offer the following thoughts:

> Eugene wanted a personal voice communicating to him, either through individual letters or specific acknowledgement, that certain information was in response to the questions he had asked. He and others of the class resisted moving away from the highly personalized here-and-now written "conversations" they had had with the upperclassmen. Yet by the end of the term, they had learned to negotiate through oral discussion the meaning of the depersonalized and decontextualized passages of Heath's letters.[6]

As I read these two passages, I get the feeling that the ethical issue Eugene raises is valid—namely his desire for reciprocity in the exchange of letters— and that perhaps Heath and Branscombe might have reflected on it at greater length and given it more weight. Even when one seeks to teach the collective negotiation of "depersonalized and decontextualized" writing, Eugene's desire to continue the correspondence might still have played a productive role, since that desire came from his own literacy style. I can see that it was not possible for Heath to keep up a personal correspondence with every single student. But if Eugene's research motivation had been rooted in an evenhanded relationship of conversational exchange, it is reasonable for him to want that exchange to continue. I wonder if it is really possible or desirable to subtly urge students who do not naturally value depersonalization and decontextualization, to nevertheless move toward these language use styles without, at the same time, retaining the interpersonal basis of their school effort. Perhaps the style of literacy they already have might lead to new research techniques altogether, just as Evelyn Keller has implied that had women been more prominent in the development of science, science might be quite different from the way it is now. I am afraid that the pedagogical attitude might become, "Aha, ethnographic techniques are the key to the teaching of academic literacy—all our problems are solved," instead of, as I hope, "ethnographic thinking can help transform the classroom into a place where human relationships will govern the use and study of language." I think Heath and Branscombe are trying to promote this latter attitude, but I

6. Ibid., p. 24.

wonder if the values of depersonalization and decontextualization of writing do not continue to be too influential a guiding ideal in their work.

In a recent dissertation at Indiana University, entitled "The Social Uses of Language in the Classroom" (1986), Tom Fox has noted another feature of ethnographic work that seems to require decontextualization: the concept of the ethnographer as someone whose job it is to "inscribe culture, not change it."[7] Geertz, who uses the word "inscribe" in quotation marks, does not actually juxtapose inscribing with not changing; however, Fox is concerned about the seemingly nonpolitical sense of ethnographic writing that Geertz is presenting. Consider the thought that one can write about something without actually changing it. If Geertz is advocating the researcher's active involvement in the culture of interest, how can this researcher's effort—the inscription of the subject-culture in our own culture—not change both? Both the researcher's joining of the new community and the writing about it, is already a change in that community relative to both the researcher's community and the one being studied. The value of ethnographic work to begin with is that it accepts social change as being endemic to the research process. To consider research all by itself as the attempt to achieve objective knowledge is the ideal Ong advocates in his desire to reach a purified language.

In reading Heath, Fox notes that she "seeks understanding and interaction, but does not seek cultural change."[8] He argues that her analysis shows how "issues related to power, privilege, and opportunity" must necessarily be part of her subject, even though she tends not to treat them directly. Here are his thoughts about why her work presupposes the need for social change:

> Heath states that the child-rearing habits of Trackton and Roadville do not adequately prepare their children for school. But it is painfully obvious that hierarchies of social class and race correspond to success in school. Trackton kids do worst in school; Roadville kids do badly, but slightly better than Trackton kids, and mainstreamers do better than both communities. Is the correlation between wealth, race and performance in school a coincidence? . . . the fact that race is complicated by class (and vice versa) doesn't mean that it [race] is not an issue. Do mainstream blacks do as well as mainstream whites? . . . Her analysis and generous use of examples seems to indicate that language learning habits reflect and reproduce the degree of intervention parents feel they can make in the world outside of their community.[9]

7. Geertz, *Interpretation of Cultures*, p. 19, quoted in Tom Fox, "Social Uses of Language in the Classroom," Ph.D. dissertation, Indiana University, 1986 [Norwood, New Jersey: Ablex, 1989].

8. Fox, p. 56.

9. Ibid., pp. 54–55.

Fox's considerations are related to Eugene's concern: insofar as Heath was a member, in Eugene's view, of an external community, she inadvertently inhibited Eugene's attempt to join it—to intervene in the world outside his own community, to permit his style of language exchange a greater voice. Therefore, the style of decontextualized writing that Heath and others among us may value is, ironically, reflected in Eugene's feeling that *he and his community* has been decontextualized. The larger political burdens of the society seem to enter directly into the details of how people talk, write, and think. I think we should ask if the idea of decontextualized writing may not include wishes for a decontextualized community, wishes, for example, for such familiar ideals as the self-sufficiency of small-town life, of the big-city neighborhood, the state, the geographic region, or for other isolationist social attitudes.

It is true that, historically, there have always been good reasons for communities as well as nations to maintain an isolationist posture. Two recent studies, however, treat two different kinds of communities, themselves isolated from the world at large by culture and gender, but which nevertheless present models of language use and collective purpose that could successfully neutralize the inertial effects of the traditional individualist ideology of literacy. The first is Samuel Heilman's 1983 sociological study of Talmud study circles entitled *People of the Book*, and the second is Anne Ruggles Gere's 1986 discussion of women's writing groups in America, which appeared in her book *Writing Groups: History, Theory, and Implications.*

In *People of the Book*, Heilman presents a sociological inquiry into a relatively old study convention among religiously observant Jews—the Talmud study circle, whose principal activity is *Lernen*, which means both literally and metaphorically, learning—though a better English translation might be something like "active, organized study of the law." The interest of the group Heilman studied was avocational, so that the group's constituents were ordinary people who held nonacademic jobs. Periodically, sometimes as a Sabbath activity, a group of seven or eight would meet under the tutelage of a rabbi—one who really knew the texts better than anyone, and whose job it was to teach them to anyone in the community who wished to learn. In keeping with orthodox law, only men belonged to such groups, while most of the time women considered it an honor to help make it possible for the men in their family to study. This gender segregation, of course, is like the gender segregation in all other religions, in which the privileged roles are played by men.[10] There is no way to excuse this feature of the

---

10. It is probably not a coincidence, in this light, and in view of my discussion of the "game" metaphor in chapters 1 and 2, that Heilman, in the following quotation, describes the study circle exchange as a "game."

study circles. However, the style of language exchange it represents was and is common, historically, among East European Jews of both genders, as Deborah Tannen's study, *Conversational Style*, suggests. Also, as I assume throughout this book, a discourse style once used by only one gender may and ought to be integrated into the discourse styles of the other.

Here is Heilman's description of the group's activity:

> . . . active participation and spontaneous involvement [this is the term that Tannen also uses to characterize the style; she amends it slightly to read "high involvement."] from everyone present is an expected part of the game. During the *lernen*, a world of words, somehow anchored to the text, is socially constructed. Within this world, the talk is variously keyed or patterned around expressive reading of the page, translation and explanation, conversational exchange, amplifying questions and answers, echoing and cueing, and language switching (between the language of the text and the vernacular of the *lerners*). Some of the talk is conventionalized speech, either tied formally to the text and its explication or anchored in the social exigencies of relations in public. At other times the talk seems freer, a reflection of the warp and woof of social and cultural life, a part of the spectacle. In this second sort of conversation, "what talkers undertake to do is not to provide information to a recipient but to present dramas to an audience."[11]

This is a group situation that seems, to the naked eye, so to speak, to represent many of our aims to create a dynamic subject of literacy. It is a purely verbal situation; in any one situation, the teacher and the group follow the same rules of reading; involvement is expected from everyone in the group—that is, everyone must experience and "enact" membership in some way, not just declare it. Two languages are used, thus providing at least two separate contexts of understanding; two modes of talk are used— explication conventions and conversational performances; and there is a common purpose as well as space for individual action, expression, and growth. This description, however, does not really convey what the deep context of activity actually is. We are dealing, that is, with an event whose vitality and power come from a history and a set of values that are part of the inner being of each member and from a sense of belonging to others that is far stronger than what a weekly study group suggests. For example, the event takes place because these people consider it historically necessary, valuable, and pleasurable to master the laws of social life as best one can, and to express their religious devotion through this mastery. It is, to them, a period of contact with what is most important in life—the law and its history

11. Samuel C. Heilman, *The People of the Book* (Chicago: The University of Chicago Press, 1983), pp. 113–114.

of interpretation and reinterpretation. It is an inquiry into how they came to be what they are and a reflection on how one ought to behave in consequence of this knowledge. It is a chance to make contact with other learned people and to learn ever more about how to be learned. It is a time to renew a collective and individual sense of identity that each of these men *already had when they entered this group.* And, on top of all these sober purposes, it is a time to enjoy one another and the two languages they use and understand. The only contemporary analogue I know of that somewhat resembles this special concentration of serious intensity and pleasure is intercollegiate athletics. Of course, the difference is that athletics usually proceeds in the cause of escaping history, while the study groups immerse themselves in it.

Heilman is careful not to extract the event from this generally unseen historically grounded context. But if we saw it only as a procedure, a method, or a style of study, we would be missing the point. The kind of knowledge each group member acquires depends not simply on his participation in the group practice, but on his unquestioned feeling of belonging to the Jewish people and its history. What is learned under these circumstances cannot be described as mastery of the text of law alone. Rather, to know these texts is to have made one's own connections with them in the contexts of history and of community value. To have made contact with these texts is an instance of fulfilling divine commandment and is a public validation of one's *citizenship*—not just one's membership—in the community and in the Jewish people. The experimental token of this citizenship is the feeling of solidarity with the thought style—the paradigm of knowledge and language use—and with the thought collective[12]—the specific group of real people who carry on the study in this and other groups.

With this example, I have tried to suggest that the context of practicing literacy for us teachers and students in the majority secular community is as socially complicated and tied to past practices and beliefs as it is for the members of the Talmud study circle. It is clear, in this light, that even conversation as a new guiding idea for the study of literacy is just as bound to specific community contexts as was the individualist approach to literacy. Productive conversations just will not take place unless the classroom membership can find consequential reasons for belonging and grounds for an internalized sense of citizenship analogous to that of the amateur Talmud scholars. One way of finding such reasons and grounds is to remind ourselves of at least part of the history of group activity in this country, a task undertaken by Anne Ruggles Gere in her book on writing groups.

12. Here I think I am using these two terms in the same sense that Fleck described, and as is discussed in chapter 2.

Early in her book Gere observes that most composition teachers would place the origin of writing groups somewhere in the 1960s. But in documenting how such groups are traceable back to at least the eighteenth century in the United States, she offers the following observation: "Writing groups are new *and* old."[13] While this point may not seem spectacular, it reflects an essential thought, namely, that however new and enlightened we think our own initiatives are, they are themselves historically rooted in political interests that existed long before we did. It will pay us, as the presumed and responsible leaders, to make contact with that history and thereby to understand our own level of citizenship as a first step in socializing the literacy classroom.

Gere reports that throughout the history of language education in America, there was a constant drumbeat signaling the superior value of such styles of classroom functioning, but an equally constant and much louder voice, coming from such establishmentarian institutions as Harvard, which confined the teaching of writing to "little more than instruction in grammar and the mechanics of writing, motivated almost solely by the idea of superficial correctness."[14] Although Gere does not come right out and say it, she provides considerable evidence that writing groups were not taken seriously because of the dominant social value of individualism, which uncritically invokes hierarchical thought patterns and automatically assumes an essentialistic approach to language as an isolated, noncommunal, noncollective phenomenon. Her book shows that those who had the most academic influence—which she implies was not even a majority—simply imposed these values through prestigious institutions exercising autocratic authority. In her section on the history of writing groups, she brings up dozens of instances of university writing groups—made up only of men—which existed only on the periphery of university life, and which popped up in spontaneous alliances, though without an inner sense of social and political solidarity with the university leadership. In contrast to the Talmud study circles, which arose with rabbinic encouragement and which shared access to the texts with the rabbis, the university writing groups were on their own a *de facto* fifth column or splinter group.

In reviewing the history of writing groups outside the academic institutions, Gere focuses on the hundreds of such groups formed by women starting about the middle of the nineteenth century. She outlines how the masculine-dominated fields of medicine and theology pressured women out of organized cultural pursuits until women finally succeeded in establishing the public legitimacy of merely gathering in the service of their own needs:

13. Anne Ruggles Gere, *Writing Groups: History, Theory, and Implications* (Carbondale: Southern Illinois University Press, 1987), p. 4.

14. Ibid., p. 25. From Albert Kitzhaber, "Rhetoric in American Colleges, 1850–1900" (1953), p. 120.

Women's clubs frequently expressed purposes and carried out literacy exercises similar to those of college literary clubs, but the political motivations behind women's literacy societies differed. For nineteenth century women, literary clubs provided one of the few socially acceptable alternatives to domestic imprisonment, while for young male students it constituted one of several forms of self-enrichment.[15]

Here is a statement of Jane Cunningham Croly, the founder of one of those societies, Sorosis, which called for membership. She sought those who were

> hungry for the society of women, that is, for the society of those whose deeper nature had been roused to activity, who had been seized by the divine spirit of inquiry and aspiration, who were interested in the thought and progress of the age, and in what other women were thinking and doing.[16]

These clubs embodied a combination of political, social, personal, and, probably, religious feeling in their purposes and reasons for forming. Unlike the masculine writing groups at the periphery of the university, these groups mattered in the larger contexts of society in ways similar to how the Talmud study circles mattered. Their sense of themselves was related to their sense of the total constituency, their wish not to oppose the men but to share in the "divine spirit of inquiry and aspiration," as well as to see their own lives in a more individuated sense. One piece of evidence for their concern for the character of the total society, Gere reports, is that "in 1933 the American Library Association credited women's clubs with initiating seventy-five percent of the public libraries in the United States."[17] Women's clubs showed how to combine self-interest, local interest, and public interest in the same movement and in this way unified literacy and citizenship.

Another salient value of these clubs, now more visible in the light of work by Heath and Tannen, is the interdependence of oral and written uses of language—a value also present in the Talmud study circles. Gere cites one nineteenth-century club member reporting that reading papers at a club "gave us the habit of expressing ourselves on paper; they taught us not to fear the sound of our own voices."[18] This interesting statement might easily be read as a *non sequitur*. Yet it is clear that the assumption behind "expressing oneself on paper" is that it requires and goes along with hearing the sound of your own voice, an assumption that I use every time I prepare a paper for public presentation: the moment of writing, while technically

15. Gere, p. 4.
16. Ibid., p. 42.
17. Ibid., p. 44.
18. Ibid.

separate from the moment of reading, may actually be understood as the same moment. From a social point of view, the moments of my writing and your reading make up the *same moment of literacy*—of vision, speech, thought, and motor action, of private behavior and public sharing. The unity of larger political, personal, and practical aims that these women felt is not coincidentally related to the intuitive unity of the oral and the written which we all share, and which is routinely demonstrated in most collective procedures in the literacy classroom.

It takes no great imaginative leap to see the oral and the written as mutually implicated, and we ought to pursue teaching and research with this understanding in mind. It will be harder, on the other hand, to associate ourselves with the history that Gere outlines, since to do so imposes on us an awareness of our political responsibility, which may require those of us who are more peacably inclined to nevertheless oppose what most English department chairs and most composition program directors will recommend. Both the Talmud study circles and the women's literary groups functioned in opposition to an established style (though not necessarily a majority style). Though we no longer hold this value, gender-segregated groups now show us certain political facts of our lives and provide early models, ironically, of how we ought to organize integrated groups. I juxtapose these two sorts of groups as historical examples of serious collective initiative; but I also wish to show some grounds for intergender solidarity, and for recognizing that while each gender may be different, each is also *like and with* the other and shares an intuitive sense of mutual implication.

The aim of socializing the classroom and integrating it with the academy, then, requires adapting ourselves, for the foreseeable future, to living and working in peaceful (but unrelenting) opposition to community ignorance, social inertia, ideological superstition. Tom Fox's dissertation gives further insight into the phenomenological character of the opposition as well as what it might take to overcome it. Fox shows, first, that almost all of the students assume traditional individualist values, namely, that they are in the literacy classroom to improve their individual skill, and that the unquestioned path to that end is to secure, in a one-to-one relationship with the teacher, either authorized approval or official instruction in a problem-solving way, to achieve the real ultimate end—a high grade. His announcement that his class would study the ethnic, gender, and class-generated accents on each student's use of language, was interpreted by students to mean that that was the path to "better writing," rather than, as Fox intended, that it was a paradigmatically new subject matter. This means that it will take Fox, me, and all of us who think we ought to do this, years of teaching in this way for students to finally *expect* a revised subject matter united with a politically generous community.

Yet the picture Fox paints may be somewhat less bleak. While he is duly skeptical of his several instances of "success" (could they be mere compliance, he wonders?), he is nevertheless able to cite texts produced by students whose new awareness cannot be wholly understood as attempts to please the teacher. What the students are writing about obviously matters to them and clearly demonstrates both their sense of location in the class as well as in society. Here is one of the more convincing instances. Ms. N, a young black student, is reflecting on her history of writing experiences:

> While growing up I use to love to write. I wrote down all my feelings and thoughts. This was the best way I could express myself. I use to take my time and make sure that all my commas were in the right place and all my sentences were complete ones and not run ons. I always had to go back and double check and sometimes triple check that all my grammar were correct. I never could figure out why I made so many grammar errors and I knew all the rules for them and what to use and when to use them. Since I've been to college my whole outlook on writing has changed. Its gotten to the point where instead of me actually sitting down, thinking the situation or problem out that I have to write about, I just write what I feel the teacher might want to hear. Yes, I even done this in my class with you . . . Writing has become like an enemy to me lately.[19]

While Fox observes with some disappointment, "I didn't achieve the influence I had wished,"[20] I wonder what more influence he could have had on this student. To finally come out and announce that she has been compliant, to finally say to the English teacher—not to a friend or other confidant, but to the white male English teacher himself—that "writing has become like an enemy to me lately," isn't this the first and the essential step that every student must take? Isn't this the moment of conviction in students we are all waiting for?

Ms. N had written a series of essays which described her ability to adapt her language use in different social environments—the street, the family, the school. Fox shows how this ability to adapt is due in part to being a black schoolgirl bussed into a white school and feeling pressured by her parents to continue their own struggle to be recognized as ordinary citizens. Finally Ms. N arrives in college where the cheerful white male teacher announces his high-minded program to a class that is all white—but for Ms. N and another black student. Perhaps Fox would have considered himself more successful had Ms. N come right out and said that he was the enemy, not writing. I don't know. It is to me quite an insight for the students to blame writing,

19. Fox, "Social Uses of Language," p. 192.
20. Ibid., p. 193.

because it seems very much to me to have been the enemy, especially in the sense that Ong extols it as Western Man's path to Arnoldian excellence. Fox describes why writing is the enemy by noting how Ms. N already "knew" that black literacy styles are

> evidence of inabilities: the inability to analyze, the inability to be logical, the inability to concentrate, the inability to be serious, the inability to work hard, the inability to be precise.[21]

The fact is that Ms. N, like countless other black students, already entered school with a rich style of literacy in which writing was just not as important as it is to whites. As Shirley Heath's work documents, that well-developed, sophisticated style is immediately undermined and dismantled in primary school. Instead of Ms. N having become a teacher of her own literacy style to others, she became yet again a victim of the white majority's naive and constricting ideas of linguistic decorum. To defend against the personal and social damage this has done, Ms. N enters all classrooms with suspicion: "Yes, I even done this in my class with you." Although it may have been disappointing to Fox to have to see this observation, it is nevertheless an authentic mark of the political scene in Fox's class. The student got up the courage even for a moment to name the situation as it was defined by *her* social history and *her* school experience: writing has become like an enemy. Isn't the courage to name things as they really are in our lives what we mean by literacy? Isn't the reduced citizenship of this student apparent when she decides that writing is the enemy, and isn't that citizenship momentarily regained when she *writes* this fact, making it available to others in the class? Every mode of concealment we find in our classes—particularly the kind practiced by us teachers—is likewise a sign of reduced citizenship and of a resigned and often cynical compliance. Fox gives many examples of such concealment in the name of gender and class as well as of race, as he patiently urges the students to write a new essay which conceals less, and slowly a few more students name—disclose—a few more of the thoughts they at first dared not present in public. Fox's work shows that most students really believe that they must conceal or deny the true terms of their citizenship in the class and in the society, that school is no place to interrogate their "background" or their history. Because of this belief, which most of us teachers have also grown up holding, we—teachers and students—have learned not to name or identify in school most of the consequential things in our lives, and we have few ways of teaching others a literacy that shows conviction, motivation, and social and political purpose.

---

21. Ibid.

But Fox's work also shows that the study of literacy is an inquiry into how to say what matters to other people that matter. It shows how teachers and students have always been spontaneously important to one another, but the deep, monastic, monadic, and individualist urge to depersonalize and decontextualize language use gradually paralyzes people's natural tendency to let human relationships shape language and knowledge. It shows, finally, that to socialize the classroom is to teach that each member has already brought a living literacy to class, and that this literacy has been brought to be named and renamed in collaboration with others. The classroom becomes a public place where each member sees that what each says both emerges from a history and participates in one, where literacy is created by the exchange of language and the common pursuit of social purpose.

Throughout this book, I have reviewed a variety of double perspectives in the hope of showing their value as instruments of thought. However, it would be wrong to assume that I have some abstract standard of correct thinking about language. My concern with these issues began in the practical problems of everyday work in the classroom, with frustrations that I and some of my colleagues and students have shared with one another over the past twenty-five years or so. My concern similarly has been with what Dorothy Dinnerstein described as systematic failures of communication between men and women, with squabbles, hostilities, and struggles which seem to descend painfully on individuals, families, communities, and societies all at once. I have gradually come to see these pedagogical and intergender frustrations as having a great deal in common, and that one of the keys to their amelioration is to become more enlightened about the simplest initiative one human being can take with another—talk. This book aims, first and last, for practical results in the classroom, in the academy, at home, and in public. It tries to see language as everyone's subject, not just the school's. If language is not soon enfranchised by recognition of its social shape, if the classroom is not soon understood as the scene of regular, consequential, even urgent human action, then all the knowledge we have traditionally valued is in danger of falling into the hands of gunsmiths, bureaucrats, and those who still believe that slavery and freedom can exist in the same society.

APPENDIX A

Instructions for Final Essays, 1981–1982

The aim of the final essay is to come up with a substantive, well-documented discussion of how you use language, spoken and written. The essay should pay attention to the personal relationships and other social circumstances where your use of language plays a significant role.

The main source for this essay is your written work in this course. But also quite important is your use of language in class—to the teacher, your colleagues, and your subgroup—your speech among those you live with here, and your verbal interactions with your parents and family while you are in this course. All situations in which you speak or write are potentially relevant to your work in this essay.

While you are studying your own language, you should also be studying the work of the two others in your subgroup. One of the main reasons for our working in small groups is that when you study your language, looking at other people's language closely makes it easier to spot analogous features of your own work.

Here are eleven general areas in which to look for language patterns in your and your partners' work. There can be more and other categories. The ones mentioned are meant to provide you with an early sense of the general direction of this course. However, you are urged to find new categories or even do without categories, so long as you are able to present disciplined understanding of your and your partners' language.

You should try out these categories as soon as you start work in this course. In this way you will begin to train yourself in the analysis of language use. As you become familiar with the task of language analysis, you will find it easier to use your imagination, and then to collaborate with your partners.

The first six topics below are meant to guide you in finding the patterns in *what you write about*, while the last five topics should help you study the *actual language*. You will know that you are "catching on" when you begin to see connections and similarities between the patterns of the first six areas and those of the last five.

PREFERRED TOPICS. Most of the essay assignments will not specify a topic in the traditional sense; *you* will have chosen the actual subject matter. When you start work, look to see if you preferred to write on a certain topic rather than some other

331

one, like sports, or school, or career, or social life, for example. Pay attention to if and how these preferred topics made you use certain kinds of language, and to whether your language grows out of a long interest in these topics—like someone who uses sports language because that person was interested in sports for as long as he or she can remember. Also, consider if there were some topics that were very important to you, but you did not write about them because they were "too" important or "too" private.

RELATIONSHIPS IN YOUR FAMILY. The essay topics will not tell you which of your family relationships to discuss; you will have mentioned those relationships which you think best suit your purpose. Make notes on which family relationships you do discuss and observe how your discussion of them relates to your language you now use. For example, you may have learned certain expressions from your parents, siblings, grandparents, or other relatives, or, you find you speak in certain ways just because they are different from the ways people in your family speak. In examining these relationships (as they appear in your work), try to discern *motives* and *reasons* for your usages; for example, you use certain phrases because you feel that is how to deal with your parents best. Always bear in mind that your language, like everyone else's, began in a family situation, and it is therefore likely that you will find some of the origins of your present language by thinking about how you spoke in your own home.

RELATIONSHIPS WITH TEACHERS. Teachers are usually the first "outsiders" with whom one develops a relationship. In various ways, we are influenced by our teachers, in the past and now, and they often contribute, in ways we are not aware of at the time, to our language repertoire. Discover if you cite such relationships, and then see if you can tell if they were the occasion of some new development in your language. Also see if your language use with your teachers of today reveals interesting features that you don't see in your language use with others.

RELATIONSHIPS WITH PEERS. All of us "pick up" a great deal from whatever peer group we are in. From preschool age on, we often consciously emulate the language of our peer groups. By searching through your work for allusions to your experiences in various peer groups at any age, see if you can tell if and/or how these groups influenced how you now use language. At the same time see if you can tell from how you speak to others in the class and in your own subgroup, what connections there are between your language use and your relationship with these peers. Typical peer groups include living groups, teams, clubs, student organizations, religious groups, music groups, and so on.

RELATIONSHIPS WITH STRANGERS. We have certain ways of speaking to those with whom we do business—store managers, the bursar, service station people, and so on. Sometimes we are friends with such people, but most of the time, even if we deal with them for many years, they remain "strangers" to us. See if you cite any such relationships and what forms your language takes when dealing with such people. Do you have a conventional language, or do you think you are just as free as when you speak with friends and family? In what sense is your language connected to how much you "really trust" a business person? What sort of language do you use to someone sitting next to you at a game? When you meet a stranger how do you judge how to speak to him or her?

EXPRESSIONS OF FEELING. This area covers two things—how you announce feelings directly ("I was enraged") and how they appear in your language indirectly, through the expression of hesitations, doubts, emphases, certainties, or judgments. How does your language express how sure you are, and how confident you are of what you are saying? You can feel confident without feeling sure, as when you articulate doubt confidently. Also involved here are considerations of diplomacy and social decorum. Try to determine how you and perhaps others regulate the difference between what you are "really" thinking and what you write or say. How much of your feeling comes out "by itself" and to what extent are you able to control what is written "between the lines"?

ESSAY STRUCTURE. This generally refers to how you start and end essays, and how you arrive at your "point." Most people have habits of starting and ending and are not aware of what these habits are. After identifying such habits in your work, try to explain why you think they are as they appear. Only part of your explanation will be, "this is the way I was taught." Many people are taught things and still do it their own way. If you think you write the way you were taught, see if you think it was a good way, or if you were just following orders, so to speak. Try to note connections between how you start and end written work and how you start and end conversations or letters. Also, check your paragraph structure for starting and ending habits, not to discover how competent you are, but to find what things appear in your language automatically. Consider if you tend toward long or short paragraphs, or if you purposely vary them according to some principles. Is there anything useful or natural about your way of writing an essay?

ESSAY LENGTH. This is not just the physical length. How much explanation of things do you naturally feel is necessary? How do you know when things are clear? How much mental revision do you go through before writing something down, or before saying something? How often do you revise the previous sentence with the next sentence, and how do you decide that something "new" is going to be said? Some people try to make every sentence count; others use larger units of thought. Try to find times when you write something and then crossed it out, and see if there are any patterns to your crossings-out. What are the connections between the length of your essays and your standards of how much to talk, say, and reveal?

SENTENCES. Inspect your work for preferred sentence types. Almost no one writes only one sort of sentence, but most people use only a few kinds and tend to stress some over others: simple versus compound; conditional versus indicative; subjunctive versus declarative, and so on. You may like sentences that start with "and" or "but"; or you may habitually link clauses with those words. In general, you have to decide *whether* a particular group of sentences is a type or not, since it may not be a type when someone else uses it; you can check such things while studying the work of others. To determine sentence types you have to concentrate and re-read your work many times. If necessary, you can even make a chart, or otherwise count the types in each essay. In most cases, we are so used to our own sentence types that it seems strange to ask whether such-and-such is a type. We think, rather, "well, how else would you say it?"

PREFERRED WORDS AND PHRASES. For example, everyone uses "seems." But it is necessary to understand how *you* use it. Look at all your vocabulary and try not only to pick out the words that reappear, but ones that are used less often yet in an especially important way. Look at classes or types of words—the ordinary classes like nouns, but also other sorts of classes like "simple" versus "complicated" words. Try to discern characteristic word combinations, like pairs of adjectives, or participial sentence openers. Note when you depart from what is otherwise "ordinary language." Some people will use slang most of the time and then come up with words like "trenchant" or "pusillanimous." Why should this happen? If you count certain kinds of words, be sure to *interpret* whatever statistics you find.

TECHNICAL PROFICIENCY. What is your competence in the traditional areas of spelling, punctuation, and grammar? Decide how important such competence is to you. If, for example, you are a habitually poor speller, try to explain why this is the case, and what it may have to do with the other areas of your language you are studying. Some people write fluently and articulately but have little to say. Some have simple vocabularies but seem to use language in a forceful way. What connections are there between your level of technical competence and your degree of enjoyment of speaking and writing? When you admire someone who uses language "well," what are you actually seeing in that person?

APPENDIX B

Ms. K's Essay 12

Question 1

Give your affective and associative response to the story [Shirley Jackson's "The Lottery"]: your strongest feelings, your general feelings, etc. Give relationship analogies to elaborate on these feelings; indicate if and to what extent you identified with those in the story.

Ms. K 1

Well, how *would* someone react to this story? I have mixed feelings about it. Of course, it's a shame that a society would go to such extremes just to follow a tradition. Its kind of like when no one questions authority. No one questioned the practicing of their tradition. I'm really amazed that something like that could really take place in the first place and then for it to continue is unbelievable. It really makes me kind of mad that people could be so yielding and unresponsive to what was going on. I found it interesting that Mrs. Hutchinson's closest friends take extra efforts in the process of stoning her.

I don't know if I can say I identify with anyone in the story. Of course, I know or have felt like the whole world has turned on me—and the kind of helpless desperation you feel. The way in which Mr. Summers took care of the whole situation I could understand. He wanted to get the job done and over with with the least amount of hassles. His way of handling the unpleasant task which "had" to be done reminds me of what I do while contemplating house cleaning or something.

In the relationship aspect—I can't understand how anyone could stand by and watch let alone participate in the killing of a close relative or friend. Even Mrs. Hutchinson's little kids do as they are told—by throwing stones at their own mother. I'm sure these people felt *something* as they found out their wife, mother, or friend was going to be killed. What they choose to do in response to it is just a whole different story. It would just really tick me off if I couldn't make people see what they were actually doing. If I couldn't make them see the way I felt about the whole situation (kind of like how Mrs. Hutchinson probably felt). If I couldn't convince them of how stupid they were acting.

Question 2 [twenty-five minutes later]

The story is often understood as an allegory of the fact that every community has a scapegoat whether they know it or not. Tell the extent to which your response contributes to this interpretation, and the extent to which your response leads to a new meaning for the story altogether.

Ms K 2

I agree with the fact that every society has a scapegoat. I think this can even be broken down further. Not just in society are there scapegoats but also in smaller groups. Wherever people form associations, whether for the purposes of work or leisure, there are people or a single person to whom the group goes against. Yes, Mrs. Hutchinson was a scapegoat, but if you take the whole situation and turn it around so that there was just ridicule or sarcasm this story would not be the same. This story goes to extremes in explaining. I would interpret the story differently. There always is going to be a scapegoat in society and no matter how wrong you think it is or how much you do to stop it—you just can't change people's set attitudes and personalities. In the story, though, if you like [*sic*; should be, "look"] at it like a death is involved for the sake of the scapegoating there is a different meaning. Sure criticism and being used by others for their own benefit is a pretty bad situation but it can't compare to the extreme example of where a death would be involved.

If just taking the story as criticism and being used for the benefit of others it just says it shouldn't be done. We all know that to have scapegoats is not the best thing in the world but there have always been scapegoats and there will always be scapegoats in a society. No matter how much you want to change things and take efforts to change things—there really isn't too much you can do to change the nature of mankind. I really wouldn't be as upset if I couldn't bring people to my way of thinking—because in this situation I feel it is quite helpless [*sic*].

Index